D1131244

LAW AND JUSTICE IN TOKUGAWA JAPAN

This series will consist of the following volumes:

Comparative legal science teaches us how nations having a common origin may develop independently their original inheritance of legal ideas . . . and, on the other hand, how the legal systems of nations having no association in history may advance along common lines of development. . . . Investigations carried on in the region of a single system serve to smooth the path for the advent of comparative legal science. Each enlargement of our view, each addition to our available material, is a gain of the greatest moment for that science.

Bernhöft, in Zeitschrift für vergleichende Rechtswissenschaft, 1878

LAW AND JUSTICE IN TOKUGAWA JAPAN

*Materials for the History
of Japanese Law and Justice under
the Tokugawa Shogunate 1603-1867*

PART IV–A
Contract: Commercial Customary Law

Edited by
John Henry Wigmore

Translated and Published under the Auspices of
The Japan Foundation

UNIVERSITY OF TOKYO PRESS
1985

© 1985 by The Japan Foundation
3-6 Kioi-cho, Chiyoda-ku,
Tokyo, Japan

ISBN 4-13-007050-9/UTP 09111
ISBN 0-86008-375-6

Contents

BOOKS I AND II*
COMMERCIAL CUSTOMS

Preface by the Editor of the Japanese Printed Edition

This work, *Collection of Commercial Customs*, consisting of three Books, is further subdivided into chapters on (1) merchants, commerce and commercial account-books, (2) commercial mortgages and their liens; (3) agents for buying and selling; (4) buying and selling; (5) breach of contract; (6) vendors; (7) vendees; (8) transport (in Books I and II of the Printed Edition); (1) contracts; (2) performance of contracts; (3) restitution of price, damages, and discount; (4) damages for breach of contract; (5) agency; and (6) account current (Book III). It consists of reports, including verbatim notes, submitted by merchants, business organizations, and provincial governments, in answer to questionnaires about the commercial customs that obtained in the various parts of Japan in the period from the closing years of the Tokugawa regime to the early years of Meiji. It forms a good reference volume for all the commercial customs that generally prevailed in the country in the days preceding the Meiji era.

As there is no explicit enumeration of the names of those issuing and answering the questionnaires, their identity cannot be definitely stated. But as there is a recital at the end of Book I, "Published in July in the 16th year of Meiji [1883]" and at the end of Book II "Published in February in the 17th year of Meiji [1884]", we are inclined to believe that these Books were the work of the Compilation Committee on a Code of Commerce[1] that had been organized under the then Central Government[2] and which was later replaced by a reorganized body known by the name of "Committee for the Investigation of Commercial Law."[3] Our belief is that these Committees, organized for the purpose of expediting the speedy enactment of a commercial code as a part of the policy of the then government, sent out questionnaires to all the parties concerned with a view to obtain helpful information for drafting the commercial code, and after arranging and classifying the reports thus obtained, to publish them. The result was these Books. The party who was in charge of drafting the Commercial Code was the eminent German scholar Dr.

---

[1] Shôhô Hensan Iin.
[2] Dajôkan.
[3] Shôhô Torishirabe Iin.

Hermann Roesler,[1] and his bulky draft code was completed at about this time (in January of the 17th year of Meiji, 1884). In his report on his draft code, he says, "The native commercial customs have not been incorporated in this Draft Code, because they were not made definitely known at the time the work of drafting was in progress." He also says in his report "It would not have been unsuitable to preserve the old Japanese legal conceptions and customs, and to adopt in the Code those which do not conflict with the general principles of commercial law. Although it is regrettable that these Japanese legal ideas and customs have not so far been brought to the notice of the draftsman of the Code, yet it is earnestly hoped that this may still be done." Considering that this report of Dr. Roesler was presented to the Emperor in the month preceding the one when this work (that is, the Book II of the Collection of Commercial Customs) was completed and printed (Book II of the Collection being printed in February of the 17th year of Meiji [1884] and Dr. Roesler's report being dated January 19th of the same year), it seems incomprehensible that the Japanese Committee for the Investigation of Commercial Laws should not have informed the German jurist of the materials thus collected. But that this Collection was made with the object of supplying materials for drafting the code, there can be no doubt. In the light of today's knowledge, there is not a little contained in it which is mere speculation or guessing on the part of those who furnished the answers to the questionnaire, and is hardly worthy of classification as statements of facts. But there is also much reliable information that was clearly based on the memory of the older generation. The use of the Volumes, therefore, needs some care on the part of the reader; but those who make use of them, using such care, though they may find some answers not to be depended upon, yet will reap not a little profit. That is the reason why the present editor has put the whole materials, as they were originally collected, into the present Collection, in spite of their being somewhat confused and crude in their composition.

1930
Takimoto Seiichi

[1] Karl Friedrich Hermann Roesler (1834–94). He was invited by the Japanese Government in 1878 and stayed in Japan for about 15 years.

EDITORIAL NOTE
by
Dr. John Henry Wigmore

A complete account of the sources from which this Series is translated will be found in the Editorial Notes (pp. xxix–xxxii) and Appendix A and B (pp. 145–156) to Part I of the Series.

This Part IV is translated from a printed Japanese volume of which the exact title is as follows:

[Title Page]

法学博士　瀧本誠一編纂
日本経済大典
第四十九巻，第五十巻

[Translated:
Edited by Takimoto Seiichi, Juris Doctor.
Collection of Economic Materials of Japan
(*Nihon Keizai Taiten*)
Volumes 49 & 50]

[Sub-title Page]

日本経済大典
第四十九巻，第五十巻
商事慣例類集

[Translated:
Collection of Economic Materials of Japan
Vols. 49 & 50
Collection of Commercial Customs
(*Shoji Kanrei Ruishû*)]

The work is printed in two volumes, dated 1930 (Shôwa V), Tokyo; the first volume contains Books I and II (236 and 496 pages); the second volume contains Book III (498 pages); the Books are paged consecutively to 1130 and also the treatise "Minji Kanrei Ruishû," translated as Part VII of this Series. This Japanese edition was a printing of a work in three volumes, prepared about 1880 by an official Commission under Count Terajima Munenori (1833–1893), that had been charged with collecting and reporting on the commercial customs, with a view to assisting the preparation of a Commercial Code. A translation of it was begun for him in 1892, but only a fragment of the first draft was done. At that time the volumes consulted for the purpose in the Department of Justice were in manuscript; there were five volumes in all, one of Book I, two of Book II, and two of Book III. The Preface of the printed edition of 1930 refers to the Commission's report as having been "published" in Meiji 16 and 17 (1883–84); but that printed edition has not been seen by the Editor.

It may here be noted that though the Japanese work is divided into three parts, here termed "Books," the topics reported on in Books I and II are identical; the answers reported, however, represent answers from different parties—in Book I, the regional commercial committees; Book II, the local officials and trades. Both are useful. But for clearness' sake, the answers from the two Books have here been placed together under the respective topics.

LIST OF THE TOPICS OF THE QUESTIONNAIRES IN BOOKS I & II[1]

Chapter I Merchants, Commerce, and Merchants' Books

Topic 1: Is there any customary standard by which to distinguish between a merchant and a non-merchant?

Topic 2: Is any distinction made between civil and commercial matters according to the nature of the enterprise or contract?

Topic 3: Does a married woman trade apart from her husband? If so, what will be her relation to her husband with respect to her property?

Topic 4:

Sub-topic 1: How many kinds of trade' books are there? What are their respective names, their uses; and how long are they supposed to be preserved?

Sub-topic 2: Is there any fixed form of entries? Are different kinds of books used in different trades?

Sub-topic 3: Is the Occidental method of bookkeeping by single and double entry becoming prevalent?

Topic 5: Have merchants' trade books any legal force as evidence against another person?

Topic 6:

Sub-topic 1: Is there any difference of treatment in legal proceedings depending upon whether the trade books are properly kept?

Sub-topic 2: Is it desirable to have some fixed rules for the supervision of a merchant's books? If so, what should be the principles?

Chapter II Commercial Mortgages and Liens

Topic 1: Is there any difference between commercial and civil mortgages?

Topic 2: When an obligor does not pay his debt at the expiration of the agreed term, payment being secured by a

---

[1] The divisions of Book II are identical with those of Book I. See Translation Editor's Note.

mortgage, is it the usual practice for the creditor to appropriate the entire property to compensate for the loss
he incurs, even when the value of the mortgaged property exceeds the amount of the debt, including its principal and interest? Or is it the custom for the creditor to
sell the mortgaged property, reimburse himself out of the
money received from the sale, and return the balance to
the obligor?

Topic   3:   When an obligor becomes insolvent, does any obligee
besides the holder of a mortgage take priority[1] over other
(general) creditors? (For example, is there any custom
according to which a land rent,[2] a house rent,[3] an employee's wage, or money due for food supplied to the
obligor, etc., takes priority over other general claims?)

Topic   4:   May a merchant who is holding a mortgage given by
another merchant execute a second mortgage[4] on the
security in favor of a third merchant, without obtaining
the consent of the second merchant?

Chapter III   Agents for Sale

Topic   1:   What marks the difference between the trade of a *toiya*
and that of a *nakagai*?[5]

Topic   2:   Is there any class of persons who, acting as agents for
sale between two parties, receive a commission, other
than those who are publicly called *toiya* and *nakagai*? If
there are, what are the varieties?

Topic   3:   Does the agent[6] make contracts with other parties in
his own name, when executing any sale or purchase
transaction committed to him? Or does he act as representative of his principal,[7] concluding a contract in the
name of his principal?

Topic   4:   If the agent advances money to his principal on goods

---

[1] *Sakidori-tokken.*

[2] *Jidai.*

[3] *Yachin.*

[4] *Fuku-teitô.*

[5] Lit., "middle-man."

[6] *Baikainin.*

[7] *Iraisha.*

---

[1] *Ninushi.*

[2] *Senchu.*

[3] *Shaba-mochinushi.*

[4] *Baibai.*

[5] *Shôsho.*

[6] *Matauri.*

[7] *Tsumini-mokuroku.*

[8] *Unsô-jô.*

of sale is concluded, but after the delivery of the goods?
If so, how is the price fixed?

Topic   7:   If the time of the delivery of goods or the term of payment is not set at the time of the formation of a contract
of sale, when should the delivery or payment be made?

Topic   8:   Does it sometimes occur that a creditor with a debtor's
loan-receipt[1] or a bill of sale[2] in his possession endorses
the document and transfers his creditor-right[3] to others?
If so, what form[4] is used? What advantages and disadvantages are derived from such a practice?

Topic   9:   How many sorts of notes,[5] tickets,[6] and the like are
used in commerce? Are those notes or tickets issued with
government permission or by private individuals?

Topic 10:   What is the ordinary time limit for the payment[7] of a
commercial debt? What is the maximum time limit?
What is the minimum time limit?

Topic 11:   Is there any custom, in the case of several obligors in
connection with a commercial sale or loan,[8] of the whole
liability being jointly assumed?[9]

Topic 12:   Does the word *torihiki* (transaction) in commerce include everything from the making of a sale-contract to
the delivery of the goods and the payment of the price?
Or does it refer only to acts carried out at the time of the
delivery of the goods or the payment of the price?

Topic 13:   What is the difference between a wholesale merchant[10]
and a retail merchant?[11] Are there any wholesale merchants who deal only with retailers, but never directly
with ordinary customers?[12]

---

[1]   *Shakuyo-shôsho.*
[2]   *Kaiuke-shôsho.*
[3]   *Saishu-ken.*
[4]   *Shoshiki.*
[5]   *Tegata.*
[6]   *Kitte.*
[7]   *Harai-kigen.*
[8]   *Taishaku.*
[9]   *Rentai-tantô.*
[10]   *Oroshiuri.*
[11]   *Kouri.*
[12]   *Tsujô-nin.*

Chapter V Rescission of Contract[1]

Topic 1: When the earnest-money[2] for a sale is forfeited,[3] does the sale-contract become rescissible?

Topic 2: If the amount of damages for breach of contract has not been fixed beforehand, how is the amount to be determined when such a breach takes place?

Topic 3: If the seller does not deliver goods[4] to the buyer, or the buyer does not take delivery[5] of them when the time limit is due, is the sale contract rescissible, or is it still in force?

Chapter VI Seller[6]

Topic 1: If the specifications of the goods, including their quality[7] and grade,[8] have not been named in the sales contract, what kind[9] of goods is to be delivered by the seller to the buyer?

Topic 2: If a seller accepts an offer of a customer to buy some goods after examining the samples or the actual merchandise, is the seller under obligation not to sell the goods to another person before they have been examined by the first customer?

Topic 3: If the buyer forfeits his earnest-money when he breaks a contract, may not the seller claim damages?

Topic 4: Is the seller implied to be held to a warranty that the goods he sells are perfectly fitted for use? Or does such a warranty arise only when it is expressly provided in the contract?

Topic 5: Is the sales contract valid when the vendor sells an article to which he has no title (for example, stolen goods)?

[1] *Hayaku.*
[2] *Tetsuke-kin.*
[3] *Nagareru.*
[4] *Hikiwatasu.*
[5] *Hikitoru.*
[6] *Urinushi.*
[7] *Seishitsu.*
[8] *Hin-i.*
[9] *Shinagara.*

Chapter VII   Vendee

Topic   1:   When the goods delivered turn out to be different from
the samples on which a contract of sale has been based,
is the buyer entitled, at any time, to claim replacement[1]
of the goods by proper ones, or to rescind the contract?

Topic   2:   Is a buyer who has offered to buy a specified article[2]
from a seller free to buy it from another without the consent of the first seller before he receives the latter's reply
to his offer, and then to cancel the offer with the first
seller?

Topic   3:   If payment of the price of an article is overdue, does
any interest[3] accrue thereon? If so, from what date is the
interest computed?

Topic   4:   If goods which have been warranted by the seller are
found to be defective,[4] is the buyer entitled, at any time,
to claim replacement of them by other goods, or to
rescind the sales contract?

Chapter VIII   Transportation[5]

Topic   1:   Is it always the practice to set a time limit for the arrival of goods in a contract of transportation? If so, what
are the responsibilities of the forwarding agent?[6] If otherwise, what are his responsibilities?

Topic   2:   When goods in transit are transshipped[7] from one vessel to another due to unavoidable circumstances before
they reach their destination, what are the responsibilities
of the second vessel?

Topic   3:   When the buyer refuses to take delivery of the goods
on arrival, how shall the goods be disposed of if the seller
or the forwarding agent is not present on the spot?

---

[1] *Torikae.*
[2] *Kakutei-butsu.*
[3] *Rishi.*
[4] *Furyô.*
[5] *Unsô.*
[6] *Unsônin.*
[7] *Tsumikae.*

Appendix to Book I: Items Not Included in the
Questionnaires on Commercial Customs

(A)   On Associations of Merchants of the Same Trade[1]
(B)   On Negotiable Instruments[2]
  (1) Bills of Exchange[3]
  (2) Deposit Certificate for Money[4]
  (3) *Sekidashi-tegata* (Check Addressed to Exchange Broker)
  (4) *Furisagami* (Note Issued by Exchange Broker)
  (5) *O-tegata* (Bill Used for Clearing Balance)
  (6) Promissory Notes[5]
  (7) Warehouse Certificates[6]
(C)   On Sales for Future Delivery[7]
(D)   On the Disposition of Wrecked Ships[8]
(E)   On Employees
(F)   On Wholesalers' Books
(G)   On the Uses and Names of Different Kinds of Books
(H)   On the Period of the Preservation of Books
(I)   On Retailers' Books

[1] *Kabunakama.*
[2] *Tegata-ryûtsû.*
[3] *Kawase-tegata.*
[4] *Azukari-tegata.*
[5] *Nobe-tegata.*
[6] *Kura-azukari-tegata.*
[7] *Nobe-baibai.*
[8] *Nampa-sen.*

LIST OF THE TOPICS OF THE QUESTIONNAIRES IN BOOK III

Chapter I Contract[1]

Topic 1: In the absence of an express oral agreement, or a written contract between two parties, does one party's silence imply acceptance[2] of the other party's proposal in such a way as to become a binding contract?

Topic 2: What degree of care must be exercised in commercial transactions in order to protect the interests of another party?

Topic 3: 1. When the party who has made an offer fails to receive the acceptance of his offer by the other party, at once, within a specified period, or within a supposedly reasonable time[3] should the offer be regarded as rejected?

2. On the other hand, may it not occur that when the party receives an offer from another party with whom he has been accustomed to deal, and fails to express his rejection of the offer, the offer may be regarded as accepted?

Topic 4: When an offer of contract is made by one party, does it become binding from the moment when the offeree accepts it, or from the moment when the offeror[4] receives the notification of acceptance?

Topic 5: Suppose a notice of acceptance of an offer is sent to the offeror. Can the notification of acceptance be cancelled if this is done before the notice has reached the offeror, or at the same time the notice is received by the offeror?

Topic 6: When a party who receives an offer accompanied with samples, or the goods themselves, finds that the samples or goods cannot be returned to the offeror due to certain circumstances, what should the offeree do?

If the samples or goods left with the offeree cost him

---

[1] *Keiyaku.*
[2] *Mokudaku.*
[3] *Mihakarai-kigen-nai.*
[4] *Môshikomi-nin.*

some expense or are lost, what should he do? If the goods are liable to perish, may not the offeree sell them and keep the money for the offeror?

Topic 7: After approval[1] has been given to an account, or payment based on it has been made, is it permissible to raise an objection[2] if some error of computation or some misrepresentation is subsequently found?[3]

Chapter II   Performance of Contract[4]

Topic 1: It is a matter of course that the obligor must obtain the permission of the obligee[5] to fulfill a contract by delivery of goods other than those agreed upon in the contract—by fulfilling,[6] for instance, a contract for grain by delivery of dry goods; but is there any situation in which permission of this nature, though not expressed, is implied?

Topic 2: When the obligee refuses to accept without any sufficient reason an article the obligor[7] duly[8] delivers in fulfillment of a contract, how should the obligor dispose of said article? If the article is money, how should the interest accruing to it after its rejection by the obligee be treated? If it is something other than money and is impaired by delay, whose loss is it deemed to be?

Topic 3: When the obligor makes only part payment[9] without previous agreement to that effect, is the obligee allowed to reject it?

Topic 4: If the time limit set in a contract is indicated by such expressions as "for a certain number of days,"[10] "for a certain number of months,"[11] or "for a certain number

---

[1] *Shôdaku.*
[2] *Koshô-o-môshitateru.*
[3] *Itsuwari.*
[4] *Keiyaku-no-rikô.*
[5] *Kenrisha.*
[6] *Hensai.*
[7] *Gimusha.*
[8] *Tôzenni.*
[9] *Uchibarai.*
[10] *Nankanichi-kan.*
[11] *Nankagetsu-kan.*

of years,"[1] what date should be fixed upon as the time for performing the contract? If the time limit is indicated by such expressions as "within the period of a certain number of days," or "within the period of a certain number of months," or "within the period of a certain number of years," is the contract performable at any time within the period thus indicated, and is the obligee entitled to demand the performance of the contract at any time within the period?

Topic   5:   Is the time limit set in a contract computable from the day when the contract is made, or from the day following the day when the contract is made?

Topic   6:   In commercial transactions, is the period of one month or half a month computable by the number of days? Or is there any other method for its computation?

Topic   7:   If the time limit set in a contract is due on a general holiday, or a local holiday, or the holiday of the store (that is, one of the parties to the contract), how should the transaction be handled?

Topic   8:   In commercial transactions, is the period of one day computable by the number of hours? Or is there any other method for its computation?

Topic   9:   If an extension[2] of the time limit for a contract is agreed upon but there is no stipulation as to the time when the computation of the extended period should start, is it computable from the day when the new contract about the extension is made, or from the day when the time limit set in the original contract expires?

Topic 10:   If no stipulations have been made in the contract as to the place where payment should be made and received, or where the goods should be delivered or taken delivery of, where should the payment or the delivery take place?

Topic 11:   If there is no specific stipulation in the contract regarding the obligation on the part of an obligor to forward goods, should the goods be forwarded to the dwelling[3]

---

[1] *Nankanen-kan.*
[2] *Enki.*
[3] *Jūsho.*

of the obligee, or to the ordinary unloading place[1] in the locality of his abode?[2] Or is it regarded as adequate for the obligor to deliver the goods to the obligee at the ordinary unloading-place of the locality of the former's abode?

Topic 12: If there is no specific stipulation in the contract as to the details of the method of delivery, such as weights,[3] measures,[4] tare,[5] and the like, should the customs[6] of the place of delivery[7] be followed; or should the usual practices of forwarder,[8] or the practices usually observed in connection with goods to be delivered, be followed?

Topic 13: If no stipulation has been made as to what kind of goods should be delivered by the obligor to the obligee by way of repaying what the former owes the latter, is the obligor free to repay the obligee with any sort of goods the former chooses; or is it a matter about which the obligee may dictate to the obligor?

If it is stipulated in the contract that repayment by the obligor to the obligee should be made with one of two articles specially mentioned, but both of the articles have been lost through the fault of the obligor, who is supposed to decide the article to be substituted for the lost ones?

Chapter III Restitution of Price,[9] Damages,[10] and Discount[11]

Topic 1: If the obligor does not fulfill his obligation within a prescribed time,[12] is the obligee free to rescind[13] the con-

---

[1] *Nioroshiba.*
[2] *Jûchi.*
[3] *Ryômoku.*
[4] *Masume.*
[5] *Fûtai.*
[6] *Shikitari.*
[7] *Hikiwatashi-chi.*
[8] *Hikiwatashi-nin.*
[9] *Kakaku-hoshô.*
[10] *Songai-baishô.*
[11] *Waribiki.*
[12] *Teiki.*
[13] *Hayaku.*

tract, or demand restitution of price from the obligor? If any loss for the obligee results from it, does the obligee sometimes make to the obligor restitution for it?

Topic   2:   Is any interest supposed to accrue on the restitution of price referred to in Topic 1? If it does, from what date should the computation of interest commence?

Topic   3:   Is any interest supposed to accrue to money one has paid on behalf of another or money advanced on behalf of another?

Topic   4:   When damage has been done, whether intentionally[1] or not, may compensation be claimed?

Topic   5:   Is compensation limited to the amount of damage actually done, or does it include the probable profit that would have accrued were it not for the damage?

In the latter case, how is the amount of the damage to be estimated?

Topic   6:   When it is found that the amount of restitution of price[2] or the amount of loss[3] which has been agreed upon beforehand does not conform to the current prices, what should be done?

Topic   7:   If an obligor repays his debt before it falls due, is he still supposed to pay the interest that would accrue between the date of the repayment and the original date of maturity? Or is the obligation of the payment of interest supposed to extend no further than the day when the repayment is made?

Topic   8:   When a contract is rescinded due to negligence[4] on the part of a seller, and the goods which have already been delivered to the obligee are returned to the obligor, is he bound to accept the goods, as they are returned, if they are fewer than the amount delivered of if they are impaired through no fault of the obligee; or may compensation be claimed for the damage?

In the latter case, as to the goods which should be returned to the obligee by the obligor, are those goods

[1] *Koi.*
[2] *Kakaku-hoshōgaku.*
[3] *Sonshitsu-kakaku.*
[4] *Okotari.*

which happen to have been reduced in quantity or impaired to be returned, as they are found, to the obligee? Or should compensation be paid for the damage?

Appendix: If any expense is incurred through negligence[1] on the part of the obligor, should the amount be added to the price as provided in Topic 2? Or should a separate claim be made?

Chapter IV Penalty for Breach of Contract[2]

Topic 1: May payment of penalty for breach of contract be demanded only when it has been stipulated beforehand in the contract? When there is no previous agreement to the effect, may such penalty be demanded when an occasion therefor occurs? May it happen that penalty for breach of contract and compensation for damage in general[3] are cumulative and the use of one remedy is not taken to exclude or waive the use of another?

Topic 2: When the obligee receives penalty for breach of contract, does he still have the right to demand performance of the contract, or is this right nullified?[4]

Chapter V Agency[5]

Topic 1: Is there any situation in which agency in a commercial transaction may be assumed by one to whom no letter of attorney[6] has been issued?

Topic 2: In a business transaction in which an agent is acting on behalf of his principal,[7] which one of the two, the agent or the principal, is supposed to assume directly the rights and the obligations toward the other party?[8]

In the case of the other party concluding a transaction with an agent without knowledge of the status of

---

[1] *Okotari.*
[2] *Iyaku-kin.*
[3] *Songai-baishô.*
[4] *Shômetsu.*
[5] *Dairi.*
[6] *Ininjô.*
[7] *Honnin.*
[8] *Aitekata.*

the latter, what are the rights and obligations assumable by the principal toward the other party?

Topic   3:   When an agent acts beyond his powers,[1] but the other party is not aware of this, is a contract thus concluded between the two parties valid? If it is, what should be done about the loss incurred by the principal as a result of his agent having acted in excess of his power?

Topic   4:   When an agent alone is held responsible for a business transaction which has been conducted in the name of his principal, is the principal entitled to retain the goods, if any, which have already come into his possession, or may he be dispossessed of such goods?

Although it seems apparent that the restoration of the goods to the other party should be made by the agent, does it ever happen that the other party tries to recover the goods for himself?

Topic   5:   Is the commission of authority[3] (to an agent) supposed to terminate naturally when the principal or the agent dies?

Topic   6:   Is it possible for an agent to delegate to somebody else the authority which has been committed to him? Is this possible only when the consent of the principal is obtained?

Chapter VI   Account Current[4]

Topic   1:   Is there any practice whereby merchants who are engaged in continuous transactions with one another, assuming in turn the roles of a creditor or a debtor, settle their accounts not at each transaction but after several months or half a year of transactions, balance and settle accounts for the whole period, or carry the balance over into next term's account?

Is this method of balancing accounts[5] (at one time for a whole period) practiced only when it is stipulated be-

---

[1] *Kengen-o-koeru.*

[2] *Torimodosaru.*

[3] *Dairi-no-inin.*

[4] *Sogo-keisan.*

[5] *Sashihiki-kanjô.*

forehand in a contract, or is it observed, even if there is no stipulation to that effect, when the mutual accounts reach a large amount?

When this practice is stipulated in a contract, what is the usual length of period for settling an account?

Is any interest supposed to accrue on this account?

Is there any special name by which this practice is designated?

Appendices: (a) Time-limit for initiating a lawsuit[1] (Chiba Prefecture).

(b) Conditions for the circulation of bills[2]: Advantages of bills; Disadvantages of bills (Tochigi Prefecture).

[1] *Shusso-kigen.*
[2] *Tegata.*

Law and Justice in
Tokugawa Japan

PART IV-A

CONTRACT: COMMERCIAL CUSTOMARY LAW

MATERIALS FOR THE STUDY OF
PRIVATE LAW IN OLD JAPAN

PART IV
CONTRACT: COMMERCIAL CUSTOMS

BOOKS I AND II[1]

CHAPTER I
MERCHANTS, COMMERCE, AND
COMMERCIAL BOOKS

Topic 1:   Is There Any Customary Standard by Which to
Distinguish between a Merchant[2] and a Non-merchant?

GROUP I—ANSWERS[3]

Tokyo.

Our Explanation Committee notifies us that we are to point out
in what manner merchants have hitherto been and are now being
distinguished from non-merchants (i.e., by custom). Although our
examination of this important topic leads us to conclude that there
has been no such custom, we think that the existence of *noren*
[signs], payment of the business tax or registration of vocation in
the census list may serve as criteria by which to publicly distinguish
a merchant from a non-merchant.

Kyoto.

As we consider this question of yours the most important one in
this whole subject, we have endeavoured to make a full explanation. When we look back to the origin of commerce we find that it
consists in the exchange of various articles among different classes

---

[1] The answers for each locality in Books I and II are here assembled in sequence,
the Titles and Topics being identical, as has already been explained in the Editorial
Preface.

[2] *Shônin.*

[3] These are the answers in Book I.

of consumers. For instance, a mountain tract produces fuel but wants salt, while a seacoast produces salt but wants fuel. Now it is the business of a merchant to procure the exchange of these products between the inhabitants of the two regions, so as to supply their respective wants. These various articles or products may be classified into natural products and manufactured products. To the first class belong all natural products, such as rice, salt, coal, mineral substances, grass, timber, etc. The labor of extracting these products is termed agriculture.[1] To the second class belong all useful articles made of these various natural products thus extracted by human labor, such, for example, as wine, vinegar, oil, silk, cotton, paper, tobacco, etc. The labor of producing these articles is called manufacture.[2] Now there are of course persons who make it their occupation to buy these articles, both natural and industrial, and resell them directly to consumers—such persons are called merchants.[3] There is another set of persons, to whom these products are always brought in the first instance, called wholesalers.[4] These wholesalers, when they take such goods, resell them to retailers[5] either directly or through the agency of a person employed as a middleman between buyer and seller. This last class of person is called broker.[6] There are also others who themselves go to the producers, buy their products and resell them to wholesalers. These are also called brokers. There are still others, also called wholesellers, to whom merchants bring their goods, either by sea or by land, and to whom they entrust their sale. Sea-merchants[7] transport the goods on board their ships to different ports and deposit them with a wholesaler for future sale, while land merchants deposit their goods in like manner to be sold to sea merchants through the agency of a wholesaler. There are still others, farmers, who occupy themselves during intervals in their chief livelihood as retailers or brokers. In this instance, the farmer becomes a merchant. Again, there are others, manufacturers, who deal in articles other than those of their

---

[1] *Nôji.*
[2] *Kôgyô.*
[3] *Shônin.*
[4] *Toiya.*
[5] *Kourimise* or *Oroshiuri-shônin.*
[6] *Nakagaishônin.*
[7] *Kaisen-shônin.*

own making which they buy from another person e.g., when a tobacco-cutter sells tobacco cut by another tobacco-cutter. In this instance, the manufacturer becomes a merchant. There are still others who are not ordinarily merchants but who occasionally sell or buy certain commodities. These are not properly called merchants.

Persons properly called merchants are those who make it their occupation day and night to buy and sell various kinds of commodities. The various occupations followed by these merchants are in this country customarily called *shôbai*. But the word *shôbai*, restricted in its proper sense to the mercantile occupations, is sometimes indiscriminately used to denote any sort of occupation whatever, thus countenancing the notion that it is a general name for all occupations. Hence such appellations as *shichiya* (pawnhouse) *shôbai*, *furoya* (bath-house) *shôbai* (public bath), and many others, such as *kanin* (officers) *shôbai* and *isha* (physician) *shôbai*. No wonder the distinction between merchants and non-merchants is obscure and indistinct. Indeed under the government of the Shogunate, "merchants" were universally despised and treated almost like slaves. Thus no samurai or farmer was allowed to become a "merchant" without relinquishing his own occupation, and any samurai who, dismissed by his master or lord, carried on a trade in order to support himself was prohibited from again becoming a samurai, though he might become a farmer or manufacturer. But nowadays there is much looseness with respect to usage of house-signs, business taxes, the civil status list, etc.

Therefore you, the Government, when you enact any commercial code, should first take care to fix as clearly as possible the distinction, not only between merchants and non-merchants, but also between different kinds of trades. We think it only right that you placed this important subject at the head of your list of questions.

GROUP II—ANSWERS[1]

Tokyo Metropolis
  Salt Wholesalers.
  A signboard is usually hung out for recognition, at the commis-

---

[1] These answers are from Book II.

sion house[1] or the local wholesalers,[2] or else many baskets are placed on show. They are thus easily recognized, in contrast with the wholesalers who come from the provinces of Kansai[3] who use no signboards.

Fish Wholesalers.

As these wholesalers have no signboard or shop curtain as other wholesalers do, not a few merchants have their shops in the fish market, a wide drain at the entrance, with the various kinds of fish arranged at the shop front. These displays make it easy to recognize them. However, those who habitually remain in the market with their lattice doors shut are hard to recognize.

Pawnshops.

In former days the number of pawnshops was limited, and a signboard was put up at the shop front. In the 9th year of Meiji, an order came from the Metropolitan Police Board for pawners to join the pawners' guild and to obtain a permit from the authorities with the word "pawnshop" written on it. It is thus easy to recognize such shops, inasmuch as they have the permit at the shop front.

Oil Wholesalers.

These wholesalers make a habit of posting the regulations of the guild. They are easily recognized as oil kegs are displayed at the wholesalers' or at the commission house where they do business.

Drapery Wholesalers.

These tradesmen are very easily recognized as they always hang a shop curtain inscribed with the word "drapery."

Timber Wholesalers.

Since ancient times, wholesalers, commission houses and retailers have had signboards at their shop fronts. Moreover, as these merchants set aside a place for displaying piles of timber in front of or alongside their shops, they are easily recognizable.

Grain Wholesalers.

Wholesalers and retailers have used signboards since ancient times, from when too they were prohibited from carrying on business unless they were members of the guild. This rule is still in effect and has been observed. The guild is known as "three-kind grains."[4]

---

[1] *Nakagai.*
[2] *Jimawari-toiya.*
[3] *Kudari-toiya.*
[4] *Beikoku-sangyô-kumiai.*

There is also a commission house called "three-percent house,"[1] the proprietor of which arranges, according to custom, the samples of rice[2] at the shop front; he therefore can plainly be identified as a merchant at first sight. There are also, however, wholesalers and retailers who do their business shut up within their shops; there is nothing special about their outward appearance to indicate they are merchants.

Fuel Wholesalers.

Wholesalers hang out a signboard at the shop entrance inscribed with the words "fuel wholesalers." Although retailers have no signboards, they are easily recognizable by the area in front of, or at the side of, the shop where the various kinds of fuel[3] are arranged. It is thus very easy to recognize this kind of merchant.

Saké Wholesalers.

Wholesalers and commission houses keep their shop counters in their own residences and hang signboards[4] at the shop front. The retailers also have an unfloored space in their home, called "storage place,"[5] in addition to a stand for selling,[6] upon which the liquor bottles are arranged for carrying on business; they are thus identified at a glance as merchants.

Dried Bonito Wholesalers.

A placard containing the rules of the guild is hung in the shops of wholesalers and commission houses, and casks containing dried bonito are arranged at the shop fronts. Boxes of dried bonito are displayed at retailers' shops, and a signboard, inscribed "dried bonito," is hung at the shop front. This shows clearly that they are merchants.

TOKYO METROPOLIS

Kôjimachi Ward.

Official recognition is authorized on the basis of whether the business tax[7] is paid or not; as in other cases, it varies according to circumstances.

[1] *San-punya.*

[2] *Sashi-mae.*

[3] *Shin-tan.*

[4] The wholesaler's signboard says "wholesaler of liquor," while the retailer's says "shop for liquor sale."

[5] *Tsugi-ba.*

[6] *Uriba-dai.*

[7] *Eigyô-zei.*

Nihombashi Ward.

In former days, merchants who attempted to carry on business privately were prohibited from doing so by means of protests by the guild. After the Meiji Restoration, however, this rule was not observed, owing to the dissolution of the guilds. Official recognition has gradually become necessary in connection with the tax on business, etc.

Kyôbashi Ward.

No answer.

Yotsuya Ward and Ushigome Ward.

The situation now with respect to the distinction between merchants and non-merchants is that anyone engaged in one of the "eight businesses"[1] who obtains the right to do business by payment of the state tax,[2] or who sells to another what he has bought, whether he has a shop or not, and who thus becomes liable for the local business tax,[3] is termed a merchant.

Asakusa Ward.

There is a clear distinction between a merchant and a non-merchant. But it is difficult to point out an authorized standard. It would be, in my opinion, on the basis of whether or not a business or local tax is levied. If it is, the person is a merchant in terms of the authorized standard. Otherwise, he is a non-merchant. No other standard seems to be known. A merchant can be rather well discriminated from a non-merchant by character, though this is a vague standard. First of all, merchants aim at simplicity, so much so that even one who is rich wears cotton clothes and an apron. Generally speaking, they always try to seek the good will of anyone they meet.[4] They are sociable, amicable, and obedient as well. Whenever they converse, they refer to fluctuations of market prices, the prosperity of their business and gains or losses from interest. They never wander from the main subject. All these traits are certain to indicate that the person is a merchant.

These peculiarities, however, are not noticeable nowadays, because the present status of merchants is very different. In fact, mer-

---

[1] *Hachinin-shô.*

[2] *Kokuzei-eigyô.*

[3] *Chihô-eigyô-zei.*

[4] This attitude towards others is very different from that of a buffoon, whose demeanor is usually fawning.

chants engaged in shipping business are prominent and live luxu-
riously. There are no merchants in this ward engaged in business
on a large scale.

This explanation of the status of ordinary merchants, people who
might be called "old-fashioned,"[1] will make it possible to distinguish between merchants and non-merchants.

Honjo Ward.

This depends on the nature of the trade. When the business tax
is imposed, the difference between merchants and non-merchants
is clear.

Ebara *kôri*.

There are no circumstances of trade by which to distinguish merchants from non-merchants.

Higashi-tama *kôri* and Minami-toshima *kôri*.

A business tax is imposed on merchants but not on non-merchants and we can thus recognize the two types fairly well. Those
on whom a business tax is imposed in both of these counties number a little less than one thousand. Only a very few do a really
large business, the others being half-farmers,[2] half-merchants[3] or
small traders.[4] In the last group, there are more than one thousand
not subject to tax; so to judge only from the point of taxation is
insufficient. There are thus no special distinguishing circumstances
in business.

Kita-toshima *kôri*.

Merchants are persons who must pay the "businesses of eight
kinds"[5] tax and the state tax. Let us say we have a timber merchant
and a grain wholesaler. If the latter wants to buy timber from the
former, he should be called a non-merchant. If, furthermore, the
timber merchant does not happen to have as many pieces of timber
as the grain wholesaler wants, he could satisfy the latter's demand
by purchasing the required remaining amount. Something the non-
merchant is not able to do.

Minami-adachi *kôri*.

It is difficult to state circumstances of trade which mark a dis-

---

[1] *Mukashikatagi.*
[2] *Han-nô.*
[3] *Hanshô.*
[4] *Saishô-no-shônin.*
[5] *Hachihinzei.*

tinction between merchants and non-merchants. In ordinary usage, we generally call one who sells to buyers things purchased from farmers or manufacturers a merchant. However, included among the merchants in "the businesses of eight kinds," as licensed by the Metropolitan Police Office, are those who deal in goldwork for ornamentation and tortoise-shell work. According to local tax regulations, an inn is subject to the business tax, while a restaurant is subject to the tax on sundry articles.[1] There is thus no clear distinction nowadays between the two groups.

Shitaya Ward.

People who pay the business tax or the tax on sundry articles may be called merchants.

Kanda Ward.

The distinction between merchants and non-merchants is made on the basis of what is recorded in the census register.

Akasaka Ward and Azabu Ward.

We call one who regularly engages in a business a merchant. Those who are called wholesalers, commission house proprietors, or retailers are allowed to carry on their businesses under license. There are, however, many merchants carrying on a side-business in addition to their main business, a practice that is called "selling in private"[2] or "buying in private."[3] Sometimes a merchant is mistakenly called a manufacturer for reasons deriving from the nature of his occupation: comb-sellers, for instance, who make combs and wooden clogs, usually call themselves merchants. Occasionally persons make a living by both selling and manufacturing. Those who let wagons for hire[4] are not called merchants.

Hongô Ward.

One who engages in the sale of goods, using invoice books, sales books, etc. is called a merchant.

CHIBA PREFECTURE

Awa *kôri*, Hei *kôri*, Asai *kôri*, and Nagasa *kôri*.

In truth, the distinction between merchants and non-merchants is difficult to state. And when it comes to collecting the business

---

[1] *Zatsu shu-zei.*
[2] *Nuke-uri.*
[3] *Nuke-gai.*
[4] *Kashiguruma-tosei.*

tax[1] and the local tax, opinions of the authorities differ. For instance, when the authorities seek to require a license at the tax rate from one who sells goods made or gathered by himself,[2] the dilemma is that if such persons are treated as merchants, the poor among them will be greatly distressed; if they are not, however, designation of business status will become chaotic. Though the establishment of some distinction between merchants and non-merchants is indispensable in business regulation and is desired by genuine merchants, nevertheless it is difficult to draw the line.

Katori *kôri*.

Pawnbrokers, book-lenders, "lenders-[of clothes, etc.] for-fee,"[3] are not called merchants.

Yamabe *kôri* and Muza *kôri*.

The only thing distinguishing a merchant is payment of the business tax.

Unakami *kôri* and Sôsa *kôri*.

One significant circumstance is that merchants generally use account books appropriate to the business.

Nishi-katsushika *kôri*.

There are no circumstances officially marking a distinction between the two groups.

IBARAGI PREFECTURE

Nishi-katsushika *kôri* and Sashima *kôri*.

Generally speaking, a merchant is one who makes his living by buying and selling goods which others have made. If a farmer raises and sells goods, for example tea or tobacco, from his farm, he is called an "agriculture off-season merchant."[4] He is distinguished from ordinary merchants.

KANAGAWA PREFECTURE

Miura *kôri*.

Merchant guilds were formerly established to ensure strict ob-

---

[1] *Shôgyô-zei.*

[2] Examples are farmers who go out and sell the vegetables and refined rice that they raise, or fishermen who go out to villages to sell fish which they have caught. These men can hardly be said to be merchants, in view of the limited extent of their traffic. But on the whole, they do have an influence on the market price.

[3] *Sonryô-kashi.*

[4] *Nôkan-shônin.*

servance of commercial law. One guild was called "the first guild,"[1] and the other "the second guild."[2] Persons not belonging to these two guilds were non-merchants. Since the dissolution of these guilds at the Meiji Restoration, there has been no way to distinguish merchants from non-merchants.

Tachibana *kôri*.

Various circumstances mark the difference; for instance, merchants differ from non-merchants in being subject to the tax on business.

Kita-tama *kôri*.

In general, merchants, are those who pay a business tax commensurate with the amount of their commodities and sales, or those who have a shop or travel and sell goods. All others are regarded as non-merchants.

Ashigara-shimo *kôri*.

Merchants customarily arrange their commodities at their shopfront, and those regarded as merchants usually have a shop curtain.

Prefectural Industry Bureau.

There is no way to distinguish merchants from non-merchants. Merchants, however, regularly engage in business and enter the goods sold in their account books for evidence in case of a controversy concerning trade. Though non-merchants may make entries of commodities in a memorandum book, they are not able to use this book as evidence. Thus, the distinction between merchants and non-merchants depends on the existence of a regular account book.

Tochigi Prefecture

Tochigi *kôri*.

It is customary to designate as merchants those who sell goods which they have bought without making any improvement on them by labor.[3]

Shimo-tsuga *kôri* and Samukawa *kôri*.

Conditions indispensable for distinguishing a merchant from a

---

[1] Merchants on a large scale.

[2] Merchants generally below the average in scale of business.

[3] Apart from such work, one who works on goods to the extent of transforming their nature is called a manufacturer. Restaurants and hotels are regarded as service-occupations.

non-merchant are: first, possession of a business license and, second, family status.

Ashikaga *kôri* and Yanada *kôri*.

The only thing that sets apart merchants is the fact that a local tax is imposed on them and that they must obtain a business license. Textile manufacturers[1] have organized a guild, "*Ashikaga-kôshô-kai*," and established certain rules which all the members must observe. A draper always affixes the trademark of the "*Ashi-kaga-shôkô-kai*" on his goods, and the goods sold by a commission-merchant have this trademark on them. Accordingly the Ashikaga-merchant can always be recognized.

MIE PREFECTURE

Suzuka *kôri*.

In former days there were no particular official circumstances that determined the distinction between marchants and non-merchants. Merchants today, however, must pay a state tax, a business tax and a tax on sundry articles in order to obtain licenses.

Isshi *kôri*.

There is no distinction in this county.

Asake *kôri*.

The state tax and the local tax are ways to discriminate merchants from non-merchants. Merchants, that is, are liable to the above taxes on business.

Nabari *kôri* and Iga *kôri*.

Nothing in particular marks the distinction, but account books, records of buying and selling, are only kept by merchants. Both merchants and non-merchants register their trademarks and engage in business.

AICHI PREFECTURE

Nakajima *kôri*.

There are two kinds of merchants in this county: those who make their living by business, and those who carry on business during slack seasons in agricultural work. Merchants—not only the former but also the latter—must be legally recognized and pay taxes whether they carry on a small or a large business. From the stand-

---

[1] These manufacturers do not themselves fabricate, but send the materials to other quarters. Many of them sell stocks when the opportunity offers.

point of commerce, however, the half-farmer merchants should be called farmer-manufacturers. It is hard to distinguish between merchants and manufacturers when they pay taxes on both business and manufacture. The distinction is also hard to make in the numerous cases of merchants in this county who engage in agriculture as a subsidiary occupation.

Nagoya Ward.

Any person who calls himself a merchant and who pays the business tax when registering the opening of his business is called a merchant. No other circumstance serves to distinguish merchants.

Chita *kôri*.

There are no special circumstances for official classification. Those persons are customarily called merchants who buy and sell goods bought from others; or who have a signboard or a trademark on their shop-front.

Minami-shidara *kôri*.

There is no distinguishing circumstance other than the fact that merchants do business in a business quarter, even though they are engaged in both business and farming or do business only as a secondary vocation. Census classification of farmers is based on the fact that a person living in the country is always a farmer, regardless of whether his main occupation is agriculture or business.

Atsumi *kôri*.

Nothing distinguishes a merchant from a non-merchant other than payment of the local tax or the business tax. There are, in fact, merchants engaged in farming, farmers in business and manufacturers who also do business.

Kaitô *kôri* and Kaisai *kôri*.

In both of these counties, merchants have no special mark. Most of them are "half-merchant farmers."[1]

Aichi *kôri*.

Merchants include only those who buy and sell goods as a regular occupation.

Niwa *kôri* and Haguri *kôri*.

Under the regulations for local taxation, merchants must report their occupation to the authorities and pay a tax, but non-merchants are not required to do so.

---

[1] *Hanshô-hannô.*

SHIZUOKA PREFECTURE

Shizuoka Province.

No circumstance distinguishes merchants, except that such persons buy and sell goods.

Udo *kôri* and Abe *kôri*.

The essential mark of merchants is that they sell to others goods which they bought not for consumption. Otherwise they are not merchants, even though they buy or sell goods.

Ina *kôri* and Aratama *kôri*.

No mark of distinction exists.

Kamo *kôri* and Naka *kôri*.

The distinction between merchants and non-merchants depends on the classification made in the local business tax regulation.

Saya *kôri* and Kitô *kôri*.

The essential mark is that merchants engage in commerce only; this distinguishes merchants from non-merchants. Farmers who also carry on a business, or merchants who also do farming, are often found in these counties. Unusual as this may be thought, this causes inactivity in regular business.

GIFU PREFECTURE

Mugi *kôri*.

No special circumstance marks the distinction.[1]

Ampachi *kôri*.

Merchants are usually those who carry on business by buying and selling goods for profit. No other special circumstance distinguishes them.

Fuwa *kôri*.

The only circumstance distinguishing merchants is that they study the values of goods and make a profit by applying the law of supply and demand to their trade.

Atsumi *kôri*, Kakami *kôri* and Katagata *kôri*.

The social position of merchants notably affects their rights and duties. Therefore the distinction between merchants and non-merchants should be made clear. Merchants are those who regularly pursue commerce and strictly observe its obligations.

---

[1] In general, one who engages in manufacturing, mixing seven parts manufacture with three parts business, is called a manufacturer; while one who carries on business, mixing seven parts business with three parts farming, is called a merchant.

Tagi *kôri* and Kamiishizu *kôri*.

By local custom, every merchant must hang his name-sign on the front of his shop.

Ono *kôri* and Ikeda *kôri*.

The term "business" means to make a profit in buying and selling goods, and this occupation is to be discriminated from such occupations as lending money. Nowadays, however, there are no special circumstances that distinguish merchants from non-merchants.

Haguri *kôri* and Nakajima *kôri*.

No special circumstances exist.

Ena *kôri*.

No special circumstances exist.

Kamo *kôri*.

As regards the distinction between merchants and non-merchants, it often occurs that farmers and manufacturers who do buying and selling in the intervals of their regular occupations are called merchants.

Kani *kôri*.

There are "merchants" who are not really merchants and "farmers" who are in fact merchants. Merchants include wholesalers, commission-house proprietors and retailers. Their trades are varied. Some sell natural products or products partly worked over; some sell products raised by themselves or partly worked over; some sell manufactured goods which others have raised; and some sell goods purchased from others. In short, not all persons who profit by selling goods can be termed merchants. The above-mentioned classes of persons are commonly called merchants, but from the standpoint of the commercial world, they perhaps ought not to be called merchants. In fact, it is not easy to discriminate merchants from non-merchants.

Atsumi *kôri*, Gifu Township.

One who makes business his regular work is to be called a merchant.

Ogaki Township.

One who makes business his regular work and makes a profit is to be called a merchant. There is no other customary standard to recognize a merchant.

Ena *kôri*, Nakatsu Village.

There is no special mark of distinction.

Shimoishizu *kôri*, Takasu Township.

In general, there is no distinction between merchants and non-merchants. But one who deals in large quantities of commodities is inevitably termed a merchant.

Haguri *kôri*, Takegahana Village.

Only those are merchants who take out a business license at the local office.

Yamagata *kôri*, Takatomi Village.

Those persons are usually called merchants who live in a city or town, even though they engage in farming at intervals. On the other hand, persons who live in a village, though they carry on business at intervals, are not called merchants.

Mugi *kôri*, Kôzu Village.

No distinction exists between merchants and non-merchants.

Haguri *kôri*, Kasamatsu Village.

No special circumstance of distinction exists.

Fuwa *kôri*, Tarui Village.

Non-merchants include such persons as officials, instructors, physicians and farmers; others are usually termed merchants.

Ôno *kôri*, Miwa Village.

No distinction exists.

Ampachi *kôri*, Gôdo Village.

There are four main kinds of occupation, namely, merchants, artisans, merchants engaged in farming at intervals and farmers.

Tagi *kôri*, Shimade Village.

Merchants commonly hang up a name-sign, inscribed with the name of their business, at the shop-front. Non-merchants put up only a name-sign on the post of their front gate.

Ena *kôri*, Iwa Village.

No distinction exists.

Toki *kôri*, Tajimi Village.

Merchants are those who sell goods to non-merchants retail and keep records in a sales book.

Kamo *kôri*, Hosome Village.

Because of the small number of real merchants in this village, there is no clear distinction between merchants and non-merchants. Those who obtain a business license from the local government are usually called merchants, but most of them are half-farmers. Nevertheless there are a few specialized merchants who do not engage in farming, but engage only in business.

Toki *kôri*, Takayama Village.

No distinction exists.

Ena *kôri*, Mitake Village.

Merchants take out a license according to the kind of business they engage in and keep the necessary account-books, while non-merchants do not.

Ena *kôri*, Akechi Village.

No distinguishing circumstances exist.

Mugi *kôri*, Seki Village.

It seems that there are no special circumstances marking a distinction between merchants and non-merchants, although there are, of course, various distinctions of occupation.

Ono *kôri*, Takayama Township.

Merchants are classified as such merely by having applied for a license and paid the local tax. Those who buy goods for their own use and sell goods made by themselves need no official license.

Motosu *kôri*, Kita-kata Village.

Merchants are persons above twenty years of age, regardless of sex, who carry on business regularly. Persons who are not under guardianship, are over fifteen years of age, have received their fathers' consent, or the mothers' in case of the fathers' death, incompetency or disappearance, or have recorded the approval of their relatives where there are no parents are entitled to be licensed as merchants as they are capable of making business contracts.

Kamo *kôri*, Ôta Village.

Merchants are distinguished from non-merchants merely by the fact of whether they have a license or not, for there have been many merchants engaged in other occupations in this village. Only a few merchants engage in business alone.

Gujô *kôri*.

There are no circumstances marking the distinction.

Topic 2:   Is Any Distinction Made between Civil and Commercial Matters According to the Nature of the Enterprise or Contract?

GROUP I—ANSWERS

Tokyo.

Any distinction made between a commercial and non-commercial affair, according to the nature of the transaction or contract, is purely a matter of opinion. No such distinction is sanctioned by custom. To express in a simpler form our answer to this question, as stated by our Explanation Committee:

People may say that, in their personal opinion, such and such transactions are by their nature ordinary (i.e., non-commercial) transactions, and such and such contracts are by their nature commercial contracts. But there is hardly any general custom recognizing such a distinction.

Kyoto.

The business of a merchant is the most active and precarious of all affairs. He is, as it were, daily fighting, sword in hand, on the battlefield. The quality of various manufactured articles depends on the state of climate and land, but it is only through the operation of a merchant that they are brought into use by mankind in general. For instance, although a dyer furnishes material and dyeing machines for coloring and printing cotton or silk cloth, he could not proceed in his work were it not for the rapidity with which the merchant sells his products for him. Hence every manufacturer naturally looks out for orders from merchants. As for the merchant, on the other hand, he must be careful to buy goods that are in fashion, or he would suffer a loss, not only now, but later as well, because the goods might remain unsold for a long time. Moreover, all natural products such as rice, raw silk, salt, iron, cotton, flax, paper-tree bark, rapeseed, mulberry leaves, tea tree buds, tobacco, etc., and manufactured articles, such as silk thread, flaxen and cotton cloth, paper, tea, sugar, wine, oil, etc., whether such manufacture be carried on in one general region or in a family, are collected by brokers, carried different places, both by land and sea, and finally deposited with wholesalers who again sell them to retailers in different districts who in turn distributed them among the consumers. Throughout all these transactions the merchant must be very watchful as to whether the price of a particular commodity is high or low or whether it is in fashion or not. He must always keep in touch with the actual market conditions of the three chief cities (i.e., Tokyo, Kyoto and Osaka) and other districts, and see which commodities are in demand and which are not. He must consider whether the circulation of money is rapid or slow and whether the interest on loans is high or low, etc. His task is so great that even a veteran merchant often incurs a great loss in spite of all his precautions. Of all mercantile undertakings, only one out of ten is a success; many or most retailers can only support themselves. Nor do the wholesale merchants[1] profit much by their transactions with retailers.[2] They lose their reputation when the goods they supply to the retailers are bad or dear, and they soon become bankrupt when business is slack. There is probably no occupation in the world in which so much peril is incurred and so much thought expended. Again, there is a certain class of merchants called *Tôki-shônin* (i.e., speculators), many of whom are to be seen nowadays, who are nevertheless no better than gamblers. There have been many speculators in the rice market. They cannot be said to be genuine merchants, they are merely dealers in craftiness.

As to commercial contracts,[3] it has been the custom, since former times, that contracts of sale between merchants themselves are concluded as soon as the seller and the buyer meet and strike hands on their bargain, however great the amount of goods to be sold may be. Such contracts, once thus concluded, have never been violated. Sometimes the parties settle by agreement the time for delivery of the thing sold, the seller receiving from the buyer a certain sum of money as earnest.[4] Earnest-money is also sometimes paid when an order is given for making a thing. If the buyer breaks his engagement, the earnest money is sometimes irrecoverably forfeited.[5] When an order is given for a thing, the details are

---

[1] *Oroshiuri-shônin.*

[2] *Kouri-shônin* or *misesaki-shônin.*

[3] The following paragraphs are presumably in answer to Topic 2 of Chapter 4, and are inserted here by mistake.

[4] *Tetsukekin.*

[5] *Nagareru.*

entered in the books of both parties and nothing further is done. In certain cases, orders are even given by post or telegraph, but this is not attended by breach of contract by either party. It sometimes happens that a contract of sale is concluded and the thing delivered, but payment by the buyer is postponed to a certain future time. Even in such cases either the contract is concluded by word of mouth (although the transaction is entered in the books of both parties), or a bill of sale, stating the goods sold and their price,[1] is delivered by the seller to the buyer. But in either case no breach of contract takes place and the buyer pays the price punctually at the stipulated time. Moreover, when a merchant sends his goods some distance for sale, the person to whom the goods are consigned deposits them in his store on their arrival, protects them against the danger of fire and theft and would never dispose of them in any manner unless assented to by their owner.

As to retailers,[2] the fixed terms for payment by customers of accounts current are in some regions six terms annually,[3] while in others twice a year, at *bon*[4] and *kure*,[5] according to the old custom. In these and other cases, when the term arrives, every merchant sends around his agent to his different customers with bills to receive payment. Such payment fails to be made in only one case out of ten. Such punctuality has been the custom from old times, although it has often been violated due to bankruptcy, absconding, etc., occasioned by famine, bad weather and other calamities.

Thus, as has already been said, merchants' contracts have never been distinguished by any formal written document handed by the buyer to the seller. Yet fewer law suits have been brought over such contracts than is the case for non-commercial contracts certified by the signature of local officers, such as contracts of mortgage, pledges, etc. This state of affairs is due to the press of commercial transactions and to the mutual confidence which exists between buyer and

---

[1] *Shikirisho.*

[2] *Kouri* and *Oroshiuri.*

[3] Six *sekki*: literally 6 ends of seasons or terms, so called because the debt is paid at the end of a month. In the above-mentioned system, payment falls due on 28th February, 30th April, 30th June, 31st August, 31st October and 31st December. In the case of monthly terms, it would be on the 31st, 30th or 28th of the respective months.

[4] In July.

[5] In December.

seller. Hence the superiority of a commercial contract, devoid of formal proof though it may be, to a non-commercial one certified by an official signature.

Such is the difference between commercial and non-commercial contracts.

Yokohama.

There is no practical custom distinguishing commercial and non-commercial matters according to the nature of the transaction or contract. The only distinction is theoretical.

Osaka.

As the meaning of the question is vague, we have found it difficult to answer. The distinction between commercial and non-commercial transactions is not well defined. However, there is some distinction. For instance, it is a commercial transaction to "stand" between producers and consumers and effect an exchange of commodities, while it is a non-commercial act to plant mulberry trees, to feed silk worms or to cultivate the land. Again, as to contracts, it is commercial to contract for the selling and buying of goods in order to profit by the transaction, while it is non-commercial to lend or borrow money, rice, etc.

Hyôgo.

Sometimes such a distinction is made.

(Quoted from the Proceedings of the local Committee):

"No. 33 (Kawanishi) said: 'We cannot answer this question immediately; we must think it over before we can answer. Therefore, would it not be better for us to lay aside this Topic for the present and proceed to Topic II?'

"All members agreed to this proposal, so we decided to lay aside this Topic for the present and proceed to consider Topic II."

Ôtsu.

Regarding the distinction between civil and commercial matters according to the nature of the enterprise or contract, there has been no established criterion in custom to distinguish these. People made distinctions according to their respective opinions.

Kumamoto.

There is such a distinction. In mercantile transactions, the parties contract by means of telegrams, postal cards, memoranda of sales, etc., mutual confidence and expedition being their principal objects. Furthermore they do not use ruled paper or sealed instru-

ments as they normally do in ordinary civil transactions.
Okayama.
Such distinction is made practically.
Yamaguchi.
No such custom exists.
Sakai.
No clear distinction between commercial and non-commercial transaction is made. The nature of the transaction or contract determines whether a particular transaction is called a commercial one or not. But when we look back to the practice hitherto observed we find there is some distinction. For example, almost all contracts of debt or sale between non-merchants are effected by the interchange of some formal written instrument; while on the other hand, among merchants, almost all contracts of sale, even of goods to the value of tens of thousands of *yen*, are effected without interchanging any sort of written documents between buyer and seller, but are concluded as soon as the parties strike their bargain. Such a transaction might at first sight seem loose and careless. But in practice very few persons break their contract, because in the commercial world a good reputation and mutual confidence are highly esteemed.
Iida.
No such custom exists. But we think that, unless we are greatly mistaken, whether one is supplying one's own demand, or supplying another's demand for the purpose of gain, may constitute the real difference.
Takamatsu.
There has been no custom to make distinction between civil and commercial matters according to the nature of the enterprise or contract, though people often think that such and such an enterprise is to be done by ordinary people and that such and such a contract is to be made by merchants.
Fukui.
Such a distinction is sometimes made.
Tokushima.
No such distinction exists by custom.
Takefu.
No such distinction exists by custom. But in a case of a contract being broken, the nature of the document decides the matter.

Miyagi.

There is no fixed criterion by which to distinguish commercial and non-commercial transactions. But we think that when a person makes it his ordinary business to "stand" between producers and consumers and to buy and sell commodities his transaction is commercial; while when he occasionally buys and sells some commodities, but does not make selling and buying his ordinary business, then his transaction is non-commercial. And as to contracts, contracts of sale of any commodity for the purpose of pecuniary profit are commercial, while those which do not aim at pecuniary profit are non-commercial.

Matsuyama.

There is naturally a distinction between persons who make it their ordinary business to sell goods or lend money for the purpose of pecuniary profit and persons who only occasionally sell things they do not want or lend money out of kindness. But we do not know of any custom to distinguish between civil and commercial matters according to the nature of the enterprise or contract.

GROUP II—ANSWERS

Tokyo Metropolis

Oil Wholesalers.

No such distinction is made.

Grain Wholesalers.

No distinction is made, either in actual business or in contract laws, between civil and commercial matters.

Timber Wholesalers.

There is naturally a distinction between civil and commercial matters.

Fuel Wholesalers.

No one in this trade carries on business with such a distinction in mind.

Salt Wholesalers.

The only contracts are commercial ones.

Dried Bonito Wholesalers.

There may be such a distinction, depending on the nature of the contract.

Dry Goods Wholesalers.

There is such a distinction.

Saké Wholesalers.

The distinction is sometimes made.

Kôjimachi Ward.

There is no clear distinction between civil and commercial matters. But in commercial usage the account book of the creditor is regarded as constituting evidence (of the transaction), no document from the debtor being needed.

Nihombashi Ward.

Many of the banks and commercial firms are limited in their liability in connection with their business and contracts, and their liabilities do not extend to individual property as in the case of ordinary merchants—a situation which makes for a distinction, based on the nature of the enterprise or contract, between civil and commercial matters.

Kyôbashi Ward.

We have nothing to say in reply to your questionnaire.

Yotsuya Ward and Ushigome Ward.

As to the distinction between civil and commercial matters depending on the nature of the enterprise or contract, those contracts made by merchants regarding transactions in commodities are contracts in the commercial sense, while all other sorts of contracts are civil. Contracts, for instance, regarding the sale of a residence, its land and furniture, for personal use, may appear to be commercial contracts, but in fact they are civil contracts.

Asakusa Ward.

There is such a distinction depending on the nature of the enterprise or contract.

Honjo Ward.

Such a distinction sometimes exists, depending on the nature of the enterprise or contract. Suppose a fuel merchant, for instance, borrows money in advance from a fuel wholesaler by hypothecating his commodities and performs his contract. In this case his transaction is commercial. If he does not perform his contract and payment is demanded of the money advanced, then the case is civil.

Ebara *kôri*.

There is no fixed distinction made between civil and commercial matters, depends on the nature of the enterprise or contract.

Higashi-tama *kôri* and Minami-tama *kôri*.

There is an implied customary distinction between civil and commercial matters, depending on the nature of the enterprise or contract. Commercial contracts are simple and brief and not so formal as civil contracts, as will be seen later.

Kita-toshima *kôri*.

The reply has already been given in connection with Topic 1.

Minami-adachi *kôri*.

There is no distinction made between civil and commercial matters.

Shitaya Ward.

We believe that there is no custom of distinguishing between civil and commercial matters according to the nature of the enterprise or contract.

Kanda Ward.

We have never noticed any distinction made between civil and commercial matters.

Akasaka Ward and Azabu Ward.

There is naturally a distinction between civil and commercial matters, depending on the nature of the enterprise and contract, but no clear distinction is made in ordinary practice. Merchants have a practice known as a transaction among guild members,[1] which is different from their transactions with ordinary persons[2] as regards market quotation,[3] manner of bargaining[4] and discount in prices.[5] An ordinary bond[6] is not required for a loan in the commercial sense, and no interest is supposed to accrue on it. But as to the period of settling the account,[7] it is no different from that in the case of a loan in the civil sense. As to the form of a commercial contract, such contracts are made by the parties concerned, there being no fixed form in use.

Hongô Ward.

There is no clear distinction depending on the nature of the enterprise or contract, but there is naturally a distinction between

[1] *Torihiki.*
[2] *Tsûjô-nin.*
[3] *Sôba.*
[4] *Kakehiki.*
[5] *Daika-no-bubiki.*
[6] *Shôsho.*
[7] *Seisan-no-kigen.*

transactions[1] between merchants and those between a merchant and a non-merchant.

CHIBA PREFECTURE

Awa *kôri*, Hei *kôri*, Asai *kôri* and Nagasa *kôri*.

Naturally there is a distinction between civil and commercial matters. We would like to cite instances of it, but as there is something in the questionnaire we cannot comprehend, we refrain from doing so.

Katori *kôri*.

Commercial matters differ from civil matters in that, except in matters relating to money loans,[2] no registered legal seal[3] is needed, a seal stamped in the statement of account[4] being sufficient proof of the transaction.

Yamabe *kôri* and Muza *kôri*.

There is naturally a general distinction between civil and commercial matters, depending on the nature of the enterprise or contract, but no such distinction in terms of particular rules has hitherto been made.

Unakami *kôri* and Sôsa *kôri*.

There is no distinction made between civil and commercial matters depending on the nature of the enterprise or contract.

Higashi-katsushika *kôri*.

There is no distinction made between civil and commercial matters, regardless of the nature of the enterprise or contract.

IBARAGI PREFECTURE

Nishi-katsushika *kôri* and Sashima *kôri*.

Suppose a company were established, the soil cultivated, young mulberry trees planted, silkworms raised and the silkreeling manufacture started. The contract dealing with these things belongs under civil matters, while a contract for the purchase and exportation of the silk thus produced belongs under commercial matters.

KANAGAWA PREFECTURE

Miura *kôri*.

There is no distinction.

Tachibana *kôri*.

---

[1] *Hikiai.*
[2] *Kingin-taishaku.*
[3] *Jitsuin.*
[4] *Shikiri-ban.*

There should be a distinction between civil and commercial matters.

Kita-tama *kôri.*

Enterprises may be classified as agricultural, industrial, and commercial. But as to the nature of the contracts, there is no particular standard by which to distinguish between civil and commercial matters.

Ashigara-shimo *kôri.*

As for the distinction between civil and commercial matters, it is customary to regard them as separate.

Prefectual Industry Bureau.

There is no practice in vogue distinguishing civil and commercial matters.

TOCHIGI PREFECTURE

Prefectural Office.

There is a considerable difference between civil and commercial contracts. In commercial contracts, for instance, the forfeiture of the earnest-money brings about the rescission of a sales contract. When a sum of money twice the amount of the earnest-money is paid back to the party who paid, the contract, even if a breach of contract has occurred, is regarded as rescinded, regardless of whether the contract is a written one or not.

Furthermore, the parties to a contract may express their agreement to it by clapping their hands. These are some of the practices that are never departed from in commercial circles.

Shimo-tsuga *kôri* and Samukawa *kôri.*

Sometimes a situation occurs in which civil and commercial matters are distinguished according to the nature of the enterprise or contract, but there is customarily no clear distinction between the two.

Ashikaga *kôri* and Yanada *kôri.*

There is no clear distinction between civil and commercial matters. When a commercial contract is made on receipt of a verbal communication[1] or an order,[2] the promisee, putting his trust in the party who has given the order and demanding no written confirmation of it, will forward the goods even without making a reply

---

[1] *Kôjô.*
[2] *Chûmon.*

of acceptance. In short, commercial transactions are very informal, compared with civil dealings.

MIE PREFECTURE

Suzuka *kôri.*

No distinction is made between civil and commercial matters, according to the nature of the enterprise or contract.

Isshi *kôri.*

There is a distinction between civil and commercial matters. In terms of occupation, for instance, there is a distinction between a pawnbroker[1] and a moneylender,[2] and in contracts, a distinction between a bond[3] and a passbook.[4]

Asake *kôri.*

There is no perceptible distinction between civil and commercial matters, depending on the nature of the enterprise or contract.

Nabari *kôri* and Iga *kôri.*

In commercial transactions, in most case no bond or contract document is given. The names of the parties to a transaction[5] are entered in a book and are used, if need be, as evidence of the transactions. Furthermore, a contract for sale on credit[6] to a customer is entered in the book of the vendor alone, and the settlement of the account is customarily made afterwards on the basis of a bill[7] or a statement of account[8] prepared by the vendor.

AICHI PREFECTURE

Nakajima *kôri.*

Regarding the distinction between civil and commercial matters depending on the nature of an enterprise, when a farmer sells the grain of his own growing, for instance, it is a civil act. If the same farmer engages in trade and buys and sells the grain of others' growing, however, it is a commercial act.

As to the distinction depending on the nature of a contract, when a buyer proposes to buy dried sardines on credit and, after this

---

[1] *Shichiya.*
[2] *Kanekashi.*
[3] *Shôsho.*
[4] *Kayoichô.*
[5] *Shiaisaki.*
[6] *Kashiuri-keiyaku.*
[7] *Nedan-sho.*
[8] *Sashihiki-sho.*

proposal is rejected, still insists on its acceptance by the vendor, the vendor might, on receipt of a bond of debt from the vendee, deliver the goods to the latter. Here the vendee originally wanted the debt to be one of a commercial nature, but it finally became a debt in the civil sense.

Nagoya Ward.

Suppose a company were established and were to engage in a commercial enterprise. The contracts formed between the company and its shareholders would be civil, while the contract concluded by the company with regard to its enterprises would be of a commercial nature. This is an example of a distinction made according to the nature of the transaction.

Chita *kôri*.

No such distinction is made.

Minami-shidara *kôri*.

Not only is no such fixed distinction made, but also there would be few persons who could distinguish between civil and commercial matters, which could be expected from the frequent carelessness in omitting to date a contract.

Kaitô *kôri* and Kaisai *kôri*.

A distinction is sometimes made between civil and commercial matters, depending on the nature of the enterprise or contract.

Atsumi *kôri*.

There is naturally a distinction between civil and commercial matters, depending on the nature of the enterprise or contract, but it is impossible to give any definition of particular instances.

Aichi *kôri*.

We have never come across anyone who makes a distinction between civil and commercial matters.

Niwa *kôri* and Haguri *kôri*.

There is a distinction between civil and commercial matters depending on the nature of the enterprise, but none depending on the nature of the contract. As to the distinction depending on the nature of the enterprise, the act of a merchant in selling and buying articles in business is commercial, while the act of non-merchant B in buying from A an article the latter can spare and in using it for the former's own purposes is entirely civil. The sale of land, buildings, ships, etc., belongs in this class.

SHIZUOKA PREFECTURE

Prefectural Office.

There is no clear distinction between civil and commercial matters, depending on the nature of the enterprise or contract.

Udo *kôri* and Abe *kôri*.

Those acts of a merchant that directly aim at his own benefit may be called commercial. But there is no customary distinction between civil and commercial matters.

Ina *kôri* and Aratama *kôri*.

No such distinction is made.

Kamo *kôri* and Naka *kôri*.

There are many instances of this distinction, but one or two of them will suffice here. Suppose a silk-reeling company makes two sorts of contract. One provides for the company's taking over the cocoons of A and reeling silk out of them for A at a certain fixed rate of charge. The other provides that the company shall take over the cocoons of B and reel silk out of them for no fixed rate of charge, but the company receives a certain proportion of the proceeds when it sells the silk manufactured out of B's cocoons. If law suits arose over these contracts, A's case would be civil and B's case commercial.

If a contract for building a bridge or opening a road provides for the amount of cost and the time limit for payment, it is a purely civil contract; while if, without fixing the amount of cost, it provides that the contractors shall receive the bridge tolls or road tolls to be collected from the travellers for a certain number of months or years after the completion of the work, it is probably a commercial contract.

Saya *kôri* and Kitô *kôri*.

There has hitherto been no distinction between civil and commercial matters depending on the nature of the enterprise or contract. As commercial transactions, however, are of such a nature as to require performance in strict faith,[1] it would be very inconvenient for commercial purposes to class them with civil contracts. It is desirable, therefore, that a distinction between civil and commercial matters be made in future and that it become an established practice to recognize entries in a merchant's book as evidence of transactions, and to recognize even a piece of paper giving a sales

[1] *Shingi.*

account as constituting sufficient evidence in a court of law.

GIFU PREFECTURE

Mugi *kôri*.

There is no distinction between civil and commercial matters, except that a civil contract is apparently a little more formal than a commercial contract.

Ampachi *kôri*.

If we look at the customs, there actually exists a distinction between civil and commercial matters, depending on the nature of the enterprise or contract. Suppose one or more men undertake some enterprise. If it relates to the good of the general public, it is usually what is called a civil enterprise; while if the enterprise, in the course of business, aims at the benefit of one or more men, it is commercial. A commercial contract is more simple and informal than an ordinary contract, which is complicated and requires the exchange of formal documents between the parties, with a surety. Also, speed in transaction and the parties' commercial credit are valued in commercial contracts, so these are usually concluded merely by means of oral communication or the clapping of hands.

Fuwa *kôri*.

Suppose A started a development enterprise,[1] and B entered into a contract[2] for the work but invited bids[3] for the work from the general public granting subcontracts[4] to C, D and so on. If B aims at reaping profits as a middleman, his enterprise is commercial. If not, it is civil. When merchant E proceeds to buy goods from merchant F, contracting for the payment of the price at such and such times, the contract is commercial. If, however, he defaults in payment for some reason, resulting in the hypothecation of (say) his house, and another contract is made for the payment of price and interest within a certain fixed period, then an alteration in the contract situation for credit between the parties takes place, and questions relating thereto will be civil.

Atsumi *kôri*, Kagami *kôri* and Katagata *kôri*.

No such distinction has ever been made.

---

[1] *Kaitaku-jigyô.*
[2] *Ukeoi.*
[3] *Nyûsatsu.*
[4] *Mata-ukeoi.*

Tagi *kôri* and Kami-ishizu *kôri*.

There is naturally a distinction between civil and commercial matters, according to the nature of the enterprise and contract.

Ôno *kôri* and Ikeda *kôri*.

There are no fixed commercial customs regarding sale of goods, credits and the making of contracts between merchants. Therefore, a commercial contract, of whatever sort it may be, is not different from a civil contract. Thus there is no distinction nowadays between civil and commercial matters.

Haguri *kôri* and Nakajima *kôri*.

There is naturally a distinction between civil and commercial matters. A civil contract is generally a written contract and a commercial contract is usually oral.

Ena *kôri*.

There is such a distinction.

Kamo *kôri*.

Suppose two ordinary people,[1] A and B, who are not merchants, make a contract for the sale of some goods, and B gives earnest-money to A. Later if the contract is rescinded by B for some reason of his own, then A must return the earnest-money to B, while if A desires to have the contract rescinded, all he has to do is to return the earnest-money to B. In a commercial transaction, however, if B proposes the rescission of such a contract, he is not entitled to reclaim the earnest-money he has paid to A; and if A proposes the rescission, he usually returns to B a sum of money twice as large as the earnest-money he has received from B. Except for such practices, however, no distinction between civil and commercial contracts has ever been noted.

Kani *kôri*.

They do not take the trouble to distinguish between civil and commercial matters; but there is naturally such a distinction according to the nature of the enterprise or contract.

Atsumi *kôri*, Gifu Township.

No distinction whatever is made between civil and commercial matters.

Ôgaki Township.

If we observe the customs, there is naturally a distinction be-

---

[1] *Tsûjô-jimmin.*

tween civil and commercial matters, depending on the nature of the enterprise or contract. Suppose one or more men undertook some enterprise. If it relates to the good of the general public, it is what is called a civil enterprise; while if the enterprise, in the course of business, aims at the benefit of the one or more men, it is commercial. As to a commercial contract, it is simple and informal, compared with an ordinary contract, which is complicated and requires the exchange of formal documents between the parties, with a surety.

Also speed in transaction, as well as the parties' commercial credit, are important in commercial contracts, so that commercial contracts are usually concluded merely by means of oral communication or the clapping of hands.

Ena *kôri*, Nakatsugawa Village.

Merchants' contracts are mostly oral, and so sometimes are to be distinguished from civil contracts.

Shimoishizu *kôri*, Takasu Township.

As for the distinction between civil and commercial matters, the civil contract is made on the basis of fixed rules and is definite. But the commercial contract is very elastic in practice, even if it is concluded observing the fixed rule and is definite.

Haguri *kôri*, Takegahana Village.

There is no clear distinction yet between civil and commercial matters.

Yamagata *kôri*, Takatomi Village.

No definite distinction between civil and commercial matters depending on the nature of the enterprise or contract has been noted.

Mugi *kôri*, Kôzuchi Village.

There is no distinction between civil and commercial matters depending on the nature of the enterprise or contract.

Haguri *kôri*, Kasamatsu Village.

Civil contracts are generally concluded by means of formal documents, while most commercial contracts are oral; hence there is naturally a distinction between the two.

Fuwa *kôri*, Tarui Village.

Suppose A started a development enterprise, and B entered into a contract for the work, but, inviting bids for the work from the general public and otherwise, granted subcontracts to C, D, and so on. B's enterprise, if it aims at reaping profits for B as a middle-man, is commercial, but if not, it is civil.

When, however, a merchant buys from a farmer some rice the latter has cultivated[1] at the current market price, and according to custom makes a contract fixing a time limit for the payment of the price and interest and gives a contract document to the farmer, it would probably be considered a case in which the merchant has started by acting commercially but ended up with the conclusion of a civil contract.

Ôno *kôri*, Miwa Village.

No such distinction is made.

Ampachi *kôri*, Gôdo Village.

There is no distinction made between civil and commercial mat-ters.

Tagi *kôri*, Shimada Village.

There is no such distinction.

Ena *kôri*, Iwa Village.

There is a distinction.

Toki *kôri*, Tajimi Village.

As far as contracts are concerned, a civil matter is different from a commercial matter.

Kamo *kôri*, Hosome Village.

Regarding sales contracts, those who are not members of some merchants' guild or are non-merchants have been called *motokata* or *kuwasaki*. Those who are true merchants will under no circum-stances break their commercial contracts.

Motokata, however, have a bad habit of breaking a contract and withholding the delivery of goods as promised if they happen to be caught in a fluctuating market. Thus merchants who are parties to contracts with *motokata*, though resenting the attitude of the latter, desiring to avoid unnecessary loss of time, will sometimes break their contracts, or even offer higher prices for the goods. Such vicious civil practices should be avoided by both parties to con-tracts.

Toki *kôri*, Takayama Village.

No such distinction is made.

Kani *kôri*, Mitake Village.

[1] *Sakutoku-mai.*

There is no definite distinction.

Ena *kôri*, Akechi Village.

There is such a distinction.

Mugi *kôri*, Seki Village.

Suppose an enterprise were organized and run on the understanding that each merchant partner should contribute a hundred
yen toward the enterprise. Merchant A immediately makes his contribution of the sum agreed upon, but B, unable to make the contribution, hypothecates his farm to A and starts working as an
employee of the firm instead. The contract between A and B was
originally a commercial one, but owing to its later change to a contract for credit between the two, it has become a civil one. However, all questions relating to the enterprise will be treated as of a
commercial nature. Herein lies the distinction between civil and
commercial matters.

Ôno *kôri*, Takayama Township.

There is of course a distinction between civil and commercial
matters with respect to enterprises, but with respect to contracts,
civil matters do not differ from commercial ones.

Motosu *kôri*, Kita-kata Village.

What makes for the distinction between civil and commercial
matters according to the nature of the enterprise or contract? A
commercial enterprise aims at profits, while a civil undertaking
aims at the good of the public.[1] If a firm is organized by a contract between certain people with the interest of the firm as its
chief aim and the good of the public as its secondary object, it will
be a commercial enterprise, while if a firm is organized by a contract having the welfare and security[2] of the public as its chief aim
and the interest of a firm or an organization as its secondary object,
it is our custom to regard it as a civil undertaking.

Kamo *kôri*, Ôta Village.

As to the distinction between civil and commercial matters depending on the nature of the enterprise or contract, let us say that
two men, A and B, conclude a sales contract in a commercial transaction, and B pays to A some earnest-money. If later B rescinds
the contract for some reason, then B cannot reclaim the earnest-

---

[1] *Kôeki.*

[2] *Kôfuku-annei.*

money which he has paid to A. However, if A proposes the rescission of the contract, he will have to return to B a sum of money twice the amount of the earnest-money which he has received from B.

Gujô *kôri*.

No such distinction has ever been noted.

Topic 3:   Does a Married Woman Trade Apart from Her Husband? If So, What Will Be Her Relation to Her Husband with Respect to Her Property?

GROUP I—ANSWERS

Tokyo.

Married women sometimes live and trade apart from their husbands. To the question put by our local committee, of whether in such cases the husband becomes the wife's sole "money master," or whether he contributes a portion of the capital, we answer that this depends on the mutual agreement between the husband and wife. Again, to the question of whether, in the case of the wife becoming bankrupt, the creditors' claims extend to the estate of the husband, we reply that there is no fixed custom about that.

Kyoto.

It often happens that a married woman carries on trade independently of her husband, but most such instances are met with in the middle and lower classes. For example, there is the case of the wife of a man who is an outdoor laborer, carpenter, mason, etc.; she might remain in the house and keep a shop with certain commodities. Another case might be of a wife whose husband is a craftsman working at home; she might go out and peddle goods. Sometimes daughters or sisters carry on occupations independently of their fathers or brothers. In all these cases the capital employed by the female trader is lent by either her husband, father, or brother, as the case may be, or by some other "money master," or, in the case of a wife trading apart from her husband, the husband may contribute a portion of it. In short, there is no fixed custom about this.

In cases where a wife or daughter appears to be carrying on a trade in her own name, it sometimes happens that in reality, though not nominally, her husband or father has a joint interest. But in such cases the husband or father cannot be made jointly responsible with the wife or daughter, because although the husband or father contributed a certain sum of money to form a part of the capital of the concern, a contribution of this kind is similar in nature to contributions from relatives. But the above statement has no general application to all cases, because circumstances are different in different cases.

Osaka.

A married woman was formerly prohibited by the law of guild-shares from trading apart from her husband, but such women sometimes kept harlot-houses or restaurants or carried on various other occupations in their own names. However, owing to the inadequacy of the old census law[1] it cannot be stated whether in such case the wife was an independent mistress of the family, or was an independent trader in name only. The married woman was entirely under the control of her husband, however, with regard to property.

Yokohama.

This is often the case. But respecting the relation of husband and wife as to property, it can be said that there is no fixed custom, this depending upon mutual agreement.

Hyôgo.

Married women never trade apart from their husbands. (Quoted from the Proceedings: No. 27 (Arima): "I do not know of any instance of a wife's trading apart from her husband in Hyôgo and Kobe. It sometimes happens in the case of harlot keepers that a married woman trades in her own name, without disclosing her husband's name; but there is nothing similar in other occupations."

No. 17 (Murai): "Not only has there been no instance in former times of a husband and wife trading separately by dividing their property between them to be held in separate rights, we have never ourselves heard of an instance of a wife's trading apart from her husband."

No. 34 (Fujita): "I am decidedly of the opinion that a wife, if she is a true wife, recognized as such in the census list, never trades apart from her husband."

President (Kajima): "Adopting now the opinion of the members who have just spoken, we shall report to the Government to the effect that no married woman trades apart from her husband.")

Ôtsu.

Although there are some instances in which a married woman trades separately, as when a married woman acts as a "room-

[1] *Koseki-ho.*

letter," or a restaurateur, or some minor trader, even in such cases her husband is the owner of her property.

Kumamoto.

There are often married women who trade apart from their husbands. However, there is customarily no situation regarding such women's property in which the husband is in no way related.

Okayama.

Some married women trade separately; but respecting their relation to their husbands with regard to property, there is no clear distinction.

Yamaguchi.

There are married women who trade apart from their husbands. However, regarding their relation to their husbands in respect to their property, no clear separations seem to be made.

Sakai.

No married woman trades separately, but we think that in future many will do so. In such cases, we fear it might sometimes happen that either husband or wife would transfer his or her property to the other, so as to defraud third parties' rights, a consequence which might lead to the detriment of commerce. It is our earnest wish, therefore, that the government should enact a law that all property should, with the consent of the husband, be made common property and that no partition should be allowed.

Iida.

There are one or two instances of a married woman trading separately, as for example a hair-binder[1] or peddler dealing in second-hand clothing or sundries. But her husband is the joint owner with her[2] of her property.

Takamatsu.

Married women often have a separate shop and trade apart from their husbands. But whether the husband is the wife's "money-master," the wife furnishes the capital herself, or the husband and wife trade on a joint account depends entirely on their mutual agreement. There is thus no fixed custom as to whether the wife's creditor can claim against her husband's estate in a case of her going bankrupt.

---

[1] *Kamiyui.*

[2] *Kyôtsû.*

Fukui.

No married woman trades separately.

Tokushima.

A married woman may trade separately, but her property is in most cases under the control of her husband.

Takefu.

No such custom exists. As to her relation to her husband respecting property, she is only entitled to the things which she brought with her when she came to her husband's house to marry.

Miyagi.

This often happens. The matter of to whom the property belongs depends on mutual agreement. Whether on not the property is apportioned between the husband and wife may depend on whether the wife trades on her own account or for the benefit of her family. But as against other persons, the husband is the owner of all property except the goods for sale.

Matsuyama.

This sometimes happens. But we have not heard of any special instances of property being apportioned between husband and wife.

GROUP II—ANSWERS

Tokyo Metropolis

Oil Wholesalers.

No answer.

Grain Wholesalers.

There have been no instances of this. Even if there be any, it is not regarded as desirable to have an interest in other persons' property.

Timber Wholesalers.

No instances of this in this guild.

Fuel Wholesalers.

No instances in this guild.

Salt Wholesalers.

Not a single instance of this.

Dried Bonito Wholesalers.

There have been no instances of a married woman carrying on an independent business apart from her husband.

Dry Goods Wholesalers.

No experience of this.

Saké Wholesalers.

Though there are some instances in commercial society, there is not a single instance in this guild.

Kôjimachi Ward.

Not a single instance in this ward of a woman doing this.

Nihombashi Ward.

A married woman is often found possessing land and a house with the consent of her husband, in order to increase her property, or being a stock holder in a company or a moneylender. It would seem, however, that a married woman has no property rights except by consent of her husband. The number of married women among our people who operate restaurants is recently on the increase. There is, however, no fixed custom with respect to their property.

Kyôbashi Ward.

A few married women engage in business independently of their husbands. We cannot answer as to property rights.

Yotsuya Ward and Ushigome Ward.

Not a few married women are engaged in business. There is, however, no distinction between her husband's and her own property.

Asakusa Ward.

There is not a single married woman independently carrying on business in this ward under her own name. Even if a woman carries on an independent business, there is no distinction between her husband's and her own property.

Honjo Ward.

Sometimes a married woman engages independently in business, in which case she has a special relation to her husband as to property. For example, if she goes bankrupt, under the business law her property is separated from her husband's.

Ebara *kôri*.

We rarely find a married woman engaged in business. As for property, this depends upon the agreement between husband and wife.

Higashi-tama *kôri* and Minami-toshima *kôri*.

No married woman in this county is engaged in business independently of her husband. If there were such a case however, all property would belong to the woman's husband, unless she takes proceedings for authorization (real property) or has positive proof (movable property). But all commodities which are indispensable for business belong to her.

Kita-toshima *kôri*.

It is rare that a married woman engages in business independently of her husband. It is difficult to distinguish her property from her husband's. In the case of a married woman operating a restaurant or a brothel in her own name, a distinction is made between her own and her husband's property for convenience' sake.

Minami-adachi *kôri*.

We rarely find a married woman engaged in business independently of her husband. There are, however, married women who carry on a paying profession apart from their husbands. Concerning property, no clear distinction exists between her husband's and her own property.

Shitaya *kôri*.

No married woman here carries on business independently except in the case of a restaurant or a teahouse affiliated with a brothel. As for property, this depends largely on the agreement of husband and wife; there is no fixed custom.

Kanda Ward.

Sometimes a married woman and her husband are living apart and the former engages in business. In order to protect her property, she has the house and land in her own name; there is no mingling of her property with her husband's.

Akasaka Ward and Azabu Ward.

Before the Meiji Restoration, no married woman engaged in business independently. If she was the head of the family, she had to have a guardian. Since the Meiji Restoration, however, not a few married women have operated restaurants, houses of assignation, clubs, riverside teahouses and variety-halls. Those who manage businesses of this sort usually own property separately.

Hongô Ward.

It is hard to find a married woman, except a so-called "concubine," engaged in business. As for property, there is no fixed custom.

CHIBA PREFECTURE

Awa *kôri*, Hei *kôri*, Asai *kôri* and Nagasa *kôri*.

No married woman engages in business apart from her husband or in her own name. There are often, however, married women carrying on business in their households with capital[1] acquired by themselves. For example, a husband and wife in fishery[2] might engage separately in the pawn business apart from their own business, using the profits for buying the children's clothes, for expenses on ceremonial occasions, or old-age pensions. Regardless of the particular understanding between wife and husband as to domestic finance, all rights and duties towards other persons[3] are treated in the husband's name. Thus, the wife's business cannot be considered to be an independent one. On the other hand, there may be emergency cases when, though it is usually distinguished, their property should be treated as common property. When a wife dies, all her property is reckoned as her husband's unless it is given to the children according to her will.

Katori *kôri*.

Sometimes there are married women engaging independently in business; we often find, however, that the capital, as property, belongs to the husband, while the profit derived from it is given to the wife.

Yamabe *kôri* and Muza *kôri*.

No married women engage in independent business.

Unakami *kôri* and Sôsa *kôri*.

There are a few married women carrying on business by themselves. But as to their property, there is no distinction.

Higashikatsushika *kôri*.

No married women carry on business independently.

IBARAGI PREFECTURE

Nishi-katsushika *kôri* and Sashima *kôri*.

In the case of a married woman dealing with goods and money in her own name, all the property belongs to her husband, unless there is proof that it is her own.

KANAGAWA PREFECTURE

Miura *kôri*.

There has been no such experience here.

---

[1] For example, the dowry which the bride brought when she was married, or money saved during her married life, etc.

[2] Managing a fishery with full right of fishing by employing fishermen.

[3] License of commerce and transaction with other persons.

Tachibana *kôri*.

With respect to property, a wife's contracts do not affect her husband. For instance, if a wife is adjudicated bankrupt under the business law, this has no effect on the husband's property.

Kita-tama *kôri*.

Some married women carry on business by themselves. All property is under the control of the head of the family, whether the wife carries on business in her own name or in her husband's name, if he is the family head.

Ashigarashimo *kôri*.

We often find a married woman engaged in independent business among retailers. Husband and wife own property together.

Prefectural Industry Bureau.

A married woman often engages in business by herself. Ownership of property depends on the agreement between husband and wife; there is no fixed custom.

Tochigi Prefecture

Prefectural Office.

Not a single married woman engages independently in business. According to local custom, many married women carry on business[1] independently. But their properties seem to belong to their husbands. It is customary to recognize a woman who is a concubine[2] and who carries on business by herself as having independent property.

Shimo-tsuga *kôri* and Samukawa *kôri*.

We rarely find that a married woman engages independently in business. It is clear that there is no distinction between her property and that of her husband.

Ashikaga *kôri* and Harita *kôri*.

In Ashikaga *kôri* more than half of the merchants are engaged in textile manufacture, and they are mostly women. Thus it may be said that there are many married women managing a business. They are, however, not carrying on business apart from their husbands financially. We may merely say that they are assisting their husbands' business. Consequently there is no distinction as regards property.

---

[1] Most of them are retailers or peddlers.

[2] A woman who does not belong to the family register of her husband.

MIE PREFECTURE

Suzuka *kôri*.

Married women often engage in business by themselves. As for property, some of them have a joint interest with their husbands, while others do not.

Isshi *kôri*.

Not a single married woman engages in business.

Asake *kôri*.

None.

Nabari *kôri* and Iga *kôri*.

A married woman rarely engages in business independently. A husband, for instance, may manufacture goods, while his wife does the trading. With respect to property, no separation is made.

AICHI PREFECTURE

Nakashima *kôri*.

None of the married women engage in business.

Nagoya Ward.

None.

Chita *kôri*.

Married women rarely engage in business by themselves; those few who do are confined to the humbler classes. Their properties belong to their husbands.

Minami-shidara *kôri*.

Though a few married women carry on business independently, there is no separation of properties between husband and wife, as the wife shares her husband's fortunes. If there is any separation, it is made at the time of a divorce.

Atsumi *kôri*.

Sometimes we find a married woman occupied in an independent business. But there is no separation of her property from her husband's.

Kaitô *kôri* and Kaisai *kôri*.

Whether a married woman carries on business independently depends on the kind of business.[1] There is no distinction as to properties.

Aichi *kôri*.

Married women often engage in business independently. How-

[1] There are some kinds of business suitable to women, for instance, drapery or old clothes.

ever they are not family heads and cannot have separate properties from their husbands.

Niwa *kôri* and Haguri *kôri*.

There are a few married women carrying on business by themselves, and their business is separate as to property, capital and profits.

SHIZUOKA PREFECTURE

Prefectural Office.

Not a single married woman engages in business independently.

Udo *kôri* and Abe *kôri*.

There are some. With respect to property, the husband is not allowed to manage it, but there is no clear distinction between husband's and wife's ownership. If the husband is unable to manage the business, the wife usually carries on the business by herself.

Ina *kôri* and Aratama *kôri*.

There are married women engaged in business independently, but they share losses and profits with their husbands.

Kamo *kôri* and Naka *kôri*.

Unless there is an agreement otherwise between husband and wife, all properties belong to the husband.

Saya *kôri* and Kitô *kôri*.

On rare occasions we find married women engaged in business by themselves. If the husband, due to mental or moral incapacity, is unable to manage his property, there may be a separation of his property from hers by agreement between them, the husband being put under the guardianship of relatives. Otherwise there is no distinction, even though they have their own separate properties. This question is, from an ethical standpoint, beyond debate.

GIFU PREFECTURE

Mugi *kôri*.

There are some married women carrying on business by themselves. The property relation between husband and wife is not uniform.

Ampachi *kôri*.

Sometimes we find a married woman carrying on business independently. Customarily husband and wife have common properties.

Fuwa *kôri*.

There are some married women doing as stated in the question, but their properties are held in common with those of their husbands.

Tagi *kôri* and Kami-ishizu *kôri*.

There are some such women. There is no separation of properties.

Ôno *kôri* and Ikeda *kôri*.

There are few married women carrying on business independently in these counties. No matter how property may actually be divided betwzen husband and wife, the legal relation between them recognizes no separation of property. This is inevitable, for there is no legal way to separate the properties.

Haguri *kôri* and Nakashima *kôri*.

There have been no married woman engaged in business independently.

Ena *kôri*.

We often find such instances. With respect to property, there is no clear distinction in point of fact.

Kamo *kôri*.

There are some, but no distinction is made as to property.

Kani *kôri*.

We often find instances of this. The husband's property is shared with his wife.

Atsumi *kôri*, Gifu Town.

Few married women engage independently in business. Generally speaking, no distinction is made as to properties.

Ôgaki Town.

A married woman seldom engages in business independently. The husband's property is usually shared with his wife.

Ena *kôri*, Nakatsugawa Village.

There are some instances. The properties are held in common by both spouses.

Shimo-ishizu *kôri*, Takasu Town.

There are some instances. The properties are held in common by both spouses.

Haguri *kôri*, Takegahana Village.

There are some poor merchants whose wives carry on business independently;[1] but such people are too poor to make any clear

---

[1] Selling haberdashery and second-hand goods in villages near their own.

distinction between husband and wife as to property.

Yamagata *kôri*, Takatomi Village.

None. If there were, there would be no ownership separate from the husband.

Mugi *kôri*, Kôzu Village.

There are a few such married women, but their property is owned in common with their husbands.

Haguri *kôri*, Kasamatsu Village.

We have none.

Fuwa *kôri*, Tarui Village.

There are some instances of this. Property is held in common.

Ôno *kôri*, Miwa Village.

There are some instances of this.

Ampachi *kôri*, Gôdo Village.

There are some instances, mostly in the humbler classes. The spouses have separate properties.

Tagi *kôri*, Shimada Village.

There are a few married women engaged in business independently, usually selling haberdashery and second-hand goods in villages a mile or two from their own. Their properties are held in common with their husbands.

Ena *kôri*, Iwa Village.

No interest separate from the husband.

Toki *kôri*, Tajimi Village.

Some married women engage in business independently, but their properties are held in common with their husbands. We sometimes find that a married woman has an interest in a bank or a company.

Kamo *kôri*, Hosome Village.

There are some instances. In such cases the separation of property between husband and wife is clear, because in most cases the wife is above average (in intelligence).

Toki *kôri*, Takayama Village.

If there are any married women engaging in business independently, no general statement as to property relations can be made. For instance, in the case of a married woman engaging in business with capital given to her by her husband, the capital itself belongs to her. Other than that capital, she cannot claim anything as hers, unless she is head of the family.

Kani *kôri*, Mitake Village.

There are some instances of this. All property interests are usually regarded as the husband's.

Ena *kôri*, Akechi Village.

Such women are sometimes found. Though there is some distinction as to their properties, it is not easy to define it.

Mugi *kôri*, Seki Village.

Not a single married woman engages in business by herself.

Ono *kôri*, Takayama Town.

There are some instances of this. For example, a husband may be an artisan and his wife an old-clothes dealer. They sometimes carry on business with the husband's consent. If the capital was given to her by her husband, the distinction cannot be made. But if the bulk of the capital came from the wife, the distinction is clear.

Motosu *kôri*, Kitakata Village.

A married woman sometimes sells at retail the husband's commodities by consent of her husband. But she is not officially recognized as a merchant.

Kamo *kôri*, Ôta Village.

There are some instances of this. No distinction is made between husband and wife as to properties.

Gujô *kôri*.

None.

Topic 4:
   Subtopic 1: How Many Kinds of Trade Books Are There? What Are Their Respective Names, Their Uses; and How Long Are They Supposed to Be Preserved?
   Subtopic 2: Is There Any Fixed Form of Entries? Are Different Kinds of Books Used in Different Trades?
   Subtopic 3: Is the Occidental Method of Bookkeeping by Single and Double Entry Becoming Prevalent?

GROUP I—ANSWERS

Tokyo. (Answers to Topic 4, Subtopics 1 and 2)

Different kinds of trade books are required in different trades or for different kinds of commercial transactions. There are scores of different kinds of trade books in use. However, in general there are nine kinds of trade books which are indispensable to any trader engaged in wholesale business, regardless of the trade. These are as follows:

Tôza-chô, Daifuku-chô, Shiire-chô, Shikiri-chô, Kuraire-chô, Mizuage-chô, Kinsen-hantori-chô, Nimotsu-hantori-chô, Kinsen-shutsunyû-chô.

However, the names by which these books are known are not the same for every trader. For example, the *tôza-chô* may be called *chûmon-chô* by some and *shoyô-chô* by others; the *daifuku-chô, kake-chô* or *moto-chô;* the *shiire-chô, kaitsuke-chô;* the *kuraire-chô, kura-dashiire-chô;* and the *kinsen-deiri-chô, ryôgae-deiri-chô.* Their uses, however, are essentially the same, by whatever name they may be called.

There is no fixed form of entries for these books, except those used by pawnbrokers and bankers, and these are rather an exception.

A brief explanation of the uses of each of these nine kinds of books will be given below.

1. *Tôza-chô.* The *tôza-chô*, also called *chûmon-chô*, or *shoyô-chô*, is a kind of journal of commercial transactions. In it are entered the quality, quantity and price of every article sold or bought by a commercial house, the date of the delivery of the article, the names of the party to which the article was sold or from which it was bought, etc., in short, all details concerning the sale of goods. Some houses divide the book into two parts, in one of which are entered

all transactions within the city of Tokyo and in the other those with other parts of the country. Besides this, a book called a "sales journal"[1] is sometimes prepared, into which are transcribed from the *tôza-chô* the essentials regarding payment of the articles sold.

This book, i.e., *tôza-chô*, is used exactly like the journals in use in the Western countries, which are kept according to the method of single entry. However, the book is very coarsely bound in most cases and is usually made of old sheets of paper which have once been used in making other books and then discarded, entries being made on the backs of the paper. Moreover, the form of the entries is very irregular, and sometimes ciphers are used to indicate the quality of the goods to prevent those unaccustomed to the system from understanding what has been entered.

2. *Daifuku-chô*, also called *kake-chô* or *moto-chô*. This book is used to clearly record every sale on credit. The form of entry is not identical in different houses. For example, those who carry on their transactions with traders from different provinces sometimes divide the book into several parts, allotting each part to a different province and facilitating reference by means of index slips attached to the margin of the leaves. In other cases it is divided into only two parts, one for entries of transactions within the metropolitan district[2] and the other for those in the outside districts.[3] Whichever method is used, each part is again subdivided into several parts according to the locality of the buyers, i.e., debtors to the house. Of the daily transactions, all of which have been entered in the *tôza-chô*, those sales for which cash payment has not been made are entered first in the *shikiri-chô* (to which reference will be made later) in all their details, including of course the prices of the goods and the expenses incurred in the transactions. They are then posted into the *daifuku-chô* under the various names, so that anyone on looking at it may learn the amount of the claims of the house against trader A of Hakodate, B of Akita, etc. When the settlement day[4] is at hand, all the claims of the house against each debtor are summed up and a bill is sent requesting payment due. The debts thus paid off are struck out of the book. Every subsequent credit

---

[1] *Uri-nikki.*
[2] *Funai.*
[3] *Jikata.*
[4] *Kessan-kijitsu.*

sale is entered and accounted for in like manner.

In some houses, besides the *daifuku-chô*, a separate book called *kake-chô* is kept, and in it are entered all transactions outside the city, while in the *daifuku-chô* are entered the transactions within the city. In other houses, the *daifuku-chô* is divided into two parts, or into several parts numbered 1, 2, 3, etc. However, there is no fixed rule about these points, these being matters to be decided upon by the nature of the transactions or the convenience of the individual trader.

The *daifuku-chô* is used in exactly the same way as the ledger used in Western countries and is kept according to the single-entry method. This book, usually bound in oblong form, is made of best-quality paper called *hashikirazu*, and the title on the cover is usually written in a peculiar style of script. It is probably the most important trade book in Japan. Of late it is occasionally made of *hanshi*[1] paper, sometimes ruled, and bound somewhat in imitation of European books, although that is rare. Some traders keep the *daifuku-chô* as a kind of ornament for the counter and use the *shikiri-chô* (see below), etc. instead, but these are rather exceptional cases. In sum, the *daifuku-chô* is one of the most important books generally used by traders.

3. *Shiire-chô*, also called *kaitsuke-chô*. The purpose of this book is to record in a clear manner every purchase made by a business house, with all the details relating thereto, such as the quality, quantity and price of the purchased goods and the date of the transaction. The book is usually divided into several parts, a part for each of the different provinces from which the purchases come. It may also be divided into two parts for entering the transactions with parties within the city of Tokyo and vicinity and those in other districts separately. There is no fixed form for entries. Some houses represent the quality of a commodity by some sign, such as 舎 for a kind of hair-oil, 萬 for a kind of soy-sauce, etc. However, it is used in the same way by all traders. This and the *shikiri-chô* (see below) are by far the most important books for showing the account of profit or loss of a concern.

4. *Shikiri-chô*. This book is used to enter in a clear manner every sale of goods, with all the details relating thereto, such as the names

---

[1] Common Japanese paper.

of the buyers, the quality and quantity of the goods sold, the expenses incurred in the transactions and the date of delivery. Those entries relating to sales on credit are always posted up into the *daifuku-chô*. Some traders also make entry in the *shikiri-chô* of the names of the ships transporting the goods and of the Tokyo forwarding agents[1] with whom they entrust the shipment of the goods. Others, in lieu of the *daifuku-chô*, use the *shikiri-chô* for the same purpose, and when the settlement day arrives, go to the book to ascertain their account of sales on credit. But such is not the usual method of using the book by traders. Because this book is used in exactly the same way as the account-of-sales book of Western bookkeeping, with entries made according to the single-entry method, it is, like the above-mentioned *shiire-chô*, a very important book for traders.

5. *Kura-ire-chô*, also called *kura-deire-chô*. This is a journal of goods, and its main object is to make clear entry of the receipt[2] and shipment of goods. If, for instance, a stock of goods bought by a trader arrives from Osaka, the goods are entered in the *mizuage-chô* (see below) and checked against the bill of lading.[3] Then, when they are put in the warehouse,[4] the name and the quantity of the goods and the date of their receipt are entered in the book. Or again, if some goods sold are to be transported to Hokkaido, the name and the quantity of the goods and the date of shipment are first entered in the book and then given over to the forwarding agents, who in turn are required to write their receipt for the goods under seal in the *nimotsu-hantori-chô* (see below) or the delivery-book of the consignor. In a similar manner, whenever some goods are received or sent out by a commercial house, they are entered in the *kura-ire-chô*, so that the house may easily learn the amount of goods in stock. If they have warehouses at several places, many traders keep

---

[1] *Tsumikomi-toiya.* The forwarding agents are called *tsumikomi-toiya* when they act in the capacity of shippers, i.e., those who ship the goods entrusted to them for shipment, while they are called *hikitori-toiya* when they act in the capacity of recipients of shipments on behalf of the consignee of the goods.

[2] *Shiire-kamotsu.*

[3] *Okuri-jô.* This term sometimes signifies merely the consignor's invoice, sometimes the carrier's bill of lading.

[4] *Kuraire* (warehouse-put).

several copies of the books called for example, *nishi-gashi*[1] *kura-ire-chô, koami-chô-gashi*[2] *kura-ire-chô*, etc. As the use of this book is limited to recording the quantity of the goods received or sent out, it may be regarded as less important than other kinds of books used by traders.

6. *Mizuage-chô* (arrivals-book). The object of this book is to make clear entry of the arrivals of goods bought by a commercial house. If some goods are to arrive from Osaka, for instance, on receipt of the invoice, the quantity of the goods, the name of the ship in which the goods have been carried, etc. are entered in detail in a book called *tsumitsuke-chô*. When the goods actually arrive, they are checked against the invoice and all the details relating to the goods are entered in the *mizuage-chô*. There is no fixed form for the entries, but the dates of shipment and arrival of the goods, their quantity, the name of the Tokyo forwarding agents who receive and handle the goods on their arrival,[3] etc. are usually entered in the book.

If any of the goods received are found damaged, the matter is first communicated to the forwarding agents that received the goods from the consignor. From them, the forwarding agents that loaded the goods at the place of origin[4] are informed; they in turn inform the original vendor of the goods. Then the vendor compensates for the damages, according to the existing customs or the contract.

When, for example, a thousand pieces of goods are bought in a lump, it happens sometimes that the goods are divided into several parts and loaded separately on several ships, due to some transportation circumstance. In such a case, as those ships will not reach port simultaneously, entries of the goods in the book are sometimes numbered Cargo No. 1 for the first five hundred pieces received and Cargo No. 2 for the second five hundred. The *shiire-chô* (see above) is for entering the details of the goods the purchase of which has been agreed upon, while the *mizuage-chô* is for entering only the goods received by the purchaser. These two books, therefore, serve almost the same purpose as the invoice book[5] used in single-

---

[1] & [2] The names of places where the warehouses are situated.

[3] *Hikitori-toiya.*

[4] *Sanchi-tsumikomi-toiya;* literally, "the forwarding agents who take care of shipment of goods at the place where they are produced."

[5] *Okurijô-hikae-chô.*

entry Western bookkeeping. In short, the *mizuage-chô* is also one of those books that are indispensable to a commercial house.

7. & 8.   *Kinsen* (money)-*hantori-chô* and *Nimotsu* (freight)-*hantori-chô*. Both of these books are used to be sealed for the receipt of money paid or goods delivered. The former is generally used to receive the seal of the vendor when a trader pays the price of the goods he has bought, of the forwarding agent when the trader has paid for the carriage of the goods, or sometimes even of the retailers from whom he has bought sundry goods.[1] A book called *kawase* (exchange)-*hantori-chô* is also kept by some merchants, and is used to secure the impress of the seal of the person who is responsible for the issue of a money order sent by the merchant to some country district, although the *kinsen-hantori-chô* serves the purpose in most cases. As to the *nimotsu-hantori-chô*, this is used to receive the seal of the vendee which is required when goods are sold and delivered to a merchant within the metropolitan district. When the goods are sold and to be delivered to some merchant outside the metropolis, the forwarding agent is usually asked to stamp his seal in the book on receipt of the goods to be shipped by him.

In short, these two are, so to speak, mere receipt books in which the recipient of money or goods is asked to affix his seal as proof of receipt. The entry is very simple, there being no fixed form. In the *nimotsu-hantori-chô*, for example, are entered the quantity of the goods, the name of the provincial person who has bought the goods, the date of delivery and the name of the person who is to receive the goods from the vendor, that is, the forwarding agent in this case. A book called *funatsuki* (ship)-*chô* is also kept by some commercial houses. When goods are sold and to be delivered to some provincial district, the kind of goods, the name of the buyer, the name of the ship to take on the goods, the date of delivery, and the name of the forwarding agent shipping the goods are entered in the book, so that it may be used for ready reference. However, this book is rather seldom used, the *nimotsu-hantori-chô* being generally used for the purpose. The latter is always divided into several parts because the parties to whom payment is made or goods are to be delivered are located in various parts of the country, and it is necessary to allot different parts of the book to these different localities. The

---

[1] *Kokaimono.*

book is mostly made of *hashikirazu* quarto paper, or a kind of paper whose edge is untrimmed. It is always provided with a case and this case is tied with a flat braid for convenient carrying by an errand boy.

9. *Kinsen* (money)-*deiri* (outgo)-*chô;* also called *ryôgae* (money-change)-*deiri-chô*. This is a book for entering in a clear manner every payment and receipt of money by a trader in connection with the purchase or sale of goods, etc. The trader makes it a rule to verify each day's account every evening by balancing the payments and the receipts. This book is also indispensable to a commercial house. There is no fixed rule as to the form of the entries, but generally speaking, entries are irregular.

Another book in use in addition to the above-mentioned books, is one called *seri-chô*. When some goods that are not in stock are in urgent demand, a trader may write down in the book the name and quantity of the goods he wants and dispatch his errand boy with it to search for such goods among his fellow tradesmen. When they are found, the errand boy may secure in the book the seal of the merchant in whose stock the goods have been found and bring them back to his master without paying the price on the spot.

There is also a book in use by traders called *sôba* (price)-*chô*. It is used when oil merchants, for instance, wish to enter, every day, the prices of foreign silver[1] and, every other day, the prices of petroleum, as well as the prices of other goods related to the petroleum business. There is also a book known as *kawase-chô*, or bill-of-exchange book, used for entering, in detail, the day a money order is drawn,[2] the amount and issuing number, the name of the drawer[3] and the drawee, the date of payment,[4] etc. A book called *kyûkin-chô* is used for entering the name of employees, the date of employment, the amount of wages paid, etc. There is also a book called *unsô-kayoi-chô*.[5] These books may be very important to some trades but cannot be regarded as indispensable to all trades in general.

To sum up, the first nine kinds of book mentioned above are

---

[1] *Yogin.*
[2] *Torikumi-bi.*
[3] *Furidashi-nin.*
[4] *Uketori-nichigen.*
[5] Literally, "carriage pass book."

necessary to wholesale merchants, while seven of them, the *tôza-chô*, the *daifuku-chô*, the *shiire-chô*, the *shikiri-chô*, the *kinsen-deiri-chô*, the *nimotsu-hantori-chô* and the *kinsen-deiri-chô*, are always indispensable in commerce, even to middlemen and retailers.

There is no fixed custom as to the length of the period during which these books are to be preserved. Many wholesale merchants of Ôdenma-chô, Tokyo, sometimes preserve these old books for as long as fifty years. But the fact is that those old books were preserved not because there was any fixed practice regarding this but simply for the sake of convenience. Since the Meiji Restoration very few traders keep the books any longer than ten years, and especially in recent years, the books are preserved by most traders for only two or three years and then discarded to be remanufactured into fresh paper or sold to a ragman.

Tokyo. (Answers to Topic 4, Subtopic 3)

Most of the national and private banks and other various companies have adopted the exclusive use of the Western method of bookkeeping, but we hear that its use has not yet come into much vogue among other traders. The reason is not because the Western method is not convenient enough, but because the traders find it hard to break with their old methods and to take to the new. It is our belief, however, that as commercial prosperity increases and commercial transactions become more complicated, the Western method is certain to find its way among the general public here.

Kyoto. (Answers to Topic 4, Subtopic 1)

The trade books are all meant for practical use in the various trades, and there is only a slight difference in the names by which these books are called and the items entered in them. This is the rule, without any exception, in the three metropolises, Tokyo, Kyoto and Osaka, and in all the provinces.

When traders buy goods for commercial purpose, this is called *shiire*; hence the book for entering all such purchases is called *shiire-chô*.

Whenever sales for cash,[1] sales on credit, or transportation of the goods to a customer take place, such transactions are temporarily entered in a book called *tôza-chô*.

Entries relating to sales on credit are taken from these temporary

---

[1] *Genkin-uri.*

entries in the *tôza-chô* and re-entered in a book called *daifuku-chô*. This book is usually divided into as many parts as there are regular customers of the commercial house. The division is made proportionately according to the estimated yearly number of purchases of each customer, one part, headed with the name of a customer, being allotted to each. Each part thus divided may also be numbered and, for convenience of reference, an index prepared. All the sales on credit which have been temporarily entered in the *tôza-chô* are usually transcribed in this book. The same is true for entries in the *shiire-chô*.

The *chûmon-chô* is used for entering all orders, whether by letter or by oral communication.

The book in which are entered payments for sales on credit, remittances accompanying orders and payments on the spot for sales is called *nyûkin-chô*.

The book in which are entered payments for merchandise bought and all other payments made by a trader is called *shukkin-chô*.

The *hikanjô-chô* is a book in which each day's account is made, daily payments and receipts are balanced and the balance from the preceding day carried over.

The *nimotsu-deiri-chô* is a book in which are entered the arrivals and departures of goods when they are received from, or given over from for transportation elsewhere, some forwarding agents or an express messenger.[1]

The *kinsen-hantori-chô* is a book in which every payment made by a commercial house is entered. The book has a (revenue) stamp affixed upon it, and whenever a payment is made, the payee is required to sign his name and put his seal in the book.

When the materials to be recorded, regardless of the nature of the materials, fill a book, as many separate volumes as are required for the purpose are prepared. Depending on the trade, there is a difference in the degree of pressure of business, in the variety of activities, or in the circumstances, hence different books are needed. The period these books are preserved depends upon the nature of the book. There is no fixed rule, some books being preserved for several years and others being discarded after use for one year. This practice differs according to the firm. However, some books,

---

[1] *Hikyaku.*

such as the *daifuku-chô* and the *kinsen-hantori-chô*, are usually preserved for several years by most traders, although each firm has
its own rule as to the exact number of years of preservation.

Kyoto. (Answers to Topic 4, Subtopics 2 & 3)

The method of bookkeeping prevalent here has been described
in the preceding paragraphs. As to the practice of putting a tally-
impression,[1] in the case of a *hantori-chô*, the recipient of a payment
is required to put his tally-impression in the book to acknowledge
his receipt of the payment. On the arrival of goods, a trader will
stamp his tally-impression[2] over his receipt and his entry in the
nyû-chô, a book in which are entered the arrivals of goods.

In connection with the entry in the *daifuku-chô* of a sale on credit,
the debtor is not required to stamp his seal in the book. Suppose,
however, some goods have been delivered through a forwarding
agent[3] to a trader in a provincial district and the bill-collecting
book[4] which the collector takes along with him shows that the trader
owes one thousand yen, including the price of the goods and freight
charges. However for some reason or other, such as shortage of
ready money or the fact that the goods delivered include, besides
his orders, other merchandise not of his line, he wishes to pay seven
hundred of the one thousand yen now, promising to remit and pay
off the rest by a certain month or to return the unordered goods
if they are later found unmarketable. In such a case, he will negotiate with the bill collector and, upon their agreement over the
terms, he may be asked to write the terms down in the *kake-chô* and
stamp his legal[5] or commercial seal[6] over the line containing the
words, "300 yen yet unpaid,"[7] as proof of his debt. Otherwise, in
no kind of trade do merchants (whether as a creditor or debtor)
have, in our opinion, the practice of stamping their seals or having
the merchants' seals stamped in a commercial book.

As to the Western method of bookkeeping, we believe it is not in
use by any commercial firms except banks, even in the three me-

---

[1] *Kiri-han*, also called *wari-han*.

[2] *Wari-in*, same as *wari-han*.

[3] *Unsô-shônin*, same as *toiya*.

[4] *Kake-chô*.

[5] *Jitsu-in*, literally, true seal.

[6] *Shôyô-in*, literally, seal for commercial use.

[7] *Zankin sanbyaku-en kashioki*.

tropolises (Tokyo, Kyoto and Osaka), much less in the provincial districts.

However, we do not know about how business transactions are done in cities devoted to foreign trade.

Even in future it will be difficult, we believe, for the Western method to find its way here, even in the three metropolises, because, as the merchants in the various provinces of the country are related in business transactions to one another, the Western method cannot be adopted unless it is universally adopted simultaneously throughout the county.

Osaka. (Answers to Topic 4, Subtopic 1)

1. The *daifuku-chô*, also called *moto-chô* or *dai-chô*. This book is used exclusively for recording sales on credit. Entries of the names of the goods and their quantity and prices are transcribed to this book from the *uri-chô*, or sales book, and entries regarding the receipt of money are posted here from the *kingin-deiri-chô*, to enable a trader to balance the account and learn at once the sum paid or still due to him. This is the most important book for an ordinary merchant. So important is it that, although other books may be attended to by ordinary clerks[1] who may occasionally make entries in them, with this book alone it is the practice in every commercial firm that only the head, or the chief clerk, or some other important man of the house should attend to it. Sometimes, to the exclusion of all employees, the master may keep it without allowing others even to look at it.

2. The *kai-chô*, or purchase book; also called by some wholesale merchants *shikiri-chô*,[2] *mokuroku-chô*,[3] or *uri-nikki*,[4] etc., and by middlemen such-and-such-*kaiire-chô* or *shiire-chô*.

In this book are entered, in a clear manner, the purchases of goods. With wholesalers, entries regarding the quantity and prices of goods purchased and the expenses incurred in the purchase are re-entered in this book from each particular book, and the state-

---

[1] *Tedai.*
[2] Invoice book.
[3] Inventory book.
[4] Sales journal.

ment of account[1] and the inventory[2] to be given to a consignor are prepared on the basis of the entries in this book.

Payments made by middlemen are re-entered in this book from the *kingin-deiri-chô* or cash book and accounts are balanced.

With some wholesalers, however, entries in this book are limited to the names of buyers, the quantity and the prices of the goods sold and the date of delivery (in this use, it serves as a sales diary). The balancing of accounts is done in a separate book, such as the *shikiri-chô* or the *mokuroku-chô*.

Whether entries of purchases are made in two or three separate books instead of one depends upon the volume or variety of trade.

3. The *uri-chô*, or sales book; called by wholesalers *jikigumi-chô* [?] or *ichiuri-chô*, and by middlemen *tôza-chô*, *uriage-chô*, or *ichiuri-chô*. In this book are entered, in a clear manner, all sales of goods. With wholesalers, when goods are sold to middlemen, the quantity and price of the goods sold are entered in this book at the time of transaction.

With middlemen, when sales of goods are made to fellow middlemen, the quantity and price of the goods are entered in the *ichiuri-chô*. When sales are made to merchants or non-merchant customers of other provinces, the names, the quantity, the prices of the goods sold, the payments, etc., are re-entered in the *tôza-chô* from the *chûmon-chô* (see below) and other books for each particular purpose after the goods are laden aboard a ship for transportation, so that the account may be balanced in the *tôza-chô* and a *shikiri-chô*[3] and inventory prepared therefrom.

4. The *chûmon-chô*. This book is used for recording the quality, quantity and price of the goods and the date of delivery, when an order is sent in by, or a contract for the sale of goods is concluded with, a trader from some other province.

5. The *kingin-deiri-chô*, or cash book. This book is used by traders for entering every payment and receipt of money.

6. The *kingin-uketori-chô*, or receipt book. When a payment is made by a trader, the recipient is required to record the receipt in

---

[1] *Shikiri-sho. Shikiri-chô* sometimes means an invoice in the sense of a list of goods shipped with price and charges that accompanies each shipment, and is distinguished from a periodical or final statement of account.

[2] *Mokuroku-sho.*

[3] Statement of account.

this book for future proof.

7. The *nimotsu-watashi-chô*, or delivery book. When goods are delivered, the recipient is required to record the receipt in this book for future proof.

The above seven books are indispensable to a trader, though any of them may be subdivided again into two or three different books or be called by a different name or names, as the case may be, depending on the volume or variety of trade.

One or more of the following books are also needed by some traders according to the nature of their trade:

The *kake-chô*, also called *kake-kin-chô*.[1]

The *mizuage-chô*.[2]

The *kakidashi-chô*, also called the *kakidashi-tome*.[3]

The *nimotsu-deiri-chô*.[4]

The *ukigashi-chô*.[5]

The *kamme-chô*.[6]

The *ai-nikki*.[7]

The *shukka-chô*.[8]

The *urihin-torihiki-kayoi*.[9]

The *uwani-chô*.[10]

The *kakekazu-chô*.[11]

The *kawase-unchin-watashi-chô*.[12]

The *tsumidashi-nimotsu-meisai-chô*.[13]

The *nyushin-nimotsu-meisai-chô*.[14]

The *nichiyô-chô*.[15]

[1] Credit sales book.

[2] A book used for entry of goods unloaded from a ship.

[3] A book used for entry of bills (demanding payment) issued.

[4] A book used for entry of arrivals and departures of goods.

[5] See below.

[6] A book used for entry of the weights of goods.

[7] Obscure.

[8] A book used for entry of all shipments of goods.

[9] A book used for entry of goods bought by a regular customer and presented to him for examination and payment.

[10] A book used for entry of goods in a warehouse ready for shipment.

[11] Obscure.

[12] A book used for entry of fees paid for sending money orders.

[13] A book used for entry of details of goods shipped, a kind of manifest.

[14] A book used for entry of details of cargo discharged from a ship.

[15] A book used for entry of daily expenses of a commercial house.

The *shohin-hantori-chô*.[1]
The *tsumi-dashi-chô*.[2]
The *irifune-chô*.[3]
The *kudarimono-uri-chô*.[4]
The *kudarimono-kai-chô*.[5]
The *niuke-chô*.[6]
The *mokuroku-sashihiki-chô*.[7]
The *budomari-chô*.[8]
The *kanjô-chô*.[9]
The *Edo-zumi-nikki*.[10]
The *nikki-chô*.[11]
The *nizukuri-chô*.[12]
The *shokoku-tsumiire-chô*.[13]
The *sashihiki-chô*.[14]
The *mirare-chô*.[15]
The *uriage-chô*.[16]
The *keisan-chô*.[17]
The *shokutema-hikae-chô*.[18]
The *nimotsu-motowari-chô*.[19]
The *shikiri-utsushi*.[20]

[1] Obscure.
[2] A book used for entry of goods shipped.
[3] A book used for entry of the names of ships entering port.
[4] A book used for entry of the sale of goods delivered to Edo.
[5] A bood used for entry of the purchase of goods delivered to Edo.
[6] A book used for entry of goods received.
[7] Obscure.
[8] A book recording rate of profits.
[9] Account book.
[10] A book used for entry of goods shipped for Edo.
[11] A book which records the credit account before it is formally entered in the credit sales book. [?]
[12] A book used for entry of goods packed for shipment.
[13] A book which registers goods laden aboard a ship for shipment to the provinces.
[14] A balance book.
[15] Obscure.
[16] Sales book which registers all sales of goods.
[17] Account book.
[18] Wage book which registers the names of workmen employed and wages for work done.
[19] Obscure.
[20] A book in which a copy of statement of account is made.

The *kawase-chô*.[1]
The *kawase-unchin-chô*.[2]
The *fûtai-chô*.[3]
The *mizuage-tawara-awase-chô*.[4]
The *torikae-chô*.[5]
The *sôba-chô*.[6]
The *masumawashi-chô*.[7]
The *buntsû-chô*.[8]
The *raijô-hikae*.[9]

However, there are three books which are indispensable to a trader, the *kai-chô*, the *uri-chô* and the *kingin-shutsunyû-chô*. The entries in these books are re-entered in the *daifuku-chô*. The other books record only a certain part of a business transaction.

Among metropolitan traders, there are certain fixed rules regarding the rate of commission and discount in reference to fellow retailers and wholesalers of the same trade. When delivery of goods is made directly from one party to another, the goods delivered are counted or measured in the presence of, and respectively by, both parties. Consequently the procedure is simple. However, when the sale is made to a trader or other customer from another province, the packing fee, the lighterage, the stevedores' fees and other expenses incurred in connection with the sale, as well as the weight and measure of the goods are entered in detail in a book. Hence with wholesalers, entries in the *kaichô* must naturally be detailed but entries in the *uri-chô* are simple; while with retailers, entries in the *kai-chô* are simple and those in the *uri-chô* detailed.

There is no fixed rule regarding the length of period during which a book is (supposed) to be preserved, this depending on the nature

[1] A book used for entry of money orders issued.

[2] A book used for entry of fees paid for money orders.

[3] A tare book.

[4] A book used for entry of the number of bales of grain discharged from a ship.

[5] A book used for entry of every exchange of an article, after its purchase by or delivery to a customer, for another, at his demand.

[6] A book which records the market prices of goods.

[7] A book used for entry of the inspection, for quantity and quality, of rice kept in a warehouse to be delivered from one trader to another. (This usually refers to the practice of inspection of rice in a warehouse by grain exchange officials.)

[8] A book which records the correspondence of a commercial house.

[9] A book used for entry of letters received.

of the book, the nature of the trade and the practice of each house. However, the seven books mentioned above and those books whose entries may be used as some sort of proof in future reference, are usually preserved for ten years at the longest, though they may be discarded by some in a shorter time. Materials which may serve as proof of some old loan will customarily be regarded as void after the lapse of ten years. Therefore, books which may be used within ten years as such proof will not be discarded unless there is some special reason for doing so. Such is the case not only with books but also with correspondence. It even occurs sometimes that such books and letters may be preserved in a commercial house for over a hundred years, being handed down from one generation to the next.

Osaka. (Answers to Topic 4, Subtopic 2)

The form of entries in these books is different with different trades. Similar forms prevail, of course, in the same trade although details are not the same.

The books used by merchants are different in different trades. However, with respect to the seven kinds of books mentioned in the answer to Subtopic 1, although they may be called different names by different traders, the nature of their use is the same. As far as any one trade is concerned, the types of books used are generally the same.

Osaka. (Answers to Topic 4, Subtopic 3)

The European method of bookkeeping has been adopted by traders of some trades, but there is hardly any chance of its being generally adopted. The European method of entry will gradually come into vogue for some kinds of books, though it is far from being likely that this method will be adopted in every sort of trades in the near future.

Yokohama. (Answers to Topic 4, Subtopic 1)

The types and names of books used by traders are different in different trades, and it is almost impossible to know how many different kinds of books are actually in use among the traders. The more common of those now used are: *daifuku-chô, tôza-chô, shiire-chô, shikiri-chô, yakujô-chô, nimotsu-tsumidashi-chô, yôgin-baibai-chô, kinsen-hantori-chô, nimotsu-hantori-chô, kinsen-deiri-chô* and *urikomi-chô*.

A brief explanation of each of the eleven books mentioned above will be given below.

1.   The *daifuku-chô* is used for entering sales on credit.

2. The *tôza-chô* is used for entering the quality[1] of goods [?] sold or bought by a trader, quantity, prices, date of delivery and the name and address of the other party in the transaction. As the name *tôza*[2] indicates, the book is used for temporary entries. Hence the manner of making entries is very flexible.

3. The *shiire-chô* is used for entering *shiire* or *kaitsuke-kata*, or purchases of goods by a trader. Hence entries include the quality, the quantity, and the purchase prices of the goods, the date of transactions, etc. As this book forms the basis of computation of profits or losses by commercial houses, it is the most important of trade books.

4. The *shikiri-chô* is used for entering, in a clear manner, the sales of goods. The entries, made in detail, include, therefore, the name of the vendee, the quality and quantity of the goods, the expenses incurred in the transaction, the date of the sale, etc. All those sales which turn out to be sales on credit, meanwhile, are as a rule entered in the *daifuku-chô*. Like the *shiire-chô*, this book is also very important for traders.

5. The *nimotsu-tsumidashi-chô* is used for entering, in a clear manner, the grade, the quantity and the price of the goods, the date of the transaction, the name of the vendee, etc., when the wholesalers are going to ship goods sold to a provincial customer.

6. The *yôgin-baibai-chô* is used by those dealing in foreign silver currency for entering amounts traded in with brokers, dates of transaction, names of brokers, etc.

7. The *yakujô-chô* is used exclusively by those engaged in foreign trade for entering contracts made with foreign merchants for import of goods. The entries include the name of the ship that will carry the goods, date of arrival, quality, quantity and price of the goods, etc.

8. & 9. The *kinsen-hantori-chô* and the *nimotsu-hantori-chô*. The one is used for securing the impression of the seal of the recipient of money as proof of receipt, and the other, the seal of the recipient of goods. The entries in the latter include quantity, name of the provincial buyer, date of receipt and name of the recipient.

10. The *kinsen-deiri-chô* is used for entering every receipt and

[1] *Hin.*
[2] Temporary.

payment of money by a trader in connection with daily purchases and sales, so that every night, i.e. at the end of each business day, he may make a balance to verify the account.

11. The *urikomi-chô* is used by a salesman,[1] when he has entered into a contract for sale of goods with a business firm, for entering in detail the quality, quantity and price of the goods, date of delivery,[2] house number of the firm, name (of the proprietor), etc.

There is no fixed rule as to the length of time these books are preserved. They may be preserved for a year or two, or may be discarded after being preserved for ten years.

Yokohama. (Answers for Topic 4, Subtopic 2)

There is no fixed form of entry in a book, each firm having its own form. The kinds of books used are also different according to the nature of business of each firm.

Yokohama. (Answers for Topic 4, Subtopic 3)

In banks and other business corporations, the entries in a book follow the Western method of bookkeeping, but this method is very seldom used by traders outside of those circles. Traders in general will, it is believed, come to adopt this method, when they have learned its use.

Hyôgo. (Answers for Topic 4, Subtopics 1 & 2)

The trade books used by traders are different in different trades. Of the scores of different kinds of books now in use among traders, the following nine are indispensable to most wholesalers and middlemen: the *yorozu-uri-chô*, the *daifuku-chô*, the *shikiri-chô*, the *mizu-age-chô*, the *kinsen-deiri-chô*, the *nimotsu-deiri-chô*, the *kanjô-chô*, the *nimotsu-hantori-chô* and the *kinsen-hantori-chô*.

The names by which they are called may be different in each firm, but the uses to which they are put are almost the same at all firms. Some of the different appellations and the uses of these books will be briefly given below.

1. The *yorozu-uri-chô*; also called *uriage-chô*, *uriwatashi-nikki* or *tôza-chô*. This book is used for entering, in a clear manner, all sales of goods. The entries include in detail the names of the vendees, the quality, quantity and prices of the goods sold, the day of payment, day of delivery, etc. Sales on credit are usually culled and

---

[1] *Urikomi-sho.*

[2] *Hikikomi.*

re-entered in the *daifuku-chô* (see the following).

2. The *daifuku-chô*; also called *yorozu-tome-chô*, *dai-chô*, or *moto-chô*. This is the most important of books for a trader and is used for entering, in a clear manner, all sales on credit. There is no fixed form of entry, but, generally speaking, wholesale merchants divide the book into several sections and allot a section to each of the middlemen with whom they have dealings. Middlemen and other traders divide the book into two sections, one for the customers in their home province and the other for those in other provinces, and further subdivide each section into smaller parts, allotting a part to each of the customers in their home province and other provinces. Some traders divide the book into two sections, for the municipal district and for outlying villages, respectively. The book is sometimes divided into sections representing provinces. Sometimes at the end of the book a special section is prepared for those customers with whom they do not have constant dealings. To facilitate reference, index-slips, similar to the fins of a fish, with the name of each section are attached to the edge of the page where each section starts. The entries in this book follow the above-mentioned *yorozu-uri-chô* in the order of sections as well as customers. When the day of final accounts[1] is close at hand, a balance of accounts is made with each of the customers and a bill[2] is sent. The entries are struck out when payments are made, and blank spaces left in the book are ready for new entries.

3. The *shikiri-chô*; also called *shiire-chô*, *kai-nikki*, or *shikomi-chô*. This book is used for entering, in a clear manner, prices of goods purchased by a trader. The names of customers are classified in the book according to the provinces where they live, or are divided into two classes, customers who trade within the same province as the trader and those in other provinces. The entries usually include in detail the grade, quantity and purchase price of the goods, the date of the transaction, etc. The use of this book is somewhat similar to that of the *uri-chô*, and along with the latter it is an important book for a trader.

4. The *mizuage-chô* is used for entering, in a clear manner, the arrival of goods purchased. The entries include the grade and quan-

[1] *Kessanki.*
[2] *Kakidashi.*

tity of the goods, the name of the ship carrying the goods, date of arrival, etc. When the goods have been delivered, the entries in the book will be posted into the *shikiri-chô* mentioned above.

5.   The *kingin-deiri-chô* is used for entering, in a clear manner, all payments and receipts of money, so that every evening at the end of business hours or at the end of each ten days, accounts may be made and the balance of cash may be readily learned. This is the most indispensable book for a trader.

6.   The *nimotsu-deiri-chô*; also called *kuragura-deiri-chô*, *arimono-chô* or *kuraire-chô*. This is used exclusively for entering all receipts and shipments of goods, the entries, which include the name and quantity of the goods, being transcribed from the *shikiri-chô* (see above) and the *uri-chô* (see above) and classified according to different classes for easy examination of goods received or shipped.

7.   The *kanjô-chô*; also called *sashihiki-chô*, or *san'yô-chô*. All prices of the purchased goods are summed up according to the *shikiri-chô* and entered in this book. The quantity and prices of the goods sold are transcribed from the *uri-chô* to this book. This is used for balancing the accounts in connection with purchase and sales and making clear the profits and losses of a commercial house. It is an important book for a trader.

8. & 9.   The *nimotsu-hantori-chô* and the *kinsen-hantori-chô*. When delivery of goods is made to the vendee, the name and price of the goods and the name of the vendee are entered by the vendor in this book, and the vendee is asked to impress his seal therein as proof of receipt of the goods. If the goods are to be delivered to a trader in another province, the forwarding agent who takes care of the shipment or the owner of the ship which will transport the goods will be asked to impress his seal in the book.

The *kinsen-hantori-chô* is a book in which, when payment for goods is made by a trader, the vendor is asked to impress his seal as proof of receipt of the money.

Both of these books are made use of as proof for the future.

Besides the books mentioned above, there is a book called *irifune-*(arrive)(ship)-*chô* that is in use among wholesalers. On the occasion of the arrival of a ship at a port, the wholesaler who has to deal with the goods on board the ship makes entries in the book of the nature and quantity of the goods, and the name of the consignor,[1] etc., on the basis of information obtained beforehand from the consignor.

This is thus a kind of preparatory entry book, occupying a position similar to that of an usher[2] in relation to other books. There is also a book called *kiridashi-chô*. It is used to enter the *kiridashi*, a kind of commission given to the crew of a ship when goods are taken on board for transportation, so that any possible damage or loss of the goods may be prevented. The *kiridashi* is given by forwarding agents on behalf of the consignor of the goods or the owner of the ship, on the understanding that the crew will be given a portion of the profits when the goods are sold. There is also a *chinsen-chô*, which records stevedores' wages or freight charges paid. The above three books are necessary for wholesalers, and the third one is used by all middlemen as well. The middleman also uses a *chûmon-chô*, a book which records the quantity of the goods, the name of the vendee, etc., when a contract of sale of goods is entered into. This book is needed as long as the delivery or shipment of the goods has not yet been completed and the goods are still in the hands of the vendor. It may also be occasionally used by some wholesalers and other traders, but for middlemen it is indispensable. Also in use among some traders according to the trade are: the *tsumi-nikki*, the *shikiri-junban-chô*, the *shoharaikata-chô*, the *shômon-chô*, the *atsume-chô*, the *ryôgae-chô*, the *ie-tsuie-chô*, the *yachin-chô*, the *uki-gashi-chô*, the *nimotsu-azuke-chô*, the *nedate-chô*, the *sôba-chô*, etc. However, these are, after all, auxiliary books, necessary for some trades, but not for all. Of the above-mentioned nine books required by wholesalers and middlemen, seven—the *yorozu-uri-chô*, the *daifuku-chô*, the *kinsen-deiri-chô*, the *nimotsu-deiri-chô*, the *kinsen-hantori-chô*, and the *nimotsu-hantori-chô*—are indispensable for any trader, regardless of his trade, who is engaged in business. Although there is no fixed form of entry in these books, in practice it is almost the same, though there may be slight differences between one trader and another.

There is also no fixed rule as to the length of time a book is pre-

---

[1] *Ninushi* (freight master). It also sometimes means the owner of a cargo; so in this sense it can be a consignor, a consignee, or somebody else.

[2] *Uketsuke*.

served. The books are usually discarded after having been preserved from ten to twenty years. The chief ledger, *daifuku-chô*, however, is preserved by some almost indefinitely.

Hyôgo. (Answers for Topic 4, Subtopic 3)

The Western method of bookkeeping will gradually come into vogue, according to present prospects.

(Quoted from the Proceedings of the local committee=Re Topic 4, Sub-topics 1 & 2)

No. 5 [Inoue] said: "The *daifuku-chô*, the *tôza-chô* and the *kingin-deiri-chô* are the most important books. The *daifuku-chô* is a ledger,[1] and the *tôza-chô* is a trader's journal. There are many books of minor importance, but they are not indispensable. As to the three above-mentioned books, though they are called by different names, their uses are the same, and other than these three, there are no other books indispensable to a trader."

No. 19 [Funai] said: "Speaking from the standpoint of a pawnbroker, which I am, the most important books are the *shichi-mono-chô* and the *shichi-dashi-chô*. Other books, such as the *shichi-fuda-chô*[2] and the *kayoi-chô*[3] are not as important as the above two books. The *kinsen-deiri-chô* concerns only the receipt and payment of money, and is not indispensable to our trade. The *shichi-mono-chô* is used for entering clearly every receipt of things pledged,[4] and the *shichidashi-chô*[5] is used for entering every restoration of things pledged."

No. 14 [Funai] said: "If the trade books are classified into those of wholesalers, middlemen and retailers, and the uses and kinds of these books used in those trades which deal in the most important goods (rice, dried sardines and saké) studied, the matter will be greatly simplified."

No. 6 [Hamada] said: "I second the proposition of No. 14. Moreover, the books used in the various trades are not very different from one another. Three kinds of books, i.e., the *uri-chô*, the *kaiire-chô* and the *dai-chô* are the most important, and there is little difference among the rest of the books."

No. 27 [Arima] said: "There are about thirteen books that are necessary in commerce. Besides these, there are twenty-odd books in use."

No. 32 [Okajima] said: "There are six or seven books used among

---

[1] *Daichô.*
[2] Pledge card-book.
[3] Obscure.
[4] *Shichi-motsu,* a thing pledged.
[5] Pledge-reliever-book.

traders engaged in foreign trade besides the sales book[1] and the transaction book.[2] If the less important books are counted, books in use would total some twenty altogether."

No. 4 [Kishi] said: "There are considerable differences in commercial customs between Kôbe and Hyôgo. Kôbe has recently shown a great advance in commerce, but hitherto few were engaged in business. The present traders have mostly come from different provinces of the country, hence their commercial customs are different and the books used by them also differ. On the other hand, Hyôgo is inhabited by a large number of old families and old firms which have been engaged in business from olden times, and most of these firms are related to one another as branch families. Hence there is not much difference among them as to their commercial customs, and the trade books used by them are also, I believe, substantially the same. Consequently it is hoped that Hyôgo and Kôbe be treated separately. Furthermore, as No. 14 has suggested, this matter should be studied with reference to wholesalers, middlemen and retailers."

No. 19 [Funai] said: "I insist that Hyôgo and Kôbe be treated as one in the investigation."

No. 32 [Okajima] said: "I ask you to vote for the study of the three classes of trades."

No. 27 [Arima] said: "There are differences in commercial customs between Hyôgo and Kôbe, even in the same trades of the three classes. Therefore, I second the proposition of No. 4."

Chairman of the Local Committee [Kashima] said: "I move you appoint a committee for the investigation of the three classes of trade books, without making any distinction between Hyôgo and Kôbe."

No. 14 [Funai] said: "I am going to present to the Chairman, in writing, the names of my choices, and I would like you to consult other members of this committee present here and decide upon the members of the commercial book committee."

Hereupon, the Chairman read the names of No. 14's choices: Mr. Arima for the investigation of wholesalers' books, Mr. Kishi for middlemen's books, and Mr. Tamba for retailers' books. As there was no objection, the Chairman entrusted the task to these three gentlemen.

No. 27 [Arima] said: "I am a middleman, so I would like to investigate middlemen's books. Also I suggest that you ask Mr. Kitakaze to investigate wholesalers' books."

The Chairman [Kashima]: "Then I will appoint Mr. Kitakaze and

[1] *Urikomi-chô.*
[2] *Hikitori-chô.*

Mr. Arima for the investigation of wholesalers' books, Mr. Arima and Mr. Kishi for middlemen's books, and Mr. Tamba and Ômori for retailers' books, and ask them to make investigations with reference to the present Topic, Subtopics 1 and 2. Then I will consult you all again."

[Re: Topic 4, Subtopic 3]

No. 11 [Horiuchi]: "There is the prospect of the Western method of bookkeeping gradually being adopted."

No. 2 [Tamba]: "There are far more traders in this district (Hyôgo) who have adopted the Western method of bookkeeping than in other districts. Before many years elapse, the Western method will come into vogue here."

No. 19 [Funai]: "Those who have taken to the Western method are still as scarce as stars on a rainy night. The Western method is hard to learn, but as the commercial sciences advance here, it will, I believe, gradually come into vogue."

Chairman [Kashima]: "As there is no dissenting opinion on this subject, I will present a report saying, 'There is a prospect of the Western method gradually coming into vogue.' "

Ôtsu. (Answer to Topic 4, Subtopic 1)

Every trader keeps the following five kinds of books, namely the *tôza-chô* (also called *uriage-chô* and, by rice traders, *uma-nikki*), the *shikiri-chô* (also called *kai-ire-chô*), the *kingin-deiri-chô*, the *kingin-hantori-chô* and the *daifuku-chô*. Besides these, a book called *nimotsu-hantori-chô* is kept by forwarding agents and wholesalers. The quality of goods sold, the price, the name of the vendee, the date of sale, etc. are entered in the *tôza-chô* on a daily basis. The *shikiri-chô* records all the particulars regarding purchases by a trader. Entries in the *tôza-chô* and the *shikiri-chô* are classified and reentered, in a more detailed manner, in the *daifuku-chô*. The *kingin-deiri-chô* contains daily entries of every payment and receipt of money. The *kinsen-hantori-chô* is customarily sealed by the payee as proof of receipt of money when payment has been made by a trader. The period during which these books are preserved is usually ten years, but sometimes it even runs to fifty years. There are not a few books, however, which may be preserved only for two or three years.

Ôtsu. (Answer to Topic 4, Subtopic 2)

There is no fixed rule as to the form of entries in these books, but in most cases the entries, usually classified into two sorts, are made under the headings of payment[1] and receipt.[2] The kinds of books used always differ with different trades, but in most cases they are mere variations of the sorts enumerated in Answers to Subtopic 1 above.

Ôtsu. (Answer to Topic 4, Subtopic 3)

The method of bookkeeping by single and double entry is gradually coming into vogue of late among banks and companies, but there are as yet no private traders who have taken to the Western method.

Kumamoto. (Answer to Topic 4, Subtopic 1)

The following six kinds of trade books, namely, the *daifuku-chô*, the *kaiire-chô*, the *uritate-chô*, the *tôza-chô*, the *kinsen-hantori-chô*, and the *nimotsu-hantori-chô*, are indispensable to any trader, regardless of the kind of trade in which he is engaged. Besides these, there are numerous auxiliary books used. There is no fixed custom regarding the period during which these books are preserved.

Kumamoto. (Answer to Topic 4, Subtopic 2)

The matters to be entered in the books are the same, but there is no fixed custom as to the form of their entry. Sometimes the books used are different in different trades, the pawnbroker, for instance, equipping himself with the following books: the *shichimono-toriire-dai-chô*,[3] the *uke-jichi-chô*,[4] the *nagaremono-chôsa-chô*,[5] and the *ukenin-ren'in-chô*[6] which is used when a pledge check is lost by the pledgor. Again, a saké brewer keeps a *shuzômai-kaiire-chô*,[7] *tsukizome-chô*,[8] *shikomi-chô*,[9] *saké-kuradashi-chô*,[10] *saké-uriage-chô*,[11] *saké-kashi-chô*,[12] *shuzô-*

---

[1] *De-no-bu.*

[2] *Iri-no-bu.*

[3] A ledger which records the things pledged.

[4] The book in which the redemption of things pledged is entered.

[5] A book which records the foreclosure of the things pledged.

[6] A book in which those who stand surety for another write their name and stamp their seals side by side with the pledger, in proof of their suretyship.

[7] A book which records the rice bought by the brewer for brewing saké.

[8] A book to record the rice which has been cleaned.

[9] A book to enter the materials bought by a brewer.

[10] A book to record the saké which has been taken out of a warehouse.

[11] A book to record the saké sold.

[12] A book used for entering sales of saké on credit.

mai-shiharai-chô,[1] *tsumidashi-chô,*[2] *sakékasunuka-uriharai-chô*[3] and *saké-kasu-mekata-hikae-chô.*[4]

Wholesale merchants keep a *mizuage-chô*[5] and *tabibito-tachi-tsuki-hikae-chô.*[6] These are some example of how different books are used in different trades.

Kumamoto. (Answer to Topic 4, Subtopic 3)

The Western method of bookkeeping is in use, at present, only at the banks and other companies and a few private firms, there being little prospect of its easy, general acceptance in the near future.

Okayama. (Answer to Topic 4, Subtopic 1)

There are numerous kinds of trade books, and the number and names of these books are different in different houses, depending upon the trade and the customs. Nevertheless, the following books are indispensable to commercial houses in general.

1.   The *tôza-chô* is a book in which daily entries are made of the names of the goods, their quality, quantity, prices, date of delivery, names of the vendors or vendees and all other matters relating to commercial transactions.

2.   The *moto-chô* is a book in which all sales on credit[7] are recorded.

3.   The *kaitsuke-chô* is a book in which particulars relating to purchases of goods are recorded.

4.   The *uriage-chô* is a book used for entering particulars relating to sales of goods.

5.   The *mizuage-chô* is a book in which particulars relative to discharges from ships are recorded.

6.   The *kinsen-hantori-chô* is a book used for securing the impress of the seal of a payee in proof of his receipt of money paid.

7.   The *kamotsu-hantori-chô* is a book used for securing the impress of the seal of a recipient of goods in proof of his receiving them.

---

[1] A book used for entering the payments for the rice for brewing bought by a brewer.

[2] A book to record the shipments (of saké).

[3] A book used for entering the sale of lees (*kasu*) and rice-bran (*nuka*) which have been procured as by-products in saké brewing.

[4] A book used for entering the weight of lees of saké.

[5] A book to record the goods unloaded from a ship.

[6] A book used for entering the departures and arrivals of passengers.

[7] *Urikake.*

The *kinsen-deiri-chô* is a book used for entering in detail daily payment and receipt of money. Entries are made every time a payment or receipt is made.

Okayama. (Answer to Topic 4, Subtopic 2)

There is no fixed form of entry for trade books. Sometimes, however, different books are used in different trades, depending upon the nature of the latter.

Okayama. (Answer to Topic 4, Subtopic 3)

The Western method of bookkeeping by single and double entry has not yet come into vogue except among banks and companies. However, there is a prospect that the method will gradually be increasingly adopted as its conveniences come to be recognized by an increasing number of people.

Bakan. (Answer to Topic 4, Subtopic 1)

Some commercial houses use as many as a dozen kinds of books, and some only three. These books are ordinarily called respectively *shohin-hantori-chô*,[1] *hama* (port)-*chô*,[2] *gembai-chô*,[3] *shôbaihin-tôzagashi-chô*,[4] *kinsen-deiri-chô*,[5] *kai-chô*,[6] *sashihiki-kanjô-chô*,[7] *kinsen-hantori-chô*,[8] *daifuku-cho*,[9] etc. As to the uses of these books, *daifuku-chô* is the principal book, the other books being used as their respective names indicate, with the possible exception of some traders who may make slightly different use of these books and their names. The length of time these books are preserved is usually eight or nine years, but some traders preserve them for as long as sixty or seventy years.

Bakan. (Answer to Topic 4, Subtopic 2)

There is no fixed form of entry for these books. Different books are used in different trades.

---

[1] A book used to be sealed by others in connection with (delivery or purchase of) various goods.

[2] A book used for entering goods loaded on board or discharged from a ship.

[3] A book used for entering sales made on the spot.

[4] A book used for entering goods that are loaned on demand by other persons for temporary or trial use [which may eventually result in purchase by the borrower, or those that are consigned to other traders for sale]. See also *ukigashi-cho* below.

[5] A book used for entering payment and receipt of money.

[6] A book used for entering purchases.

[7] A book used for recording the balance of debts and credits.

[8] A book to be sealed by a recipient of money in proof of receipt.

[9] A ledger.

Bakan. (Answer to Topic 4, Subtopic 3)

With the exception of banks and other commercial corporations, there is no prospect that entries in trade books will be made according to the Western method of bookkeeping.

Sakai. (Answer to Topic 4, Subtopic 1)

There are a great number of different kinds of trade books in use depending on the different needs of each merchant. It would be impossible to enumerate them all. However, there are no more than thirteen books which are indispensable to every trader; and their names and uses are as follows.

1. The *tôza-chô*, also called *uri-chô* or *tsukekomi-chô*. In this book are entered the quantities of goods sold, prices, date of delivery, names of the vendees and everything else relating to sales.

2. The *ukigashi-chô*. In this book are recorded the kinds of goods that are loaned to a trader or non-trader at his request (for trial use) preparatory to purchase for disposal to others. Items which are returned will be struck out, and those which have been disposed of will be culled and posted up to the sales book.

3. The *daifuku-chô*, also called *kake-chô* or *moto-chô*. This is used exclusively for entering sales on credit.

4. The *mizuage-chô*. This is used chiefly for entering the amount of the goods that have been bought and delivered which have been received, or of those that have been delivered with the request to forward to another.

5. The *shikiri-chô*, also called *kai-chô*, *kai-nikki*, or *shiire-chô*. This is used for entering, and summing up, the quantity, grades and prices of goods which, having been purchased and delivered or delivered with the request to forward to another, have been entered in the *mizuage-chô*, and of those of which the contract for purchase has been concluded. However, besides the above items, wholesalers make it a rule to make entries of the various charges[1] and other expenses, and the commission fees[2] that have been paid in connection with the goods.

6. The *nimotsu-azukari* (deposit)-*chô*. This is used for recording goods for which the sales transaction, except for details of payment, has been concluded, and the quantity of those goods which have

[1] *Sho-kakarimono.*
[2] *Kosen.*

been left on deposit with the vendor at the request of the vendee, as well as any sum of money which might be loaned to the vendee in connection with the deposit.

7. The *kawase* (exchange)-*chô*. This book is used for entering the bank discount on a cashed bill of exchange,[1] and the amount of a bill of exchange drawn between traders A and B for convenience. This book is also used to record exchanges of goods.

8. The *kinsen-deiri-chô*. This is used for entering the prices of sales, purchases of goods and all other matters with regard to payment and receipt of money, for frequent balancing of accounts in order to verify the payment and receipt figures.

9. & 10. The *kinsen-watashi-chô*, also called *kinsen-hantori-chô*; and the *nimotsu-watashi-chô*, also called *nimotsu-hantori-chô*. These books are used to prove receipt by the recipient at the time of payment of money and delivery of goods.

11. The *shiire-kashitsuke-chô*. This is used to record the loan of a business advance[2] which has been requested by a trader from whom purchases of one's goods for sale are made. In this case the debtor must gradually pay back his debt by supplying goods to the creditor whenever he has goods to deliver. Until the debtor has repaid the entire advance, he is not allowed, according to custom, to freely dispose of these goods to other traders.

12. The *chûmon-chô*. This is used to enter the quality of the goods, prices, date of their delivery, etc. at the time when the orders are received.

13. The *daichô*. This book is used by pawnbrokers only. In the days of the old government, in December every year, pawnbrokers used to prepare their books with the number of sheets which they estimated were necessary for use for the next year and bring them to the pawnbrokers' meeting-place.[3] Here the number of sheets in the books were examined by copyists[4] under the direction of the general secretary[5] of the pawnbrokers' association. Then, the number of sheets thus examined and the rules of the association were

---

[1] Not quite clear.

[2] *Eigyô-shihon.*

[3] *Shichi-kaishô.*

[4] *Hissei.*

[5] *Nen-gyôji.* "At present this term denotes the superintendent (*torishimari-nin*) or chief representative" (*sôdai-nin*). [Compilers]

written down in detail and the seal of approval[1] of the association was impressed on the first page of each book. Furthermore, the seal was put on the side edge of the book, so that no sheets might be replaced by new ones undetected.

This book is used for daily entries of the names of things pledged[2] and the amount of money loaned, the addresses and names of the pledgor[3] and the names of sureties.[4] And on the 7th, 15th, 22nd, and 30th of every month, the entries in the *daichô* are copied in the *shichimotsu-deiri-chô*, also called *efu-chô* or *uchiwake-chô*. As a rule a tally-seal is impressed whenever things are pledged or redeemed.

For the thirteen book types mentioned above, new books are prepared every January to replace the old ones. There is no fixed custom as to the period they are preserved, but they are usually kept for ten years or more.

Besides these thirteen books, there are two more books in use, the *seri-chô* and the *kaimono-chô*. The *seri-chô* is used for the following purpose. The trader enters in this book the names, quality and quantity, of goods which a customer unexpectedly applies to buy but which the trader does not have in stock, and borrows them for the time being from a fellow trader who does have them in stock. If the goods satisfy the customer and can be sold, the trader will then pay over the purchase-money to the fellow trader from whom he obtained them. If the goods cannot be sold, they will be returned to the original owner.

The *kaimono-chô* is used on the occasion of a purchase of a daily necessities. The vendee brings the book to the vendor, and the latter enters in it the quality and price of the goods he has sold and returns it immediately to the former. As long as these books are returned to, and kept by, the vendee it means that evidence of sale is in the hands of the vendee, but vendors do not seem to mind this.

Sakai. (Answer to Topic 4, Subtopic 2)

There is no fixed rule as to the form of entries. There are some slight differences in the kinds of books used depending on the nature of the trade, but the chief books are the thirteen mentioned

[1] Ken-in.
[2] *Shichi-motsu (azukarihin).*
[3] *Oki-nushi.*
[4] *Ukenin.*

in the answers to the questions in Subtopic 1.

Sakai. (Answer to Topic 4, Subtopic 3)

The practice of keeping books according to the Western method is not yet in use here except at the national banks.

Iida. (Answer to Topic 4, Subtopic 1)

1. The *tôza-chô*. This book is used for making daily entries of all sales, whether in cash or on credit.

2. The *daifuku-chô*. This book is used exclusively for entering sales on credit. Prices of the goods are posted up to this book from the *tôza-chô*, and receipts of money in payment are also copied here from the *kingin-deiri-chô*. The accounts are then balanced and verified. This is the most important book for a mercantile house.

3. The *kingin-deiri-chô*. This book is used, as the name indicates, to enter every payment and receipt of money.

4. The *kaiire-chô*, also called *shiire-chô*. This is used to enter the original prices[1] of goods [bought from the wholesalers or the manufacturers].

5. The *uriage-chô*. This is used to enter the sales prices of the goods sold.

6. The *nimotsu-deiri-chô*. This is used to enter in detail the receipt and forwarding of goods.

7. The *hantori-chô*. Upon the occasion of payment of money, the recipient is required to write down the receipt in this book, and to seal it, so that the entry may be kept for future proof.

8. The *urikake-kakinuki-chô*. This book is used, as its name indicates, for extracting those entries concerning sales on credit from the *daifuku-chô*. Thus this book may be made use of for collecting bills.

9. The *kayoi-chô*. This book is used for the entry of sales on credit and is given to the most trustworthy customers. In it are entered the names and prices of goods sold, and it is left in the keeping of the customer.

10. The *zappi-chô*. The book is used for the entry of all sundry expenses.

These books are usually preserved for at least ten years, and sometimes for as long as fifty years.

Iida. (Answer to Topic 4, Subtopic 2)

---

[1] *Genka.*

In our district, there is no fixed form of entry, nor are different kinds of books recognized according to the nature of the trade.

Iida. (Answer to Topic 4, Subtopic 3)

In our district, the Western method of bookkeeping has not yet been adopted except at the national banks, and there is no indication that it will become prevalent.

Takamatsu. (Answer to Topic 4, Subtopic 1)

The trader's books in use here are different, depending upon the nature of the trade (whether it is, for instance, a wholesale or retail business or pawnbroking, etc.) and upon the manner of transaction (whether it is carried on, for instance, interprovincially, inter-*go*,[1] or within the city, or for cash or on credit, etc.). Also the same sort of book may sometimes be called by different names. There are more than a hundred kinds of books altogether, but the more essential of those commonly used by traders are presumably the following eleven:

The *tôza-chô*, the *moto-chô*, the *shiire-chô*, the *shikiri-chô*, the *kinsen-suitô-chô*, the *san'yô-chô*, the *mokuroku-chô*, the *kaneiri-chô*, the *nimotsu-azukari-chô*, the *hantori-chô* and the *shichiya-daichô*.

The form of entry for these books depends upon the convenience and custom of each mercantile house and there is no fixed rule about this. Pawnshops and banks have rather fixed forms for entry (but even this cannot be invariably asserted). The period of preservation of these books differs. However, as the object of their preservation is to provide for future proof, needless to say, they must be preserved until the matters entered therein are finished. Consequently, the preservation period of these books is short if the matters entered therein are completed soon, and long if otherwise. The period is sometimes as short as one year or as long as ten. Such are the ordinary customs regarding form of entry and period of preservation of trade books.

The following is a brief account of the uses of these eleven books.

1. The *tôza-chô*. This is a day book, in which everything relating to sales transaction is entered for later selective transfer to other books. In it are entered, one by one, the names of the goods, their quality, quantity, and prices, the date of their delivery and the

---

[1] *Go* used to stand for a district consisting of several villages, within a *gun* or *kôri*. It was bigger than a village but smaller than a *gun*.

name and domicile of the other party to the transaction. In keeping with the needs of the individual mercantile house, several copies of the book are sometimes prepared and numbered. Or, the book may be divided into two parts, one for the town and the other for the country. The book is usually composed of a certain number of sheets estimated to be required for one year's use. Some mercantile houses prepare the *uriage-chô* (literally, "sales book") as well as the *tôza-chô*, entering in the former all sales in cash and in the latter all sales on credit. In this case, the *uriage-chô* is prefixed with the name of the goods with which it deals, e.g., an oil dealer will write "*aburarui-uriage-chô.*"[1]

The *tôza-chô* is the most important of all books for a trader.

2. The *moto-chô*, also called *kake-moto-chô*. This is used for transferring entries from the *tôza-chô* for easy location of all sales on credit. Depending on different circumstances, the book is sometimes divided into a number of parts representing streets [where the other parties to the transactions have their domicile or their stores], or into two parts, one for the town and the other for the country, or into two parts representing the Eastern and the Western districts. Each part is again subdivided according to the name and domicile of each purchaser, and reference is facilitated by index-slips attached to the margin of the leaves.

With wholesalers, every sale on credit, complete with particulars, including prices of goods sold and miscellaneous expenses incurred in connection with the sale, is first entered in the *shikiri-chô* (see below), and then are re-entered in this book, separated for each customer according to the locality.

For transactions within the city, a supplementary book called *kaketori-chô*[2] is usually prepared for bill collectors making their rounds. In this only the prices of the goods sold and the names of vendees, abstracted from the *moto-chô*, are entered, when the bills have been collected, they are entered in the *tôza-chô* on the very day of collection, and then the entries are checked against each individual's section of the *moto-chô*. If all the bills of a customer have been paid up, the old entries will be struck out, and usually entries of new sales on credit will follow.

[1] Lit., "oil sale book."

[2] *Kake*, bill, and *tori*, collection.

The *moto-chô* is a most important book for a commercial house.[1]

3.   The *kinsen-suitô-chô*. This is used for entry of every payment and receipt of money that is made in connection with purchases and sales of goods, etc. in business transactions. In some commercial houses accounts are balanced daily, in others, semi-monthly, or monthly. Or sometimes retailers[2] balance their accounts in the *tôza-chô*, while wholesalers[3] balance theirs in the *kinsen-suitô-chô*. The form of entry in this book is more irregular than in others.

4.   The *san'yô-chô*. This book is used for entering net profit and loss relating to commercial matters. Consequently, retailers and wholesalers usually transcribe to this book the proceeds and purchase costs from the *tôza-chô* and *shiire-chô*, so that they may calculate their profit and loss at the end of each month or year. The form of entry and the period of account is different with different traders.

5.   The *mokuroku-chô*. This book belongs chiefly (or exclusively) to the commission agent (or the wholesaler)[4] and is entered with the balance account[5] of the prices of goods sold and purchased by the transporter.[6] Entries are made separately for each of the customers, and the book is divided into two parts, one for customers and the other for transporters, each part having been indexed. At first all prices of goods sold by the transporter are summed up from the *shikiri-chô*, and then they are entered in the *mokuroku-chô*. Then the balance is made, entering all prices of goods purchased, the number and kind of which are stated. When money is paid [to the transporter?] it is usually balanced with that to be received [from him in selling goods?]

6.   The *shiire-chô*, also called *shikomi-chô*. This book is an important book and is indispensable to a trader. It is used for entering, not only the goods purchased, in detail, but also all the particulars relating to the purchases. Suppose a box of petroleum cans worth

---

[1]   [In the original text this is written "sho-kyaku" (customer), but a marginal explanation says that this is perhaps a clerical mistake for *shoka* (commercial house).]

[2]   *Misekata.*

[3]   *Motokata.*

[4]   *Toiya.*

[5]   *Sashihiki-kanjô.*

[6]   *Funakata;* this literally means "ship-crews," and in this case probably signifies the common carrier by sea or river.

¥3.80 is bought at Osaka and shipped to the place of consumption, and that the freight, commission[1] and the reward for trouble amounted,[2] in all, to 20 *sen*. The goods will be regarded as if the original purchase price[3] were ¥3.90,[4] and this figure will be the basis for calculating the sales price.

7. The *shikiri-chô*. This is used exclusively by wholesalers, of whatever trade. All the particulars relating to sales and purchases, from the standpoint of middlemen between the sellers and the buyers, are entered in this book. Every time money received from the buyers is handed over to the sellers, a detailed invoice[5] is made from the entries in this book.

8. The *nimotsu-azukari-chô*. This book is used exclusively by wholesalers, who, while the sale of deposited goods has not yet been decided upon, make a detailed entry of the quantity of the goods and the date when the goods were first placed in their charge. Thus when there is a demand for the goods and they are called for by the owner, calculation of storage[6] and other charges may be made from the entries in this book.

9. The *hantori-chô*. There are two kinds of *hantori-chô*, that is, the *kinsen-hantori-chô* and the *nimotsu-hantori-chô*. When delivery of goods is made, the deliverer himself enters into the latter the quantity of the goods delivered and requires the recipient to impress his firm seal[7] or the receipt seal[8] to prove that the goods have, without doubt, been received. The former book is similarly used at the time of payment to prove that the money has actually been received.

10. The *shichiya-daichô*. This book, used exclusively by pawn-brokers, is the most important one, having a decisive legal effect in any future dispute. It is used to secure the pledgor's[9] acknowl-edgement that he has obtained the loan of a certain amount of money from the pawnbroker. Suppose a poor man wishes to pledge

---

[1] *Kosen.*

[2] *Dachin.*

[3] *Genka.*

[4] [Probably should be ¥4.00.]

[5] *Shikiri-sho.*

[6] *Kurashiki-hi*, *Kurashiki*, and *Kurashiki-ryô* mean the same thing.

[7] *Yagô-in.*

[8] *Uketori-han;* that is, a seal indicating receipt (of goods or money).

[9] *Shichi-ire-sha.*

a lined garment for spring and autumn wear[1] for a certain sum of money. He himself must enter in this book the sum of money he receives on loan and immediately below this, the item, e.g. a "lined garment,"[2] and to the right of the sum, the date. Then he signs his name and puts his seal[2] to the left of "lined garment." Then the pawnbroker will affix a tally-impression on a page of the *daichô* and the pledge-ticket,[3] made of *yatsugiri*-sized[4] or *jûgiri*-sized[5] *Senka-gami*[6] or *uda-gami*[7] paper, and give the ticket to the pledgor. If the pledged goods are redeemed within the prescribed period, the goods are returned to the pledgor in exchange for the ticket. After the expiration of the prescribed period, practice has it that the ticket becomes entirely invalid. If the ticket is lost during the prescribed period, the pledgor is required to find a proper surety who will guarantee that, even if the lost ticket is found in the future, it shall be uncollectable. The goods are then returned to the pledgor. The pledge period is usually six months for *erimono*[8] and three months for grain and hardware. Also, when the sum loaned to the pledgor is more than ten *yen*, a one-*sen* revenue stamp (a one-*sen* stamp is required for every ten *yen*) is affixed to the ticket which is given to

---

[1] *Awase.*

[2] The way the entry is made by the pledgor is illustrated as follows:

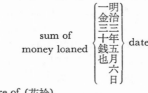

[3] *Shichimotsu-tefuda;* also called *kofuda,* or *shichifuda.*

[4] Literally, "octavo"; however, this does not represent the same size as in the Western system.

[5] Literally, "decimally-divided size."

[6] A thick sort of Japanese paper, believed to have been first manufactured by a Senka Hyôdô. It was formerly used as the material for paper bags or oilskin made of paper.

[7] Obscure.

[8] In the Tokugawa period and the early years of Meiji, people of the lower classes used to have an *eri* or collar attached to their clothes for daily wear or work; hence *erimono* here means clothes for daily wear of the lower classes.

the pledgor. Thus there is little fear that a dispute will arise for trial. However, people who wish to pledge goods like *erimono* (collared clothes) belong to the needy classes who live in nine-by-twelve[1] houses in the back-streets.[2] They are mostly illiterate and unable to sign their name in the *daichô*, and seldom have even their own seal to put in the book. (If pawnbrokers were to try to require these customers to impress a seal, the latter would cease to patronize their shops. Therefore pawnbrokers usually leave it up to their customers whether to stamp their seal or not.) When a dispute arises, therefore, there is no way to verify the transaction, so that in such cases the book might as well be ignored. Therefore we hope that in future in compiling the commercial code regulations may be enacted to prevent disputes, even where there is no pledgor's seal in the *daichô*.

11.   The *kane-iri-chô*. This book is used by commercial houses carrying on an active business and having a large number of domestic employees.[3] A servant, dispatched to collect bills, for instance, is given this book to take with him. If the person, pressed for payment, wishes to pay his debt on that occasion, he is supposed to write in the book that such and such an amount has been given in payment, and to stamp his shop-name seal[4] or shop seal[5] as positive proof that the sum has been paid.

Takamatsu. (Answer to Topic 4, Subtopic 2) [Missing]

Takamatsu. (Answer to Topic 4, Subtopic 3)

Since the Western method of bookkeeping was introduced recently into our country, there are some ambitious traders here who, hearing how remarkably convenient it is, have bought some books and studied it, and have become the more convinced of its advantages. However, to abandon the old system which has been adhered to for many years and adopt a new one is certainly irksome. Hence with the exception of the national bank here, there is not a single trader yet who has adopted the Western method in actual practice.

---

[1] *Kushaku-niken*, lit., "nine *shaku* by two *ken* (= 12 *shaku*)"; an expression used to denote a humble dwelling.

[2] *Uradana*, equivalent to "slum quarters."

[3] Formerly, in small mercantile houses, there was often no distinction between domestic employees and commercial employees.

[4] *Yago-ban.*

[5] *Mise-ban.*

It is our firm belief, however, that the time will come when, as our foreign trade becomes more prosperous and we come to allow our foreign residents to live alongside our own people, our business relations with them will become closer, and we shall be obliged, by force of circumstances, to adopt it, even against our will.

Fukui. (Answer to Topic 4, Subtopic 1)

1.   The *genkin-uriage-chô*. In this book are entered all daily sales in cash.

2.   The *buppin-ukigashi-chô*. In this book are entered goods which have been delivered for which contracts of sale have not yet been concluded.

3.   The *kashitsuke-uriage-chô*.[1] In this book are entered goods which have been sold but have not yet been paid for.

4.   The *shôbaihin-ichijigashi-chô*, also called *daifuku-chô*. The entries in the *kashitsuke-uriage-chô* of names of goods sold, prices, etc., are selected and recorded in the present book under the names of the debtors.

5.   The *kinsen-deiri-chô*. In this book all payments and receipts of money are entered for the purpose of daily settlement of accounts.

6.   The *kinsen-taishaku-chô*. In this book only loans of money are entered.

7.   The *kinsen-watashi-chô*. Whenever delivery of money is made, the recipient is required to enter in the present book the sum he has received.

8.   The *buppin-hantori-chô*. When delivery of promised goods[2] is made, the recipient is required to enter his name in the present book and stamp his seal.

9.   The *shôbaihin-shiire-chô*. In this book are entered all purchases of goods for sale.[3]

10.   The *buppin-chôsa-chô*. In this book the amount of goods bought is balanced against the amount sold in order to verify the remaining stock.[4]

11.   The *shichimotsu-daichô*. In this book are entered the kinds and quantity of goods pledged, and the sum loaned.

The period of preservation of these books depends on the circum-

---

[1] Book for sales on credit.
[2] *Uke-buppin.*
[3] *Eigyô-hin.*
[4] *Zampin.*

stances of the individual trader. Some keep them for a year, others for more than ten years.

Fukui. (Answer to Topic 4, Subtopic 2)

There is no fixed form of entry in these books. Also, very different kinds of books are used, depending on the nature of the trade. Pawnbrokers, for example, carry on their business using the *shichimotsu-daichô* and the *kinsen-suitô-chô*;[1] saké brewers use sixteen books, according to the regulations of the Ministry of Finance. Thus there are too many books to enumerate here.

Fukui. (Answer to Topic 4, Subtopic 3)

The Western method of bookkeeping has come slightly into use here, and there is the prospect that it will gradually be adopted generally.

Tokushima. (Answer to Topic 4, Subtopic 1)

There are some eight kinds of trade books in use here. They are generally known as *kaiire-chô*,[2] *kane-suitô-chô*,[3] *uriage-chô*,[4] *uketori-chô*,[5] *nimotsu-hantori-chô*,[6] *tôza-chô* [which records daily sales on credit], *yorozu-ne-chô*[7] and *keisan-chô*[8] and are respectively used as their names indicate.

As to the period of preservation, this differs with the individual mercantile house.

Tokushima. (Answer to Topic 4, Subtopic 2)

Almost the same sorts of books are used in different trades, but the form of entry is different, depending upon the nature of the trade.

Tokushima. (Answer to Topic 4, Subtopic 3)

The method of bookkeeping by single and double entries, such as is employed in the European and American countries, has hardly penetrated here.

Takefu (Fukui Prefecture). (Answers to Topic 4, Subtopics 1 & 2)

---

[1] Same as *kinsen-deiri-chô*; see above.
[2] Purchases book.
[3] Cash book.
[4] Sales book.
[5] Receipt book.
[6] See above.
[7] Same as *moto-chô* or *daichô*, i.e., ledger.
[8] Account book.

There are so many different kinds of books in use, such as *shiire-chô*,[1] *kashi-tsuke-chô*,[2] *tôza-chô*, *hikae-chô*,[3] and *genkin-chô*,[4] that it is impossible to know how many there are in all. Their nature is generally as mentioned above. However there is no fixed rule as to their appellation and use. Apparently each mercantile house has its own rule, and we cannot presume to know what such rules are.

The period of preservation is generally from one to five years.

Takefu. (Answer to Topic 4, Subtopic 3)

There is no trader here using the Western method of bookkeeping, nor is there any prospect of its gradual adoption.

Miyagi. (Answer to Topic 4, Subtopic 1)

The kinds of books required depend upon the amount of business and the nature of the trade. There are scores of books in use, but the more important of them, those usually regarded as indispensable to a trader, are the following five:

1. The *kingin-deiri-chô*. In this are entered all payments and receipts of money in connection with daily purchases and sales of goods, etc., for the purpose of accurately balancing the accounts at the end of each day or week.

2. The *shiire-chô*. In this are entered the particulars regarding purchase of goods for sale, based upon the statement of account[5] or invoice,[6] etc. Consequently the entries include names of goods bought, quantities, purchase prices and the nature of transactions, such as cash or credit or term,[7] etc.

3. The *urisabaki-chô*. In this are entered all sales of goods. Entries cover the quality, quantity, purchase prices, etc. for every sale of goods, and are largely similar to those in the *shiire-chô*.

4. The *hatori-chô*. Those to whom payment of money or delivery of goods has been made are required to stamp their seal in the present book as proof of receipt. Consequently, there are two sorts of *hantori-chô*.

5. The *daifuku-chô*. In this are entered sales on credit. Entries

---

[1] A book that records purchases of goods for sale. See *shôbai-hin-shiire-chô* above.

[2] A book that records all sales on credit. See *kashitsuke-uriage-chô* above.

[3] A memorandum.

[4] A cashbook.

[5] *Shikiri-sho.*

[6] *Okurijô.*

[7] *Gengetsu.*

regarding the receipt and payment of money as well as the loan of money are usually transferred to the present book from the particular books dealing with these items.

As has been indicated above, these five constitute the most common kinds of books. Besides these, we have, for instance, the *tôza-chô* and others, but no reference to them will here be made.

There is no fixed period of preservation. However, with the exception of the *daifuku-chô* and the *hantori-chô* mentioned above, the other books are usually replaced every year. The *daifuku-chô* is used for one year or several years, there being no fixed period.

Miyagi. (Answer to Topic 4, Subtopic 2)

There is no fixed form of entry in the books. Further, each trader classifies the books according to his own convenience, and different kinds of books are used even by traders of the same trade. In short, there is confusion, at present, about the manner in which these books are used.

Miyagi. (Answer to Topic 4, Subtopic 3)

As it is generally known that the Western method of bookkeeping is a very convenient one, there is every likelihood that it will come into vogue in future. However, at present no one here has adopted it, with the exception of banks. The day is far off when merchants will come to follow the Western method in their entries in all their books, and it is probably impossible to assert that this will happen within a space of several years.

Matsuyama. (Answer to Topic 4, Subtopic 1)

1. The *chûmon-chô*. When a trader wants to lay in a stock of something, it is entered in the present book as a preparation for the actual dispatch of the order. The book is usually preserved for one year.

2. The *mizuage-chô*, also called *hamamizu-chô*; the *niwairi-chô*; and the *niuke-chô*. Upon the arrival of a cargo, receipt of the goods is entered in the present book. It is usually preserved for one year.

3. The *irifune-chô*. At every arrival of a ship in port, entries are made in this book of the descriptions of its cargo, the names and addresses of the consignors,[1] etc. The book is usually preserved for one year.

4. The *kaichô*; the *shikiri-chô*; and the *shinari-chô*. When goods

[1] *Ninushi*.

are purchased, prices, quantity and other salient points are entered here. The book is usually preserved for five years.

5. The *banzuke-chô*;[1] the *urikeshi-chô*.[2] Goods in stock are inventoried, and the amounts are registered in the appropriate book. At each sale of the goods, the corresponding number of entries in these books are struck out, so that the stock in hand may be verified. The period of preservation is generally from one to two years.

6. The *kinsen-hantori-chô*, and the *nimotsu-hantori-chô*. On the occasion of payment of money or delivery of goods, the recipient is required to impress his seal in the appropriate book, as proof of receipt. These books are usually preserved for five years.

7. The *tôza-chô*; the *ukigashi-chô*. In these books are entered records of goods for sale to be sent to a customer. The books are usually preserved for one year.

8. The *nimotsu-tsumiire-chô*, or *niharai-chô*; and the *jôsen-chô*. In these books are entered goods to be forwarded or names of passengers, respectively. There is no fixed period of preservation, but they are usually preserved for three years.

9. The *tôzakashi-chô*; the *urikake-tôza-chô*; and the *kashi-uri-chô*. In these books are entered all sales on credit. The period of preservation is five years.

10. The *genkin-uri-chô*; the *uriage-chô*. In these books are entered all daily sales in cash. They are usually preserved for one year.

11. The *moto-cho*;[3] the *daifuku-chô*; the *moto-chô*; and the *daichô*. Entries in other particular books are posted up in each of these books. Therefore, these books are used for summing up various entries. They are usually preserved for five years.

12. The *kinsen-suitô-chô*. In this book are entered daily receipts and payments of money to enable a trader to estimate the sum he has in hand. This book is usually preserved for one year.

13. The *irejichi-chô*; the *shichi-daichô*. These books are, so to speak, ledgers of money loans, and are usually preserved for five years.

14. The *nagarejichi-chô*. Goods pledged that are not redeemed at the prescribed time are transcribed to the present book from the

[1] "Numbering" book.

[2] "Striking-out-at-sale" book.

[3] Different characters are used in these two names, but they are pronounced in the same way.

shichi-daichô. The book is usually preserved for one year.

15. The *kake-iri-chô*. In this are entered payments made for sales on credit. The book is usually preserved for one year.

16. The *kanjô-chô*. In this are entered sums paid or received in connection with sales or purchases of various goods, as well as profits and losses, to enable a trader to balance accounts at the end of every month, every year, or every five years.

17. The *kinsen-kayoi-chô*. In this are entered all moneys paid and received for the purpose of accomodation between individual traders. The book is usually preserved for one year.

18. The *otoshi-mono-chô*. The *otoshi-mono* here refers to the by-products in a manufacturing industry. Among rice dealers, for instance, this would refer to things such as rice bran,[1] broken rice,[2] straw bags[3] and straw rope. The book is usually preserved for one year.

Matsuyama. (Answer to Topic 4, Subtopic 2)

There is no fixed form of entry. Different kinds of books may be used, depending upon the nature of the trade. Saké brewers, and wholesalers, for instance, employ special books with different names and uses. However, the brevity of the entries seems rather common to all persons of the same trade.

Matsuyama. (Answer to Topic 4, Subtopic 3)

The Western method of bookkeeping is in use at banks and a few companies, but we have never heard of any other mercantile houses that have adopted it. However, as they are apparently aware of the certainty and clearness of this method, we believe it will gradually come into vogue.

GROUP II—ANSWERS

Tokyo Metropolis (Answers to Topic 4, Subtopic 1)

Pawnshops.

Usually there are about four kinds of trade books in use:

1. The *meisai-chô* (to which is affixed a revenue stamp) is used for making entry of the quantity of goods pledged, for instance, an entry that such-and-such goods were received from so-and-so and

---

[1] *Nuka.*

[2] *Kogome.*

[3] *Tawara.*

such-and-such a sum of money was loaned for them.

2. The *ukeoi-chô*. This is used for entering the time of redemption, the quality of the goods as entered in the *meisai-chô*, the principal and interest,[1] etc.

3. The *irekae-chô* is used for making entry of goods pledged as a substitute for goods which have already been pledged.

4. The *nagare-jichi-chô* is used for making entry of forfeited pledges[2] and the principal and interest, when the time of redemption has passed [over six months from pledging].

These books are preserved for five to ten years. As to the form of entry, the old one still prevails, the Western method having not yet been adopted.

Oil Wholesalers.

Books differ according to the circumstances of each wholesaler. However, the following five books are generally indispensable to all oil dealers, regardless of the special circumstances of each dealer:

1. the *tôza-chô*;
2. the *shiire-chô*;
3. the *uri-chô*;
4. the *kinsen-hantori-chô*;
5. the *nimotsu-hantori-chô*.

The names by which these books are called differ with the firm, but their usage is apparently generally the same. There is no fixed form of entry. There are none who want to take up the Western method of bookkeeping.

Dry Goods Wholesalers.[3]

There are about ten kinds of books in use.

1. The *shokoku-kaiire-chô* contains the so-called "immediate entry,"[4] i.e., entry of names[5] of kinds of goods bought in various provinces, their quantity and prices.

2. The *uri-chô*, also called *daifuku-chô*. This is used for making entry of sales of goods to customers.[6]

3. The *tôza-chô*. This is used for making temporary entry of

---

[1] *Ganri-kin.*

[2] *Nagare-jichi;* or often, *shichi-nagare.*

[3] *Gofuku-futomono-ya*, same as *gofuku-tanmono-ya.*

[4] *Jikigaki.*

[5] *Mei.*

[6] *Torihiki-saki.*

sales on credit in various provinces. The entries in the present book are posted up to the *uri-chô* every six months or every year. Hence it is also called *hikae-chô*, or memorandum book.

4. The *kingin-deiri-chô*.[1]

5. The *irifune-nimotsu-kisai-chô*, also called *kura-ire-chô* or *mizuage-chô*. Whenever goods arrive from various provinces and are put in a warehouse, traders make entry in the present book of the kinds of the goods, their quantity and by whose ship the goods were carried.

6. The *tana-oroshi-chô*. When the settlement of account of stock takes place in June and December, an inventory of stock is made in the present book.

7. The *somemono-chô*. In this are entered the quantity of goods that are sent to a dyer's[2] or a fuller's.[3]

8. The *somemono-uketori-chô*. In this are entered goods which, after having been dyed or fulled, are returned from the dyer's or the fuller's.

9. The *nimotsu-hantori-chô*.[4]

10. The *kingin-hantori-chô*.[5]

Besides the above, other books may sometimes be in use, depending upon the convenience of each firm, but they are not essentially different from the above-mentioned books.

These books are usually preserved for from three to ten years.

Generally, there is a definite form of entry for these books, but, except for the *hantori-chô*[6] there is no practice of having a seal impressed in a trade book.

Timber Wholesalers.

There are about twelve kinds of book in use.

1. The *okurijô-dome*.[7] This is used to copy the invoice from a consignor, giving the kind and the quantity of the lumber that has been shipped to the wholesalers.

---

[1] The cash book, in which are entered receipts and payments of money.

[2] *Kon-ya* or *kou-ya*, same as *somemono-ya*.

[3] *Arai-hari-ya*.

[4] See page 56, above.

[5] Same as *kinsen-hantori-chô*. See page 56, above.

[6] Chit-book, or delivery book.

[7] *Dome* or *tome* signifies a memorandum.

2. The *mizuage-chô*; also called *shiwake-chô* or *kenchi-chô*.[1] This is used for checking the invoice with the goods actually delivered and entering details regarding the square timbers, classifying them according to length, width, etc.

3. The *chûmon-chô*. This is used for copying entries from the *mizuage-chô*. It is taken to the sales yard[2] for making entry of timber sold.

4. The *uri-chô*. This is used for entering sales of planks,[3] as for instance, the sale of a certain quantity, in *soku*,[4] of planks, and the name of the vendee. The following memorandum slip[5] is then delivered to the vendee.

> Memo
> Cryptomeria board....................*soku*
> (or *hon* or *sai*)
> Date..........
> Mr. _____ (name of the vendee)

5. The *kake-chô*. This is used for entry of goods sold on credit and sent by ship or raft[6] to the vendee.

6. The *tôza-chô*. This is used for entry of temporary sales on credit, credit for one or two days, for instance.

7. The *dai-chô*; also called *sashihiki-chô* or *daifuku-chô*. This is used for entry of loans[7] of money and advances,[8] etc.

8. The *kingin-deiri-chô*.[9]

9. The *kingin-hantori-chô*.[9]

10. The *nimotsu-hantori-chô*.[9]

11. The *shikiri-chô*.[9]

12. The *kai-chô*. This is used by middlemen and retailers for entry of purchases from wholesalers.

---

[1] Pronunciation questionable.

[2] *Uriba*, the open place where timbers are arranged for sale; in ordinary cases, a sales room.

[3] *Ita*.

[4] *Soku*, a unit of measuring board which stands for three pieces of board, each of which is 2 *ken* (=12 feet) long by 3 *shaku* (about 35 inches) wide.

[5] *Hagaki*. In modern usage, *hagaki* means a postcard.

[6] *Ikada*.

[7] *Kashi-kin*.

[8] *Shikin*.

[9] These terms have already been explained.

There are also some other different sorts of books with different names in use by some merchants, but the above list will in most cases cover the books in use in the trade.

These books are generally preserved for one year, with the exception of the *daifuku-chô*, which is usually preserved for an indefinite period.

Grain Wholesalers.[1]

There are some five sorts of books in use in the trade, including 1) the *daifuku-chô*, 2) the *mizuage-chô*, 3) the *chûmon-chô*, 4) the *nimotsu-hantori-chô*, and 5) *kane-hantori-chô*. Apart from these, other books are in use, different in appellation and number, depending on the convenience of each individual trader. They cannot be uniformly classified.

There is no fixed period of preservation for these books. They used to be preserved for at least two or three years. But as few rice wholesalers sell on credit nowadays, they are often discarded after being preserved for a period ranging from two or three months to one year.

Fish Wholesalers.

There are seven sorts of books in use in the trade.

1. The *shitatsuke-chô* is used for entering sales to a particular vendee (middleman). Under each entry of a vendee are written the kinds and quantities of goods sold and the wholesaler's estimation (e.g. sea bream, *xx* [quantity], *xx sen* [value] per fish). Some vendees draw a bill of exchange immediately after they sum up the amount (e.g. they draw a bill of 80 *yen* if the estimation is 100 *yen*). Then after winding up the sales the next day, the wholesaler will record the balance as credit to the vendee. After entering the above items in the book, the wholesaler immediately delivers the goods to the vendee (middleman).

2. The *uri-nikki*. The entries in this book include the price, name and quantity of the goods sold, payments received and sales on credit.

3. The *mizuage-chô*; also called *kakinuki-chô*. This is used for posting up entries of the names and quantities of goods from the *shitatsuke-chô* as well as the prices at which the goods have actually been

---

[1] *Beikoku*, which may also mean "rice and other cereals," or simply "cereals."

disposed of. Statements of account[1] will be prepared on the basis of the entries in the present book.

4. The *shikiri-chô*. This is used for copying statements of account as prepared in the above manner, and then subtracting the commission[2] and advance[3] (out of the figures representing sales) to show the balance.

5. The *kake-chô*. Entries relating to sales on credit are transcribed from the *uri-nikki*.

6. The *kingin-hantori-chô*. This is used when loans (of money) are made to a consignor or retailer, or when a sealed envelope containing money[4] is sent to a consignor through the courtesy of some third person.

7. The *iri-chô*. This is used for entering the amount of money advanced in connection with laying goods in stock as well as the agreement regarding repayment.

This is called a ten percent loan.[5] It will be cleared at the time of *shikiri* (winding up).

There are five kinds of books in use among middlemen of this trade.

1. The *watari-chô*. This is used for making entry of the amount of goods delivered to middlemen by wholesalers.

2. The *tsuke-nikki*. This is used for making entry of the kind and amount of goods and the sum total of sales prices.

3. The *hantori-chô*. This is exclusively used when middlemen settle their account with wholesalers.

The above three books are indispensable to the middlemen of the trade. As to the remaining two books, the *kingin-deiri-cho* and the *kake-chô*, they are not very important and may or may not be kept, according to the convenience of the individual middleman.

The *shiire-chô*, the *hantori-chô* and such books are usually preserved for a period of ten years, while other books are discarded after one or one and a half years.

There is a settled form of entry for almost all these books.

Fuel Wholesalers.

---

[1] *Shikiri.*

[2] *Kôsen.*

[3] *Tome-gane* = *kashi-kin.*

[4] *Fûkin* ("sealed-money").

[5] *Ichiwari-dome; tome* = loan.

There are generally seven kinds of books in use in the trade.

1. The *mizuage-chô*; also called *okurijô-dome*. This is used for checking the goods delivered with the invoice, and for copying the same.

2. The *shikiri-chô*; also called *shiire-chô*. After the receipt of goods (from the consignor), prices are fixed and entered in the present book.

3. The *tôza-chô*. This is used for entry of daily sales, loans, and the like.

4. The *daifuku-chô*. This is used for copying the entries in the *tôza-chô*.

5. The *kashikin-chô*. In this are entered the advances made to the consignor.

6. The *kinsen-hantori-chô*.

7. The *nimotsu-hantori-chô*.

These books are usually preserved for five years.

There is no prescribed form of entry for these books, but there are standard forms which prevail.

Saké Wholesalers.

There are some six kinds of books in use in the trade.

1. The *tsuritsuke-chô*; also called *annai-chô*, or *yorozu-oboe-chô*. In this is entered advice from a consignor regarding shipment of the goods, the entry including the name of the ship, the date of shipment, the trademark of the goods and the quantity.

2. The *mizuage-chô*; also called *kura-ire-chô*, or *inifune-chô*. In this are entered arrival of goods, the entry including the name of the ship, the quantity of the goods, the trademark and the name of the consignor.

3. The *daifuku-chô*; also called *uriage-chô*, or *daiju-chô*. In this are entered sales, the entry including the name of the vendee, the quantity, the trade mark of the goods and the price. Such thing as whether the goods have been sold on credit or for cash are also noted.

4. The *kura-dashi-chô*. In this is entered delivery of goods, the entry including the name of the deliveree, the date, and the trademark and quantity of the goods. It is used merely for showing the amount of the goods left in stock.

5. The *ninushi-torihiki-chô*; also called *nimotsu-torishirabe-chô* or *daifuku-chô*. This is used for copying entries from the *uriage-chô*. The

statement of account to be sent to the consignor is prepared on the basis of this book.

6. The *moto-daifuku-chô*; also called *yorozu-oboe-chô*. In this are entered payments and receipts of money in connection with domestic matters.

Besides these books, there are others which may be kept according to the convenience of each individual trader.

There is no definite rule about the period of preservation of these books, but most of them are usually preserved for seven or eight years. There are some persons, however, who discard them after one or two years.

The books used by middlemen of the trade are almost the same as those used by wholesalers, but there is a difference in usage. As they regard wholesalers as their consignors, the middlemen and even the retailers prepare their books and leave them with the wholesalers, so that at every transaction the latter make entry in them of the name, quantity and price of the goods sold, for proof of their delivery.

Dried Bonito Wholesalers.

There are eight kinds of book in use in the trade.

1. The *mizuage-chô*. When a shipment arrives in port, the invoice is copied in the present book.

2. The *shikiri-chô*. This is used to make entry of the goods when they are sold, and to prepare a sales report[1] for the consignor of the goods sold, the entry including the name of the consignor (who has shipped the goods to the wholesalers), the trademark of the goods, quantity in *taru*[2] and sales price.

3. The *uri-chô*. This is used for entry of sales in cash and on credit.

4. The *daifuku-chô*. This is used for entry of sales on credit. These entries are culled from the entries in the *uri-chô* and are

---

[1] *Shikiru*. This may mean one of the following five things: (1) to make an invoice (a price list of goods shipped to a purchaser, consignee, or the like); (2) to fix the sales or purchase price (said of wholesalers or middlemen); (3) to make a sales or purchase report to be presented to a consignor or purchaser; (4) to balance an account; (5) to balance an account and send a statement of account. In case No. 3 referred to above, the purchase report is called *uri-jikiri* (lit., "sales report") and the sales report *kai-jikiri* (lit., "purchase report").

[2] Barrel.

transferred to the present book.

5. The *mannen-chô*. This is used for entry of arrears of sales on credit, entries which are culled from the entries in the *daifuku-chô*.

6. The *kingin-hantori-chô*.

7. The *nimotsu-hantori-chô*.

8. The *kingin-deiri-chô*.

Besides the above, there are some other kinds of books in use called by different names, but the above eight kinds of books are generally sufficient for most practical purposes.

These books are usually preserved for ten years.

Salt Wholesalers.

There are eight kinds of book in use in the trade:

(1) the *nimotsu-waritsuke-chô*,

(2) the *nimotsu-hantori-chô*,

(3) the *sedori-shiwake-chô*,

(4) the *tawara-barai-chô* [?],

(5) the *shikiri-chô*,

(6) the *uri-chô*,

(7) the *kinsen-hantori-chô* and

(8) the *mokuroku-chô*.

The first book above is used for entry of prices of goods upon their arrival in port, these prices being fixed at a middlemen's session,[1] as well as the amount of goods each of the middlemen agrees to handle.

The second is used for entry of the amount of goods which, as a result of a sales transaction between traders through the medium of commission agents,[2] have been unloaded from a ship and delivered or received.

The third is used for entry, under the names of the traders, of the details of the delivered goods, as well as the total amount of the above.

The fourth is used for entry of the total amount of goods which, as a result of sales transactions, have all been unloaded from a ship and delivered to middlemen.

The fifth is used for making a sales report to the consignor.

---

[1] *Tachiai.*

[2] *Sedori.* This may signify either the middlemen or traders who work for a commission, or their business.

The sixth book is divided into parts marked with index slips attached[1] to the margins of the leaves. Each part, conveniently allotted to the account[2] of each individual middleman, is used for entry of the amount of the goods which have been delivered.

The seventh is used for entry of payments and receipts of money.

The eighth is used for balancing the accounts with each consignor on the basis of consignments and sales.

These books are usually preserved for a period of ten years.

Kanda Ward.

There are generally nine kinds of trade books in use here: the *shiire-chô*; the *uriage-chô*; the *urikake-chô*; the *kinsen-hantori-chô*; the *shukka-hantori-chô*;[3] the *nimotsu-mizuage-chô*;[4] the *nakama-seri-chô*;[5] the *tôza-chô* and the *kinsen-deiri-chô*.

However, the names by which these books are called are not the same with all traders, and there is no fixed rule as to how long they should be preserved.

Kôjimachi Ward. (Answer to Topic 4, Subtopic 1)

The books in general use are the *kingin-deiri-chô*, the *hantori-chô*,[6] the *shiire-chô*, the *uriage-chô*, the *kayoi-chô*[7] and the *buppin-hantori-chô*.

The last two books are usually preserved for one year, but there is no fixed rule regarding the others.

Nihombashi Ward.

As to the variety and the names of trade books, each individual commercial house has its own custom, books often being called by lucky names. However, there are probably no more than the following eleven kinds of books which can be considered indispensable to a firm whether it is large or small.

These are: the *tôza-chô*, the *yorozu-oboe-chô*, the *daifuku-chô*, the *shiire-chô*, the *shikiri-chô*, the *hantori-chô*, the *seri-chô*,[8] the *unsô-chô*,[9] the *mizuage-chô*, the *chûmon-chô* and the *kingin-deiri-chô*.

---

[1] *Kuchitori.*

[2] *Shikiri-kanjô.*

[3] A *hantori-chô* for shipments.

[4] Same as *mizuage-chô.*

[5] Used for recording sales for commission among traders of the same trade.

[6] Here this means *kinsen-hantori-chô.*

[7] A chit book.

[8] See page 57.

[9] Shipment book.

The *tôza-chô* and the *yorozu-oboe-chô*, both being a sort of commercial journal, are used for daily entry of all sorts of commercial matters.

The *daifuku-chô* is generally used for classified entries[1] of sales on credit, the classification being according to customer.

The *deiri-chô* serves a purpose similar to that of the account book of present-day bookkeeping.

It is understood that no definite rule prevails regarding the period of their preservation, but all large firms make it a rule to preserve these books [for an indefinite period].

Kyôbashi Ward.

There are seven kinds of books in use here.

The *daifuku-chô*. This is used for entries, classified by customer, of sales on credit, which are transcribed to the present book from the *tôza-chô*. These sales on credit are commonly called *chôai-uri*.[2]

The *tôza-chô*. This is used for general entry of all sales, be they in cash or on credit. Sales on credit will be posted up to the *daifuku-chô*.

The *shiire-chô*. This is used for entry of purchases of goods from *kunigata* and *jikata*. Here *jikata*[3] refers to Tokyo and *kunigata* to the provinces.

The *kingin-deiri-chô*. This is used for entry of daily receipts and payments of money for purposes of balancing the account.

The *kingin-watashi-hantori-chô*.[4] This is used by a payor for securing the impress of the seal of the payee as proof of receipt of payment for purchases.

The *nimotsu-watashi-hantori-chô*.[5] This is used for securing the impress of the seal of the deliveree as proof of receipt of goods.

The *uriage-chô*. This is used for entry of daily sales, retail or wholesale.

These books are preserved for a period ranging from five to fifteen years.

Yotsuya Ward and Ushigome Ward.

---

[1] *Kuchitori;* lit., "an index slip attached to the margin of a leaf."

[2] Sales on the books.

[3] *Jikata* more often means "the provinces." In modern usage, it usually means "the provinces" and is pronounced "*chihô.*"

[4] Same as *kingin-hantori-chô* or *kinsen-hantori-chô*.

[5] Same as *nimotsu-hantori-chô*.

The trade books in use here are different depending upon the trade, but the following books are generally in use: the *tôza-chô*, the *shiire-chô*, the *hantori-chô* and the *kake-chô*.[1]

Asakusa Ward.

The following books are generally used in commerce.

The *daifuku-chô*. Used for entry of sales classified according to customer.

The *tôza-chô*. Used for entry of all daily sales.

The *kingin-deiri-chô*. Used for entry of daily receipts and payments of money.

The *mizuage-chô*. Used for entry of daily arrivals of shipments.

The *shikiri-chô*. Used for re-entry, classified by consignor, of all consignments transcribable from the *mizuage-chô*. Also used for entry of purchase prices[2] of consignments, reports of which are to be presented to the consignor.

The *kaiire-chô*; also called *shiire-chô*. This is a book of the same sort as the *shikiri-chô*. Wholesalers generally call it *shikiri-chô*, while retailers call it *kaiire-chô* or *shiire-chô*.

The *kingin-hantori-chô*. This is kept for proof of payment or receipt of money.

The *nimotsu-hantori-chô*. This is kept for proof of receipt or delivery of goods.

The following books are used by pawnbrokers.

The *meisai-chô*; also commonly called *daichô*. In this are entered the name of the pawner, details regarding the pawned goods and the pawn number. The pawner is required to impress his seal in it.

The *dejichi-chô*; also called *riagari-dome*. In this are entered each pawned item that has been redeemed and the amount of the loan and interest.

The *shichimotsu-kanjô-chô*. In this are entered daily pledgings and redemptions of pawns and the account of receipt and payment of money. It is a pawnbroker's journal, the entries of which are posted up to each special book.

The *nagare-jichi*[3]*-chô*. In this are entered forfeited pawns, the pawn

[1] A book for entry of sales on credit; same as *kake-uri-chô*.
[2] *Shikiri-daikin*.
[3] Forfeited pawn.

numbers and name of the pawner. These items are transcribed to the present book from the *meisai-chô*.

The *nagare-jichi-uriharai-chô*. In this are entered, when forfeited pawned goods are sold, the date of sale, the name of the goods, the sales price, the name and address of the vendee, etc.

The *gofukoku-funshitsu-todoke*.[1] In this are entered official notices[2] of lost articles.[3]

The *inkan-bo*. This is a book in which pawners are required to leave the impression of their seals (for future identification).

The *shichimotsu-torihiki-chô*. The pawner is supplied with this book, and whenever he goes to a pawnshop, he takes it with him and has entered in it the amount of his loan and the article pledged. He makes use of the entry as proof when he redeems the pawn.

The above are the more important trade books in use here, and they are usually preserved for ten years. There are other minor books in use, too, but they are all discarded after a year of use.

Honjo Ward.

There are many kinds of trade book in use here, such as those called *daifuku-chô, tsukekomi-chô*,[4] *shikiri-chô, kingin-deiri-chô, tôza-chô, urikomi-chô* and *hantori-chô*.

These books are kept or not according to the convenience of the trader. Similarly, there is no fixed rule about the period of preservation.

Ebara *kôri*.

The following trade books are in use here:

The *shiire-chô*, used for entry of purchases of goods, and preserved for ten years.

The *kingin-deiri-chô*, used for entry of payments and receipts of money in connection with business as well as household matters,[5] and preserved for an indefinite period.

The *daifuku-chô*, used for entry of all sales on credit, and preserved for three years.

---

[1] *Gofukoku* = government proclamation, *funshitsu* = lost (articles), *todoke* = notice.

[2] *Fure*.

[3] *Funshitsu-hin*.

[4] A book in which various sorts of things are entered, as they occur, regardless of their nature.

[5] *Keizai-yô*, i.e., "for economic purposes," but here, presumably for household economy.

The *nikki-chô*, used for entry of payments and receipts of money in connection with sales, and preserved for three years.

The *mizuage-chô*, used for examination of a shipment received, and preserved for three years.

The *kingin-hantori-chô*, preserved for ten years.

The *nimotsu-hantori-chô*, preserved for ten years.

Higashi-tama *kôri* and Minami-toshima *kôri*.

The books used in commerce are roughly as follows:

The *kingin-hantori-chô* (subject to stamp duty).[1] In this are entered, for future proof, payments and receipts of money regarding stocks.

The *nimotsu-hantori-chô* (subject to stamp duty). This is used for entry of a shipment, and includes such things as the amount and the name of the goods. The customers (i.e., the consignees) are asked to impress their seals (upon receipt of the shipment). The book is used as the basis from which to prepare a statement of account. Prices are usually recorded on a separate sheet of paper or in a chit-book. However, the present book is not necessary to a retail trader.

The *kingin-deiri-chô*. This is used for entry of the amount of money received and paid in connection with sales and purchases for the purpose of adjustment of the variation of the balance.[2]

The *shiire-chô*. This is used for entry of purchases, i.e., the quantity and the name of the goods bought and the freightage. The book will be referred to for preparing a statement of account, although for entry of payments and receipts of money the *kingin-hantori-chô* is used.

The *daifuku-chô*. In this are entered, as a reminder for each individual trader, the goods sold, the sales prices and the vendee.

The *urikomi-chô*. This book is divided into parts, each part being allotted to one customer, and the orders of each customer being entered in the respective part. The goods are then forwarded to the customer, along with the invoice. Upon delivery of the order, the recipient is presented with the *nimotsu-hantori-chô* and asked to

---

[1] *Yûzei.* This refers here to the practice of requiring a bond or a trade book to bear a revenue stamp of a certain value, by way of paying duty incident to the bond or trade book.

[2] *Koshi-kin;* this literally means a balance carried forward to the next account.

impress his firm seal in it (in proof of receipt). This book is called *chûmon-chô* by some and, like the preceding book, is used by wholesalers.

The *kayoi-chô*. Subject to stamp duty. Used by commission agents, wholesalers, etc. when they ship goods to the customer, to enter the name of the goods, their quantity and price. This book is not used by every wholesaler.

The *shichimotsu-daichô*. Subject to stamp duty. This book is used by pawnbrokers, who enter in it the articles pawned, the amount of the loan, the date, the name of the pawner, etc. This book, large in size and containing many leaves, is indispensable to a pawnbroker.

The *nagarejichi-uriwatashi-chô*. When a forfeited pawn is sold, the pawnbroker enters in this the sale price, the name of the article, the name of the vendee, the date, etc.

The *dashijichi-chô*. When a pawn is redeemed by a pawner, the pawnbroker enters in this the amount of the loan repaid, the name of the article, the name of the pawner and the date (of redemption). The broker may thus strike out the entries regarding the pawn in the *shichimotsu-daichô*.

The *meisai-chô*. This is used by "dealers in the eight goods"[1] ("thirty-six goods" now), who enter in it their names and addresses, the names and prices of the goods sold by them, etc. Now, by regulation of the Metropolitan Police,[2] every merchant is required to provide this book for himself and get it inspected and sealed[3] by the head[4] of the association of the "dealers in the eight goods."

These are the books used by every merchant of our *kôri*, and they are usually kept for two or three years, sometimes even longer. Some books may be renewed every year.

There is no fixed rule as to the period of their preservation, but the *kingin-hantori-chô*, the *nimotsu-hantori-chô*, the *daifuku-chô*, the *shiire-chô*, the *shichimotsu-daichô*, etc., are usually preserved for about thirty years, sometimes being handed down to posterity. Other books will only be discarded after they have been preserved for some ten years.

[1] See below, under Akasaka-ku.
[2] *Keishichô*.
[3] *Ken-in*.
[4] *Tôdori*.

Kita-toshima *kôri.*

No rule prevails, even in the same trade, about the variety and appellations of the books used by traders. There is also no fixed rule about the period of preservation, but usually these books are preserved for reference's sake for about two years. However, the time of discarding them differs according to the nature of the trade. Pawnbrokers usually observe the practice of preserving their books for six years.

The Western method of bookkeeping is in use only at two or three firms here. Not only are there no other firms adopting this method, but there are very few people who know anything about it.

Minami-adachi *kôri.*

There are differences in the kind of trade books in use here, depending upon the nature of the trade. Those books which are in use among two or three kinds of traders here are as follows:

Books used by pawnshops:

1. The *shichimotsu-meisai-chô.* In this are entered articles pawned, the sum of money loaned, name and address of the pawner, name and the address of his surety, etc. This is the pawnbroker's journal. The items in this book should be added or deleted according to the change of transaction.

2. The *uke-jichi-chô.* In this are entered redeemed pawns.

3. The *nagare-jichi-chô.* The journal is gone through to ascertain the pawns forfeited with a view to selling them. The pawns thus disposed of are entered in the present book, the entry including the address and name of the vendee, the price, the name of the article, etc.

4. The *kingin-deiri-chô.* In this are entered important payments and receipts of money.

5. The *kanjô-chô.* Every time money is paid or received, it is entered in the present book, regardless of the sum.

Books used by rice merchants, paper merchants, wine merchants, dry goods, and lumber merchants:

There is some difference in the appellation of the books used by these traders, but none in their use. They are classified as follows:

1. The *tôza-chô*; the *niwa-chô*;[1] and the *mizuage-chô.* These books

---

[1] Formerly, a book called by this name was used for entry of the *nengu,* land tax or ground rent paid, rice usually being used for the payment.

are used for entry of transactions as soon as they are concluded, the entries forming the material for re-entry in other books.

2. The *shiire-chô*. This is used for detailed entry of the goods purchased, their quantity and the prices and the names of the people from whom they have been bought.

3. The *uriwatashi-chô* and the *daifuku-chô*. These books are used for entry, according to customer, of sales on credit and payments made on them, each customer being allotted his portion in the books.

4. The *kingin-deiri-chô*. This is used for entry, in the evening, of that day's payments and receipts of money, entries which are respectively totalled and balanced. Thus, sales in cash, which as a rule are not entered in the above-mentioned *uriwatashi-chô*, will be reflected in the results in this book.

5. The *nimotsu-hantori-chô*. When a shipment of goods is made, this book is used for securing the impression of the seal of the deliveree in proof of receipt of the goods.

6. The *kinsen-hantori-chô*. When payment of money is made between merchants of the same trade, the payee is required to impress his seal in the present book in proof of receipt. However, when goods are purchased by a trader from a farmer, neither their delivery nor receipt is customarily accompanied by any voucher. The use of the present book is limited to transactions between merchants of the same trade.

Shitaya Ward.

The variety and number of books that are used in commerce differ according to the trade, but there are five which are indispensable to ordinary commercial activities, the *tôza-chô*, the *shiire-chô*, the *daifuku-chô*, the *kinsen-deiri-chô* and the *hantori-chô*.

However, to those engaged in wholesale business, the following ten books are usually indispensable: the *okurijô-dome*, the *mizuage-chô*, the *shikiri-chô*, the *sainyû-chô*, the *tôza-chô*, the *daifuku-chô*, the *shiire-chô*, the *kinsen-hantori-chô* and the *nimotsu-hantori-chô*.

The names by which these books are called are not the same with all commercial firms, but the uses of the books and the methods of entry in them are practically the same with all traders.

There is no fixed rule regarding the period of preservation of these books. In former times there were some leading wholesalers who sometimes preserved these books as long as a hundred years.

But the Meiji Restoration brought about a change in this practice, and there are now few traders who preserve their books any longer than two or three years. This is said to be the general rule at present.

Akasaka Ward and Azabu Ward.

The kinds and names of trade books in use here are as follows:

1. The *shiire-chô*. In this are entered goods laid in and their purchase prices.

2. The *daifuku-chô*. This name is written by some merchants on the cover of every one of their trade books, in addition to a subtitle indicating the use of each respective book. A ledger with entry of one's property is sometimes called by this name.

3. The *tôza-chô*. In this are entered daily sales on credit.

4. The *seri-chô*. This book is used for commercial cull loans.

5. *The mizuage-chô*. This is used for entry of all arrivals of goods, shipped on land or by sea, from various places.

6. The *kingin-hantori-chô* and the *nimotsu-hantori-chô*. These two books are used as substitutes for receipts.

7. The *kingin-deiri-chô*, the *chûmon-chô* and the *kayoichô*. These three books are used as each of the names indicates.

Some of the above books are called by some traders *kura-nimotsu-deiri-chô*,[1] *urikake-chô*, *meisai-chô*, or any other name they like.

Regarding the period of the preservation of these books, before the Meiji Restoration, pawnbrokers, sellers of second-hand clothes,[2] buyers of second-hand clothes,[3] dealers in second-hand furniture,[4] dealers in sword fittings,[5] buyers of old copper goods or junk,[6] dealers in (foreign) fancy goods[7] and dealers in old copper goods,[8] those referred to as merchants of the eight trades, were to preserve

---

[1] *Kura-nimotsu* means goods in warehouse. Hence it is a book in which are entered the arrivals and departures of goods.

[2] *Furugi-ya*. This more commonly means a dealer in old clothes, but here the word is apparently used in a special sense, distinct from the *furugi-kai* that follows.

[3] *Furugi-kai*.

[4] *Furu-dôgu-ya*.

[5] *Kodôgu-ya*. It also means a dealer in second-hand furniture.

[6] *Furu-dô-kai*.

[7] *Tôbutsuya*, also pronounced *karamono-ya*. This originally referred to dealers in foreign fancy goods, but later came to also mean any dealer in fancy goods or dry goods, whether imported or not.

[8] *Furu-dô-ya*.

their books for an indefinite period. If these books happened to be lost in consequence of some natural calamity or eaten by worms, their owners had to report this in writing to the town magistrate,[1] after getting, by way of endorsement, the signature and seal of the headman of the district,[2] along with their own. Since the Restoration, however, there is no fixed rule about this matter.

Hongô Ward.

The trade books in use here are generally made of *mino-gami* paper or *torinouchi* [?] paper in quarto or side-folding [?].

Although they are often called by different names and their uses are not always the same, the books generally used include the *chûmon-chô*, the *suitô-chô*,[3] the *kinsen-hantori-chô*, the *nimotsu-hantori-chô*, the *urihin-daichô* and the *shiire-chô*.

CHIBA PREFECTURE

Awa *kôri*, Hei *kôri*, Asai *kôri* and Nagasa *kôri*.

The kinds, uses and periods of preservation of trade books that are in use here are generally as follows:

1. The *kinsen-deiri-chô*. In this are entered, at every payment or receipt of money, the sum paid or received, the name of the payee or payor, and other remarks in detail. Then the sums paid and received are balanced, and the balance is checked with the actual cash in hand. If the cash does not agree with the balance, this means that there must be some omission in entry or some mistake in handling cash in connection with payment or receipt. Consequently the whole process will be examined over and over again until the actual cash and the balance in the book are in agreement. Therefore, if in future doubt arises about some payment or receipt of money, the traders will be able to solve the doubt by referring to the present book.

Thus this is an indispensable book to a trader, and is said to be usually preserved indefinitely for as long as a firm remains in existence.

2. The *shiire-chô*. This book is divided into parts, and the parts are allotted to the different wholesalers with whom a trader has regular business dealings. Whenever a shipment is made to him

---

[1] *Machi-bugyô.*

[2] *Nanushi.*

[3] *Cashbook.*

[4] *Sales ledger.*

by a wholesaler, the trader makes entry, in the section allotted to the wholesaler, of the name of the goods shipped and the wholesale prices.

A sundries section[1] is also reserved in the book for the entry of purchases from those wholesalers with whom he has not enough business dealings to allot a separate section.

Thus the book is used for making clear the purchases from a wholesaler and the purchase prices.

Though there may be differences in practice according to the firm, this book is usually preserved for five years before it is discarded.

3. The *tôza-chô*. In this are entered sales of goods on credit,[2] from which a selection is later made for posting up to the *daifuku-chô*, also called *daichô*, to show payments in arrears. However, if payments are made for such sales on credit before the entries are transferred from the *tôza-chô* to the *daifuku-chô*, then a stamp with the letters "相済" meaning "paid," is affixed on the entries in the *tôza-chô*, and instead of posting up the *tôza-chô* entry to the *daifuku-chô*, the payments are simply entered in the *kinsen-deiri-chô*. Although this is called *tôza-chô*, or temporary book, because it supplies materials for entry to the *daifuku-chô*, it may be referred to when a perplexing situation about some old transaction presents itself in future, and help to clarify the situation.

Regarding the period of preservation, the *tôza-chô* is said to be generally preserved for an indefinite period, like the *kinsen-deiri-chô*.

In some firms, however, the *tôza-chô* is used for entry of anything and everything done in a shop, including sales of goods on credit and loans of money. Thus, in this case, the present book is treated as a journal, whose entries will be posted up to the *daifuku-chô* or to the *kinsen-deiri-chô*; this is a different use of the book.

4. The *mizuage-chô*. In this are entered all goods unloaded from a ship, enabling the trader to verify, at will, the date of some shipment, the name and amount of the goods, the name of the wholesaler who made the shipment and the name of the ship which

---

[1] *Zatsu-no-bu.*
[2] *Toki-gashi;* lit., "temporary loan" or "loan for a short period."

discharged the goods.[1] Traders may also find it useful for payment of freight charges.

If the trader is a land merchant,[2] he makes entry in the book in accordance with the invoice. If he is a fishmonger,[3] he makes entry in it in accordance with the *hama-nikki*.[4]

There is no fixed rule about the period of preservation of the book, but it is the usual practice here to discard it once the settlement of account is made.

5. The *okuridome-chô*. In this are entered goods to be shipped to customers in distant places such as Tokyo. A tally impression is put on the entry and the invoice to be issued with the shipment. The entry includes the date of the shipment, the name and the quantity of the goods and the name of the ship. Thus the book has a function just opposite to that of the *mizuage-chô*.

In some firms, however, the *okuridome-chô* is used for making entry of the prices at which the goods have been invoiced, the market prices and the settlement of the invoice.

Regarding the period of the preservation of the book, a practice similar to that for the *mizuage-chô* prevails.

6. The *kane-hantori-chô*. This book is used for securing the impression of the seal of the payee, by way of confirmation of receipt. Thus it is most often used on occasions when collectors from wholesalers of Tokyo or elsewhere are paid.

The book is preserved for an indefinite period.

7. The *nimotsu-hantori-chô*. This is used for securing the impression of the seal of the deliveree of goods, when delivery is made. The book is usually preserved until the prices of the goods are paid, hence usually for not more than two years.

8. The *daifuku-chô*; also called *daichô*. This book is divided into parts, one for each customer. In each part are entered the sales on credit which are granted to the customer, treated as assets. A bill[5] called *kakidashi*, demanding payment of a customer, will be pre-

---

[1] *Ryôchi* (領置). This is now more often used as a technical word, meaning a legal disposition by the government of some property belonging to a suspect, an accused or a prisoner.

[2] *Oka-shô*, probably used here in contrast to the fishmonger dealing in sea products.

[3] *Gyo-shô*.

[4] Shore journal. See below.

[5] *Kanjô-gaki*.

pared annually on the basis of the entries in the present book.

The book is said to be preserved for an indefinite period.

9. The *uriage-chô*. In this are entered daily sales. The book is also necessary for examination of sales in connection with taxes.

The length of period of preserving the book varies according to the trader, but it is usually said to be discarded after two or three years of use.

10. The *hama-nikki*.[1] This book is exclusively used by fish mongers[2] and never by dealers in land products.[3] When a fishing boat enters port from an expedition for which some money has been advanced[4] by a fish-monger, the latter takes the book with him and goes to the boat to make entry of the varieties and the amount of the fish caught. Entry in the *mizuage-chô* of the amount of fish received by the trader will then be made on the basis of the entry in the present book. This book thus has the nature of a temporary note. However, the book is indispensable to a trader, because in the confusion that attends the fishing ship's arrival and the landing of its catch[5] he cannot make entries in the book in the ordinary careful manner, and is apt to make unintended errors.

Once the entries in the present book are posted up to the *mizuage-chô*, the *hama-nikki* would appear to be useless, but it is said to be usually preserved for two years for prevention of possible mistakes in future.

11. The *hama-shiire*[6]*-chô*; also called such-and-such *shiire-kashi-tsuke*[7]*-chô*. In this are entered advance loans and the terms of repayment for certain goods. Let us say, for example, that some advances are made to the owners of a fishing boat equipped with an eight-armed scoop-net,[8] and in return a promise to repay with their haul is secured. Or let us say that some advances are made to a charcoalmaker[9] in return for his promise to repay the debt with his

---

[1] Shore journal.
[2] *Gyô-shô.*
[3] *Riku-shô;* land merchant.
[4] *Shiire-kin;* fund or money for laying in stock.
[5] *Seigyô;* live or fresh fish.
[6] *Hama* means shore and *shiire*, laying in stock.
[7] Loan of a fund for laying in stock.
[8] *Yatsude-ami.*
[9] *Sumi-yaki.*

products. These are the kinds of things entered in the *hama-shiire-chô*.

12. The *chûmon-chô*. Whenever an order for goods is received, it is entered in this book in order to expedite the shipment of the order. However, the use of the book is limited, it is said, to those traders who carry on an extensive trade, most traders being content with the *okuridome-chô*.

Katori *kôri*.

There are about ten kinds of book in use here: the *uriage-chô*, the *tôzakashi-chô*, the *hantori-chô*, the *shiire-chô*, the *shikiri-chô*, the *daifuku-chô*, the *kingin-deiri-chô*, the *shinagashi-chô*,[1] the *chûmon-chô* and the *shichimotsu-meisai-chô*. Their uses are not the same, but each book is used in the way its name indicates. These books are generally preserved for one year.

Yamabe *kôri* and Muza *kôri*.

Those kinds of book that are in use here are given below, along with their uses. There is no definite rule about the period of their preservation.

1. The *shiire-chô*. This is used, in every trade, for entry of the goods bought to be laid in and their prices.

2. The *uriage-chô*. This is used, also in every trade, for entry of daily sales.

3. The *tôza-chô*. This is used, also in every trade, for entry of temporary sales on credit.[2]

4. The *daifuku-chô*. This is used, also in every trade, for entries, classified according to customer, of sales on credit.

5. The *kinsen-deiri-chô*. This is used, also in every trade, for entry of all payments and receipts of money.

6. The *kinsen-hantori-chô*. This is used, also in every trade, as proof of payment of money for laying in stock, etc.

7. The *shikiri-chô*. This is used for entry of the prices of goods fixed by the wholesalers to whom the goods have been consigned.

8. The *nimotsu-hantori-chô*. This is used as proof of receipt by a deliveree of goods delivered.

9. The *kayoi-chô*. This is left in the hands of a customer at ordinary times, and used for entry of sales on credit, etc.

10. The *shichi-daichô*. This is used (by a pawnbroker) for entry

---

[1] A book in which a loan of goods is entered.

[2] *Tôza-gashi;* temporary loan.

of goods pledged and the amounts of the loans.

11. The *suigyo-chô*. This is used by those engaged in fishing with a seine,[1] traders associated with[2] the fishermen, brokers, etc., for entry of sales and purchases of fresh (live) fish.[3]

12. The *sonryô-gashi-chô*. This is used for entry of articles lent on hire,[4] the charges for hire,[5] etc.

Unakami *kôri* and Sôsa *kôri*.

Each firm is engaged in its own special trade, and makes use of different books. Thus it is impossible to enumerate all the different books, but those most commonly in use are the following five:

1. The *daifuku-chô*. This is used for entry of temporary sales on credit.

2. The *hantori-chô*. This is used for entry of receipt by a vendor of a payment.

3. The *kinsen-deiri-chô*. This is used for payment and receipt of money.

4. The *yorozu-uri-chô*. This is used for entry of goods sold and the sales prices.[6]

5. The *yorozu-kai-chô*. This is used for entry of goods bought[7] and the purchase prices.

Some books are preserved for an indefinite period and others are not, there being no definite rule about this. But these trade books are preserved for a period varying from ten years at the shortest to fifty years at the longest.

Higashi-katsushika *kôri*.

There are five trade books in common use here, and their names and uses are given below.

1. The *kinsen-hantori-chô*. This is used in commerce to serve as receipt for payment of money.

2. The *uridaka-chô*. In this are entered daily sales. The book is sometimes called *uriage-chô*.

3. The *shiire-chô*. In this are entered purchases of a trader. It

---

[1] *Jibiki-ami.*

[2] *Fuzoku-(shônin).*

[3] *Seigyo;* live fish; also pronounced by some "*nama-uo.*"

[4] *Sonryô-gashi-buppin.*

[5] *Kashi-ryô.*

[6] *Shika;* market price.

[7] *Yunyû-shôhin;* imported goods.

is called *shikiri-chô* or *kaiire-chô* in some trades.

4.   The *tôza-chô*. In this are entered the prices of goods sold on temporary credit.

5.   The *kinsen-deiri-chô*. In this are entered daily payments and receipts of money.

There is no fixed rule about the period of preservation of these books, but it is usually from one to three years, depending on the trade.

IBARAGI PREFECTURE

Nishi-katsushika *kôri* and Sashima *kôri*.

The kinds of book that are used in commerce are as follows:

1.   The *kinsen-deiri-chô*, used for entry of payment and receipt of money.

2.   The *shiire-chô*, used for entry of goods laid in.

3.   The *shikiri-chô*, used for entry of goods shipped from others and of purchase prices, these being decided by the consignee.

4.   The *hantori-chô*, used for securing the impression of the seal of the party to whom some goods have been delivered.

5.   The *uriage-chô*, used for entry of sales.

6.   The *dai-chô*, used exclusively by pawnbrokers.

7.   The *daifuku-chô*, used for entry of sundry domestic expenses.

These books are usually discarded after ten years, with the exception of the (*shichi-*)*dai-chô*, which is preserved for a long time.

KANAGAWA PREFECTURE

Miura *kôri*.

The ordinary books in use here are:

1.   The *daifuku-chô*, used for entry of sales on credit.

2.   The *tôza-chô*, used for daily entry of all sales and purchases.

3.   The *kinsen-deiri-chô*, used for daily entry of payments and receipts of money.

4.   The *kaiire-chô*, used for entry of purchases.

5.   The *uriage-chô*, used for detailed entry of goods sold and their sales prices.

6.   The *kinsen-hantori-chô*, used for entry of payments of money.

7.   The *nimotsu-hantori-chô*, used for entry of goods delivered.

8.   The *heikin-chô*, in which balances are made of the purchase and sales prices of goods, for the computation of profits.

These books are used for just one year, and are preserved for about ten years.

Tachibana *kôri*.

There are many kinds of book in use here, some of which are called: *uriage-chô, tôza-gashi-chô, daifuku-chô, shiire-chô, kingin-hantori-chô*, and *nimotsu-hikitori-chô*.[1]

There is a difference in the length of the period of their preservation ranging from one to ten years.

Kita-tama *kôri*.

Each firm has a different practice with respect to the books it uses, so that it will be impossible to enumerate the varieties and names of all the books used. Those books that are indispensable to a firm, however, are:

1. the *buppin*[2]-*shiire-chô*;
2. the *buppin-uriage-chô*;
3. the *kingin-hantori-chô*;
4. the *nimotsu-hantori-chô*; and
5. the *kingin-deiri-chô*.

Each firm has a different practice regarding the uses of these books and the period of preservation, and it is impossible to specify these practices for every case.

Ashigara-shimo *kôri*.

The books most commonly in use are: 1. the *tôza-chô*; 2. the *daifuku-chô*; 3. the *kinsen-suitô-chô*; 4. the *kinsen-hantori-chô*, etc. Also different books are used in different trades and are named according to the convenience of the trade, examples being the pawnbroker's *shichimotsu-chô* or the rice-dealer's *beikoku-chô*.[3]

Of these books, the *daifuku-chô* is the most important and is preserved until it is regarded as being of no more use. The actual length of the period of its preservation, however, varies depending on the trader.

Prefectural Industry Bureau.[4]

There are eight trade books in general use here, and their names and uses are as follows:

1. The *kingin-deiri-chô*. In this are entered payments and receipts of money, as they occur, in connection with daily sales and purchases, so that in the evening an accurate examination and a bal-

---

[1] A book used for entry of goods taken delivery of.
[2] *Buppin*, an article or goods. Hence the *buppin-shiire-chô* is the same as the *shiire-chô*.
[3] *Beikoku* may mean (1) rice, (2) corn or grain in general, or (3) rice and other cereals.
[4] *Kangyô-ka. Kangyô* means encouragement of industry.

ance of the day's account may be made.

2.   The *nimotsu-deiri-chô*. In this are entered the names and quantity of goods received and delivered at various places, and the names of the deliverer and the deliveree.

3.   The *shiire-chô*. This is used for entry of stock laid in, that is, goods bought. The entry includes the grade, the quantity, and the purchase price of the goods, the date of the transaction, the name of the party from whom the purchase has been made, his firm name[1] and address.

This book is the most important of all, as it forms the basis upon which a firm's profit and loss is computed.

4.   The *uriage-chô*. This is used for entry of goods sold. The entry includes the grade, quantity and sales price of the goods, the date of the transaction, the name of the party to whom the sale has been made and his firm name and address. Like the *shiire-chô*, it is a very important book.

5.   The *sashihiki-daichô*. This is used for classified entry, according to consignor, of loans and repayments, shipments, etc.

6.   The *hantori-chô*. This is used for securing, as proof of receipt, the impression of the seal of the party to whom payment of money or delivery of goods has been made.

7.   The *yakujô-chô*. This is used for entry of orders of a consignor or a buyer, the entry having no reference to payment or receipt of money.

8.   The *shokan-ôfuku-chô*. This is used for making a résumé of correspondence exchanged, and is very useful.

There are innumerable books used by traders besides the above, but they will not be enumerated here as the above-mentioned eight books cover the field, and the rest are merely supplementary books.

The practice is to preserve the books for an indefinite period.

TOCHIGI PREFECTURE

Prefectural Office.

The trade books in use here are: 1) the *daifuku-chô*; 2) the *tôza-chô*; 3) the *kinsen-deiri-chô*; 4) the *shiire-chô*; 5) the *uriage-chô*; 6) the *nimotsu-hantori-chô*; 7) the *kinsen-hantori-chô*; 8) the *shikiri-chô*; 9) the *kayoi-chô*; 10) the *niuke-chô*; and 11) the *kawase-chô*.

As to their uses, the *daifuku-chô* is a ledger, and the others are

[1] *Shôin.*

used in the way their names indicate.

These books are used for one year, and are preserved for about ten years.

Shimo-tsuga *kôri* and Samukawa *kôri*.

There are many trade books in use here, but they may be reduced to the following four kinds of books: the *uri-chô*, the *kai-chô*, the *deiri-chô*[1] and the *hantori-chô*.

There is no fixed rule, but they are usually preserved for an indefinite period.

Ashikaga *kôri* and Yanada *kôri*.

The following fourteen kinds of books are in use here: 1) the *niuke-chô*; 2) the *nizukuri-chô*;[2] 3) the *hantori-chô*; 4) the *uri-chô*; 5) the *kawase-chô*; 6) the *kayoi-chô*; 7) the *chûmon-chô*; 8) the *kinsen-deiri-chô*; 9) the *kuchitori-chô*;[3] 10) the *daifuku-chô*; 11) the *shiire-chô*; 12) the *nyûhi-chô*;[4] 13) the *rieki-keisan-chô*;[5] and 14) the *tana-oroshi-chô*.[6]

MIE PREFECTURE

Suzuka *kôri*.

The trade books in use here are generally as follows:

1. The *shiire-chô*. This is used for entry of the goods purchased for laying in stock, the date of purchase, the quantity, the purchase price and the name of the party from whom the purchase has been made.

2. The *tôza-chô*. When sales on credit are made, the date of the sale, the sales prices and the quantity of the goods are entered in the book according to customer. The entry will later be posted up to the *daifuku-chô*. After their transfer to the *daifuku-chô*, entries in the *tôza-chô* will be struck out.

3. The *kinsen-deiri-chô*. This is used for entry of sales for cash and all other receipts and payments of money.

4. The *uriage-shûnyû-chô*. This is used for combined re-entry of the entries in the *tôza-chô* as well as the entries of cash sales in the

---

[1] Same as the *kinsen-deiri-chô*.

[2] Packing book, in which are entered goods packed.

[3] A book which, divided into parts and furnished with index-slips, is used for classified entries.

[4] Expense book, in which are entered expenses made.

[5] A book in which profits and losses are computed.

[6] A book used for taking account of stock.

kinsen-deiri-chô. Thus the present book shows the total amount of sales.

5. The *daifuku-chô*. This is used for re-entry, classified according to customer, of the sales on credit that were first entered in the *tôza-chô*.

6. The *hantori-chô*. When a payment is made, this book is used for securing the impression of the seal of the payee as proof of receipt.

7. The *kayoi-chô*. Goods sold on credit are first entered in the *tôza-chô*. The entry is then transferred to the *kayoi-chô*, which is left in the hands of the customer so that there may be no disagreement between trader and customer about the prices and quantity of the goods.

8. The *buppin-deiri-chô*. This book is used for entry of the quantity of goods newly bought or sold. The balance is noted also.

9. The *kaketori-chô*. When collections are made for sales on credit as entered in the *daifuku-chô*—at the end of the month, the half year[1] or the year, according to the trader—this book is used, for the convenience of the collector, for making notes of the total sum of the debt of each customer.

Each firm has its practice with regard to the period of preserving these books, but from three to five years is usual.

Isshi *kôri*.

Roughly speaking, there are three kinds of book in use here: the *genkin-kaiage-chô*, the *tôzagashi-chô* and the *daifuku-chô*. Besides these, there are a pawnbroker's *daichô* and other books.

The *genkin-chô* is used for entry of daily sales for cash.

The *tôzagashi-chô* is used for entry of sales on credit, entries including the date, the amount, the name of the goods sold and the name of the buyer. When the time for payment arrives, each entry is transferred to that part of the *daifuku-chô* allotted to the particular customer and is tagged with an index-slip bearing the customer's name. Then the sales for each customer are summed up so that the book may be used for collection.

There is no fixed rule about the period of the preservation of these books, but wealthy merchants generally have the practice of preserving the *daifuku-chô* for five or six years. The other books are

---

[1] *Hannen-matsu; matsu* = end.

usually discarded after one year of use.

Asake *kôri*.

The varieties and names of books in use here, with the period of their preservation, are usually as follows.

1.   The *tôza-chô*. This is used for entry of sales as they occur.

2.   The *kinsen-deiri-chô*; also called *kingin-suitô-chô*. In this are entered daily payments and receipts of money, including the proceeds of sales and the amount paid, and the sums borrowed and lent. The accounts are balanced every day or every three or four days.

3.   The *shiire-chô*; also called *kaiire-chô*. This is used for entry of the amount of goods laid in stock.

4.   The *daifuku-chô*. This book is divided into parts, and each part, furnished with an index-slip, is allotted to a customer or a trader from whom purchases are made. It is used for entry of prices of goods bought or sold and amounts of debt or credit, etc.

The above four books are used by traders in general, except for shipping or loading agents[1] or land or marine forwarding agents.[2] These persons, not being engaged in sale or purchase of goods, do not need the *tôza-chô* and the *shiire-chô*.

5.   The *mizuage-chô*. This is used for making entry, from an invoice, of goods shipped by a consignor. Entries include the quantity and name of the goods, the name of the ship, the name of the consignor, etc., and are checked against the goods actually received.

6.   The *tsumitsuke-chô*; also called *tsumiire-chô*. In this are entered, on the occasion of shipment, the quantity and name of the goods shipped and the name of the consignee. Then a tally impression[3] is affixed on the entry and the invoice.

The above three books are used exclusively by wholesalers.

7.   The *shikiri-chô*. Upon sale of goods consigned for sale, traders make entry in this book of the name, number or weight, and price of the goods; calculate, upon the basis of the sale, the commission,[4]

---

[1]   *Tsumini-doiya.*
[2]   *Kairiku-unsôten.*
[3]   *Oshikiri-in,* same as *wari-han* or *wari-in.* The *oshikiri-chô* is the same as the *hantori-chô.*
[4]   *Kôsen.*

fee,[1] landing charges,[2] warehousing charge[3] and storage charge; and affix their tally impression on the entry in the present book and the statement of sales to be sent to the consignor.

The above three books are used exclusively by wholesalers and commission agents.

Among the other books used as needed are the *nimotsu-kura-dashi-kura-ire-chô*,[4] the *kan-masu-chô*,[5] the *uriage-hijime-chô*,[6] the *buntsû-dome*,[7] the *baibai-kanjô-chô*[8] and the *hiyô-chô*.[9]

Retailers prepare a *kayoi-chô* and leave it with each customer. Whenever orders are given, they make entry in the book of the name of the goods and the prices, and deliver the goods to the customer. Some retailers put a tally impression over the entry in this book and the corresponding entry in the *tôza-chô*.

There is a considerable difference in the length of the period of preserving these books, depending upon the firm. Firms of moderate scale or larger have the practice of preserving the *kinsen-deiri-chô* and the *daifuku-chô* as long as the firms remain in existence and the other books for a period ranging from ten to twenty years. Nevertheless, a new copy of each of the books is prepared and put into use each January, and this is put out of use in December. However, for a book dealing with debts and credits, such as the *daifuku-chô*, balances as they are found on the thirty-first of December are transferred to a new copy of such a book. This is called *utsushi-kae* or transfer, of a ledger.

Nabari *kôri* and Iga *kôri*.

The following kinds of trade books are in use here:

1. The *tanaoroshi-chô*. This is used for making a calculation, every January, of profits and losses of the preceding twelve months and making an estimate of business for the coming twelve months.

---

[1] *Tesûryô*, which often means the same thing as *kôsen*, but, in distinction from the latter, may signify any kind of fee regardless of whether it is commercial or not.

[2] *Mizuage-chin*.

[3] *Kuraire-chin*, the fee required for carrying goods to a warehouse; distinct from storage charge.

[4] A book used for entry of goods taken into or out of a warehouse.

[5] A book which is used for entry of the weight or volume of goods.

[6] A book used for casting up accounts of daily sales.

[7] A book in which are entered letters received or sent out, or prices are noted down.

[8] A book in which an account of sales and purchases is made.

[9] A book for miscellaneous expenses.

2.　The *buppin-shiire-chô*, the *oroshiuri-chô*, the *shikiri-chô*, etc. are used for entry of goods (bought, sold wholesale, invoiced, etc.), their prices, the dates, etc.

3.　The *dai-chô* or the *daifuku-chô*. One of these books is used by clerks at the counter[1] who make classified entry, separately for sales and purchases, of the names and prices of goods sold or purchased, so that they may verify the account of the day or month, or other accounts of debt and credit.

4.　The *tôza-chô* and the *niwa-chô*.[2] Temporary entry of daily sales and purchases as they take place is made in one of these books. The daily entries are transferred into the *daifuku-chô* and other books. These are used by people at the counter to make entries on the spot.

5.　The *kinsen-hantori-chô* and the *buppin-hantori-chô*.

6.　The *kashiuri-kayoi-chô*. In this are entered sales on credit, just as in the *daifuku-chô*, when goods sold are delivered. Every half a year or sixty days customers are billed for the total sums, and the payment is demanded.

7.　The *kakidashi-chô*. This book is carried along by one who goes out for collection. The entries consist of excerpts from entries (elsewhere) of sales on credit.

There is no definite rule about the period of preserving these books, but the *kayoi-chô* is discarded after half a year of use.

AICHI PREFECTURE

Nakajima *kôri*.

The trade books that are in use here are as follows. Their uses and period of preservation are described in detail in inserted notes.[3]

1.　The *tôza-chô*. This is used for entry of daily sales. The book is usually preserved for one year, but, depending on conditions of accounting, its preservation may be extended over the following year.

2.　The *dai-chô*. This is used for re-entries of sales on credit, classified by customer, from the *tôza-chô*. At the end of the first and second six months of the year, the sales for the respective periods

---

[1] *Misekata.*

[2] More often used in the sense of a book which makes entry of the ground-rent paid in the form of rice.

[3] *Warigaki*, also called *warichû*; a two-line note inserted within the body of the text.

are summed up. The book is preserved until after all the payments are made.

3. The *kinsen-deiri-chô*. This is used for detailed entry of one's receipts and payments of money. The book is preserved until after the accounts are all settled.

4. The *shiire-chô*. This is used for entry of goods bought, including amount and prices. The book may, after a year's use, be replaced by a new volume.

5. The *kinsen-hantori-chô*. When payment of money is made, this book is used for securing the impression of the seal of the payee.

6. The *nimotsu-hantori-chô*. When delivery of goods is made, this book is used for securing the impression of the seal of the deliveree.

7. The *shichimotsu-daichô*. This book is used for detailed entry of goods pledged, the sum of the loan, interest and term.

Those books, for which there is no fixed rule regarding period of preservation, are kept in use until the accounts entered therein are all settled.

Nagoya Ward.

The books in use here vary slightly according to the trade, but the following ten are generally used: the *tôza-chô*, the *tôza-kaiire-chô*, the *daichô*, the *kinsen-deiri-chô*, the *buppin-bangô-chô*,[1] the *sashi-hiki-kanjô-chô*, the *kawase-chô*, the *unchin-mizuage-chô*, the *kinsen-hantori-chô* and the *nimotsu-hantori-chô*.

The above-mentioned *sashihiki-kanjô-chô* is used for entry of the balance of the account of sales on credit.

These books are preserved for a period ranging from three to five years from the time they are put out of use.

Chita *kôri*.

The trade books are called by different names depending upon the firm, so it is impossible to find a general name for each of them. However, those books that are called by approximately the same names and are always in use are as given below. There is no definite rule about the uses and the period of preservation of these books. These books are: 1) the *tôza-chô*, 2) the *kinsen-deiri-chô*, 3) the *kinsen-hantori-chô*, 4) the *nimotsu-hantori-chô*, 5) the *uriage-chô*, 6) the *kinsen-sashihiki-chô*,[2] 7) the *nimotsu-kuradashiire-chô*, 8) the *buppin-shiire-chô*,

---

[1] A book used to make entry of the numbers with which each individual piece of merchandise is marked.

[2] A book used for entry of the balance of account.

9) the *nyûka-chô*,[1] 10) the *kawairi-chô*, 11) the *shiwake-chô*, 12) the *tsumitsuke-chô*[2] and 13) the *zatsuyô-chô*.[3]

Minami-shitara *kôri*.

Of those books that are in general use among traders, regardless of the nature of the trade, the more important are: 1) the *shiire-chô*, 2) the *daifuku-chô*, 3) the *tôza-chô*, 4) the *kingin-deiri-chô*, 5) the *nimotsu-hantori-chô*, 6) the *kingin-hantori-chô*, and 7) the *kakinuki-chô*.

The *shiire-chô* and the *kingin-deiri-chô* are used in the way their names indicate.

The *daifuku-chô* is used for later re-entry of sales from the *tôza-chô*. Entries include the names of goods sold and their sales prices, which were originally entered daily in the *tôza-chô*.

The *nimotsu-hantori-chô* is used for detailed entry of goods delivered by one trader to another, and for securing, by way of proof of receipt, the impression of the seal of the deliveree. The *kingin-hantori-chô* is used in the same way.

The *kakinuki-chô* is used for culling from the *tôza-chô* and re-entering payments in arrears, for convenience in demanding payment.

Formerly traders provided themselves with a new volume of these books every January, but since the issue of revenue stamps[4] by the government, they sometimes use a volume for more than a year to economize on stamps.

The old books are usually thrown away after being preserved for a period ranging from five to ten years.

Atsumi *kôri*.

The trade books in use here are: 1) the *daifuku-chô*, 2) the *shiire-chô*, 3) the *deiri-chô*, 4) the *tôza-chô*, 5) the *kinsen-hantori-chô*, 6) the *nimotsu-hantori-chô*, etc.

They are preserved for three years.

The practice is to restrict looking over accounts[5] after the closing of books to the books of one (the preceding) year.

Kaitô *kôri* and Kaisai *kôri*.

---

[1] A book used for entry of the arrivals of goods.

[2] A book used to make entry of goods loaded on board a vessel for shipment.

[3] A book used for entry of sundry matters or sundry expenses.

[4] *Shoken-inshi;* also called *shûnyû-inshi*.

[5] *Chôbo-chôsa*, which also may mean "auditing the accounts."

The number of trade books[1] used here differs according to the trade, some traders requiring a large number of books and others only four or five. However, those kinds of trade books that are indispensable to all traders are: 1) the *daifuku-chô*, 2) the *tôza-chô*, 3) the *shiire-chô*, 4) the *uriage-chô*, 5) the *kinka-deiri-chô*,[2] 6) the *kinka-hantori-chô*, 7) and the *nimotsu-hantori-chô*.

Their uses are as follows:

The *tôza-tsukekomi-chô*[3] is used for entry, on the spot, of sales, including the quantity of the goods sold, their prices, and the names of the vendees. The entries are later transferred to the *daifuku-chô*, a book in which the trader's accounts with others are balanced. The *shiire-chô* is used for the entry of the purchase prices of goods. The *uriage-chô* is used for entry of the amount of sales, so that a trader may calculate the amount of his profits and losses by setting the sum total of the purchase prices of goods against that of the sales prices.

The *suitô-bo*[4] is concerned only with payments and receipts of money, and nothing else is entered. In the evening at the end of every business day it is used for checking the balance, calculated according to entries in the book, with the actual cash in hand, so that there may be no doubt as to the day's account.

These books are usually used for one year, but there is no fixed practice as to the period of their preservation. The general rule is to keep them for six or seven years.

Aichi *kôri*.

The trade books in use here, and their names, uses, and period of preservation are generally as follows:

1. The *tôza-chô*. This is used for on-the-spot[5] entry of daily sales.

2. The *daifuku-chô*. Entries in the *tôza-chô* relating to goods rented to others[6] and sales on credit are culled and posted in the *daifuku-chô*.

---

[1] *Chôai*, which usually means one of the following: 1) to check the actual goods or cash on hand against the entries in a book; 2) to make entry in a book; 3) to make a calculation of profits and losses, is clearly used here in the sense of a trade book.

[2] *Kinka*, gold coin; used here in the sense of *kingin* or *kinsen* currency.

[3] Same as the *tôza-chô* above.

[4] *Bo*, as a suffix, means the same as *chô*, i.e. book.

[5] *Tôza-ni;* this also may mean temporary.

[6] *Buppin-no-kashi;* this may mean goods consigned for sale.

3. The *shiire-chô*. This is used for entry of goods purchased.

4. The *mizuage-chô*. This is used for entry of goods, and their amount, discharged from a boat when a shipment arrives.

5. The *nimotsu-hantori-chô*. When goods are delivered, this book is used for securing, by way of proof of receipt, the impression of the seal of the deliveree.

6. The *kinsen-hantori-chô*. When money is paid, this book is used for securing, by way of proof of receipt, the impression of the seal of the payee.

7. The *shohin-hantori-chô*.[1] When sundry goods are delivered, this book is used for securing, by way of proof of receipt, the impression of the seal of the deliveree.

8. The *kinsen-deiri-chô*. This is used for entry of payments and receipts of money.

These books are generally preserved for ten years.

Niwa *kôri* and Haguri *kôri*.

There are many kinds of trade books in use here, but there is no fixed rule as to their appellations, uses and period of preservation. Generally speaking, the following books are used in commerce.

1. The *daifuku-chô*, 2. the *tôza-chô*, 3. the *kinsen-suitô-chô*, 4. the *kinsen-hantori-chô*, 5. the *buppin-kaiire-chô*, 6. the *buppin-urisabaki-chô*[2] and the *nimotsu-hantori-chô*.

SHIZUOKA PREFECTURE

Prefectural Office.

The trade books in use here, with their appellations, uses and period of preservation, are as follows:

1. The *tôza-chô*; also called *urikake-chô*. This is used for entry of sales on credit, and is preserved for one year.

2. The *kakinuki-chô*. This is used for re-entry, classified by customer, of sales on credit from the *tôza-chô*. It is preserved for three years.

3. The *sôko-chô*.[3] This is used for daily entry of goods in stock and their prices. It is preserved for three years.

4. The *sôkanjô-moto-chô*. This is used for entry of the goods in

---

[1] *Shohin*, sundry goods. The distinction between the *nimotsu-hantori-chô* and the *shohin-hantori-chô* is not clear.

[2] A book used for entry of sales of goods, same as the *uriage-chô*, etc.

[3] *Sôko*, literally, "storage," or "warehouse."

stock, the amount of cash in hand and the balance after payment. It is preserved for five years.

5.   The *daifuku-chô*. This is used for entries classified by customer, of the total of sales on credit to each customer. It is preserved for five years.

6.   The *kaiire-chô*; also called *shiire-chô*, or *kanjô-chô*. This is used for entry of goods purchased. It is preserved for five years.

7.   The *uriwatashi-chô*; also called *oroshiuri-chô*. This is used for entry of wholesales. It is preserved for five years.

8.   The *uriage-chô*. This is used for entry of daily sales. It is preserved for three years.

9.   The *kingin-deiri-chô*. This is used for entry of daily payments and receipts of money. It is preserved for ten years.

10.   The *nimotsu-hantori-chô*. This is used, on delivery of goods, for securing the impression of the seal of the deliveree by way of proof of receipt. It is preserved for five years.

11.   The *kingin-hantori-chô*. This is used, on payment of money, for securing the impression of the seal of the payee by way of proof of receipt. It is preserved for ten years.

12.   The *niwatashi-chô*. This is used for entry of the distinguishing mark[1] with which a case or bale of goods to be forwarded is identified, and the quantity of the goods composing the load. It is preserved for one year.

13.   The *kayoi-chô*. This is left with each regular customer, and at every sale and delivery of goods entry is made therein of the name and quantity of the goods, and it is checked against the corresponding entry in the *kakinuki-chô*.

The above books (1–13) are used by ordinary mercantile firms, while those given below (14–33) are used by shipping agents.[2]

14.   The *wasen-funazumi-chô*. At the departure of a *wasen*,[3] this book is used for entry of the number of cases or bales it is carrying, the weight[4] of the goods and their destination. It is preserved for one year.

15.   The *jôkisen-zumi-chô*. At the departure of a steamship,[5] this

---

[1]   *Nijirushi.*

[2]   *Funadoiya.*

[3]   A ship of Japanese build or style, especially used in contrast to a steamship.

[4]   *Ryomoku.*

[5]   *Jôkisen.*

book is used in the same way. It is preserved for one year.

16.   The *mizuage-chô* in the Japanese or Western style. This book is used in the same way when a ship enters port. It is preserved for one year.

17.   The *daifuku-chô*. This is used for entry of the freight charges, commission, etc., due to the shipping agents. It is preserved for five years.

18.   The *yushutsu-chô*.[1] This is used for entry of shipments. It is preserved temporarily.

19.   The *tôza-chô*. This is used for copying entries from the *yushutsu-chô*. It is preserved for one year.

20.   The *shitate-chô*. This is used for entry of the destinations of shipments. It is preserved for one year.

21.   The *kingin-hantori-chô*. When payment of money is made, this book is used for securing, by way of proof of receipt, the impression of the seal of the payee. It is preserved for ten years.

22.   The *niuke-chô*. At the arrival in port of a ship,[2] this book is used for entry of the number of cases (or bales) of goods it has carried, the weight of the goods and their destinations. It is preserved temporarily.

23.   The *niwatashi-chô*. At the departure of a ship,[3] this book is used for entry of the number of the cases (or bales) it is carrying, the weight of the goods and their destinations. It is preserved temporarily.

24.   The *deharai-chô*. This is used for entry of shipments. It is preserved for two years.

25.   The *nimotsu-azukari-chô*. This is used for entry of the number of articles left in temporary charge of shipping agents. It is preserved for five years.

---

[1] *Yushutsu*, export.

[2] *Chakusen; chaku* = arrival, *sen* = ship.

[3] *Hassen*, a contracted form of *hatsu sen; hatsu* means departure.

26. The *niuke-chô*.[1] This is used for copying from the *teita*,[2] or invoice. It is preserved for one year.

27. The *nizumi-chô*. This is used for copying from the *niwatashi-chô*. It is preserved for five years.

28. The *umpan-kôsen-chô*. This is used for entry of carriage charges.[3] It is preserved for five years.

29. The *kurashiki-ryô-chô*. This is used for entry of storage[4] charged for articles left temporarily with shipping agents.

30. The *unchin-shiharai-chô*. This is used for entry of payment, for their customer,[5] of carriage charges by the shipping agents. It is preserved for five years.

31. The *nimotsu-hikiawase-chô*. This is used for checking articles that have been sent and those that remain to be sent. It is preserved for five years.

32. The *nimotsu-hantori-chô*. At the delivery of articles, this book is used for securing, by way of proof of receipt, the impression of the seal of the deliveree. It is preserved for five years.

33. The *kinsen-deiri-chô*. This is used for entry of daily payments and receipts of money. It is preserved for ten years.

Udo *kôri* and Abe *kôri*.

The types of trade books used depend upon the trade. They are not the same for all traders here, with the exception of the *kingin-deiri-chô* and the *tôza-chô*, both of which are used in every firm. These two books are generally preserved for just one year.

Inasa *kôri* and Aratama *kôri*.

The kinds of book in use here, with their names, uses and periods of preservation, are as follows:

---

[1] This *niuke-chô* apparently serves a slightly different purpose from the *niuke-chô* mentioned above (22).

[2] *Teita* was a special form of invoice employed in the dispatch of articles or money in the Tokugawa period. In it were given the name of the sender, the name of the addressee, the name of the article and the name of the *hikyaku* or courier with whom the conveyance was entrusted, the sender and the courier affixing their seals. On the completion of delivery, the deliveree affixed his seal by way of proof of receipt and returned the *teita* to the sender; thus the *teita* functioned also as a sort of *nimotsu-hantori-chô*. The name *teita*, meaning, literally, hand-board, was originally derived from the practice of using a small piece of board for the purpose.

[3] *Unchin*.

[4] *Kurashi-ryô*; which more often refers to the rates charged by warehouse people.

[5] *Torikae*. Payment for another is also expressed in Japanese by *tatekae*.

1. The *kinsen-suitô-bo*. Every payment and receipt of money by a house is entered in this book. It is preserved as long as there is blank space for entries.

2. The *shiire-chô*. This is used for entry of goods laid in and their cost prices, freight charges, etc. Entries of the goods[1] brought into the shop and their sales are also made in this book. The goods are sold according to this book. It is preserved for one year.

3. The *uri-chô*. This is used for entry of goods sold, their sales prices, and also the amount, if any, of overpayment[2] or shortage. The book is preserved for one year.

4. The *tôza-chô*. When commercial transactions, i.e. sales and purchases of goods, the payment and receipt of money, take place, they are entered in the present book. It is preserved for one year.

5. The *kinsen-hantori-chô*. When payment of money is made, it is entered in this book. Also, the payee is asked to sign his name and impress his seal in it. The book is preserved until there is no space left for further entry.

6. The *yushutsu-chô*. All goods exported[3] are entered in this book, the entries including the names of the goods, the party to whom the sales have been made, the destination of the goods, the sales prices, the vessel carrying the goods, the party to whom delivery of the goods has been made, etc. The book is preserved until there is no space left for further entry.

Kamo *kôri* and Naka *kôri*.

The names by which trade books are called, and the kinds of trade book in use here, are many and different, depending on the trade in which they are used; but generally the more common of them are as follows:

1. The *tôza-chô*;
2. The *kingin-deiri-chô*;
3. The *daifuku-chô*.

These books are used for miscellaneous[4] entries of daily payments and receipts of money.

4. The *shiire-chô*;

---

[1] *Niwairi*. The ensuing passage is obscure.

[2] *Ka-fusoku.*

[3] *Yushutsu;* referring here to domestic trade carried on by sea.

[4] *Zakki:* lit., "sundry."

5. The *kaiire-chô*;
6. The *shikiri-chô*;
7. The *moto-chô*.

These books are used for entry of the cost prices of the goods laid in.

8. The *uriage-chô*;
9. The *mizuage-chô*.

These books are used for daily entry of the sales prices of the goods sold.

10. The *hantori-chô*. This book is used for entry of the sum of money involved in such commercial transactions as *shikiri*,[1] laying in stock, and lending or borrowing money. Those who have thus received money are required to impress their seal in connection with such an entry.

11. The *eitai-chô*, also called *mannen-chô*. Entries of sales on credit, payment for which has long been in arrears, are culled from the *uriage-chô*, the *mizuage-chô*, the *hantori-chô* and other books of similar nature and posted up to the present book.

12. The *chûmon-chô*. Suppose certain goods are found to be sold out or short, and orders for them are sent out to such and such a firm on a certain date; or suppose orders for certain goods are accepted at a certain date: these are the sorts of things entered in the present book.

There is no fixed rule about the period of preservation of these books. However, firms of the middle class and above make it a rule to preserve the old books handed down from generation to generation, books which are mostly concerned with the loan of money or goods.

Saya *kôri* and Kitô *kôri*.

The following kinds of book are in use here:

1. The *daifuku-chô*. This is used for re-entry from the *tôza-chô* of sales on credit, classified according to customer.
2. The *kaiage-chô*. This is used for entry of goods laid in.
3. The *uriage-chô*. This is used for entry of sales for cash.
4. The *tôza-chô*. This is used for entry of sales on cash-credit.[2]
5. The *hantori-chô*. This is used for entry of receipt of money.

[1] Clearance of balance, debt and credit, etc.
[2] *Tôza-kashitsuke* = *tôza-gashi*.

6. The *kinsen-deiri-chô*. This is used for daily entry of payment and receipt of money.

The above books would be used, for instance, by a draper.

The *daifuku-chô*, the *baibai-chô* and the *deiri-chô* would be used, for instance, by a rice dealer.

As to the period of preservation of these books, the *daifuku-chô* is usually preserved for an indefinite period; the *deiri-chô* for over ten years; and the *tôza-chô*, the *uriage-chô*, the *hantori-chô* and others for a period ranging from three to five years.

GIFU PREFECTURE

Mugi *kôri*.

Each of the trade books is preserved for over one year. The kinds of book in use here are as follows:

1. The *shôbaihin-tôzagashi-kayoi-chô*;[1]
2. The *tôza-chô*. Everything connected with commerce is entered in this book.
3. The *kinsen-deiri-chô*;
4. The *buppin-uriage-chô*;[2]
5. The *buppin-shiire-chô*;
6. The *niuke-chô*;[3]
7. The *niharai-chô*;[4]
8. The *kinsen-hantori-chô*;
9. The *nimotsu-hantori-chô*.

Ampachi *kôri*.

It is difficult to make a generalized statement about the kinds of trade books in use here, but the more common books and their uses are as follows:

1. The *buppin-kaiire-chô*. This book, which used to be called *shiire-chô*, is used for entry of the prices of goods laid in for trade.

2. The *genkin-uriage-chô*. This is used for daily entry of sales for cash.

3. The *shôbaihin-tôza-gashikayoi-chô*. This book, which used to be called *tôza-chô*, is used for temporary entry of daily occasional sales of goods on cash-credit. These entries are subsequently posted up to the *tsukeage-chô*.

---

[1] Book in which short-term loans for commercial goods are entered.
[2] Same as the *uriage-chô*; *buppin*, goods or articles.
[3] A book used for entry of goods received; *ni* = goods, freight, *uke* = receipt.
[4] A book used for shipping of goods sold.

4. The *tsukeage-chô*. This book, popularly called *daifuku-chô*, is used for the entry of goods sold on credit and their sales prices from *tôzagashi-kayoi-chô* (see above).

The above three books are used in connection with sales.

5. The *kinsen-deiri-chô*. This is a journal for entry of daily payments and receipts of money connected with ordinary affairs of daily life.[1]

6. The *kinsen-hantori-chô*. This is used for securing proof of receipt from a payee to whom payment connected with ordinary affairs has been made.

7. The *nimotsu-hantori-chô*. This is used for commercial purposes alone, for securing proof of receipt from a party to whom delivery of goods has been made.

Besides the above, there are various other books in use, depending on the trade.

There is no fixed rule regarding the period of preservation of these books, but they are preserved for at least five years and usually longer by traders of middle class and above.

Fuwa *kôri*.

The trade books in use here include the following:

1. The *tôza-chô*. This is used for daily entry of goods sold on credit.

2. The *daifuku-chô*, also called *shôbaihin-kashi-chô*. This is a book in which credit accounts of individual vendees are entered from the *tôza-chô*. Every six months the balances of individual vendees are calculated based on this book.

3. The *genkin-uriage-chô*. This is used for entry of the daily amount of sales.

4. The *shiire-chô*. This is used for entry of the quantity and cost prices of the goods laid in stock.

5. The *kinsen-deiri-chô*. This is used for daily entry of every payment and receipt of money.

6. The *kinsen-hantori-chô*. This is used for securing proof of receipt for the party to whom payment of money has been paid.

7. The *nizumi-chô*. This is used for entry of goods to be forwarded to a customer in a different district.

These books are preserved for from one to ten years.

[1] As distinct from commercial matters.

Atsumi *kôri*, Kagami *kôri* and Katagata *kôri*.

There is a difference in the kinds of trade books in use, as well as in their uses and period of preservation, depending upon the trade, but the more common of them may be generally given as follows:

1. The *tôza-chô*. This book is a journal for entry of sales and purchases as they take place. According to some, the entry is limited to sales or purchases only, while others make entry in it of both sales and purchases. In short, it serves as a memorandum preparatory for later transfer to the ledger.

2. The *uri-chô*. This is used for entry of the sales prices of the goods sold, and for recording the credits granted.

Besides the *uri-chô*, the *daifuku-chô*, the *daihôe*,[1] the *daikichi*,[2] the *mampuku-yorozuoboe-chô*,[3] the *shôbaihin-kashi-chô*, and others are also used. Their usage, however, is no different from that of the *uri-chô*.

These books are preserved for a period ranging from ten to twenty years.

3. The *kai-chô*. This is used for entry of purchases of goods for sale.

The *shiire-chô*, the *shikiri-chô* and the *moto-chô* are used for a purpose similar to that of the *kai-chô*.

These books are preserved for the same length of period as the *uri-chô* mentioned above.

4. The *kinsen-deiri-chô*. This is used for the purpose indicated by its name. Its period of preservation is the same as those of the preceding books.

5. The *nimotsu-hantori-chô*.

In addition to the above, there are the *uma-nikki*,[4] the *mizuage-chô*, the *nizukuri-chô*, and many other books, but it is impossible to describe them all.

Tagi *kôri* and Kami-ishizu *kôri*.

The trade books in use here are generally as described below.

As to the period of their preservation, they are preserved or dis-

---

[1] 大宝恵, these local terms are obscure.

[2] 大吉, lit., "great luck."

[3] 万福万覚帳, lit., "ten-thousand-luck-all-memoranda-book."

[4] 馬日記, lit., "horse journal." It is used for entry of goods forwarded from others by horse.

c arded in accordance with the convenience of each firm, after the credit and debit accounts entered in each book have all been settled.

1. The *tôza-chô*. This book, not subject to the legal requirement of affixing a revenue stamp, is used for all and sundry entry of goods sold, regardless of whether the sales are for cash or on credit.

2. The *shôbaihin-tôza-taishaku-kayoi-chô*. This book is subject to the requirement of affixing a revenue stamp, and is used for selective re-entry from the *tôza-chô* of those entries connected with sales on credit. Traders make it a rule to sum up the sales on credit, for each customer, twice a year, at the times of settlement[1] in February and August, and make demands for payment.

3. The *kinsen-hantori-chô*. This book is subject to the requirement of affixing a revenue stamp, and is used for securing proof of receipt from the payee for payment connected with goods bought or ordinary[2] matters.

Ôno *kôri* and Ikeda *kôri*.

There is no uniformity in the kinds of book used by traders here, but only the following few are commonly in use:

1. The *shiire-chô*;
2. The *deiri-chô*;
3. The *uriage-chô*;
4. The *misegashi-chô*;
5. The *hantori-chô*; etc.

There is no definite custom regarding the period of preservation, this varying with the convenience of the trader.

Haguri *kôri* and Nakajima *kôri*.

Those trade books that are used here include:

1. The *daifuku-chô*, used for detailed entry of sales of goods;
2. The *shiire-chô*;
3. The *tôza-chô*, a journal;
4. The *kinsen-deiri-chô*;
5. The *hantori*; etc.

Books like the *daifuku-chô*, *shiire-chô* and *hantori-chô* are usually preserved as long as possible, but there is no definite rule about the period.

---

[1] *Sekki*. The term was originally used to mean the year-end period (for settlement).

[2] *Tsûjô*. Here the term presumably means non-mercantile as distinct from mercantile.

Ena *kôri*.

The trade books used here are generally as follows:

1. The *daifuku-chô*;
2. The *shôbaihin-tôzagashi-kayoi-chô*;
3. The *kaiage-chô*;
4. The *shiire-chô*;
5. The *kinsen-hantori-chô*;
6. The *kinsen-deiri-chô*;
7. The *nimotsu-deiri-chô*;
8. The *nimotsu-hantori-chô*; etc.

There is no definite rule about the uses of these books.

The period of preservation varies according to the nature of the trade and the custom of the house.

Thus some books are preserved forever, and some for only one year.

Kamo *kôri*.

The kinds of trade books used here are as follows. The period of preservation is one year.

Lumber Merchants.

1. The *hiyatoi-chô*. This book is used for entry of hands employed on a daily basis and their attendance.[1] The wage fixed with each worker is also entered in the present book.

2. The *juyô-chô*. This book is used for entry of the amount of purchases of food and anything else needed by lumbermen when they are engaged in felling trees.

3. The *batsuboku-kenshaku-chô*. This book is used for entry of the number of trees felled daily, and their sizes.

4. The *kyûhaku-chô*. This is used for entry of the expenses for food and other expenditures which are paid during the transportation of timber by river.[2]

5. The *kinsen-deiri-chô*. This is used for entry of daily payments and receipts of money.

The above books are needed in connection with the work from the cutting of the timber to transporting it by river.

6. The *kôbatsu-kenchi-chô*. This is used for recording, daily,

---

[1] *Kinda;* "diligence-and-idleness."
[2] Ensuing passage obscure.

amount of timber collected from a raft, its size, etc.

7. The *kaiire-chô* for *tô* (rattan) and other goods. This is used for entry of purchases of materials for the transportation of timber in the form of raft.

8. The *minato-hiyatoi-chô*. This is used for entry of the hands employed on a daily basis and their wages, etc.

9. The *ikada-hantori-chô*. This is used for securing the impression of the seal of the party to whom a raft has been sold (and delivered), or merely delivered.

10. The *shonyûhi-shiharai-chô*. This is used for entry of the sums paid for purchases of necessaries and other expenditures.

11. The *kinsen-suitô-chô*. This is used for entry of daily payments and receipts of money.

The above books (6 to 11) are needed by lumber merchants in connection with that part of their business that involves the transportation of lumber. Included are things such as the raft, sale of the raft and settlement of the transaction.

In other lines of business, the following books are generally used.

1. The *shiire-chô*. This is used for entry of goods laid in.

2. The *tôza-chô*. This is used for all and sundry entries of daily sales.

3. The *shôbaihin-kashi-chô*. Those entries of sales in the *tôza-chô* for which payment has not yet been received are culled and posted up to the present book.

4. The *kinsen-deiri-chô*. This is used for entry of daily payments and receipts of money.

Kani *kôri*.

The trade books used here are classified into three types: those used in connection with laying in goods; those dealing with sales; those dealing with payments and receipts of money.

The kinds and names of these books are as follows:

I. 1. The *shiire-chô*;
   2. The *nimotsu-niwaire-chô*;
II. 3. The *uriage-chô*;
   4. The *nimotsu-hantori-chô*;
   5. The *tôzagashi-kayoi-chô*;
   6. The *tôzagashi-chô*;
III. 7. The *kinsen-deiri-chô*;
   8. The *kinsen-hantori-chô*.

The uses of these books are clearly indicated by their names, with the exception of the *tôzagashi-chô*, in the second class, which contains two different books. The first, which is subject to the legal requirement of having a revenue stamp affixed, is used for entry of sales on credit, payment for which is due in June and December; while the second, which used to be called *daifuku-chô* or *tôza-oboe-chô*, is used for entry of sales on temporary credit.

These books are generally preserved for five or six years after the trader has discontinued making entries in them.

Atsumi *kôri*, Gifu Township.

There are a great number of different books used here, depending upon the different trades, and their uses, names and periods of preservation are hard to standardize. But the more common of them, with their names, uses and periods of preservation, are as follows:

1. The *tôza-chô*. This is used by some traders as a journal for temporary entry of either sales or purchases, and by others, for both sales and purchases. In short, it serves as a memorandum until the entry is transferred to the *moto-chô*, which is kept separately. The book is not preserved (after the trader has discontinued making entries in it).

2. The *uri-chô*. This is used for entry of the sales prices of goods bought, and serves for recording sales on credit. The book is usually preserved for a period ranging from ten to twenty years, but may be preserved for an indefinite period by some traders. It is called by many different names, including *daifuku-chô*, *daihôe*, *daikichi-manpuku-chô*, *yorozu-oboe-chô*, *shôbaihin-kashi-chô*, etc.

3. The *kai-chô*. This is used for entry of purchases of goods for sale, and is preserved for the same length of period as the *uri-chô*. The book is also called *shiire-chô*, *shikiri-chô* or *moto-chô*, etc.

4. The *kinsen-deiri-chô*. This is used for entry of payments and receipts of money. It is preserved for the same period as the preceding books.

5. The *kinsen-hantori-chô*. This is used as proof of payment of money, and is preserved for the same length of period as the preceding books.

6. The *nimotsu-hantori-chô*. This is used as proof of delivery of goods, and is preserved by a few traders (after they have discontinued making entries in it).

7. The *uma-nikki*; also called *mizuage-chô*. This is used for entry of goods forwarded from others by ship, wagon, or horse, and serves as proof of the arrival or non-arrival of the goods. The book is preserved by a few traders (after they have discontinued making entries in it).

8. The *nizukuri-chô*. This is used for entry of the number of packages of goods that have been shipped. The book is used by some traders as a *tôza-chô*.

Ôgaki Township.

It is difficult to standardize the varieties of trade books used here, but the more common of them and their uses are given below.

1. The *buppin-kaiire-chô*. This used to be called *shiire-chô*, and is used for entry of purchases of goods for sale.

2. The *genkin-uriage-chô*. This is used for daily entry of sales for cash.

3. The *shôbaihin-tôzagashi-kayoi-chô*. This book, which used to be called *tôza-chô*, is used for daily miscellaneous entry[1] of goods sold on credit and their prices for later transfer to the *tsukeage-chô*.

4. The *tsukeage-chô*, popularly called *daifuku-chô*, is used for the re-entry of the goods sold on credit and their prices from the *tôzagashi-kayoi-chô*.

The above three books are used in connection with sales.

5. The *kinsen-deiri-chô*. This is a journal for entry of daily ordinary general payments and receipts of money.

6. The *kinsen-hantori-chô*. This is used for securing a receipt for an ordinary general payment.

7. The *nimotsu-hantori-chô*. This book, which is used exclusively in commerce, is for securing a receipt for goods delivered.

There are also various other books used, depending upon the trade.

There is no fixed rule about the period of preservation of these books, but in commercial firms of middle class and above they are usually preserved for more than five years at least.

Ena *kôri*, Nakatsugawa Village.

The books used here are:

1. The *daifuku-chô*, used for entry of sales on credit;

---

[1] *Zakki.*

2. The *kinsendeiri-sashihiki-chô*;[1]
3. The *kaiire-chô*;
4. The *uri-chô*;
5. The *shôbaihin-tôzagashi-kayoi-chô*;
6. The *kinsen-hantori-chô*.

These books are preserved for a year or two.

Shimo-ishizu *kôri*, Takasu Village.

Different books are used depending upon the trade, and it will be impossible to enumerate all of them. Those that are more commonly used are:

1. The *kinsen-hantori-chô*;
2. The *kinsen-deiri-chô*;
3. The *shiire-chô*;
4. The *uriage-chô*;
5. The *tôzagashi-chô*; etc.

There is no fixed rule about the period of preservation.

Haguri *kôri*, Takegahana Village.

There are many different trade books in use here, but the names and uses of the more important of them are as follows:

1. The *tôza-chô*. The use of this book consists in making entry of all and sundry matters connected with purchases and sales. Sales for cash or on credit, and purchases for cash or on credit are all entered in the present book.

2. The *daifuku-chô*. Those entries in the *tôza-chô* that relate to sales on credit and purchases on credit are culled and re-entered in the present book in order to balance the account.

3. The *kinsen-deiri-chô*. This is used for daily entry of payments and receipts of money to insure freedom from error in the account.

4. The *shiire-chô*. This is a book for making entry, for future reference, of the purchase prices of the goods laid in and the amount of money paid to the party from whom the purchase was made.

5. The *kingin-hantori-chô*. When payment is made, this book is used for the payee to write down the sum and receipt for the same.

6. The *nimotsu-hantori-chô*. When goods sold are delivered, this book is used to have the deliveree write a receipt for the same for future proof.

---

[1] A book used for making entry of payments and receipts of money and their balances.

These constitute the trade books generally kept by ordinary firms. But, depending upon the trade, there are also various other books used by each firm for its own particular needs.

These books are all preserved for one year. If some space is left for further entry at the end of the year, the trader may sometimes extend the use of such a book over into the next year. But this is the case with petty merchants; a merchant of good standing[1] never does this.

Yamagata *kôri*, Takatomi Village.

The books used here are, 1) the *shôbaihin-tôzagashi-chô*, 2) the *kinsen-hantori-chô*, 3) the *shiire-chô*, 4) the *uriage-chô*, etc.

These books are generally renewed every twelve months.

Mugi *kôri*, Kôzuchi Village.

The trade books used here are:

1. The *tôza-chô*;
2. The *kinsen-deiri-chô*;
3. The *shiire-chô*;
4. The *shôbaihin-tôzagashi-kayoi-chô*;
5. The *kinsen-hantori-chô*;
6. The *niiri-chô*;[2]
7. The *nimotsu-hantori-chô*;
8. The *nidashi-chô*.[3]

The practice of ordinary commercial houses is to preserve these books for one year.

Fuwa *kôri*, Tarui Village.

The books used here are:

1. The *tôza-chô*. This is used for daily indiscriminate entry of goods sold on credit.

2. The *daifuku-chô*; also called *shôbaihin-kashiwatashi-chô*. This is a *daichô* used for selective re-entry from the *tôza-chô* for use in casting an account (with each customer) every six months.

3. The *genkin-uriage-chô*. This is used for entry of goods sold for cash.

4. The *shiire-chô*. This is used for entry of the cost prices of goods purchased.

---

[1] More literally, "of independent means."
[2] A book used for entry of the arrivals of goods.
[3] A book used for entry of the shipments of goods.

5. The *kinsen-deiri-chô*. This is used for keeping accounts of daily payments and receipts of money.

6. The *hantori-chô*. This is used for securing proof of payment of money.

These books are preserved for a period ranging from three to five years.

Ôno *kôri*, Miwa Village.

The trade books used here are so numerous that it would be impossible to enumerate every one of them. They are usually preserved for one year.

Ampachi *kôri*, Gôdo Village.

The trade books used here are very numerous, and their names differ with the trade, as do their uses. The period of the preservation of these books also differs with different trades. Most traders have the practice of preserving them for one year. Pawnbrokers make it a rule to preserve their books for a period of from seven to nine years.

Tagi *kôri*, Shimada Village.

The kinds of trade books kept by each firm differ according to different trades. The only exceptions are:

1. The *kinsen-hantori-chô*;
2. The *shôbaihin-tôzagashi-kayoi-chô*;
3. The *uriage-chô*;

which are all used by every firm. The period of preservation of these books is different with each firm and it would be impossible to give any definite statement.

Ena *kôri*, Iwa Village.

The kinds of trade books used here are generally as follows.

1. The *daifuku-chô*;
2. The *shôbaihin-tôzagashi-kayoi-chô*;
3. The *uriage-chô*;
4. The *shiire-chô*;
5. The *kinsen-hantori-chô*;
6. The *kinsen-deiri-chô*;
7. The *nimotsu-deiri-chô*;
8. The *nimotsu-hantori-chô*; etc.

There is no fixed rule for the uses of these respective books.

Some of the books are preserved for an indefinite period, and others for two or three years only.

Toki *kôri*, Tajimi Village.
The books used by the various traders are as follows:
1. The *shiirehin-kanjô-chô*;[1]
2. The *shiirenimotsu-uketori-chô*;[2]
3. The *oroshiuri-kinyû-chô*;[3]
4. The *kouri-nikki-chô*;[4]
5. The *baihin-sashihiki-kanjô-chô*;[5]
6. The *urini-okuridashi-chô*;[6]
7. The *kinsen-deiri-chô*;
8. The *kinsen-hantori-chô*.

The books used by manufacturers are as follows:
9. The *shoshiki-shiire-kanjô-chô*;[7]
10. The *shokkô-hiyatoi-kanjô-chô*;[8]
11. The *shoshiki-uketori-chô*;
12. The *seizôhin-urisabaki-chô*;[9]
13. The *baihin-okuridashi-chô*;[10]
14. The *kinsen-hantori-chô*;
15. The *kinsen-deiri-chô*.

Kamo *kôri*, Hosome Village.
The books used here are:
1. The *shiire-chô*;
2. The *shôbaihin-kashi-chô*;
3. The *tôza-chô*;
4. The *kinsen-deiri-chô*;
5. The *kinsen-watashi-chô*;[11]
6. The *nimotsu-hantori-chô*;
7. The *kayoi-chô*.

---

[1] Obscure.

[2] A book used for entry of the delivery of goods purchased for laying in stock.

[3] A book used for entry of wholesale sales.

[4] A journal for entry of retail sales.

[5] Obscure.

[6] A book used for entry of shipments of goods sold.

[7] Obscure.

[8] A book used for entry of factory hands employed on a daily basis and the wages paid them.

[9] A book used for entry of sales of manufactured goods.

[10] A book used for entry of shipment of goods sold.

[11] A book used for entry of money paid to others.

The merchants make daily entries in these books and preserve them for one year.

Toki *kôri*, Takayama Village.

The names and uses of trade books are so different according to the various firms that it is impossible to enumerate them all.

These books are usually preserved for about ten years.

Kani *kôri*, Mitake Village.

Although there is some difference in the variety of trade books used here, depending upon the trade, the more common of them are as follows. Their uses are indicated by their names. They are usually preserved for a period ranging from three to five years.

1. The *shôbaihin-tôzagashi-chô*;
2. The *uriage-chô*;
3. The *kinsen-deiri-tôza-chô*;
4. The *kinsen-hantori-chô*;
5. The *shiire-chô*;
6. The *kinsen-ichijigashi-chô*.[1]

Ena *kôri*, Akechi Village.

The kinds of trade books generally used here are:

1. The *daifuku-chô*;
2. The *shôbaihin-tôzagashi-kayoi-chô*;
3. The *uriage-chô*;
4. The *shiire-chô*;
5. The *kinsen-hantori-chô*;
6. The *kinsen-deiri-chô*;
7. The *nimotsu-deiri-chô*, etc.

There is no fixed rule for the respective uses of these books.

As to the period of preservation, some of the books are customarily preserved for an indefinite period, and others for one year only.

Mugi *kôri*, Seki Village.

The books used here include:

1. The *tôza-chô*. This book is used to make entry of sales of goods on credit or for cash. The book is generally used for entries for one year only. But when space remains for further entry, it is used by some for continuous entry regardless of the year.

There is no fixed rule about the period of preservation, but it is usually preserved for fourteen to fifteen years.

---

[1] Obscure.

2. The *shôbaihin-tôzagashi-kayoi-chô*. This is used for re-entry, classified by customer, from the *tôza-chô* of sales on credit. It is used for one year.

The period of preservation is the same as that of the *tôza-chô*.

3. The *kinsen-deiri-chô*. This is used for entry of all payments and receipts of money.

The length of the period of its use and preservation is the same as for the *tôza-chô*.

4. The *kinsen-hantori-chô*. This book is used in accordance with the government regulation.

5. The *nimotsu-hantori-chô*. The same is the case with this book.

Ôno *kôri*, Takayama Township.

There are many kinds of trade books in use here, such as the *shiire-chô*, the *tôza-chô*, the *niaratame-chô*[1] and the *nidashi-chô*.[2] Each book has its own special use. Five years may be regarded as the limit of their preservation.

Motosu *kôri*, Kita-kata Village.

There are many kinds of books used here in commerce. They are called by different names, but those who call themselves merchants mostly make use of:

1. The *baibai-torihiki-kisai-chô*;[3]
2. The *shôbaihin-kashi-chô*;
3. The *tôzagashi-kiokudome*, more often called *daifuku-chô*;
4. The *kinsen-hantori-chô*;
5. The *chûmon-shiire-chô*;
6. The *nimotsu-tsumidashi-chô*.

There is no fixed rule for the period of the preservation of these books. Some of them are preserved, at the shortest, for three to five years, and the rest for an indefinite period.

Those merchants who are engaged in a trade subject to national tax,[4] keep certain trade books in accordance with the government regulations.

Kamo *kôri*, Ôta Village.

The trade books commonly used here are given below. They are preserved for a full year.

---

[1] A book used for the entry of goods purchased.
[2] A book used for the entry of goods sold.
[3] A book used for entry of sales and purchases.
[4] *Koku-zei; koku*, national, *zei*, tax.

1. The *shiire-chô*;
2. The *shôbaihin-kashi-chô*;
3. The *tôza-chô*;
4. The *kinsen-deiri-chô*;
5. The *kinsen-watashi-chô*;[1]
6. The *nimotsu-hantori-chô*;
7. The *kayoi-chô*.

Gujô *kôri*.

There are many kinds of trade books in use here, and the more common of them are represented by (1) the *tôza-chô*, (2) the *daifuku-chô*, (3) the *kinsen-deiri-chô*, (4) the *hantori-chô*, and others. It is impossible to enumerate them all, as the uses of each book differ depending upon the nature of the trade in which it is used.

The period of preservation of these books depends upon the firm, but they are usually preserved for ten years.

Tokyo Metropolis (Answers to Topic 4, Subtopic 2)

Kôjimachi Ward.

The form of entry in each book is more or less different; there is no fixed form.

There are also differences in the form of entry between retailers and wholesalers.

Nihombashi Ward.

There is no fixed practice (about the form of entry).

Kyôbashi Ward.

There is no fixed form of entry. There is a difference in the kind of trade books used according to the nature of the trade.

Yotsuya Ward and Ushigome Ward.

There is a difference, according to the trade, in the form of entry in trade books. This is also true of the kind of trade books used.

Asakusa Ward.

There is no fixed form of entry. Sometimes there is a difference, according to the trade, in the kind of trade books kept, but the difference is rather slight. However, pawnbrokers constitute a distinct type of traders, so their trade books are also different from those of ordinary traders, as is shown above.[2]

---

[1] Obscure.

[2] See pages 104–105 above (Group I answers to Topic 4, Subtopic 1).

Honjo Ward.

Generally there is a fixed form of entry, but sometimes there is none.

Ebara *kôri*.

There is no fixed form of entry. Sometimes there is also a difference, according to the nature of the trade, in the trade books kept.

Higashi-tama *kôri* and Minami-toshima *kôri*.

The form of entry for a trade book is generally fixed. The trade books used have been described in the preceding subtopic.[1]

Of those books, the *kingin-hantori-chô*, the *nimotsu-hantori-chô*, the *kingin-deiri-chô*, the *daifuku-chô*, etc. are indispensable to every trader.

Kita-toshima *kôri*.

The answer to this question has already been given in the answer to Subtopic 1.[2]

Minami-adachi *kôri*.

There is no strictly fixed form of entry, but there is practical agreement in the forms of each firm. However, it is impossible to describe all the forms.

Shitaya Ward.

The traders here have no fixed form of entry, with the exception of pawnbrokers, who apparently have a somewhat fixed, special form of entry of their own. The variety of trade books used is naturally different, it is said, according to the trade.

Kanda Ward.

There is no fixed form of entry adopted by traders, with the exception of the merchants of the Eight Trades who are bound by a regulation of the Metropolitan Police Board to follow a definite form of entry.

Akasaka Ward and Azabu Ward.

The traders here use practically the same form of entry, but the kinds of trade books they use are naturally different according to the trade.

Recently saké brewers, tobacco merchants, and others[3]........

Hongô Ward.

---

[1] See pages 106–107 (Group I answers to Topic 4, Subtopic 1).

[2] See page 108 (Group I answers to Topic 4, Sub-topic 1).

[3] The text is not clear, as the compiler himself points out.

There is no fixed form of entry. However, following an informal regulation of the authorities, those who are engaged in the pawn-broking business have recently adopted a definite form of entry for their trade books.

The number and kind of books used by each trader is different according to the trade.

CHIBA PREFECTURE (Answers to Topic 4, Subtopic 2)

Awa *kôri*, Hei *kôri*, Asai *kôri* and Nagasa *kôri*.

The form of entry for a trade book is slightly different with each firm, but generally speaking, it is practically the same, for the traders here are said to have followed the practice of the traders in Uraga and vicinity in Sagami Province.

As to the books used by traders, pawnbrokers alone employ books different from those of other traders. There is a slight difference in the variety of books used by the merchants of marine products and those of land products.[1] But the twelve kinds of books mentioned above are said to suffice for the use of both groups of merchants.

Some merchants use certain books for provisional entry,[2] calling them by different names. But these books are, after all, only a temporary sort of memoranda.

Katori *kôri*.

No fixed form of entry prevails, except for the *shichimotsu-meisai-chô*. The forms of entry are different according to the trade.

Yamabe *kôri* and Muza *kôri*.

There is no fixed form of entry.

Unakami *kôri* and Sôsa *kôri*.

Those books, peculiar to a trade, have already been described in the answer to the preceding subtopic.[3] Although there are slight differences depending upon the trade, we say that there are regular forms of entry based upon custom. Naturally there is a difference in the books used according to the trade, but generally speaking, the books described in the first Subtopic of Topic 4[4] are the most essential.

Higashi-katsushika *kôri*.

---

[1] See pages 112–113 above.
[2] *Yobi-no-chôbo*.
[3] See page 116.
[4] See page 116.

There is no fixed form of entry. But there is a difference in the trade books, depending upon the nature of the trade.

IBARAGI PREFECTURE (Answers to Topic 4, Subtopic 2)

Nishi-katsushika *kôri* and Sashima *kôri*.

Pawnbrokers have a fixed form of entry for their books, but other traders have none, as they make entry in their books according to the traditional practices of their firms.

Sometimes there is a difference in the books used, according to the nature of the trade, for example, that of a forwarding agent and that of a pawnbroker.

KANAGAWA PREFECTURE (Answers to Topic 4, Subtopic 2)

Miura *kôri*.

In a general sense these books have a definite form of entry. Different books are used according to the nature of the trade.

Tachibana *kôri*.

There is no fixed form of entry. There is a difference in the books used, depending upon the nature of the trade.

Kita-tama *kôri*.

Traders generally make entry in their books as follows:

The paper used for their books is *hanshi*,[1] *hosokawa*,[2] *minogami*,[3] *torinouchi*,[4] etc. In the perpendicular-bound[5] books, traders merely make entries in regular sequence of dates, etc.

There is no difference in the books used, but there are differences within each trade.

Prefectural Industrial Bureau.

There is no fixed form of entry. There are some differences in the names of books, depending upon the nature of the trade, but varieties used here do not generally go beyond those already mentioned.[6]

TOCHIGI PREFECTURE (Answers to Topic 4, Subtopic 2)

Prefectural Office.

There are definite forms of entry, but the variety of trade books

---

[1] A common Japanese writing paper, 24–26 by 32.5–35 centimeters.

[2] Also called *hosokawa-gami*, or *hashi-kirazu*; a large-sized paper, mostly used for trade books.

[3] A large-sized Japanese paper of good quality.

[4] Obscure.

[5] *Tate-tsuzuri*.

[6] See pages 118–119.

used is different depending upon the nature of the trade.

Shimo-tsuga *kôri* and Samukawa *kôri*.

Generally speaking, there is a fixed form of entry, and there is naturally a difference in the variety of books used, according to the nature of the trade.

Ashikaga *kôri* and Yanada *kôri*.

Few trade books used here have a fixed form of entry. But in the books of brokers[1] and some other traders, the total number of leaves[2] comprising the book is noted on the first page. When there are no more leaves left available for further entry, another book is prepared. The books are numbered serially, so that the volumes are distinguished one from another. Also, the number of lines to be written on one page is limited, so that no later entry may be made on that page. This form of entry is especially adopted for books connected with money. There are about fourteen kinds of books in use here, as has been described in our answer to Subtopic 1 of Topic 4. Of these fourteen books, the brokers of textile fabrics use four or five kinds of books, without otherwise using any different books from other traders.

MIE PREFECTURE (Answers to Topic 4, Subtopic 2)

Suzuka *kôri*.

The forms of entry for books are generally as follows:

(As to the books used, the nature of a trade sometimes calls for the use of different books in different trades, but sometimes books of the same kind are employed in different trades):

1.   Form of entry for the *shiire-chô*:

Date _____	Name of party _____
Name of goods _____ Prices _____	Amount bought _____

---

[1] Obscure.

[2] *Mai.* One leaf of Japanese writing paper, when doubled up, is used as two pages, but otherwise it counts as one page.

2. Form of entry for the *tôza-chô*:

Date _____	Name of Buyer _____
Name of goods _____	Amount sold and Price
	Name of Buyer _____
Name of goods _____	Amount sold and Price

3. Form of entry for the *kinsen-deiri-chô*:

Date _____	
Sum paid _____	Name of goods bought _____
	and name of party to whom paid
Sum received _____	Amount of goods sold
	at sales counter _____

4. Form of entry for the *uriage-shûnyû-chô*:

Amount of money _____	Date _____
Amount of money _____	Date _____

5. Form of entry for the *daifuku-chô*:

Date _____	Mr. So-and-so _____
Price _____	Amount of goods sold _____
Price _____	Amount of goods sold _____
Sum total _____	

(The sums are totalled at the end of each month, at the
end of the first and second six months, or at the end of a
year when bills are collected.)

6. Form of entry for the *hantori-chô*:

> The roughly estimated total sum enterable in the book will be
> ¥ _____
> (This statement is made at the very beginning of the book,
> where also a revenue stamp is to be affixed in accordance with
> the Regulations.)
>
> | | |
> |---|---|
> | Date (*when the book was prepared*)[1] _____ | Name (*to whom the book belongs*)[2]
 Seal |
> | Date _____ | Name (*of payer*)[3] |
> | Amount of money _____ | Paid for what _____ |
> | The above has been duly received. | |

7. Form of entry for the *kayoi-chô*:

> | | |
> |---|---|
> | Amount of money _____ | Goods sold
 (*on credit*)[4] _____ |
> | Amount of money _____ | Goods sold
 (*on credit*)[5] _____ |

8. Form of entry for the *buppin-deiri-chô*:

> | | |
> |---|---|
> | Name of goods & amount _____ | Date when the <br> goods were laid in _____ |
> | Name of goods & amount _____ | Date when the <br> goods were sold _____ |

9. Form of entry for the *kaketori-chô*:

> | | *Collected from*[6] |
> |---|---|
> | Amount of money | Mr. So-and-so, his address |
> | _____ | _____ |
> | Amount of money | Mr. So-and-so, his address |
> | _____ | _____ |

[1,2,3] The italicized parts are annotations by the translator.
[4,5] The italicized parts are annotations by the translator.
[6] The italicized part is the translator's annotation.

Ishi *kôri*.

No form of entry prevails here. However, generally speaking, in making entry in the *tôza-chô*, the name [of the party to whom the sale on credit is made] is given first, and the amount of money is entered in the upper half of the following line and the name of the goods sold in the lower half. Whenever an entry is transferred from the *tôza-chô* to the *daifuku-chô*, the entry in question in the *tôza-chô* will be impressed with a stamp bearing the letter 圈[1] or 合[2] to indicate that the transfer has been completed.

The *daifuku-chô*, which is divided into parts allotted to each individual customer, has an index slip affixed to each part. The name and address of each customer are given at the beginning of each part. In making a regular entry, the date [of transaction] is entered in the part that may be regarded as the right shoulder[3] [i.e., the upper right-hand side of the main part of an entry], and the amount of money and the name of the goods sold, which form the main body of the entry, are entered in the upper and in the lower half of a line next to that of the date, respectively.

Different books are used according to the nature of the trade, such as the *dai-chô* of a pawnbroker. In other trades also, there is a slight difference in the kinds of books used.

Asake *kôri*.

There is no fixed form of entry, but generally speaking, those forms given in the annex prevail. The annex will not be entered here.

Nabari *kôri* and Iga *kôri*.

The trade books are essentially the same, but there is a little difference in the books used, depending on the nature of the trade.

AICHI PREFECTURE (Answers to Topic 4, Subtopic 2)

Nakajima *kôri*.

There is no fixed form of entry. Different kinds of books are used according to the nature of the trade.

Nagoya Ward.

There is no uniformity. There are differences in the form of entry according to the traditional practice of each firm and the nature of the trade.

---

[1] Obscure.
[2] Obscure.
[3] *Kata.*

Different kinds of books are used in different trades, according to the nature of the trade, as pointed out in the answers to the preceding subtopic.[1]

Chita *kôri*.

There is no fixed form of entry. Different kinds of books are used in different trades.

Minami-shitara *kôri*.

The form of entry is not fixed for all, but may be made by each trader as he thinks fit. The nature of a trade makes no difference in the variety of trade books used, as has been stated in the answers to the preceding subtopic.[2]

Atsumi *kôri*.

There is a fixed form of entry. Depending upon the nature of trade, customarily books are used for a year.

Kaitô *kôri* and Kaisai *kôri*.

There is no fixed form of entry. It has already been stated in Subtopic 1,[3] Topic 4, that different books are used in different trades according to the nature of the trade, so this does not require any further statement.

Aichi *kôri*.

Generally speaking, there are definite forms of entry, but naturally there is a slight difference among different traders. Different books are used in different trades, according to the nature of the trade.

Niwa *kôri* and Haguri *kôri*.

There is no fixed form of entry. Different books are used in different trades according to the nature of the trade.

SHIZUOKA PREFECTURE (Answers to Topic 4, Subtopic 2)

Prefectural Office.

There is no fixed form of entry for all, and each firm has its own form. A different trade requires different books, according to its nature.

Udo *kôri* and Abe *kôri*.

There is no fixed form of entry.

Inasa *kôri* and Aratama *kôri*.

There is no fixed form of entry. No different books are required

---

[1] See page 125.

[2] See page 126.

[3] See page 127.

in different trades; it depends on the nature of the trade.

Kamo *kôri* and Naka *kôri*.

There is no fixed form of entry. There is naturally a difference in the variety of trade books used, according to the nature of the trade.

Saya *kôri* and Kitô *kôri*.

There are in a general sense fixed forms of entry.

GIFU PREFECTURE (Answers to Topic 4, Subtopic 2)

Mugi *kôri*.

There is no fixed form of entry. There is a difference in the variety of trade books used, according to the nature of the trade.

Ampachi *kôri*.

There is no fixed form of entry, but there is not much difference [among the forms adopted by different traders]. There is a difference in the variety of trade books used, according to the nature of the trade.

Fuwa *kôri*.

Generally speaking, there are certain definite forms of entry; i.e., in the upper half of a line is entered the amount of money, and in the lower half the name of the goods. Different kinds of books are used according to the nature of the trade, but the difference does not amount to any more than differences in the names of the books written on its covers. Thus most books are more or less like those mentioned in Subtopic 1,[1] Topic 4.

Atsumi *kôri*, Kagami *kôri* and Katagata *kôri*.

With the exception of the *tôza-chô*, there is a fixed form of entry for the trade books. No different books are used according to the nature of the trade.

Tagi *kôri* and Kami-ishizu *kôri*.

There is no fixed form of entry. Different books are used according to the nature of the trade.

Ôno *kôri* and Ikeda *kôri*.

There is no fixed form of entry. Slightly different books are used in different trades according to the nature of the trade, but they are not much different from those mentioned in the preceding subtopic.[2]

---

[1] See page 135.
[2] See pages 137–138.

Haguri *kôri* and Nakajima *kôri*.

There is no fixed form of entry. Slightly different books are used in different trades, according to the nature of the trade.

Ena *kôri*.

There is no fixed form of entry. Different books are used in different trades.

Kamo *kôri*.

Although there is no fixed form of entry, no essential difference is found between one form and another.

It has already been stated in Subtopic 1[1] that different books are used in different trades according to the nature of the trade.

Kani *kôri*.

There is no fixed form of entry. Different books are used in different trades according to the nature of the trade.

Atsumi *kôri*, Gifu Township.

With the exception of the *tôza-chô*, there is a fixed form of entry for all books mentioned in the preceding Subtopic 1. Different books are used in different trades according to the nature of the trade.

Ôgaki Township.

There is no fixed form of entry, but the differences between one form and other are very slight. Different books are used in different trades according to the nature of the trade.

Ena *kôri*, Nakatsugawa Village.

There is a slight difference in the form of entry depending upon the trade. The six kinds of books already mentioned in the preceding Topic[2] are in use here.

Shimo-ishizu *kôri*, Takasu Village.

There is no fixed form of entry for all; and each firm follows its own practice about entries. Different kinds of books are used in different trades according to the nature of the trade.

Haguri *kôri*, Takegahana Village.

The form of entry is practically fixed. Different kinds of books are used in different trades. Thus there are no definite and fixed kinds of private trade books.

Yamagata *kôri*, Takatomi Village.

---

[1] See pages 138–139.

[2] See page 142.

There are slight differences in the form of entry according to the nature of the trade.

Mugi *kôri*, Kôzuchi Village.

Generally there is a fixed form of entry for trade books here, but in some places it is different according to the nature of the trade.

Haguri *kôri*, Kasamatsu Village.

The answer is the same as given in the preceding subtopic.[1]

Fuwa *kôri*, Tarui Village.

There is a difference, depending upon the nature of the trade, in the form of entry as well as in the kinds of trade books used, although they are generally based upon those described in the answer to Subtopic 1, Topic 4.[2]

Ôno *kôri*, Miwa Village.

There is no fixed form of entry for trade books here. The trade books to be used are also different according to the nature of the trade.

Ampachi *kôri*, Gôdo Village.

There are few trades here which have a definite form of entry for their books. Neither are there many trades which, because of their nature, make use of books different from those in common use.

Tagi *kôri*, Shimada Village.

The trade books in use here have already been described in the answer to the preceding subtopic.[3]

Ena *kôri*, Iwa Village.

There is no fixed form of entry; and different kinds of trade books are used according to the nature of the trade.

Kamo *kôri*, Hosome Village.

Generally a fixed form of entry prevails, and it is seldom that a different form is used.

Tagi *kôri*, Takayama Village.

There is no fixed form of entry, and different kinds of trade books are sometimes used according to the nature of the trade.

Kani *kôri*, Mitake Village.

A fixed form of entry prevails within a trade, but it differs ac-

---

[1] [Answers for this *kôri* seem to be missing from the compilation of Subtopic 2.]

[2] See pages 142–143.

[3] See page 144.

cording to the trade. And different books are used according to the nature of the trade.

Ena *kôri*, Akechi Village.

There is no fixed form of entry for trade books. Different kinds of trade book are used according to the nature of the trade.

Mugi *kôri*, Seki Village.

Generally, fixed forms of entry prevail, but sometimes different forms are used according to the nature of the trade. However, no different books are used according to the nature of the trade.

Ôno *kôri*, Takayama Town.

Traders have had an old, traditional form of entry for their trade books. But since the issue of the regulation calling for the adoption of a general, fixed form of entry and the *shôbaihin-kashi-kayoi-chô*, many of them have been greatly inconvenienced by changes in these old customs. Hence, they still find it convenient to follow their older practices and to make entries in separate books like the *gofuku-kashi-kayoi-chô* and the *komamono-kashi-kayoi-chô*, according to the kind of goods. Sometimes there is a slight difference in the procedure according to the trade.

Motosu *kôri*, Kita-kata Village.

As a trader makes entries in his books in a way that is convenient to him, there is no fixed form of entry for all. But in most cases the same form of entry for the third[1] and the fourth books[2] prevails that was described in our answer to the preceding subtopic.[3] Also, some slightly different kinds of books are used according to the nature of the trade.

Kamo *kôri*, Ôta Village.

There is no fixed form of entry for trade books, but it is seldom that any remarkable difference is found in the forms between one trader and another.

Gujô *kôri*.

There is no fixed form of entry. As to the trade books, however, some books, such as the *tôza-chô*, the *daifuku-chô* and the *kinsen-deiri-chô*, are used in almost every trade, although sometimes different kinds of books are used according to the nature of the trade.

---

[1] The *tôza-chô*.

[2] The *kinsen-deiri-chô*.

[3] See page 147.

Tokyo Metropolis (Answers to Topic 4, Subtopic 3)

Kôjimachi Ward.

In our ward, this method is sometimes used by traders in connection with their delivery of goods to the various government offices, as well as in transactions among booksellers, but it is never used on other occasions.

Nihombashi Ward.

There is no prospect of its wide adoption, except among banks and companies.

Kyôbashi Ward.

The Occidental method of bookkeeping is little used by ordinary firms.

Yotsuya Ward and Ushigome Ward.

There is no prospect yet of the Occidental method of bookkeeping being adopted by ordinary firms.

Honjo Ward.

None in this ward have yet adopted the method of bookkeeping according to double entry in use in the Occidental countries.

Ebara *kôri*.

The Occidental method of bookkeeping according to double entry has apparently not been adopted here yet.

Higashi-tama *kôri* and Minami-toshima *kôri*.

The Occidental method of bookkeeping has never been employed here.

Kita-toshima *kôri*.

The answer has already been given in Subtopic 1.

Minami-adachi *kôri*.

The Occidental method of bookkeeping according to double entry has not yet been put into use here.

Shitaya Ward.

Apparently no ordinary firm has yet adopted the Occidental method of bookkeeping.

Kanda Ward.

No ordinary merchant here has adopted the Occidental method of bookkeeping.

Akasaka Ward.

Only one firm in this ward has adopted the Occidental method of bookkeeping. There is no prospect of its coming into vogue here.

Azabu Ward.

No one in the ward has adopted the method of bookkeeping according to double entry.

Hongô Ward.

There is no prospect of its adoption.

CHIBA PREFECTURE (Answers to Topic 4, Subtopic 2)

Awa *kôri*, Hei *kôri*, Asai *kôri* and Nagasa *kôri*.

Not a single merchant in the four *kôri* of Awa Province has adopted the Occidental method of bookkeeping. It will be a long time before we can tell whether it will come into vogue here. However some here have recently begun to use, for the purpose of bookkeeping, the entry form[1] published by the Tokyo Bunshi Kaisha. The method and form will be improved in future.

Katori *kôri*.

There is no prospect of the Occidental method of bookkeeping being adopted by firms here.

Yamabe *kôri* and Muza *kôri*.

No one here has adopted the Occidental method of bookkeeping by double entry.

Unakami *kôri* and Sôsa *kôri*.

The Occidental method of bookkeeping by double entry has never been put into use here.

Higashi-katsushika *kôri*.

With the exception of banks, the Occidental method of bookkeeping has not been adopted by any firms here.

IBARAGI PREFECTURE (Answers to Topic 4, Subtopic 3)

Nishi-katsushika *kôri* and Sashima *kôri*.

None here make entry in their trade books in accordance with the method of bookkeeping by double entry prevalent in the Occidental countries. According to present indications, there is no prospect of its coming into vogue.

KANAGAWA PREFECTURE (Answers to Topic 4, Subtopic 3)

Miura *kôri*.

The Occidental method has never been adopted here.

Tachibana *kôri*.

The Occidental method of bookkeeping has not been adopted here yet.

Kita-tama *kôri*.

---

[1] *Yoshi;* literally, "paper to be used for some purpose."

There are only two or three companies and one or two merchants here who make entry in their trade books after the Occidental method of bookkeeping by double entry. It has not come into vogue yet.

Prefectural Industrial Bureau.

Entries in books kept by banks and other companies here are mostly made by the Occidental method of bookkeeping, but it has been adopted by only a few private merchants. However, as private merchants come to appreciate the advantages of the Occidental method, it is believed that the method will gradually come into wide use.

TOCHIGI PREFECTURE (Answers to Topic 4, Subtopic 3)

Prefectural Office.

With the exception of the national bank, the Occidental method has not been adopted by traders in general here.

Shimo-tsuga *kôri* and Samukawa *kôri*.

The Occidental method of bookkeeping is in use in the banks here, but it has not been adopted by other traders.

Ashikaga *kôri* and Yanada *kôri*.

Traders in general here have not abandoned their loose practices in keeping trade books, and do not take to the Occidental method of bookkeeping, considering it too troublesome. There are still very few people here who are favourably inclined to its adoption.

MIE PREFECTURE (Answers to Topic 4, Subtopic 3)

Suzuka *kôri*.

With the exception of the national bank, the method of bookkeeping by double entry prevalent in the Occidental countries has not been adopted here. Nor is there any prospect of its coming into wide use here in future.

Isshi *kôri*.

The Occidental method has apparently never been put into use here.

Asake *kôri*.

The Occidental method of bookkeeping has never been put into use here.

Nabari *kôri* and Iga *kôri*.

None here have begun to keep their trade books after the Occidental method of bookkeeping.

AICHI PREFECTURE (Answers to Topic 4, Subtopic 3)

Nakajima *kôri*.

With the exception of the Ichinomiya Bank here, the Occidental method of bookkeeping by double entry has not been adopted by any firms here.

Nagoya Ward.

The Occidental method of bookkeeping has been put into practice here only in the banks and companies, not in private commercial houses in general. There are no indications at present that it will come into wider use here.

Chita *kôri*.

The Occidental method of bookkeeping by double entry has not yet been adopted by firms in general here, with the exception of banks, etc. However, judging from present indications, it is believed that the method will become widely prevalent in future.

Minami-shidara *kôri*.

None here have adopted the Occidental method of bookkeeping by double entry, with the exception of the district government office.[1]

Atsumi *kôri*.

The Occidental method of bookkeeping has already been adopted by various companies here, though only a few private firms have taken it up. The indications are, however, that the method will gradually be adopted generally. Although they are fully aware that it is an advantageous method, there are only a few people engaged in business who have adopted the Occidental method of bookkeeping.

Kaitô *kôri* and Kaisai *kôri*.

Though the Occidental method of bookkeeping is well and widely known, it is rarely adopted in practice.

Aichi *kôri*.

The Occidental method of bookkeeping has not been put into use yet.

Niwa *kôri* and Haguri *kôri*.

With the exception of banks, the Occidental method of bookkeeping has not been reported to be adopted by ordinary firms.

SHIZUOKA PREFECTURE (Answers to Topic 4, Subtopic 3)

Prefectural Office.

---

[1] *Gunga;* the government office of the *kôri* (*gôri*).

There are a few companies here which make entry in their trade books after the Occidental method of bookkeeping, but other than that group, apparently few firms have adopted it.

Udo *kôri* and Abe *kôri*.

There are no indications at present that the Occidental method will come into extensive use, except in the banks and companies here.

Kamo *kôri* and Naka *kôri*.

The Occidental method has never been adopted here.

Ina *kôri* and Aratama *kôri*.

None here have adopted the Occidental method of bookkeeping by double entry.

Saya *kôri* and Kitô *kôri*.

None here have adopted the Occidental method of bookkeeping.

GIFU PREFECTURE (Answers to Topic 4, Subtopic 3)

Mugi *kôri*.

Although the Occidental method is in use in companies and private banks here, no merchants engaged in ordinary trade have adopted it. Nor is there any prospect of its coming into vogue among ordinary merchants.

Ampachi *kôri*.

With the exception of banks and companies, no firms here have adopted the Occidental method of bookkeeping by double entry.

Fuwa *kôri*.

There are no indications at present that the Occidental method will be adopted here.

Atsumi *kôri*, Kagami *kôri* and Katagata *kôri*.

None of the practices described in the questionnaire exist here yet.

Tagi *kôri* and Kami-ishizu *kôri*.

The Occidental method of bookkeeping has not come into use here.

Ôno *kôri* and Ikeda *kôri*.

From present indications, the Occidental method of bookkeeping will not be readily adopted here. But if a law should be made giving validity, as evidence, to entries made after the Occidental fashion, it may gradually come to be adopted.

Haguri *kôri* and Nakajima *kôri*.

None here have adopted the Occidental method of bookkeeping

for their trade books, although it is believed that the method will gradually come into general use.

Ena *kôri*.

There are no indications that the Occidental method of book-keeping will be adopted here.

Kamo *kôri*.

The Occidental method of bookkeeping is now in use in some banks and companies, but there is no prospect that it will gradually come into general use.

Kani *kôri*.

With the exception of companies, banks and other large firms, none has adopted the Occidental method of bookkeeping, not only the method by double entry, but even the method by single entry.

Atsumi *kôri*, Gifu Township.

Most of the partnership companies[1] here prepare and enter their trade books after the Occidental method of bookkeeping by double entry, but no private merchants have been heard to adopt its use.

Ôgaki Township.

With the exception of banks and companies, none here have adopted the Occidental method of bookkeeping by double entry.

Ena *kôri*, Nakatsugawa Village.

The Occidental method of bookkeeping has been adopted only in a few companies here, and apparently nowhere else yet.

Shimo-ishizu *kôri*, Takasu Township.

The Occidental method of bookkeeping by double entry has apparently been adopted by none in this place yet.

Haguri *kôri*, Takegahana Village.

With the exception of banks and companies, the Occidental method of bookkeeping has not been adopted by any private traders here.

Yamagata *kôri*, Takatomi Village.

The Occidental method of bookkeeping by double entry has not come into wide use here.

Mugi *kôri*, Kôzuchi Village.

The Occidental method of bookkeeping by double entry has ap-

---

[1] *Gohonkaisha*.

parently never been adopted here, even in banks and companies.

Haguri *kôri*, Kasamatsu Village.

None here have adopted the Occidental method of bookkeeping, although it is believed that the method will gradually come into general use.

Fuwa *kôri*, Tarui Village.

None at all here have adopted the method in question.

Fuwa *kôri*, Miwa Village.

The time has not yet come for its use here.

Ampachi *kôri*, Gôdo Village.

None here make entry in trade books after the Occidental method of bookkeeping.

Tagi *kôri*, Shimada Village.

None here yet follow the Occidental method in bookkeeping.

Ena *kôri*, Iwa Village.

The Occidental method has apparently not been put into use here yet.

Kamo *kôri*, Hosome Village.

None here have yet adopted the Occidental method.

Toki *kôri*, Takayama Village.

No firm here has adopted the Occidental method.

Kani *kôri*, Mitake Village.

The Occidental method of bookkeeping has apparently not been employed here.

Mugi *kôri*, Seki Village.

The Occidental method of bookkeeping is not adopted by any ordinary firms here, probably because it is rather complicated.

Ôno *kôri*, Takayama Township.

The Occidental method of bookkeeping is convenient, but no one at all here has adopted it. An early revision of the old methods will be difficult to effect.

Motosu *kôri*, Kita-kata Village.

One or two firms here have adopted the Occidental method of double entry in keeping books. As it has been found to be very simple and clear, there is no doubt that it will gradually come into more general use.

Kamo *kôri*, Ôta Village.

The Occidental method of bookkeeping is in use here in banks and companies, but not among traders in general.

Gujô *kôri*.

The Occidental method of bookkeeping by double entry has not been adopted here yet.

Topic 5: Have Merchants' Trade Books Any Legal Force as Evidence against Another Person?

GROUP I—ANSWERS

Tokyo.

Many of the trade books have legal force as evidence in business relations, at future dates. Books described in our answer to Topic 4 such as the *nimotsu-* and *kinsen-hantori-chô*, the *tôza-chô*, the *shikiri-chô* and the *seri-chô* are accorded such validity, while books like the *chûmon-chô* have little authority. Consequently it may be stated that not all trade books are given legal effect at a future date.

Kyoto.

Since a trade book is used for entry of daily happenings in a firm in order that the entries may serve for reference by the firm in the future, there is no reason why the entries of a firm should be evidence against another party. However, the entries in the trade books may sometimes prove to be evidence for the police if any doubt is raised leading to an investigation. Also, in business relations between two parties, memory may fail. In that case, the trade books may serve to settle a matter that has been lost to memory, and in that sense may become evidence in the context of the two parties' mutual relations. The *hantori-chô* and other books of like nature to which revenue stamps are affixed, and the *kake-chô* (credit account book) of the travelling merchant[1] accreditted by the seals of witness(es) will be valid as evidence in legal action.

Osaka.

Some of the trade books, depending on their nature, may be legal evidence against others. Those books, such as the *kingin-uketori-chô*, the *nimotsu-watashi-chô* and the *shichi-dai-chô*, in which the other party is made to stamp his seal, will, needless to say, be legal evidence. But books like the *tôza-chô*, the *ichiuri-chô*, the *seriuri-chô*, the *kaiage-chô* and the *negumi-chô* may also furnish legal evidence though it is only the party owning the books who makes entries. And it is especially when the pages of these books are filled with entries of

---

[1] *Tabi-shônin.*

[2] *Tachiai-chôin.*

sales or purchases, leaving no blank for further entry, that they will have the greatest validity as evidence.

The *daifuku-chô*, as stated above in the first subtopic of Topic 4, is an important book summarizing the entries of other books. But its importance, after all, is for the firm to which it belongs, and it does not have credibility as evidence against other parties. Thus it is only the *tôza-chô* and the other books mentioned above that may furnish legal evidence. Certain other books also, such as the *kamme-chô*, the *masumawashi-chô*, the *mizuage-chô* and the *kuraire-chô*, may be valid as evidence with respect to the main objects of these books.

Those books which may hereafter be valid as evidence against another party would be ones made of long, unfolded sheets of paper, called *naga-chô*. For these books do not admit of later increase or decrease in the number of pages, and are bound in a manner that gives them credibility with respect to what has been entered.

Books, such as the *daifuku-chô*, which are indispensable to the firm to which they belong but have no later validity as evidence against other parties, are made of quarto[1] paper, about twenty sheets of this paper being bound in one bundle, and several bundles being bound together to form a book. This sort of binding is called *fukuro-tsuzuri*,[2] and hence the *daifuku-chô* itself is sometimes called *fukuro-chô*.

It is true that trade books may be prepared in a way that suits the convenience of each trader, there being no fixed rule about the matter at present. But formerly the practice at the old town magistrates' office was not to recognize the validity of trade books as evidence unless they were bound in the style of *naga-tsuzuri*.

Of course some of the books kept by traders have legal force as evidence. The practice among traders, as far as their own transactions are concerned, is to accord these books the status of a notorial act,[3] the terms of which cannot be contested. The entries in the *ichiuri-chô* kept by fish wholesalers, vegetable wholesalers, lumber wholesalers and others, and the *techô*[4] of the rice brokers at Dôjima[5] are usually accepted as correct.

[1] *Yotsuori*.
[2] "Bag-binding."
[3] *Kôshô;* same as *kôseishôsho*.
[4] Memorandum book.
[5] The place in Osaka where the rice exchange is situated.

Yokohama.

There are not a few books that have legal effect as evidence against other parties, but not all of them.

Hyôgo.

The *kinsen-watashi-chô* and the *nimotsu-hantori-chô*, of course, have legal effect as evidence against other parties. As to the other books, some of them have such effect and some do not.

Below are the proceedings of the inquiry committee on the subject:

No. 3 Member [Kondô]: Only two books, the *kinsen-watashi-chô* and the *nimotsu-hantori-chô*, have legal effect as evidence against others. The other books are essential to the party to whom they belong, but they do not have legal effect against other parties.

No. 33 [Kawanishi]: It goes without saying that the *kinsen-watashi-chô* and the *nimotsu-hantori* have legal effect as evidence, as do also the *tôza-chô*, the *daifuku-chô* and the *kinsen-deiri-chô*. For when a dispute occurs with reference to an entry in the *kinsen-watashi-chô* and the *nimotsu-hantori-chô*, the books will be referred to for evidence.

No. 9 [Takahama]: In the days before the Meiji Restoration the books used to have considerable legal effect as evidence, and were quite often used as evidence in court.

No. 11 [Horiuchi]: I am a curio dealer,[1] and I had the following experience, in which my trade books proved very useful as evidence. Some time ago I bought a copper flower vase and resold[2] it to another person. Then I happened to be examined later by the authorities on the allegation that the vase was stolen goods.[3] But the particulars of the vase, including the decorative pattern, were found to have been entered in my books, and it was established that the vase in question was not the one stolen.

No. 27 [Arima]: Some trade books have validity as evidence. A book such as the *kinsen-deiri-chô* will prove particularly decisive. I once had the following experience. I delivered two kinds of goods, A and B, to a wholesaler, and disposed of A. But no agreement could be reached regarding the price of B, and it was left on deposit with the wholesaler. Later, however, the wholesaler would not return B to me, whereupon I brought a suit against him. Insisting that he was in possession of evidence that he had bought B, the wholesaler presented at the trial the receipt of payment for A that had been sold to him. It was proved, however, from the entries in my book that the date of that receipt was

---

[1] *Kottô-shô; kottô*, curio; *shô*, merchant or shop.
[2] *Tembai.*
[3] *Tôhin* (*zôhin*).

prior to the date when B was placed on deposit with the wholesaler. Thus I won the case. I mention this for your information.

No. 19 [Funai]: Books such as the *daichô* and the *kingin-deiri-chô* serve in verifying entries in the *hantori-chô* and the *uketori-chô*, but they do not have any legal effect in court.

Chairman: I will therefore present a report to the effect that trade books may have validity as evidence.

No. 27 [Arima]: Not all books have such validity. A book is valid or not according to the circumstance. Please report to that effect. I just wish to be clear about that.

Chairman: Yes, that is agreed.

Ôtsu.

The trade books that have most validity are the *daifuku-chô* and the *hantori-chô*. Other books might have validity as evidence, but this depends upon the circumstances and the party. Thus they may sometimes have no validity.

Kumamoto.

Most of the trade books have legal effect at a later date as evidence among traders. The *nimotsu-hantori-chô*, the *kinsen-hantori-chô*, the *shichimotsu-dai-chô* and some others have the greatest force of that nature.

Okayama.

In the Tokugawa Shogunate period apparently every trade book had legal effect as evidence against others. But since the Meiji Restoration, with the exception of the *kinsen-hantori-chô* and the *nimotsu-hantori-chô*, there is no book with such validity.

Bakan.

Trade books may possibly be given legal effect as evidence. Some do not have any legal effect in court, while others do.

Sakai.

Trade books generally may become evidential against others in ordinary use in relations between traders. With regard to their legal effect in court when a suit is brought by one party against another, however, the following points should be noted:

(1) The statement [in the topic] used to apply in the (former) courts of the district deputy or the esquire.

(2) Of the books mentioned in the first subtopic of Topic 4, those which used to have legal effect as evidence in the former court of the town magistrate were the *tôza-chô*, the *kinsen-deiri-chô*,

the *mizuage-chô* and the *hantori-chô*, the group of books usually called *tsukekomi-chô*.[1]

During the former Shogunate, the following regulation was in effect, among others, at the court of the magistrate:

Entries in the *tôza-chô*, the *tsukekomi-chô*, the *yorozu-oboe-chô*, the *hitazune-chô*, the *mizuage-chô*, etc. regarding sales on credit and payments and receipts of money shall be considered legal evidence, while entries in the *batori-chô*,[2] the *bubun-chô*,[3] etc., shall not. Though books may be called by different names in different commercial houses, those in which entries are made in such close succession that there is not enough blank space[4] between for later entry shall be regarded as having validity as legal evidence, regardless of what they are called.

The practice which thus came into existence still holds good among private individuals. But in court proceedings today those books may serve merely for the information of the judges and cannot be accepted as positive proof. Needless to say, however, a book such as the *hantori-chô* is legal evidence in public as well as in private relations.

Iida.

A book like the *tôza-chô* which is used for daily entry is full proof as evidence.

Takamatsu.

Trade books which may have legal effect as evidence at a later date in court include the *daichô* of the pawnbroker, and the *shikiri-chô*, the *hantori-chô* and the *haneiri-chô* used in collecting bills. It cannot be definitely stated whether other books may be used later as legal proof in court.

Fukui.

Those books whose entries appear to have been made in proper order may receive legal effect as evidence.

Tokushima.

Trade books had legal effect against others in the feudal period, but have lost it since the Meiji Restoration.

---

[1] Blank.

[2] Blank.

[3] Blank.

[4] *Raishi;* space left blank on a placard. It also may mean white paper used for wrapping a letter or a list of presents, or a postscript made at a blank corner of a letter.

Takefu.

If the buyer of the goods, that is, the "party liable for the payment of the price"[1] signed his name and affixed his seal in the book, and this was not in violation of the regulations regarding revenue stamps, the book may be considered as having legal effect as evidence against others.

Other books may not be valid legally, but since conventional custom prevails, there are few cases of breach of contract.

Miyagi.

The five kinds of books mentioned in the preceding topic may have legal effect as evidence according to custom, but the *hantori-chô* and the *daifuku-chô* are the most important of all in this respect.

Matsuyama.

Those entries in trade books which have not received the impression of the seal of the obligor are not considered legally valid now. But hitherto they were usually regarded as trustworthy by both parties [to the transaction].

GROUP II—ANSWERS

Tokyo Metropolis

Prefectural Office.

Pawnshops.

The *meisai-chô*, the *shichiuke-chô* and the *nagare-jichi-chô* are valid as evidence.

Oil Wholesalers.

Such books as the *nimotsu-hantori-chô* and the *kinsen-hantori-chô* are recognized as evidence at a later date in relations between the parties[2] [to some transaction]. Some of the other books also command credit[3] as evidence.

Dry Goods Wholesalers.

Almost all books, it may be said, are evidence between merchants in the trade. Hence no dispute in the trade has been brought to court since olden days.

Timber Wholesalers.

Most of the books used to be effective as legal evidence. How-

---

[1] *Daikin-fusai-nushi.*

[2] The original text has *sotaijo*, i.e., relative.

[3] *Shin'yô-jô;* lit., "faith" or "belief."

ever, no book except the *hantori-chô* has such force in court today.

Grain Wholesalers.

Books, as used at present, do not have any validity as evidence against others. Those books whose entries were made in proper order used to be regarded valid as evidence [in the trade?], but they are not accepted in court today. Hence they are not legal proof.

Fish Wholesalers.

The *shikiri-chô* and the *shiire-chô*, which are called *tome* (final) are regarded as valid in evidence by wholesalers and consignors because the balances therein are itemized. The *tsuke-nikki-chô* and the *hantori-chô* are treated as evidence between wholesalers.

Fuel Wholesalers.

Formerly, books like the *daifuku-chô* and the *hantori-chô* were regarded as evidence for later purposes between merchants. Also, books such as the *daifuku-chô* were accepted as valid evidence in court. But at present no book except the *hantori-chô* has any legal effect in court.

Saké Wholesalers.

Most of the books are sufficient as evidence between merchants in the trade, because merchants trust each other.

Dried Bonito Wholesalers.

The *uri-chô*, the *daifuku-chô*, the *nimotsu-hantori-chô* and the *kingin-hantori-chô* used to be accepted as evidence between merchants in the trade, but only the *hantori-chô* was accepted as evidence in court.

Salt Wholesalers.

Those books which are acceptable as evidence are the *nimotsu-hantori-chô*, the *uri-chô*, the *shikiri-mokuroku* and the *kinsen-hantori-chô*.

Kôjimachi Ward.

There is a custom among fellow merchants of regarding trade books as evidence. It does not follow however, that trade books are always valid as evidence [in court].

Nihombashi Ward.

Such books as the *hantori-chô* and the *urikake-chô* have as much validity as deeds.

Kyôbashi Ward.

Trade books are valid as evidence against others.

Yotsuya Ward and Ushigome Ward.

Some of the trade books are valid as evidence against others.

Asakusa Ward.

Trade books are valid as evidence against others.

Honjo Ward.

Some of the trade books have validity as evidence between merchants, and some do not. The *kingin-hantori-chô*, the *nimotsu-hantori-chô*, the *shikiri-chô* and other books whose entries are verified with a tally impression, for instance, do have validity as evidence.

Ebara *kôri*.

Some of the trade books are valid as evidence against others.

Higashi-tama *kôri* and Minami-toshima *kôri*.

The trade books have a general validity as evidence against others.

Kita-toshima *kôri*.

Trade books whose entries are regular and in good order[1] are valid as evidence against others. Books whose entries are irregular and disorderly not infrequently arouse distrust in court proceedings. It has not yet occurred to people in general to seek the formulation of regulations for trade books. But if this were suggested to them, many would be desirous of having such regulations. It has often been brought to our notice that irregularity of entries in books has led to disputes over transactions. In the days before the administrative readjustment of the district[2] had been effected, there were frequent disputes between villagers and the village officials regarding over-assessment[3] of the village rates,[4] embezzlement,[5] etc., much to the trouble of the police or the judicial officers.[6] When the books were called for and examined, it was found that the village officials had been inconsistent in their entries, often neglecting to make or strike out an entry. Thus when they finished their examination of the books, with much trouble, having secured the testimony[7] of both parties with reference to the entries irregularly made, it turned out in many cases that no evidence of the over-assessment of the rate or of embezzlement was found, and all doubts were dispelled. How-

---

[1] *Seiton.*

[2] *Gyôseiku-kaisei.*

[3] *Katoritate;* (*katori* or *kachô*).

[4] *Sompi.*

[5] *Ôryô.*

[6] *Hôkan.*

[7] *Môshitate.*

ever, at present there prevails generally a rather definite practice about entries in the account book, so that no disputes between villagers and village officials have been heard of recently. Nevertheless, owing to the irregular method of entry in books, there still occur, it is said, disputes between private individuals.

Minami-adachi *kôri*.

Trade books are sometimes valid as evidence against others.

Shitaya Ward.

Trade books such as the *kinsen-hantori-chô*, the *nimotsuhantori-chô* and the *shikiri-chô* are valid as evidence against others. The validity of other books depends upon the credit of the party to whom they belong.

Kanda Ward.

The *hantori-chô* is valid as evidence.

Akasaka Ward.

Books, like the *tôza-chô* and the *tsukekomi-chô*, whose entries do not permit of later alteration by addition or deletion, are valid as evidence. However, the decision as to whether a given book can be accepted as evidence depends upon the discretion of the judicial officer.

Azabu Ward.

Trade books in which entries are made daily and which cannot be altered later by addition or deletion are valid as evidence. But it is for the judicial officer to decide whether a given book can be accepted as evidence.

Hongô Ward.

If the rule of affixing a revenue stamp [on a book] is conformed to, the book may be valid as evidence.

Chiba Prefecture

Awa *kôri*, Hei *kôri*, Asai *kôri* and Nagasa *kôri*.

Trade books are valid as evidence against another. Entries in the *kinsen-deiri-chô*, for instance, are made whenever payment or receipt of money is made, and accounts are summed up and balanced each day, so that entries cannot easily be struck out or changed. Every trader makes much of such books, and their entries are valid as evidence, carrying the greatest weight.

Katori *kôri*.

Trade books which are valid as evidence against another include the *hantori-chô*, the *shikiri-chô*, etc.

Yamabe *kôri* and Muza *kôri*.

Trade books such as the *hantori-chô*, the *shikiri-chô* and the *shichi-daichô*, in which is secured the impression of the seal of the other party, are valid as evidence. Other books have no legal validity in court.

Unakami *kôri* and Sôsa *kôri*.

According to their nature, some trade books, like the *shichi-dai-chô*, the *sonryô-chô* and the *hantori-chô*, have validity.

Higashi-katsushika *kôri*.

Such books as the *nimotsu-hantori-chô*, the *kingin-hantori-chô* and the *kayoi-chô* are valid as evidence.

IBARAGI PREFECTURE

Nishi-katsushika *kôri* and Sashima *kôri*.

All the trade books are valid as evidence against another.

KANAGAWA PREFECTURE

Miura *kôri*.

We believe that trade books should be valid as evidence against another.

Tachibana *kôri*.

Some trade books, for instance, the *tôza-chô*, are valid as evidence.

Kita-tama *kôri*.

The validity of trade books, as evidence against another will be recognized if they are authenticated by the official seal.[1] However, books that are prepared by a merchant (without the official authentication) would not have such validity at all.

Ashigara-shimo *kôri*.

Trade books should be regarded as evidence against others, but their effect depends upon the particular case, as they are to be regarded as a source of information only.

Prefectural Industry Bureau.

Trade books are valid enough to be evidence at a later date, not only between fellow traders but also between a trader and a person outside the trade.

TOCHIGI PREFECTURE

Prefectural Office.

Trade books, for instance, the *hantori-chô* and the *kayoi-chô*, may

---

[1] *Kan-no-shôin.*

apparently become evidence against others. The *hantori-chô* is used for securing the impression of the seal of the payee or the deliveree whenever money is paid or goods are delivered. As to the *kayoi-chô*, whenever goods are delivered to or payment is made by a customer, this is entered in the book, and the book is usually left with him. Accounts are also settled according to its entries. Entries in the *hantori-chô* and the *kayoi-chô* are then posted up to the *tôza-chô*, from which they are again transferred to the *daifuku-chô* in order to verify the account. If this procedure is not followed strictly, the books are apparently not regarded as evidence.

Shimo-tsuga *kôri* and Samukawa *kôri*.

With the exception of the *hantori-chô*, no trade books are valid as evidence.

Ashikaga *kôri* and Yanada *kôri*.

As long as the regulation regarding the affixing of a revenue stamp is followed, the *hantori-chô* is of course valid as evidence. When the entries in other books are limited to a certain number per page, admitting of no additional entry, as has been described above,[1] these will also be valid as evidence. Again, when there are more than seven or eight different kinds of books in use and a single transaction is entered and re-entered in several different books, it can be corroborated by referring to the entry in one book or another if some omission or mistake of entry is suggested. Speaking from our actual experience, such mistakes are naturally brought to our notice when we examine our books and compare the entries with one another. The reason why traders do not like to go to law about commercial affairs is that it takes much time and money to conduct a suit. Thus they try to be patient in most matters.

Mie Prefecture

Suzuka *kôri*.

With the exception of the *hantori-chô*, there is no trade book that would be valid as evidence against others. For the *tôza-chô*, the *daifuku-chô* and other books that have been in use in commerce are intended merely to serve the memory of the vendor, and do not possess features necessary for evidence, such as the impression of the seal of the vendee.

Isshi *kôri*.

---

[1] See page 152.

There is no trade book that is valid as evidence against others. Only the *kayoi-chô* appears to have some such validity. But even this book does not contain any evidence that the vendee is in debt to the vendor, since the vendor himself makes entries in it and leaves it with the vendee.

Asake *kôri*.

Very few trade books have validity as evidence against others. Of the books enumerated in the preceding topic, the *kinsen-deiri-chô* may be regarded as probably valid as evidence. Since accounts in this book are balanced every day or every three or four days continuously for one year, it is not possible to make any later addition or deletion. However, if this procedure is neglected in balancing the accounts, the book will, of course, be unsatisfactory as evidence.

Nabari *kôri* and Iga *kôri*.

Trade books are valid as evidence against others, as, for instance, the *buppin-kashiuri-hikae-chô*, the *daifuku-chô* and the *kakidashi-chô*. As to the practice regarding sales on credit, either entries are made in the *kayoi-chô* which is then left with the customer, or the entry is just made in the *daifuku-chô*, and when the semi-annual time of settlement comes, the account is settled (thereon). The *kakidashi-chô*, which is used for selective re-entry from the *daichô*, is apparently used only temporarily. But when the accounts are settled, they sometimes just strike out the entries, giving no receipt.

AICHI PREFECTURE

Nakajima *kôri*.

With the exception of the *kinsen-hantori-chô* and the *nimotsu-hantori-chô*, no trade book has legal effect as evidence, except in the moral sense.

Nagoya Ward.

It is mainly the *kinsen-hantori-chô* and the *nimotsu-hantori-chô* that may be evidence against others. However, if the occasion arises when these two books are resorted to as evidence, other related books may become acceptable as evidence.

Chita *kôri*.

Most trade books have no validity as evidence against others, but some of those which give clear descriptions are valid as evidence.

Minami-shidara *kôri*.

Except for the *nimotsu-hantori-chô* and the *kingin-hantori-chô*, in which entries are sealed by the other party, trade books are intended for the merchant's personal use and are not valid as evidence.

Atsumi *kôri*.

Trade books have no features that make them acceptable as evidence. But in view of the importance of credit in business, they have some power of evidence.

Kaitô *kôri* and Kaisai *kôri*.

With the exception of the *kinsen-hantori-chô* and the *nimotsu-hantori-chô*, trade books are kept by the merchant to whom they belong, and the entries are not verified by the impression of the seal of the other party. Consequently these books have no validity as evidence; but depending on a trader's credibility, they customarily have some power of evidence.

Aichi *kôri*.

Trade books are regarded by merchants as "books of evidence," but whether or not they have validity as evidence against the other party depends on the nature of the book. The *nimotsu-hantori-chô* and the *kinsen-hantori-chô*, for instance, are valid as evidence, as they are stamped with a revenue stamp and their entries are sealed by the recipient of payment or goods. However, books like the *tôza-chô* and the *daifuku-chô* are intended merely to serve the trader's own memory, and do not have such validity.

Niwa *kôri* and Haguri *kôri*.

Trade books such as the *kinsen-hantori-chô* and the *nimotsu-hantori-chô* are valid as evidence.

Shizuoka Prefecture

Prefectural Office.

With the exception of the *kinsen-hantori-chô* and the *nimotsu-hantori-chô*, trade books are not acceptable as evidence.

Udo *kôri* and Abe *kôri*.

Trade books come near to having some validity as evidence. Suppose, for instance, one were making some inquiry, and, on opening a trade book, observed, "The entry here says so and so." If the entries of the book were made clearly and in good order, persons observing the entry would not infrequently believe it to be true. A book like the *hantori-chô*, whose entries are accompanied, for instance, by the impression of the seal by the other party verifying receipt, is of course acceptable as evidence, and the foregoing remark is not meant to apply to such a book as this. This is why I said above that trade books come near to having some validity.

Inasa *kôri* and Aratama *kôri*.

Some trade books are acceptable as evidence against others, and some are not.

Kamo *kôri* and Naka *kôri*.

Some trade books in which entries are made successively as each transaction take place may be regarded as valid evidence from the natural force of the circumstances.[1] Some books have to be stamped with a revenue stamp according to the regulation. The *hantori-chô* will be the most valid of all.

Saya *kôri* and Kitô *kôri*.

Trade books will be valid as evidence between traders as long as there exists trust between them. Once faith is lost between traders, the books will also lose their validity.

GIFU PREFECTURE

Mugi *kôri*.

Trade books have validity as evidence against others.

Ampachi *kôri*.

According to the old practice, trade books have a moral validity as evidence between merchants.

Fuwa *kôri*.

The *tôza-chô*, in which entries are made every day successively as each sale on credit takes place, so that no blank space is available for a later or revised entry, is accepted as evidence of credit granted. The occurrence of disputes is thereby avoided.

Atsumi *kôri*, Kagami *kôri* and Katakata *kôri*.

As there are no definite rules regulating their use, it may almost always be stated that trade books have little validity as evidence.

Tagi *kôri* and Kami-ishizu *kôri*.

A book like the *shôbaihin-tôzagashi-kayoi-chô* (or the *shôbaihin-tôzagari-kayoi-chô*) has a force entitling the party to whom it belongs to collect his bill by going to law when the debtor fails to pay. However, the majority of the people in our county[2] know nothing about this practice.

Ôno *kôri* and Ikeda *kôri*.

The trade books customarily used here cannot be regarded as sufficient proof. However, such books as the *hantori-chô* and the

---

[1] *Shizenryoku,* "natural forces."

[2] *Kôri.*

kahei-chô are exceptions to the rule, and are valid as proof. Also the *uriage-chô* and the *misegashi-chô* may be accorded such validity depending on the case.

Haguri *kôri* and Nakajima *kôri*.

According to the local custom, the *hantori-chô* is the only book that will be acceptable as evidence against others.

Ena *kôri*.

Trade books do not have any such validity except for those bearing a revenue stamp.

Kamo *kôri*.

Trade books have validity as evidence against others.

Kani *kôri*.

Most trade books have such validity, but they are not acceptable as proof in court unless their entries are sealed, by way of confirmation, by the other party.

Atsumi *kôri*, Gifu Township.

The *hantori-chô* is one trade book that is always valid as evidence against others. As for the other books, those whose entries are shown to be accurate are sometimes acceptable as evidence in a case of a commercial dispute.

Ôgaki.

According to the old custom, trade books are regarded by merchants as evidence between one another, from the point of view of commercial honor.

Ena *kôri*, Nakatsugawa Village.

The *kinsen-hantori-chô* and the *shôbaihin-tôzagashi-kayoi-chô* are valid as proof, but the other trade books do not have any definite effect as evidence.

Shimo-ishizu *kôri*, Takasu Township.

The *kinsen-hantori-chô* is the only book that is valid as evidence against others.

Haguri *kôri*, Takegahana Village.

Trade books were occasionally accepted as evidence, especially the *kinsen-hantori-chô* and the *nimotsu-hantori-chô*, as their entries are made by the party who receives the money or the goods.

Yamagata *kôri*, Takatomi Village.

Books that bear a revenue stamp provide the strongest evidence. But unless an entry is made personally by the party alleged as debtor and is also confirmed by the impression of his seal, the entry will not be valid as evidence in a case against him.

Mugi *kôri*, Kôzu Village.

Trade books are valid as evidence against others.

Haguri *kôri*, Kasamatsu Village.

According to old local custom, the *hantori-chô* is the only book that has such validity.

Fuwa *kôri*, Tarui Village.

Trade books are valid as evidence against others. But not so many comply with the legal requirements. Therefore, in practice they are not much used as evidence.

Ôno *kôri*, Miwa Village.

Most trade books have such validity, although there are some that are not valid.

Ampachi *kôri*, Gôdo Village.

The entries in trade books are made by the party to which they belong, so they are not acceptable as evidence against others.

Tagi *kôri*, Shimada Village.

The validity of trade books as evidence varies according to the firm where they are kept. The trade books of a firm which is in the habit of making entries in an orderly and clear manner may be acceptable as evidence, while those of a firm which makes entries in a loose manner may not be acceptable as evidence.

Ena *kôri*, Iwa Village.

Except for those which bear a revenue stamp, trade books do not have any such validity.

Toki *kôri*, Tajimi Village.

The evidential effect of trade books does not amount to more than appears in each case from the circumstances of daily entry, the calligraphic style[1] of the entry, the colour of ink, etc. With the exception of the *shôbaihin-kashi-chô*, an entry in a trade book is not confirmed by the impression of the seal of the other party.

Kamo *kôri*, Hosome Village.

Some trade books are acceptable as evidence, particularly the *kinsen-watashi-chô*, the *kayoi-chô*, and others, which are kept with a view to having them accepted as evidence.

Toki *kôri*, Takayama Village.

There are some trade books that are acceptable as evidence.

---

[1] *Sho-tai.*

Kani *kôri*, Mitake Village.

Such books as the *kinsen-ichijigashi-chô*, the *shôbaihin-tôzagashi-chô* and the *kinsen-hantori-chô* are supposed to have validity, as provided by law. But the regulation which requires a debtor to stamp his legal seal in confirmation of an entry in those books is not observed in actual practice. Consequently trade books are not acceptable as evidence.

Ena *kôri*, Akechi Village.

Trade books do not have such validity, except those which bear a revenue stamp.

Mugi *kôri*, Seki Village.

Such books as the *kinsen-hantori-chô* and *shôbaihin-tôzagashi-kayoi-chô* are considered to be valid as evidence against others.

Ôno *kôri*, Takayama Township.

As the *shôbaihin-kashi-chô* has validity as evidence against others, it is used as the basis of creditor's demand for payment in collecting bills.

Motosu *kôri*, Kita-kata Village.

There is no trade book which has indubitable validity as evidence against others.

Kamo *kôri*, Ôta Village.

Trade books have validity as evidence against others.

Gujô *kôri*.

Those trade books that will be valid as evidence against others are the *kinsen-deiri-chô*, the *tôza-chô* and the like.

Topic 6:
> Subtopic 1: Is There Any Difference of Treatment in Legal Proceedings Depending upon Whether the Trade Books Are Properly Kept?
>
> Subtopic 2: Is It Desirable to Have Some Fixed Rules for the Supervision of a Merchant's Books? If So, What Should Be the Principles?

GROUP I—ANSWERS

Tokyo. (Answer to Topic 6, Subtopic 1)

In expounding this topic, the Explanation Committee asked us if there is any convenience or inconvenience, in submitting a case to the court, attributable to the manner in which merchants' books are kept, according to whether they are in good order or not. In the opinion of this association, it is of course reasonable to suppose that it would be desirable, in proving a case before the court, for the trade books to be kept in good order. But as there are not yet in existence any settled rules regarding trade books, it does not always follow, even if the trade books are kept in good order, that they will prove sufficient in a trial.

Tokyo. (Answer to Topic 6, Subtopic 2)

The present topic does not refer to past or present circumstances, but asks our opinion about the future. However, as the matter would considerably affect all kinds of trades throughout the country, we will resume the discussion again at some other time and submit a report on the question.

Kyoto. (Answers to Topic 6, Subtopics 1 and 2)

As has been stated in the preceding topic, trade books are generally kept merely to serve as a reference for the commercial house itself, and would be regarded as worthless as waste paper after the lapse of one year (although some of the books, including the *daifuku-chô*, the *kinsen-hantori-chô* and also the *shiire-chô*, are preserved for several years). However, the trade books that would be valid as evidence in a trial are limited to those whose entries are confirmed by the impression of the seal of the other party. The rest of the books, regardless of whether their entries are detailed or not, are, in our opinion, not valid as evidence.

As to the desirability of uniformity in the binding and the manner of entry of trade books, it should be stated that the kinds of books differ in different regions—cultivated areas, mountains and forests, etc.—and it is natural that still other different kinds of books should be used in the various trades. Furthermore, as we have already stated in our answer to the first topic, the time will never come, in our opinion, when the same sorts of trade books will be used, even by all merchants. For some merchants are exclusively engaged in a particular trade, some in more than one trade at once, and some are only temporarily engaged in a trade. And among merchants exclusively engaged in a particular trade, there are different classes within the trade. Moreover, all merchants may be classified again not only into wealthy, middle class, and poorer groups, but also into scores of other different grades. Under such circumstances, therefore, it may be observed that there will be perhaps only one or two out of a thousand first-class firms whose trade books follow some fixed traditional precedents in the method of binding, entries, etc. Much depends upon the number of employees, and this too varies with the type of business. In some firms, the members of a family comprise the entire personnel, and not even a single boy from outside is employed. Sometimes a married couple alone, a father and his sons alone, or even a bachelor alone make up the entire work force of a firm. In these cases, bookkeeping will be a very simple and easy affair, being intended to serve merely as a record for personal use. These people probably do not, we believe, have any desire to have a fixed form of entry for their trade books.

Osaka. (Answer to Topic 6, Subtopic 1)

If the trade books are kept in order, the entries can be compared with one another and will prove convenient in an actual trial.

Osaka. (Answer to Topic 6, Subtopic 2)

As this Topic has an important bearing on the future, we will take up the discussion in due course of time and present a report on it.

Yokohama. (Answer to Topic 6, Subtopic 1)

As there are no definite rules regarding trade books, there are very few books that are kept in perfect order. Consequently these books do not serve any purpose in a trial.

Yokohama. (Answer to Topic 6, Subtopic 2)

At present there are none, we believe, who are actually desirous of having some fixed rules for the supervision of trade books, though there are sometimes those who appear to be in favor of such regulations.

Hyôgo. (Answer to Topic 6, Subtopic 1)

Trade books would prove of great service in a trial if they were kept in good order, and vice versa.

Hyôgo. (Answer to Topic 6, Subtopic 2)

We of course wish to have some fixed regulations. But we are unable to give any definite answer regarding the precise terms of such regulation under the present circumstances. However, as this is a most important matter for merchants, we will in due course make a detailed study and submit a report on this.

Below are the proceedings of the Investigation Committee on Subtopic 1.

No. 11 [Horiuchi]: My firm, *Kyôritsu-Shôten*, delivered several *koku*[1] of rice to some water-mill[2] hands, but we did not ask them to make entry in the *watashi-chô*.[3] Afterwards they insisted that they had never received the rice, whereupon we submitted the case to court. The court made a decision in our favour because we had made a detailed entry of the delivery, and we recovered payment for the rice. This decision, I believe, was entirely due to our books being kept in good order.

No. 33 [Kawanishi]: Under the Tokugawa Shogunate, it was prohibited to make a permanent sale of land, so people would effect a sale under the pretence of a free grant[4] or an exchange of gifts.[5] The latter consisted only in the seller giving a deed to the buyer; the seller received no deed from the buyer. The seller impressed his seal in the *nayose-chô*,[6] or *ôin-chô*, by way of proving that the piece of land had been given away by him to the buyer as a gift in return for a (supposed) gift from the latter. Even this book of entries proved afterwards of great value as evidence; much more so would a book kept in prescribed order.

No. 14 [Funai]: The *hantori-chô* and the *uketori-chô* are valid as evidence in court, but the other books are not.

---

[1] A unit of measurement of grain or liquids; equivalent to 49,629 bushels or 397,033 gallons.

[2] *Suisha.*

[3] Delivery book.

[4] *Yuzuri-watashi.*

[5] *Hômotsu-gaeshi.*

[6] Name-register book of the village or town; see Parts V and VI.

No. 27 [Arima]: It goes without saying that books kept in good order will be of service in court.

Chairman [Kashima]: I will submit a report to the effect that trade books are of great service or not in a trial or elsewhere, according as they are kept in good order or left in disorder.

The Investigation Committee on Subtopic 2.

No. 27 [Arima]: We should like to have some fixed regulations regarding the supervision of trade books. But I think it best to consider carefully what the most desirable details would be and then submit a report. We cannot expect to have our proposals ready at once.

The other members of the committee agreed to the proposition of No. 27, and decided to take up the matter again at some future date.

Ôtsu. (Answer to Topic 6, Subtopic 1)

It goes without saying that trade books will be of service to us in laying a case before a court. But as there are yet in existence no fixed regulations about trade books, it is impossible to affirm definitely that trade books are sufficient proof, however orderly they may be kept.

Ôtsu. (Answer to Topic 6, Subtopic 2)

The need has long been felt for some fixed regulations—regulations, for instance, requiring all merchants to keep certain books, prescribing some fixed forms of entry, the period of preservation of the books, etc.

Kumamoto. (Answer to Topic 6, Subtopic 1)

If the trade books are not kept in order, there will be inconvenience in proving a claim at a trial.

Kumamoto. (Answer to Topic 6, Subtopic 2)

Under the present circumstances there are probably very few who desire to have fixed regulations about trade books.

Okayama. (Answer to Topic 6, Subtopic 1)

If the trade books are kept in good order, they will be of service in a trial.

Okayama. (Answer to Topic 6, Subtopic 2)

There is some desire for fixed regulations for the supervision of trade books, and there is also a desire to have some regulations for determining validity of trade books as evidence against others.

Bakan. (Answer to Topic 6, Subtopic 1)

The old trade books which have hitherto been used have never led to any inconvenience in court.

Bakan. (Answer to Topic 6, Subtopic 2)

However, there is some desire for fixed regulations, although it is hard to define the provisions desired.

Sakai. (Answer to Topic 6, Sub-topic 1)

Reference has already been made in the preceding topic, Topic 5, to the legal usefulness or otherwise of trade books according as they are kept in good order or not. As a matter of fact there is a great deal of inconvenience at trials, because our trade books are not kept in accordance with fixed regulations, which we do not as yet have in our country.

Sakai. (Answer to Topic 6, Sub-topic 2)

Some fixed rules for the supervision of trade books are desired by people at large, but it would appear to be impossible to enforce them all, even if they were made. However, if rules were laid down for the supervision of trade books on the lines of the provisions of the French commercial code for trade books, provisions covering such things as insolvency,[1] (commercial) bankruptcy,[2] ordinary bankruptcy[3] and fraudulent bankruptcy,[4] we firmly believe that there would not only be no difficulty in the commercial world in bringing the rules into effect, but also that it would be to the general advantage of business affairs. But we hope that you will allow time before adoption of Article 8 (of the French commercial code?) providing that copies of letters sent out to others must be made in a book prepared for the purpose, for such a provision would be often hard to put into effect under the present circumstances of the business world in our country.

As to the method of preparing trade books, considering that it will not be easy for our businessmen to adopt the Occidental method of bookkeeping all at once, we suggest a provision that the binding of trade books should follow the old, general method of *fukuro-tsuzuri*;[5] that the paper used in making a trade book should be quarto-sized *uda-gami*, also known as *kiyonaga*, with six ruled lines; and that the pages should be numbered, and each page be

---

[1] *Kashibunsan.*
[2] *Tôsan (hasan).*
[3] *Futsû-no-tôsan.*
[4] *Sagi.*
[5] See page 170 above.

impressed with a tally[1] by the judge of the lower court,[2] the ward office[3] and the *gun* office.[4]

If books prepared in this way are used as *kai-chô*, *uri-chô*, *kinsen-deiri-chô*, *baibai-keisan-chô*, *kinsen-watashi-chô*, *nimotsu-watashi-chô*, etc., there will be no inconvenience. We also believe that the books will be accorded validity as evidence against others.

Iida. (Answer to Topic 6, Subtopic 1)

It goes without saying that trade books will be of little service at a trial if they are not kept in good order.

Iida. (Answer to Topic 6, Subtopic 2)

We earnestly desire that some fixed rules be made for the supervision of trade books, but we cannot yet determine what specifics are desirable.

Takamatsu. (Answer to Topic 6, Subtopic 1)

If trade books are kept irregularly and left in confusion, the bookkeeper himself will have difficulty in interpreting the entries he has made, even if he can read them. Hence outside parties will naturally feel dissatisfied and will be unable to understand the entries. What book can be of service at a trial that is not kept in order? One might as well ask which are better off, the rich or the poor. Unless trade books are kept in order, this association firmly believes that the court will not give sufficient consideration when they are offered.

Takamatsu. (Answer to Topic 6, Subtopic 2)

There are scores of different trade books, and the form of entry is not fixed for all. Consequently it often happens that those trade books which naturally ought to have legal validity in court unfortunately cannot receive it when needed because they are inadequately kept. It is very important, therefore, to have some fixed rules laid down for the supervision of trade books; this we earnestly desire. Supervision may be indicated, for instance, by drawing a horizontal line or by the impression of a seal. At any rate, it is desirable that rules regarding trade books be formulated in such a way as will be convenient for merchants in general.

Fukui. (Answer to Topic 6, Subtopic 1)

[1] *Kei-in;* same as *wari-in.*
[2] *Chian-saibansho.*
[3] *Ku-yakusho.*
[4] *Gun-yakusho.*

If trade books are kept in good order, they will prove most serviceable at a trial.

Fukui. (Answer to Topic 6, Subtopic 2)

This is most desirable. It is our desire that there should be enacted a law regulating kinds of trade books and the form of entry for merchants in general, and recognizing the validity as evidence of those trade books that are kept in accordance with these regulations.

Tokushima. (Answer to Topic 6, Subtopic 1)

Regardless of whether they are kept in order or not, trade books are never brought into use in a trial. Consequently, there is no question of their being of service.

Tokushima. (Answer to Topic 6, Subtopic 2)

There are no regulations in existence about the supervision of trade books. However, their supervision is earnestly desired in various trades, although we do not have any provisions to suggest.

Takefu. (Answer to Topic 6, Subtopic 1)

There are no fixed rules regarding trade books. None of the trade books are of any service at a trial, regardless of whether they are kept in order or not, with the exception of those which are subject to the revenue stamp regulations.

Takefu. (Answer to Topic 6, Subtopic 2)

The conditions which we desire to be included in the rules regarding the supervision of trade books are as follows:

1. There should be a fixed form of entry, depending on the subject, for the same kind of books.

2. There should be a provision that the entries in the *shôbaihin-kashitsuke-chô* are to be accompanied by the buyer's signature and the impression of his seal.

Miyagi. (Answer to Topic 6, Subtopic 1)

It goes without saying that if the trade books are kept in order, they will prove of service in a trial. But as there are no fixed rules regarding trade books in this district, we cannot say for sure that they will always prove of sufficient service even if they are kept in perfect order.

Miyagi. (Answer to Topic 6, Subtopic 2)

Some here are desirous of having some fixed rules for the supervision of trade books. But since this is an important matter for the future, we cannot express ourselves definitely about it at present.

Matsuyama. (Answer to Topic 6, Subtopic 1)

Trade books kept in disorder are often the cause of disputes. Thus if they are kept in good order, they will prove of service at a trial.

Matsuyama. (Answer to Topic 6, Subtopic 2)

It is desirable that there be a fixed form of entry for trade books. But if rules are made and put into force all at once by official decree,[1] they will cause trouble under the present circumstances. Therefore, what we desire is that instruction be given in the method of bookkeeping by double entry, so that merchants may gradually come to adopt the Western method.

GROUP II—ANSWERS

TOKYO METROPOLIS (Answers to Topic 6, Subtopic 1)

Tokyo Prefectural Office.

Pawnshops.

There is no such utility. Neither is there any desire on our part for enactment of a law for supervision of trade books.

Oil Wholesalers.

If trade books are kept in good order, it proves useful for the traders. It is desirable to have some fixed regulations for the supervision of trade books; but as each of the traders has had his own way of keeping his books in order, it is impossible to state here those general conditions which traders may desire to have formulated.

Dry Goods Wholesalers.

It is believed that books kept in good order will prove useful in trials, while books kept in disorderly style will prove unsatisfactory. But as it is not required by law to keep books in good order, the Association of Drapers cannot make any definite statement about this. It is desirable to have some measure of supervision of trade books, but the association does not have any definite ideas about desirable measures to be formulated, and commercial firms will not change their conventional practice.

Grain Wholesalers.

Those books which are declared by the government to be eligible

[1] *Kanrei.*

for submission at a public hearing will be legally useful (as evidence)
against another party. It is most desirable to have some fixed regulation for the supervision of trade books. But considering that the
merchants of each trade have their own way of keeping books, dif-
ferently from one another, it is hoped that such regulations will
be framed by merchants of different trades in consultation.

Fish Wholesalers.

It is best to keep trade books in good order. Suppose that a fisher-
man or a seashore merchant,[1] for example, wishes to borrow money
in advance,[2] and coming to some wholesaler, asks him to let him
have a loan of, say, 200 *yen*, offering to consign goods to him from
such and such a date on. The wholesaler may at once grant the
request and loan him the money, without making inquiries into
his status[3] and credit,[4] while others may make him sign a deed of
sale. In the latter case the borrower will make out the deed for that
amount to the wholesaler, and the wholesaler will at once hand
him 100 or 150 *yen* of the 200 with only an oral[5] promise to deliver
the remaining sum later. The borrower will consign the goods as
promised and then obtain the payment of the remaining sum. And
as to the goods received from the consignor, the wholesaler, following the ordinary procedure, will make a statement of account de-
ducting the deposit,[6] and send it to the consignor. Now suppose that
the consignor comes to the wholesaler again and asks for another
loan of 50 *yen*, and this is granted. But as it is generally presumed
that he is not the sort of man to carry along his seal with him all
the time, the wholesaler (instead of taking a note or receipt) will
simply make an entry of the advance, in his own *hantori-chô*, and
loan the sum as requested.

Then, if the debtor proves not honest enough to return the money
or to fulfill his promise to consign goods to the wholesale merchant,
the latter would take his *hantori-chô* with him and proceed to the
office of the town magistrate who was in office that term[7] and bring

---

[1] *Isojû shônin.*
[2] *Zenshaku*, or *maegari.*
[3] *Mimoto.*
[4] *Shômon (shôsho).*
[5] *Kuchi-yakusoku.*
[6] *Tomegane.*
[7] *Nen-ban.*

an action against the other party, a proceeding something like the petition for examination[1] today. In one such case, the assistants attached to the town magistrate's office[2] took up[3] a complaint summarily and, summoning the other party from the fishing village where he lived, subjected him to examination. Fish wholesalers were thus accorded a special treatment by the government, for they had been purveyors of fish to the Shogunate.

To be sure, the wholesalers, being aware that their practice of advancing money in the above manner contributed to the lowering of the rates at which they could fix their purchase prices, would not ordinarily demand payment of the money thus advanced, even if the debtor became insolvent.

We cannot make now any definite statement as to what terms for the supervision of trade books should be formulated.

Salt Wholesalers.

None.

Fuel Wholesalers.

Nothing is better than to keep trade books in good order. There is no desire on our part to have uniform regulation (of trade books). However, as to the manner in which the *hantori-chô* must be kept in order to be used as legal evidence, it is sufficient that one make the entry in one's own handwriting, and merely ask the customer to sign his name.

Saké Wholesalers.

There is no inconvenience at all, even if trade books are kept in disorder. For we rely so much on our credit with one another that no lawsuit has ever taken place in our circles. However, there is some desire for fixed regulations.

Dried Bonito Wholesalers.

Nothing is better than to keep trade books in order. It is desirable to have some uniform regulations for trade books, including the books mentioned in our answer to Topic 5,[4] so as to avoid confusion.

Kôjimachi Ward.

Trade books kept in good order will of course prove useful at a trial. The correspondence of certain entries in the *deiri-chô* with

---

[1] *Gimmi-negai; gimmi*, examination; *negai*, petition, request.

[2] *Nenban-tsuki yoriki.*

[3] *Setsuju (juri).*

[4] See page 175.

those in other books, for instance, may establish some fact. For this reason, those books which are not kept in order would be unsatisfactory at a trial, for they would not be sufficiently reliable to establish a fact.

Nihombashi Ward.

Books kept in good order are not of sufficient legal effect to be evidence in a trial, but they furnish necessary materials to refer to for ascertaining the terms of a transaction, the accounts as they stood at the time when a dispute had its origin, etc. Consequently, trade books are convenient to some degree.

Kyôbashi Ward.

We believe that trade books will prove useful or not in a trial, depending upon whether or not they are kept in good order.

Yotsuya Ward and Ushigome Ward.

As trade books possess a certain validity, as already observed in Topic 5,[1] they will be very useful at a trial, depending upon whether they are kept in order or not.

Asakusa Ward.

Does the question mean that a judge will find them useful or not depending upon whether the trade books are kept in good order or not? The question is somewhat ambiguous. If the opinion of a judge is meant, then we are evidently not in a position to guess. If the convenience of the merchant is meant, then it is needless to say that those trade books which are not kept in good order will prove inconvenient at a trial.

Honjo Ward.

We would find trade books useful or not in actual trial according to whether they are kept in good order or not.

Ebara *kôri.*

We would find trade books useful or not in actual trial according to whether they are kept in good order or not.

Higashi-tama *kôri* and Minami-toshima *kôri.*

We would find trade books useful or not in an actual trial according to whether or not they are kept in good order. Especially books such as the *kingin-hantori-chô* and the *nimotsu-hantori-chô* are sufficiently acceptable to be presumptive evidence.

Kita-toshima *kôri.*

---

[1] See page 175.

The answer to this question has already been stated under Topic 5.[1]

Minami-adachi *kôri*.

We sometimes find trade books useful or not in actual trial according to whether they are kept in good order or not.

Shitaya Ward.

We have never heard a comment on the part of ordinary traders to the effect that they benefitted in a trial because they had kept their trade books in perfect order. Also traders make so much of their mutual credibility that they very rarely go to law over a commercial affair. But in our opinion we should find it useful in a trial if our trade books were kept in good order.

Kanda Ward.

We understand that the customary usages[2] (regarding trade books) hitherto in existence have never been found unsatisfactory.

Akasaka Ward and Azabu Ward.

We should find trade books very useful or not according to whether or not they are kept in good order.

Hongô Ward.

According to the present system of justice, decisions in both commercial and other civil cases are all given upon the basis of evidence. So we should find trade books very useful or not according to whether or not they are kept in good order.

CHIBA PREFECTURE

Awa *kôri*, Hei *kôri*, Asai *kôri* and Nagasa *kôri*.

There are few people these days who go to law over commercial matters. But if trade books are kept in good order, they will, in the first place, clear up the misunderstandings of both parties, and prevent the occurrence of lawsuits. Secondly, they would no doubt prove useful in a trial if the merchants do have to go to law. We understand that those merchants who lay great store by their credibility, wishing to prosper in trade, always pay much attention to keeping their trade books in good order.

Katori *kôri*.

If trade books are kept in a disorderly way, this causes much inconvenience to us in public as well as in private matters.

---

[1] See pages 176–177.

[2] *Kanshû-hô;* literally, "customary law."

Yamabe *kôri* and Muza *kôri*.

Trade books will be useful or not in a trial (according to whether or not they are kept in good order). We have spoken of their legal validity in the preceding topic.

Unakami *kôri* and Sôsa *kôri*.

If trade books are kept in good order, we believe they will prove useful.

Higashi-katsushika *kôri*.

We presume that trade books will be useful or not according to whether or not they are kept in good order.

IBARAGI PREFECTURE

Nishi-katsushika *kôri* and Sashima *kôri*.

It often happens that trade books that are not kept in good order are the cause of unfounded disputes leading to lawsuits. Trade books kept in a disorderly way will give not a little inconvenience to the court in actual trial, and the courts (we hear) have much trouble in their examination.

KANAGAWA PREFECTURE

Miura *kôri*.

Trade books that are not kept in good order will be unsatisfactory in a trial.

Tachibana *kôri*.

Trade books will be useful or not in actual trials according to whether or not they are kept in good order.

Kita-tama *kôri*.

Trade books kept in a disorderly way often give rise to difficulty in a trial. However, it is impossible to discuss the utility of trade books. For books kept by commercial firms for entry of credits or loans of money or goods contain, for the most part, merely the creditor's memoranda, in his own handwriting, of the credit or loan granted. They are therefore useful only on moral grounds, and have no legal validity.

Ashigara-shimo *kôri*.

If trade books are to be used satisfactorily in a trial, they had best be kept in good order.

Prefectural Industrial Bureau.

Trade books are unsatisfactory in actual trials, because there are no fixed forms of entry. However, considering that there is no commercial code yet in existence, it is perhaps not right to ascribe the dissatisfaction in court use solely to the disorderly manner in which trade books are kept.

TOCHIGI PREFECTURE

Prefectural Office.

Not only does the usefulness of trade books depend very much on whether they are kept in good order or not, but also, with reference to the preceding topic, some books may be valid as evidence and others may not.

Shimo-tsuga *kôri* and Samukawa *kôri*.

If trade books are kept in good order, they will of course be useful in a trial.

Ashikaga *kôri* and Yanada *kôri*.

Trade books kept in good order have hitherto often proved useful in helping to reveal some misunderstanding or false representation on the part of some traders. In civil cases, however, no trade books are brought into court for examination, so it is impossible to know how they stand in this connection. But judging from our experience, as above stated, here too trade books will certainly be useful or not according to whether or not they are kept in good order.

MIE PREFECTURE

Suzuka *kôri*.

Trade books will of course be useful or not in actual trials according to whether or not they are kept in good order, for the reasons stated in Topic 5.[1]

Isshi *kôri*.

If trade books are kept in order they will be useful.

Asake *kôri*.

It is difficult to cite examples of trade books being useful or not in trials depending upon whether or not they were kept in good order. But if books are kept in as good order as possible, they will be of great help in providing information, even if they may not be valid as evidence.

Nabari *kôri* and Iga *kôri*.

If trade books are not kept in good order, they will be unsatisfactory in trials.

AICHI PREFECTURE

Nakajima *kôri*.

[1] See page 179.

If trade books are not kept in good order, there will be difficulty in trials.

Nagoya Ward.

Trade books will be greatly useful or not, not only in trials but in commerce also, according to whether or not they are kept in good order.

Chita *kôri*.

It makes no difference with respect to usefulness in ordinary commercial affairs whether the trade books are kept in good order or not. But in legal trials those books which are not kept in good order may sometimes give rise to some difficulty.

Minami-shidara *kôri*.

It is true that during the ancient regime of the Shogun there were various kinds of disputes regarding commercial rights, but in most cases they were settled by arbitration or in ceremonial fashion. Even after the Restoration there has been no case of lawsuits regarding this matter in this district. Therefore, people seem to have lost interest in improving their books. It is impossible to describe whether they are convenient or not.

Atsumi *kôri*.

There will be no difficulty in actual trials if the trade books are kept in order.

Kaitô *kôri* and Kaisai *kôri*.

If trade books are kept in good order, they can be very useful in trials.

Aichi *kôri*.

Trade books which are not kept in good order cannot prove payment and receipt of money, and will prove useless in trials.

Niwa *kôri* and Haguri *kôri*.

If trade books are not kept in good order, there will be difficulty in using them in actual trials.

SHIZUOKA PREFECTURE

Prefectural Office.

Though trade books (with two exceptions) cannot be given legal validity as evidence (as has been observed above), those books that are kept in good order will have some utility in legal trials.

Udo *kôri* and Abe *kôri*.

If our trade books are not kept in good order, we shall of course have difficulty.

Inasa *kôri* and Aratama *kôri*.

We sometimes have some difficulty in actual trials because trade books have not been kept in good order.

Kamo *kôri* and Naka *kôri*.

Those books that are not kept in good order will give rise to much difficulty in trials.

Saya *kôri* and Kitô *kôri*.

If trade books are kept in good order, there is no question that they will prove useful in actual trials. But no one would expect to establish proof in a suit at law merely from his trade books. For it is impossible, according to the present practice, to force the other party impress his seal upon the entries.

GIFU PREFECTURE

Mugi *kôri*.

Trade books that are not kept in good order will, we believe, give rise to difficulties (in lawsuits). However, there has been no case yet to illustrate this.

Ampachi *kôri*.

Trade books that are not kept in good order would give rise to difficulties in trial.

Fuwa *kôri*.

Disorder, negligence, etc. in making entries in trade books may cause difficulties. But it would be of great help in a trial if every transaction were entered in trade books at the time it takes place. However, few persons in this district go to law with respect to commercial affairs.

Atsumi *kôri*, Kagami *kôri* and Katagata *kôri*.

If trade books are not kept in good order, no doubt they will prove of little use at a trial. In a few cases such books would even lose their validity (as evidence).

Tagi *kôri* and Kami-ishizu *kôri*.

If trade books are not kept in good order, they will have no validity at a trial, while books kept in good order will prove useful.

Ôno *kôri* and Ikeda *kôri*.

Surely the usefulness of trade books at a trial depends on whether or not they are kept in good order. Commerce usually consists in transactions of receipt or delivery (of goods). These transactions are not accompanied by formal instruments, and a trade book alone is depended upon for recording them. Therefore, the manner in which the trade books are kept—whether they are in good order or not—will have much to do with (their legal effect) at a trial.

Haguri *kôri* and Nakajima *kôri*.

Difficulty at a trial sometimes occurs here because traders have not gotten rid yet of their old practice of keeping their books in a disorderly manner.

Ena *kôri*.

Yes.

Kamo *kôri*.

There can be much difficulty at a trial because trade books are not kept in good order, e.g., the failure to mention the purpose of a certain payment of money in an entry in the *kinsen-hantori-chô*.

Kani *kôri*.

If trade books are not kept in good order, not only will difficulty arise at trials, but also the party that has kept his trade books in disorderly manner will often lose the case.[1]

Atsumi *kôri*, Gifu Township.

If trade books are kept in disorderly manner, there will be much difficulty at trials.

Ôgaki.

If trade books are not kept in good order, there will be difficulty at trials.

Ena *kôri*, Nakatsugawa Village.

Trade books are, for the most part, imperfectly kept at present, and this gives rise to difficulty at trials.

Shimo-ishizu *kôri*, Takasu Township.

In this district, trade books are generally meant for private use, and are not intended to be used at trials. Thus they would hardly lead to difficulty at a trial.

Haguri *kôri*, Takegahana Village.

We believe it is reasonable to expect that trade books will be useful at trials according to whether or not they are kept in good order.

Yamagata *kôri*, Takatomi Village.

If trade books are kept in good order, they will prove useful in actual trials.

Mugi *kôri*, Kôzuchi Village.

---

[1] *Haiso.*

We have not yet met with any case showing any difficulty or lack thereof at a trial because of trade books.

Haguri *kôri*, Kasamatsu Village.

Difficulty occasionally arises [at trials] because people in this locality have not yet gotten rid of their old ways, so as to keep their books in good order.

Fuwa *kôri*, Tarui Village.

There is difficulty at trials because trade books are not kept in good order.

Ôno *kôri*, Miwa Village.

There is practically no utility.

Ampachi *kôri*, Gôdo Village.

Even if trade books are kept in good order, we cannot say for certain whether they will provide any usefulness at trials.

Tagi *kôri*, Shimada Village.

To a great extent, trade books are useful or not at trials, depending upon whether or not they are kept in good order.

Ena *kôri*, Iwa Village.

There is.

Toki *kôri*, Tajimi Village.

The validity as evidence against another party that one's trade book might receive depends merely upon whether its entries have been made every day, the style of penmanship, the colour of ink, etc. Buyers are never asked to stamp their seals with the entries in the trade books. An exception is the *shôbaihin-kashi-chô*, in which the other party is required to stamp his seal.

Kamo *kôri*, Hosome Village.

Trade books may or may not be useful at trials according to whether or not they are kept in good order.

Toki *kôri*, Takayama Village.

Yes.

Kani *kôri*, Mitake Village.

There is.

Ena *kôri*, Akechi Village.

Yes.

Mugi *kôri*, Seki Village.

There is certainly difficulty at trials if trade books are not kept in good order. In this locality, however, we have never heard of a commercial dispute being brought to court.

Ôno *kôri*, Takayama Township.

There is some difficulty in actual practice according to whether trade books are kept in good order or not. For instance, when goods are sold on credit, and the sale is entered temporarily in the *tôza-chô* and posted up later into the *shôbaihin-kashi-chô*, one will have to make an abstract of the entries when he is called upon to bring the book to court. However, there is no legal difficulty at all.

Motosu *kôri*, Kita-kata Village.

If trade books are kept in good order, they will serve as a basis for the findings[1] of judges at trials. But as the books are kept by each merchant for his own convenience, the entries can hardly be accepted as valid evidence unless they are admitted to be true by the defendant in the court. This is so even if the entries have been made entirely in good faith,[2] in regular order of date, with no blank spaces between the entries and without any marginal[3] entries.

Kamo *kôri*, Ôta Village.

There is a good deal of difficulty at trials if the trade books are not kept in good order.

Gujô *kôri*.

As a trade book is hardly more than the individual's assertion based on his memory, we believe it is not useful in trial.

TOKYO METROPOLIS (Answers to Topic 6, Subtopic 2)

Prefectural Office.

The answer has already been given in Subtopic 1.[4]

Kôjimachi Ward.

There are none here who are desirous of having definite rules for the supervision of trade books. They are apparently averse to the troublesome restrictions of such rules.

Nihombashi Ward.

They are apparently not desirous of having definite rules, because each of the merchants has followed the natural traditional usages and has not felt any inconvenience.

Kyôbashi Ward.

None here are desirous of having rules for the supervision of

---

[1] *Shinshô.*

[2] *Seii.*

[3] *Rangai.*

[4] See page 193.

trade books.

Yotsuya Ward and Ushigome Ward.

As for the supervision of the trade books, no merchants here are desirous of having definite regulations under the present circumstances, since they are not inconvenienced by the old customs.

Asakusa Ward.

None here are desirous of having definite rules.

Honjo Ward.

Some are desirous of having definite rules for the supervision of trade books, while the others are not.

Ebara *kôri.*

We have never heard of a merchant who entertains a desire for having definite rules for the supervision of trade books.

Higashi-tama *kôri* and Minami-toshima *kôri.*

Some of the pawnbrokers here are desirous of having definite rules, and they are the only people to entertain such a desire. The pawnbrokers apparently have detailed regulations in the form of traditional usages, but these are no more than mere agreements among themselves. In certain circumstances it sometimes happens that they cannot prove a claim to official satisfaction. Therefore they are apparently desirous of having definite rules enacted by the government.

Minami-adachi *kôri.*

None here are desirous of having definite rules for the supervision of trade books. It is very desirable, however, to have laws enacted that will validate the trade books as legal evidence in the court.

Shitaya Ward.

Some merchants have a desire for the formulation of definite rules for trade books, but they are merely expressing their own ideas. It is difficult to say for certain what the practical terms, desirable for all, would be. Our opinion is that, in view of the fact that merchants have made use of different kinds of trade books, have lacked any uniform methods of entry, and yet have never experienced any inconvenience in practice for several hundred years, it is very difficult for them to break away from the old customs.

Kanda Ward.

As the question concerns all kinds of merchants, it is impossible to say generally what their desires are.

Akasaka Ward and Azabu Ward.

It is desirable:

(I) to fix the varieties of trade books, and classify them into (a) books used for making entry of capital; (b) books for making entry of purchases; (c) books for making entry of payments and receipts of money; (d) books for making entry of debt and credit; and (e) books for making entry of sales and sales prices;

(II) to require each valid trade book to be approved and sealed[1] by the government.

Hongô Ward.

Some merchants desire rules for supervision so that they will not find themselves in possession of divergent sorts of trade books. It is difficult to point out briefly the terms they suggest, but it may be stated that they merely aim at accuracy and convenience.

CHIBA PREFECTURE

Awa *kôri*, Hei *kôri*, Asai *kôri* and Nagasa *kôri*.

It has already been stated how much the merchants here depend on their trade books. Suppose a fire breaks out, for instance. The first thing they invariably do is to try to save their trade books. From this we can see how much they value them. Hence they desire that definite rules be enacted for the supervision of trade books, and that the entries in them be given some special effect.[2] But if we consider the conditions of merchants in the rural districts, we find that there are very few firms with a complete staff, from head clerk[3] to errand boy.[4] Many of the firms are one-man shops, a single person acting at once as proprietor, head clerk, and sales clerk[5] as well as errand boy. Many are operated by husband and wife, or father and son. In most cases, these firms are engaged in the sale of many sorts of goods and require much attention but yield very small returns. This is especially the case with fishmongers. So even if definite rules were laid down for the protection of their interests, the merchants themselves might not be able to observe some of the rules. This will be especially so with those merchants today who are illiterate and unable even to make entries in the *tôza-chô*. There-

---

[1] *Ken-in.*

[2] *Kôyô.*

[3] *Bantô.*

[4] *Detchi.*

[5] *Tedai.*

fore, supervision of trade books is desirable, but it is hoped that it will not prove too burdensome.

Katori *kôri*.

The merchants here apparently have no desire for definite rules for the supervision of trade books.

Yamabe *kôri* and Muza *kôri*.

We have never heard of a person who entertains such a desire.

Unakami *kôri* and Sôsa *kôri*.

If definite rules are made, there will be some practical advantage. As to the terms, we suggest that entries about the payment and receipt of money and the purchase and sale of goods should be made in detail.

Higashi-katsushika *kôri*.

We do not have any such desire.

IBARAGI PREFECTURE

Nishi-katsushika *kôri* and Sashima *kôri*.

There is no desire on the part of merchants here for definite rules for the supervision of trade books. But considering that the disorderly conduct of business and the careless manner of keeping trade books have hitherto often given rise to confusion, it is desirable that some settled forms of entry be prescribed and that other rules be gradually made.

KANAGAWA PREFECTURE

Miura *kôri*.

There is nothing to be desired.

Tachibana *kôri*.

It is desirable to have definite rules, a rule, for instance, requiring the preparation of two kinds of *kayoi-chô* to be used for making entries of debts and credits.

Kita-tama *kôri*.

What we should like to suggest is concerned with the *mono-uriage-chô*, the book used by commercial firms for entry of sales of goods on credit. Books like the *kingin-hantori-chô* and the *nimotsu-hantori-chô* that must be approved and sealed by the authorities have legal effect in a trial, but not all sales of goods require the use of the *nimotsu-hantori-chô*. Hence, if the *uriage-chô*, used for entry of sales of goods on credit, came to require the approval and seal of the authorities, thereby acquiring legal effect, every trader would benefit thereby.

Ashigara-shimo *kôri*.

Ordinarily, no set rules are needed for trade books. But there must be a system of rules if they are to be given credence in a trial,[1] as is the *hantori-chô* today.

Prefectural Industrial Bureau.

It is desirable to have definite rules formulated for the supervision of trade books, as we believe the credit of a trader is affected by whether his trade books are kept in perfect order or not. The adoption of the Western method of bookkeeping by single and double entry is most desirable. But considering that its immediate adoption would be impracticable, it is necessary to prepare a method that is a compromise between the commercial bookkeeping methods used in the Western countries and the traditional method of commercial bookkeeping in Japan. Set forms of entry would be prescribed, so that one might examine the other party's book to verify an account.

TOCHIGI PREFECTURE

Prefectural Office.

They are apparently desirous of having some definite rules for the supervision of trade books. Such rules would stipulate, for instance, that every delivery and receipt of goods or money should be accompanied by an entry in the *hantori-chô*, and that a trade book should bear a revenue-stamp and its entries regarded as corroborative evidence[2] between one party and another. If such definite rules as these are made, they will not only make the trade books trustworthy, but will also add to the public good.

Shimo-tsuga *kôri* and Samukawa *kôri*.

It is our earnest desire to have some definite rules made for the supervision of trade books. It is especially desired that some amendment be made to the general custom regarding the *kayoi-chô*. The essential point of the desired amendment is to provide that the buyer impress his seal in the *kayoi-chô* by way of proof of his purchase from the seller.

Ashikaga *kôri* and Yanada *kôri*.

Practices here are so simple that there are few merchants who keep trade books. Thus those who are in favour of supervision of

---

[1] *Saiban-jo (no) shin'yô.*

[2] *Kaku-shô.*

trade books propose the adoption of a simplified method of book-keeping based upon the Western method, and of some settled forms of entry in current language.

MIE PREFECTURE

Suzuka *kôri.*

None here are desirous of having fixed rules for the supervision of trade books. If the *tôza-chô* and the *daifuku-chô,* for example, which do not possess legal validity as evidence, were to be validated as such, it would cause much trouble to both buyer and seller. Further, these sales are contracts entered into between parties having mutual trust. In case some special proof of a sale is desired, they can verify the transaction by means of a bill of sale or a contract note.

Isshi *kôri.*

Yes, it is. What we wish to suggest is that the buyer should affix his seal to the entry of the sale in the *kashi-watashi-chô.* We also suggest that merchants keep uniform trade books, as for instance, the following:

Books for wholesale merchants,

 (1) the *yorozu-kaiire-chô;*
 (2) the *yorozu-uriage-chô;*
 (3) the *kinsen-suitô-chô;*
 (4) the *nimotsu-deiri-chô;*
 (5) the *kinsen-uketori-chô;*
 (6) the *kinsen-watashi-chô;*
 (7) the *sho-zappi-chô;*[1]
 (8) the *rieki-seisan-chô.*[2]

For brokers,

 (1) the *kyakukata-uri-chô;*
 (2) the *kyakukata-kai-chô;*
 (3) the *kôsen-chô;*
 (4) the *kinsen-suitô-chô;*
 (5) the *kinsen-uketori-chô;*
 (6) the *kinsen-watashi-chô;*
 (7) the *nimotsu-deiri-chô;*
 (8) the *sho-zappi-chô;*

[1] Sundry expenses book.
[2] Profit-accounting book.

(9) the *rieki-seisan-chô*.

For retail merchants,

(1) the *genkin-uriage-chô*;
(2) the *kashiuri-tôza-chô*;
(3) the *daifuku-chô*;
(4) the *kinsen-suitô-cho*;
(5) the *kinsen-watashi-chô*;
(6) the *buppin-kaiire-chô*;
(7) the *sho-zappi-chô*;
(8) the *rieki-seisan-chô*, etc.

Asake *kôri*.

Some here are desirous of having fixed rules for trade books. But if we may judge the general sentiment, people here are apparently generally content with their old practices, considering them the best methods conceivable. If a uniform standard is imposed, they will regard it as so inconvenient that it will be impossible to put it into effect.

Nabari *kôri* and Iga *kôri*.

Not yet.

AICHI PREFECTURE

Nakajima *kôri*.

Occasionally there are merchants who express a desire for fixed rules. But for lack of satisfactory rules, they keep their books as they please. We are still under the impression that it would be impossible to formulate rules at once.

Nagoya Ward.

We have never heard of persons desirous of having fixed rules for trade books.

Chita *kôri*.

It is desired that some fixed rules be formulated, such as will help to make the examination of books simple and easy.

Minami-shidara *kôri*.

Apparently the merchants here are content with their old practices, and there are none who express a desire for new rules.

Atsumi *kôri*.

It is desired that fixed rules be made. That would make for greater convenience in checking entries against each other.

Kaitô *kôri* and Kaisai *kôri*.

There are few people here who express such a desire.

Aichi *kôri*.

People here are content with their trade books and with the names hitherto in use, and are abiding by them. We have never heard of any persons expressing a desire for settled rules for the supervision of trade books.

Niwa *kôri* and Haguri *kôri*.

The merchants here have a desire for settled rules for the supervision of trade books, but they have no specific terms to suggest.

SHIZUOKA PREFECTURE

Prefectural Office.

It is not known yet whether there are any persons who entertain a desire for settled rules for the supervision of trade books.

Udo *kôri* and Abe *kôri*.

We have never heard of any persons expressing a desire for settled rules.

Inasa *kôri* and Aratama *kôri*.

Only wholesale traders entertain a desire for settled rules. One such rule would be for the appointment of a group-chief[1] for every ten commercial houses. This person, on examining the trade books submitted to him for the purpose very ten or fifteen days by the members of the group, would approve the entries if he deems them proper, and stamp his seal of inspection. These entries would then have validity as evidence for the future.

Saya *kôri* and Kitô *kôri*.

It is not desirable to have settled rules about trade books for all, for it is feared that many persons are likely to be inconvenienced by such rules. However, if some forms of entry were prescribed and the traders were gradually induced to follow them, and were to learn that entries according to the prescribed forms would have considerable utility in trials, this might be expected to lead to a reform of the subject.

Kamo *kôri* and Naka *kôri*.

Apparently merchants here have a desire for some settled rules, such as the following:

1. The varieties of trade books used and their designations should be fixed.

---

[1] *Kumi-chô.*

2.   Each trade book should be made of ruled paper.

3.   Each trade book should be examined by the authorities, and, on approval, be stamped on the margin with their stamp of inspection.

4.   Entries should follow the order of dates, with no blank lines between entries.

5.   At the end of each year, entries should be made in each book of the sum total of moneys dealt with therein, etc.

GIFU PREFECTURE

Mugi *kôri.*

None here has a desire for settled rules.

Ampachi *kôri.*

It is desirable to have settled rules for the supervision of trade books, some simple rules, for instance, such as declaring the validity as evidence against others of a trade book.

Fuwa *kôri.*

Apparently none here have such a desire.

Atsumi *kôri,* Kagami *kôri* and Katagata *kôri.*

We cannot expect to have "happiness in commerce"[1] unless we are exempt from fixed control of trade books. We have no terms to suggest, but it is essential that trade books be supervised effectively.

Tagi *kôri* and Kami-ishizu *kôri.*

The merchants here are not yet advanced enough in their views to have a desire for settled rules for the supervision of trade books.

Ôno *kôri* and Ikeda *kôri.*

Needless to say, trade books are a necessity in commerce. Therefore, it is natural to expect that merchants should desire to have some settled rules for them. But they are not advanced enough in their knowledge, and none of them express such a desire. It is our own desire, however, that some settled rules be made by legislative or administrative measures. It is very difficult to specify the terms, but the essential thing is that the varieties of trade books and the forms of entry be fixed for all.

Haguri *kôri* and Nakajima *kôri.*

It is desirable to have some settled rules, but it would be difficult to put them into effect immediately under present conditions.

---

[1] *Shôgyô-jô-no kôfuku.*

Ena *kôri*.

If there is any method that is simple and worthy of trust by others, we shall be glad to have it. But the troublesome Western method of bookkeeping is impracticable.

Kamo *kôri*.

We should like to have the following type of settled rules for the supervision of trade books. They should be very simple, but should be of such a nature as to invest the trade books with sufficient validity as evidence. And the books should be so kept that when there is an error in calculation[1] or other mistake, the cause can be readily discovered.

Kani *kôri*.

Some among the wealthier class of merchants have such a desire, but on the other hand they dislike the trouble involved, which is always the case with human nature. This is even more with the merchants of the middle class and downward, who are thus apparently rather opposed to the desire of the upper-class merchants.

Such being the situation, we do not yet know the terms desired by them.

Atsumi *kôri*, Gifu Township.

It is most desirable to have some settled rules for the supervision of trade books, especially rules about the *uri-chô*, the *jai-chô*, the *tôza-chô* and the *kinsen-deiri-chô*.

Ôgaki Township.

It is desirable to have some settled rules for the supervision of trade books, some simple rules, for instance, about the validity of trade books as evidence against others.

Ena *kôri*, Nakatsugawa Village.

Since commercial transactions are based upon mutual trust, merchants have trouble when their trade book entries are not in order.

Shimo-ishizu *kôri*, Takasu Township.

As each commercial house has its own practices, we have never heard of any persons here expressing a desire for settled rules. Even though some persons may desire such rules, it would be very difficult to put them into effect under the present circumstances.

Haguri *kôri*, Takegahana Village.

[1] *Isan.*

We are unable to formulate a method for the supervision of trade books, but we believe it is necessary to have some fixed rules for such books in commerce.

Yamagata *kôri*, Takatomi Village.

We are desirous of having some fixed rules. Our suggestion is that the various kinds of merchants be required to use specific sorts of books.

Mugi *kôri*, Kôzuchi Village.

None here are desirous of having fixed rules.

Haguri *kôri*, Kasamatsu Village.

It is desirable to have some fixed rules, but we believe it would be difficult to put them into effect at present.

Fuwa *kôri*, Tarui Village.

None here express such a desire.

Ôno *kôri*, Miwa Village.

It is desirable to have some fixed rules for supervision. As to the terms of the rules, we have nothing to suggest yet, but will later give you an answer on this point.

Ampachi *kôri*, Gôdo Village.

If there were some fixed rules for the supervision of trade books, we believe it would be very useful, but none in this village have yet expressed a desire for such fixed rules.

Ena *kôri*, Iwa Village.

If there is any simple method [of entry] which would entitle a book to receive the confidence of others, we should like to have it adopted.

Toki *kôri*, Tajimi Village.

It is desirable to have some fixed rules for trade books. However, simple modes of entry are here the general practice. The adoption of the new method of bookkeeping would mean more trouble and more expense to those who adopt it. Consequently, those who preserved the simple method of entry, at less trouble and expense, would be able to undersell,[1] while those who are obliged to incur more expense would be outdone in business by their rivals and would finally be compelled to return to the simplified practice. So it would be very desirable in the keeping of books[2] if all merchants

---

[1] *Yasuuri-suru.*

[2] *Chôai;* older word for *boki.*

were required by regulation to adopt the Western method of book-keeping.

Kamo *kôri*, Hosome Village.

It would be useful, if possible, to have some fixed rules for the supervision of trade books. It is desirable that the rules should be simple and easy to understand, especially for the lower class of merchants. It would be most useful if the causes of disputes regarding debts and credits, etc., could in future be removed by such rules.

Toki *kôri*, Takayama Village.

There are no such practices in existence here.

Kani *kôri*, Mitake Village.

It is desirable. But we have not yet deliberated upon the precise terms.

Ena *kôri*, Akechi Village.

If there is any method of keeping books which is simple but will ensure their credibility, we would like to have it. But we are not skilled enough to use such a troublesome method as the European method of bookkeeping.

Mugi *kôri*, Seki Village.

We have no desire at all for any rules.

Ôno *kôri*, Takayama Township.

We believe there is no supervision of trade books in effect today. When the Civil Code comes into force, however, it is difficult at present to say whether it will bring about improvement or not.

Motosu *kôri*, Kita-kata Village.

It is desirable that a system be adopted by regulation whereby a proper official is empowered to issue a certificate recognizing the legal validity as evidence of a trade book when its entries are made in accordance with some prescribed forms.

Kamo *kôri*, Ôta Village.

If some fixed rules are to be made for the supervision of trade books, it is desirable to include some provisions whereby the validity as evidence of a trade book can be established, as well as rules which would help to settle disputes that might arise in future. However, it is also desirable that the rules should be simple and easy to understand, especially for the lower class of merchants.

CHAPTER II
COMMERCIAL MORTGAGES AND LIENS

Topic 1: Is There Any Difference between Commercial and Civil Mortgages?

GROUP I—ANSWERS

Tokyo.

There is nothing in a commercial mortgage differentiating it from a civil mortgage. It is to be noted, however, that when the forwarding agent holds goods on consignment and loans money to the consignor, it has been the practice hitherto in many cases not to require the making of any deed.

Kyoto.

We have never heard of a practice of mortgaging for commercial purposes only. Suppose, however, persons engaged in coastal trade,[1] calling at various ports and loading their ship with the local products they had purchased, arrived at a certain port, and then unloaded the goods with a view to consigning them for sale to some wholesale merchants in that port. But before they could come to terms with the wholesalers, they decided to set sail from the port to take advantage of the wind. In such a case the coastal traders may leave their goods in pledge with the wholesalers. They would set sail after making a rough estimate of the market prices of the goods and obtaining partial payment in advance from the wholesalers. They usually make a contract with the wholesalers about the prices at which they would dispose of the goods to the latter, before consigning them for sale. Settlement of the accounts may be made between the parties when the ship re-enters the port, or by exchange of correspondence, by checking the advance loan and interest thereon with the sales returns of the goods and then repaying the deficit or being paid the excess.

Ordinary merchants do not resort to a mortgage in buying or selling goods. But the lower class of merchants, when they do not

---

[1] *Kaisen-shô;* this ordinarily means shipping agents, but here it is apparently used in the sense of merchant service, or, more particularly, coastal trade.

have funds enough to buy some goods, proceed (so we hear, though it is rather rare) to purchase the goods by mortgaging their real estate to secure payment until they can pay off the mortgage with the sales proceeds of the goods.

Or again, when an artisan or a middleman finds it difficult to sell to wholesalers or other regular customers the goods he has made or purchased from various sources because of some sudden change in the market price or the unsuitable nature of the goods for the market, etc., then he may mortgage the goods [and consign them for sale] and borrow money on interest, specifying the month of repayment,[1] the rate of interest, etc. If the goods have not been sold at a price limited[2] by the "month of promise," the consignor may renounce his right to the goods. Or if the market prices of the goods fall in the "month of promise," he pays the difference. In any case, the terms of promise as first agreed upon would be adhered to.

Taking these things into consideration, we believe there is not much difference between a mortgage made by an ordinary man and that made by a merchant.

Osaka.

A mortgage is an article given by the mortgagor to the mortgagee as security that the mortgagor will do what he has promised to do when the time of promise comes. There is nothing in the nature of a mortgage that differentiates a civil mortgage from a commercial one. But they differ with respect to the occasion for mortgaging and the terms of agreement between the parties. As there has been no noticeable difference between a civil and a commercial transaction, as far as customs go, it is difficult to give a definite answer to the question. However, generally speaking, the civil mortgage requires rather elaborate procedures, while commercial mortgages are rather simple. If, in a civil transaction, one wishes to mortgage, for instance, one's real estate or chattels for the purpose of borrowing money or obtaining the loan of some grain, one would make out an instrument. In the case of real estate, one would make a "public deed,"[3] i.e., a deed attested by the head of the town or

---

[1] *Kigetsu;* more usually "month of promise."

[2] *Sashi-nedan,* or *sashine.*

[3] *Kôshô.*

village[1] where the person lives, find a surety, and seal the deed with his legal seal, etc. In a commercial mortgage he has only to give or receive a memorandum,[2] a receipt or a letter of deposit,[3] etc., and stamp his seal on it.[4]

In short, a civil mortgage arises from a loan and is mostly subject to special rules, while a commercial mortgage arises from a business transaction and is customarily arranged by contract, case by case.

In commercial language, a mortgage is sometimes called *heigô*, i.e., amalgamation.

Yokohama.

There is no essential difference between a civil mortgage and a commercial mortgage. However, if a broker,[5] who is engaged in selling to foreign traders here [at a trade port] goods consigned to him for sale by provincial merchants advances money to the consignor on the goods, the practice is, of course, that no deed is necessary. Nor is any special contract required. Furthermore, the broker is at liberty to dispose of the goods without the consent of the consignor. So it happens that some commission agents may even refuse to grant an advance[6] to the consignor on the goods if the sales price has already been fixed by the latter.

Hyôgo.

A commercial mortgage differs from a civil one.

Proceedings of the Investigation Committee meeting.

No. 3 [Kondô]: There is something in a commercial mortgage that differentiates it from a civil mortgage. In commercial language, a commercial mortgage is called *kawase*,[7] not *teitô*.[8] There is no difference between them however, with respect to the procedure for leaving an article in the hands of another party and borrowing money from him.

No. 27 [Arima]: There is considerable difference. In civil transactions a mortgagee may not execute a mortgage upon an article which he has been holding in bailment. But in commerce a merchant (such as a com-

---

[1] *Kochô.*
[2] *Hagaki.*
[3] *Azukari-shô.*
[4] *Oshikiri-ban (wari-in* or *wari-han).*
[5] *Urikomi-shô.*
[6] *Kawase-kin;* see the following passages under *Hyôgo.*
[7] *Kawase* usually means "exchange."
[8] An ordinary term for "mortgage."

mission agent) may sometimes mortgage the goods which he has been holding in bailment. Recently, certain commission agents mortgaged to a bank the goods of a consignor which they had been holding in bailment. A controversy then arose between the parties, and the case was laid before the court, which (I hear) has adjudged the mortgage [improper] on the ground that the property of the other party had been mortgaged without his consent. If this report is true, the mortgage will not have validity as such, and will surely result in a loss to the bank. In future no one will lend money to merchants on the security of their merchandise. This will affect business in an unfavourable way and bring about a tightness of the money market.[1] Not only will the money market be tight, but merchants will also be inconvenienced and at a disadvantage. Hitherto no objection has been known in the case of commission agents executing a mortgage on goods which they had been holding in bailment. Such has been the customary practice. In this respect a commercial mortgage differs from a civil mortgage.

No. 3 [Kondô]: The mortgagor is only required to make entry of a *kawase*, that is, a commercial mortgage, in his *hantori-chô*, and in many cases no instrument is required. Also, in advancing a mortgage loan in commerce, if the mortgaged goods are worth ¥100, the lender may advance as much as ¥100. But in a civil mortgage this is different. In most cases lenders will not advance any more than 70 or 80 percent of the value of the mortgaged goods.

No. 19 [Funai]: *Kawase* and *teitô* are different only in name; substantially they are the same. Therefore I believe there is no difference between a civil and a commercial mortgage.

No. 9 [Takahama]: In civil affairs, it is always necessary to affix a revenue stamp commensurate with the sum loaned to the deed of loan.[2] This is not necessary, however, for a loan on a commercial mortgage.

No. 1 [Ikeda]: If there is any demand for it, a commercial mortgage can be redeemed at any time or be sold. But a civil mortgage generally cannot be redeemed until the time when it is due.

No. 4 [Kishi]: What would be done if, after money has been loaned as described by No. 3, the money is not repaid nor the goods redeemed? I should like to ask the opinion of those of you who have had experiences with this.

No. 3 [Kondô]: Business depends so much upon mutual trust that such a dilemma never occurs. Some time ago, I was going to ship some silk to certain commission agents at Yokohama and sent a telegram to

---

[1] *Kin'yû-no-hippaku.*
[2] *Taishaku-shô.*

them asking for an advance loan as soon as the goods were stowed aboard the S.S. Hyôgo-maru. They promptly sent me a telegraphic money order[1] through the branch office here of the Daiichi Bank. This is how a commercial loan differs from a civil loan.

No. 6 [Hamada]: There is a great difference between *kawase* and *teitô*. If, for instance, a man in Tokyo has a certain sum of money due to be paid him at Kôbe, and a man in Kôbe also has a certain sum of money to be paid him at Tokyo (as it would cost them some expense to receive their moneys respectively at Kôbe and Tokyo) they can arrange the matter so that the man of Tokyo can receive what the man of Kôbe is to receive at Tokyo and vice versa. Such an arrangement is called *kawase*.[2]

Chairman of the Committee [Kashima]: Shall we then report to the effect that there are some differences between commercial mortgage and a civil mortgage?

The members present unanimously agreed to this proposal.

Ôtsu.

A commercial mortgage is naturally different from a civil mortgage. For a commercial mortgage is much more liberal in its terms than a civil mortgage. And a commercial mortgage can be arranged in such a way that the mortgaged goods can be disposed of before the loan is due (which cannot be done in a civil mortgage). The two differ in other respects as well.

Kumamoto.

There is certainly some difference between a commercial mortgage and a civil mortgage. In a commercial mortgage, it is usually the practice not to make any instrument, but to hold the goods in bailment and advance loans on them.

Okayama.

A commercial mortgage is naturally different from a civil mortgage. One point of difference is in the sort of commercial practice described later in our answer to Topic 4. A second difference that may be cited is the practice that when commission agents or middlemen hold goods in bailment and advance loans on them they do not require any instrument.

Bakan.

There is no difference.

---

[1] *Denshin-kawase.*

[2] The word is used here in the sense of exchange, or money order, which is the more ordinary meaning of the word.

Sakai.

There is some difference between a commercial and a civil mortgage. A civil mortgage usually requires an instrument, but a commercial mortgage does not. Also, there is a practice among wholesalers that, when they cannot reach an agreement with the consignor about the prices of the goods which they want to purchase or which have been consigned to them, they may hold the goods in bailment and advance money on them.

It may be added that what our association calls *teitô* in our answer to the questionnaire has been considered with reference to the following old practices:

Oki-jichi.[1] This word refers to the practice of borrowing money by leaving some articles as security[2] in the hands of a bailee.[3]

Ire-jichi. This word refers to the practice of borrowing money by bringing some article as security to an obligee.[4]

Kaitsuke-machiai. This word refers to the merchants' practice of borrowing or lending money from or to a fellow trader[5] by leaving or taking some goods as bailment in his hands or from him. The word was derived from the merchants' practice (called by the same name in the old [Tokugawa Shogunate] government days) of mutual help in financial matters among traders by lending money; for it was prohibited for a merchant who did not hold a share in the pawnbrokers' guild[6] to lend or borrow money on pledges of articles. The name is still retained to this day.

Iida.

A commercial mortgage is different from a civil mortgage. As it continues only until the goods are sold, a commercial mortgage is not accompanied by the delivery or receipt of an instrument. Even when an instrument is given, it amounts to merely a few lines on a little piece of paper, stamped with the *shikiri-ban*[7] of the two parties —a very simple affair.

Takamatsu.

---

[1] *Oki-shichi*.

[2] *Hikiate (teitô)*.

[3] *Okinushi*.

[4] *Saishu (saikensha* or creditor).

[5] *Dôgyô-sha*.

[6] *Shichi-kabu; shichi*, pawn; *kabu*, share.

[7] Trading-seals.

There is no special difference between a commercial and a civil mortgage, with the single exception that when wholesalers take some goods in bailment, it has been the usual practice hitherto not to require any instrument.

Fukui.

A commercial mortgage and a civil mortgage are sometimes different.

Tokushima.

There is no difference between a commercial and a civil mortgage.

Takefu.

Both in commercial and civil cases, mortgage is dependent upon terms stated in the contract and is treated as in the case of a civil suit.

Miyagi.

There is no special difference between a commercial and a civil mortgage. But with respect to the procedure of mortgaging, a commercial mortgage is chiefly dependent upon mutual trust between merchants, and being basically informal in nature, does not require any instrument. An example would be the case of wholesalers advancing money to consignors upon goods left in bailment.

Matsuyama.

A commercial mortgage is based mainly upon convenience, and the merchandise, trade books and bills serve as evidence of the mortgages. Therefore, it is naturally different from a civil mortgage.

GROUP II—ANSWERS

Tokyo Metropolis

Pawnshops.

There is no difference.

Oil Wholesalers.

There is no difference. But when wholesalers take goods from a consignor in bailment and advance money on them to the consignor, according to current practice they do not require any instrument, but simply make an entry in their *hantori-chô* or draw up a bill of exchange.

Dry Goods Wholesalers.

There is no practice of mortgaging in our trade.

Timber Wholesalers.

There is no distinction between a commercial and a civil mortgage. What is called *hikiate*, or mortgage, among timber traders consists in advancing (for instance) ¥700 or ¥800 upon so many thousand pieces of timber worth ¥1,000. When the mortgage is due, the obligor[1] may dispose of the goods as he likes to repay the loan, or the obligor may ask the obligee to put the goods at auction, so that he may settle the accounts of principal and interest. It may be noted, however, that the auction is not meant primarily for liquidation of the debt: a sale among fellow traders always takes place by auction.

Grain Wholesalers.

There is a practice called *kura-jichi*[2] that consists in mortgaging grain as it is warehoused. The practice is also called *hachibu-kin*,[3] and consists in advancing a sum equivalent to 80 percent of the worth of the goods in bailment. If the market price comes down, current practice dictates that the obligor give money to the obligee to cover[4] the loss due to the fall in price.

A civil mortgage is naturally different from a commercial mortgage.

Fish Wholesalers.

There is no difference. For fishmongers have a special way of advancing money to fishermen that may resemble mortgaging by wholesalers. When, for instance, fishermen make fishing nets or build fishing boats, wholesalers provide them with money equivalent to 60 to 70 percent of the necessary expense, and then lend the net or boat, the property of the wholesalers, to the fishermen or the fish dealers on the seashore. Thus the obligors never give anything in pledge. But from time to time, as they ship their catch to the wholesalers, the latter deduct by degrees the purchase prices from the advances they have granted to the fishermen whenever a settlement of account is made, until the advances are entirely repaid.

Nowadays, however, some wholesalers have changed their old practice, and require of their obligors an instrument of loan, nam-

---

[1] *Fusai-shu;* opposed to *saishu*, obligee.

[2] *Kura*, warehouse; *jichi* (*shichi*), pledge.

[3] *Hachibu*, 80 percent; *kin*, money.

[4] *Sashi-kin-o-ireuru; sashi-kin*, covering money.

ing their rice and other fields, etc. as security.[1]

Fuel Wholesalers.

Consignors may sometimes borrow money from wholesalers on the security of their timber lands.[2] This is called *purchase-mortgage*,[3] and binds the mortgagor to consign all the wood and charcoal[4] produced from the forest to the wholesaler from whom he has borrowed money until the whole loan is reapid—not more than five years. A commercial mortgage is thus very different from a civil mortgage. Among fellow traders wood and charcoal are also put in mortgage.

Saké Wholesalers.

All transactions are based upon credit, and no recourse is made to a mortgage for loans.

Dried Bonito Wholesalers.

A mortgage comes into being when, for instance, a consignor who has made a shipment to wholesalers refrains from disposing of the goods at once on account of a fall in the price, and leaving the goods in bailment with the wholesalers, borrows money from them. In such a case the practice is that if the goods are quoted at that time at (e.g.) ¥1,000 per 100 barrels, the wholesalers will grant a loan of what is called "70 percent money"[5] or "80 percent money,"[6] at the rate of ¥700 to ¥800. Thus the advance is in the nature of part payment[7] of purchase. The consignor may ask the wholesalers to sell the goods if their market price goes up to (say) ¥12 a barrel. It is the rule of the trade to charge interest on the loan and the warehouse rent, but in practice these charges are not usually levied, and when the account is settled, only the advances are deducted [from the prices got by the wholesalers]. Thus a commercial mortgage is different from a civil mortgage.

Salt Wholesalers.

There is a practice of borrowing money on the security of goods that have been stored in a warehouse. This is usually called "60

[1] *Kakiire.*

[2] *San-rin.*

[3] *Shiire-hikiate;* probably so called from the mortgagee's side.

[4] *Shin-tan; shin,* firewood; *tan,* charcoal.

[5] *Shichibu-kin.*

[6] *Hachibu-kin.*

[7] *Uchi-kin.*

percent money,"[1] and allows a loan up to an amount representing 60 percent of the value of the whole stock. The term is usually three or six months.

Kôjimachi Ward.

In this ward there is no difference at all between a commercial and a civil mortgage.

Nihombashi Ward.

There are some merchants here who make an agreement with a moneylender that they will place their land, building, share certificates, etc. in bailment with him. This is known as "foundation mortgage,"[2] and whenever there arises a need for money, it is understood that they shall at once be entitled to borrow money from him. In the point of rights and obligations,[3] a commercial mortgage is not different from a civil mortgage. There is a great difference, however, in the actual transactions of the two.

Kyôbashi Ward.

There is some difference between a commercial and a civil mortgage.

Yotsuya Ward and Ushigome Ward.

There is no settled practice about the matter, this depending upon the contract in each case.

Asakusa Ward.

There is a great difference between a commercial and a civil mortgage. For in a commercial mortgage the mortgagor often estimates roughly the sales prices of the mortgaged goods and asks the mortgagee to sell them. But there is nothing of the sort in a civil mortgage.

Honjo Ward.

There is some difference between a commercial and a civil mortgage. For when a fuel dealer mortgages his merchandise, it is a commercial mortgage, but if he mortgages his land, house, etc., it is a civil mortgage.

Ebara *kôri*.

There is no difference between a commercial and a civil mortgage.

---

[1] *Rokubu-kin.*

[2] *Ne-deitô(teito).*

[3] *Kenri*, right; *gimu*, obligation.

Higashi-tama *kôri* and Minami-toshima *kôri*.

The sort of commercial mortgage that is referred to in this question [Topic 1] is represented here by what is called *kura-jichi*,[1] and consists in holding grain or other goods in bailment, and lending money equivalent to 70 or 80 percent of the value of the goods. The storage-pledge is different from the ordinary pledge[2] in that although an instrument is made and the time of repayment is stipulated in a general way, there is no foreclosure. A commercial mortgage is different from a civil mortgage in points such as these.

Kita-toshima *kôri*.

A commercial mortgage takes place when goods have been delivered for sale, but no agreement can be reached about the prices. The consignors will leave the goods in bailment, and borrow money from the consignee, the prices to be fixed later. In such cases the loan is seldom treated as interest-bearing. For even if the loan may not be made to yield interest, the equivalent can be reckoned in fixing the sale prices. Consequently there is no practice of exchanging instruments between the parties in a commercial mortgage, and in this again it is slightly different from a civil mortgage. Furthermore, a merchant who has once had some goods consigned to him and has advanced money to the consignor usually does not like to return the goods to the consignor even if he were to be repaid the principal with interest.

Minami-adachi *kôri*.

There is nothing in a commercial mortgage that is different from a civil mortgage.

Shitaya Ward.

There is nothing particular in a civil mortgage that is different from a commercial mortgage. However, in a commercial mortgage, when wholesalers advance a loan to the consignor on the goods which have been delivered to them or have been promised to be delivered in future, it has usually not been required hitherto (it is said) to make an instrument.

Kanda Ward.

There is no particular difference. However, in commercial mortgage practice, no instrument is required.

---

[1] *Kura*, warehouse, or storage; *jichi* (*shichi*), pledge.
[2] *Shichi*.

Akasaka Ward and Azabu Ward.

There is some difference [between a commercial and a civil mortgage]. Suppose a consignee, for instance, advances money to the consignor on the arrival of a cargo.[1] Or, in the case of a wholesaler and a retail merchant, suppose the retailer deposits some money as security[2] with the wholesaler, who in turn sends to the retailer goods worth two or three times as much as the deposit. In a commercial mortgage like this, no instrument at all is required, and sometimes a loan is made on sheer credit. But if the parties do exchange instruments even though it is a commercial mortgage, it is no different from a civil mortgage.

Hongô Ward.

There is some difference. In a commercial mortgage the rate of interest is lower than in a civil mortgage. Also if the mortgagor repays the principal, he can redeem the goods in bailment at any time.

CHIBA PREFECTURE

Awa *kôri*, Hei *kôri*, Asai *kôri* and Nagasa *kôri*.

A commercial mortgage is, in most cases, different from a civil mortgage. In a civil mortgage it is mostly immovables that are put in pledge, and a notarial act attested by the town or village head, or some other elaborate procedure is required. A commercial mortgage, however, depends on mutual credit, and not on the worth of the goods pledged. When money is advanced on the goods, the mortgagee holds them in pledge. If the mortgagor fails to repay the loan, the mortgagee has only to sell the goods and recover principal and interest, etc. The procedure is very simple in a commercial mortgage.

In a fishing village they sometimes borrow money on the dried sardines[3] that are still on the drying ground[4] or on oilcakes.[5]

Under these circumstances disputes sometimes occur, as (for instance) when A advances money to another without being aware that B has also advanced money to the same person. In short the transactions mong merchants and fishermen are so lively and the

---

[1] *Chaku-ni.*

[2] *Mimoto-kin.*

[3] *Hoshi-iwashi.*

[4] *Hoshi-ba.*

[5] *Shimekasu.*

settlement term is so short that the procedure regarding the exchange of instruments is exceptionally simple.

Katori *kôri*.

A commercial mortgage is different from a civil mortgage; for among merchants it is mostly merchandise that is mortgaged.

Yamabe *kôri* and Muza *kôri*.

There is no difference at all between a commercial and a civil mortgage.

Unagami *kôri* and Sôsa *kôri*.

There is no difference between a commercial and a civil mortgage.

Higashi-katsushika *kôri*.

There is no difference between a civil and a commercial mortgage, except that, in mortgaging immovables, there is a rule in the civil mortgage requiring a notarial act attested by the town or village head.

IBARAGI PREFECTURE

Nishi-katsushika *kôri* and Sashima *kôri*.

There is no difference between a commercial and a civil mortgage with respect to procedure.

KANAGAWA PREFECTURE

Miura *kôri*.

A commercial mortgage is limited to merchandise, while a civil mortgage deals with movables and immovables.

Tachibana *kôri*.

There is some difference. When a fuel dealer, for instance, mortgages his merchandise, it is a commercial mortgage; but if he mortgages his land[1] or house,[2] it is a civil mortgage.

Kita-tama *kôri*.

In procedure, there is no difference between a commercial and a civil mortgage.

Ashigara-shimo *kôri*.

There is some difference in practice between a commercial and a civil mortgage.

Prefectural Industrial Bureau.

When the commission agents for a sale to foreign merchants

---

[1] *Jisho.*
[2] *Kaoku.*

receive a consignment of goods for sale, and advance money to the consignor upon the goods, no instrument is required. And according to the local practice, the agents are at liberty to dispose of the goods without the consent of the consignor.

TOCHIGI PREFECTURE

Prefectural Office.

There is something in a commercial mortgage that is different from a civil mortgage. Suppose a merchant mortgages his merchandise and borrows money from another merchant (an instrument may or may not be prepared depending upon each case) and fails to repay the money within the prescribed term of settlement. Then the obligee, according to the usual practice here, is at liberty to dispose of the goods and out of the sales price to recover principal and interest. If there is a surplus or shortage, it will all revert to the obligee as his gain or loss. There is never any difficulty over balancing the accounts.

Shimo-tsuga *kôri* and Samukawa *kôri*.

There is amost no difference between a commercial and a civil mortgage.

Ashikaga *kôri* and Yanada *kôri*.

A commercial mortgage is different from a civil mortgage with respect to the articles pledged and the motives for mortgaging. The articles for commercial mortgages here consist of those kinds of merchandise for which there will be no demand after certain months of the year. There are two motives for mortgaging. First, merchants mortgage goods which are not in demand during a certain period of the year (as they expect), so that they may apply the money thus borrowed to an increase in the supply of other merchandise for which there is greater demand. Or, second, in order to expedite matters they mortgage certain goods which they have in abundance and fill the immediate shortage of other goods.

The second case is the same in other localities, so no more reference will be made to it here. Regarding the first case, suppose there is a manufacturer who is in fact more of a merchant, and who, anticipating some profit, wishes to manufacture during summer an abundant quantity of textile fabrics[1] for winter clothes. Then he may place those fabrics he has already manufactured in pledge to

---

[1] *Orimono.*

some middlemen, borrow money on them, and continue manufacturing the same goods until he has a large supply of textile
fabrics ready. The middlemen, who are the mortgagees now, know
that the pledged goods will be redeemed almost without fail when
winter comes. Or, in case the mortgagor cannot redeem the goods,
they expect that they can assume the title to the goods and sell them
to their regular customers or others. Therefore, at the request of
the mortgagor, they are usually willing to lend ¥900-odd on goods
worth ¥1,000.

Thus a commercial mortgage, where the loan is granted on a
fair prospect of business, is quite different from a civil mortgage,
where the loan is granted only upon the value of the pledged goods,
and does not amount to more than one half of the value of the
goods.

MIE PREFECTURE

Suzuka *kôri.*

There is no difference between a commercial mortgage and a
civil mortgage.

Isshi *kôri.*

There is some difference. A civil mortgage is accompanied by
an instrument, while a commercial mortgage consists only in the
transfer of goods.

Asake *kôri.*

A commercial mortgage differs somewhat from a civil mortgage
in the following way. Suppose, for instance, some merchants from
a place called A consign some goods to B wholesalers for sale, but
the two sides are unable to come to terms about the sales prices.
The A merchants may then leave the goods in bailment with the
B wholesalers and borrow money on them until they can come to
agreement with the wholesalers and ask them to sell the goods at
some specified terms. This is called sale at a specified price.[1] This
is an instance of a [commercial] mortgage that does not have any
stipulated time limit [which is not the case with a civil mortgage].

Nabari *kôri* and Iga *kôri.*

Apparently there is no difference between a commercial and a
civil mortgage. However, there are some merchants who, before
they agree about the sales prices of their goods, borrow money on

---

[1] *Sashine-uri.*

them equivalent to 70 to 80 percent of the estimated sales value[1] of the goods, and balance their accounts after the sales transaction is concluded. In such a case the advance loan is usually made to bear no interest. However, the loan is sometimes interest-bearing. And when it is interest-bearing, the mortgagee is not at liberty to dispose of the pledged goods at his pleasure.

AICHI PREFECTURE

Nakajima *kôri.*

A commercial mortgage consists simply in the transfer of goods, or the signing a paper for an unsecured[2] loan.

Nagoya Ward.

There is no particular difference.

Chita *kôri.*

A commercial mortgage is executed by an ordinary contract, while a civil mortgage requires a notarial act attested by the town or village authorities. The two kinds of mortgages are different from each other in that point. But when a thing is to be mortgaged that does not need any notarial act, there is not much difference between a civil and a commercial mortgage.

Minami-shidara *kôri.*

Here they are not aware of any distinction between a commercial and a civil mortgage. In the execution of a mortgage they are apparently following the local practice in regard to the lending and borrowing of money.

Atsumi *kôri.*

There naturally is some difference between a commercial and civil mortgage. For a commercial mortgage does not need any surety, but a civil mortgage does.

Kaitô *kôri* and Kaisai *kôri.*

A commercial mortgage consists mostly of chattels, and never of real property. Hence there is a great difference between a commercial and a civil mortgage.

Aichi *kôri.*

There is no distinction between a commercial and a civil mortgage.

Niwa *kôri* and Haguri *kôri.*

---

[1] *Mitsumori-baika.*
[2] *Muteitô (mutampo).*

There is no particular difference between a commercial and a civil mortgage.

SHIZUOKA PREFECTURE

Prefectural Office.

There is no difference.

Udo *kôri* and Abe *kôri*.

A commercial mortgage consists mostly of merchandise, called "goods pledge,"[1] as, for instance, grain for a rice dealer and tea for a tea dealer. So it is naturally different from a civil mortgage.

Inasa *kôri* and Aratama *kôri*.

There is no difference at all between a commercial and a civil mortgage.

Kamo *kôri* and Naka *kôri*.

Chattels are mostly used in a commercial mortgage, and the mortgage instrument need only be signed and sealed by the mortgagor, or by the mortgagor and his surety. Such is not the case with a civil mortgage, which usually consists of real property, and needs to be signed and sealed by the mortgagor and his surety, and also to be attested by the town or village head.

Saya *kôri* and Kitô *kôri*.

Those who resort to mortgaging in commercial transactions never make use of land or a house. And a commercial mortgage is always restricted to share certificates[2] or public loan bonds.[3]

GIFU PREFECTURE

Mugi *kôri*.

In commercial mortgages chattel of a value corresponding to the sum of the loan is taken as pledge. It does not require any instrument nor any surety, being mainly dependent upon the borrower's credit. Consequently it is naturally different from a civil mortgage.

Ampachi *kôri*.

It is difficult to establish any clear distinction upon the basis of the hitherto prevailing traditional practices. But [generally speaking] a commercial mortgage is different from a civil mortgage, being simple in procedures, not so elaborate as the latter. It is executed, for instance, mostly by an oral promise. Moreover, in the case of goods like rice and oil, goods that are traded at the ex-

---

[1] *Ni-jichi.*

[2] *Kabuken.*

[3] *Kôsai-shôsho; kôsai,* public loan; *shôsho,* bond.

change,[1] merchants have a practice of fixing the term of a mortgage according to the market situation. That is, when the mortgagee wishes to terminate the mortgage because of the market situation, he will notify his intention to the mortgagor, and, immediately upon receipt of his reply, will assume title to the goods and proceed to dispose of the goods.

Fuwa *kôri*.

There is naturally some difference between a commercial and a civil mortgage. If land, for instance, is pledged, it is a civil mortgage; but if a merchant mortgages his merchandise for the benefit of his business, it is a commercial mortgage. Furthermore, as a commercial mortgage depends mostly upon the borrower's credit, it is often transacted by oral promise only. Sometimes a written contract is required in commercial transactions depending on the circumstances, but generally it is not required in a commercial mortgage.

Atsumi *kôri*, Kagami *kôri* and Katagata *kôri*.

There naturally is some difference.

Tagi *kôri* and Kami-ishizu *kôri*.

There is no difference at all between a commercial and a civil mortgage.

Haguri *kôri* and Nakajima *kôri*.

In a commercial mortgage the mortgagee merely gives a receipt for the goods to the mortgagor. In this it is apparently different from a civil mortgage.

Ena *kôri*.

Yes.

Kamo *kôri*.

There is no difference at all between a commercial and a civil mortgage.

Kani *kôri*.

In a commercial mortgage in most cases the mortgagor leaves his goods in bailment in the warehouse of the mortgagee. A civil mortgage is executed with the attestation of the town or village head, and it is mostly real property that is pledged. Such is the difference between a commercial and a civil mortgage.

Atsumi *kôri*, Gifu Township.

---

[1] *Sôba-hin;* literally, "exchange-goods."

There naturally is some difference between a commercial and a civil mortgage.

Ôgaki.

It is difficult to establish any clear distinction upon the basis of the hitherto prevailing traditional practices. But [generally speaking] a commercial mortgage is different from a civil mortgage in being simple in procedure and not so elaborate as the latter. It is executed, for instance, mostly by an oral promise. And moreover, the practice with goods like rice and oil that are traded at the exchange, is to fix the term of a mortgage according to the market situation. That is, when the mortgagee wishes to terminate the mortgage because of the market situation, he will notify his intention to the mortgagor and, immediately upon receipt of his reply, will assume title to the goods and proceed to dispose of them.

Ena *kôri*, Nakatsugawa Village.

A commercial mortgage is, in most cases, a promise based upon credit. It is thus different, in practice, from a civil mortgage.

Shimo-ishizu *kôri*, Takasu Township.

In this locality there is not much difference of rules between a commercial and a civil mortgage. But a commercial mortgage is more informal in procedure than a civil mortgage.

Haguri *kôri*, Takegahana Village.

There is no old practice in existence here pointing to a distinction between a commercial and a civil mortgage, as suggested in this topic.

Yamagata *kôri*, Takatomi Village.

A commercial mortgage is not different at all from a civil mortgage.

Mugi *kôri*, Kôzuchi Village.

A commercial mortgage is not different at all from a civil mortgage.

Haguri *kôri*, Kasamatsu Village.

In a commercial mortgage the mortgagee customarily gives the mortgagor a receipt for the pledged goods. Hence, it is slightly different from a civil mortgage.

Fuwa *kôri*, Tarui Village.

There naturally is some difference between a commercial and a civil mortgage.

Ôno *kôri*, Miwa Village.

There is no difference between a commercial and a civil mortgage.

Ampachi *kôri*, Gôdo Village.

A commercial mortgage differs greatly from a civil one.

Tagi *kôri*, Shimada Village.

There does not exist yet [any institution of] a commercial mortgage, as such.

Ena *kôri*, Iwa Village.

Yes, there is.

Toki *kôri*, Tajimi Village.

A commercial mortgage is not different from a civil mortgage.

Kamo *kôri*, Hosome Village.

A commercial mortgage consists of goods under bill of exchange,[1] goods lying in a warehouse,[2] or a "certificate of purchase,"[3] etc., the purchase referring here to that of a forest or standing timber.[4] A commercial mortgage differs from a civil mortgage in that it can be executed without attestation by the town or village head, mostly on the strength of the mortgagor's personal credit.

Toki *kôri*, Takayama Village.

There is no difference.

Kani *kôri*, Mitake Village.

A commercial mortgage consists mostly of goods lying in a warehouse and does not require any attestation by the town or village head, while a civil mortgage, whether in the form of personal or real property, requires such attestation.

Ena *kôri*, Akechi Village.

Yes, there is.

Mugi *kôri*, Seki Village.

There is some difference between a commercial and a civil mortgage. If, for instance, one's landed property is mortgaged, it is a civil mortgage. If goods handled by some commercial firm are mortgaged, it is a commercial mortgage. Suppose, on the other hand, there is a merchant who has no house of his own nor other real property, and does not have enough money to pay even the

---

[1] *Kawase-nimotsu.*

[2] *Kuraire-mono.*

[3] *Kaiuke-shôsho.*

[4] *Tachi-ki.*

national tax[1] and local charges.[2] If he mortgages goods in which he deals, it is not a commercial mortgage, and can probably be called a civil mortgage.

Ôno *kôri*, Takayama Township.

There is no difference at all between a commercial and a civil mortgage.

Motosu *kôri*, Kita-kata Village.

A civil mortgage is quite different from a commercial mortgage, as will be described under Topic 2. For in a civil mortgage, upon default of the pledgor, the practice here is that the pledgee may get some competent merchant to appraise the pledged property and sell the property to apply the proceeds to the satisfaction of the debt. If there is still a deficit for covering principal and interest, the pledgee may demand that the pledgor pay off the deficit. If there is a surplus, it is accounted for to the pledgor.

Kamo *kôri*, Ôta Village.

A commercial mortgage consists of goods under bill of exchange, goods laid in a warehouse, or a certificate of purchase, etc. The difference with a civil mortgage consists in the fact that a commercial mortgage can be executed on the strength of the mortgagor's personal credit, even without attestation by the town or village head.

Gujô *kôri*.

There is no difference between a commercial and a civil mortgage.

---

[1] *Kô-zei.*
[2] *Kyôgi-hi.*

Topic 2:   When An Obligor Does Not Pay His Debt at the Ex-
           piration of the Agreed Term, Payment Being Secured by
           a Mortgage, Is It the Usual Practice for the Creditor to
           Appropriate the Entire Property to Compensate for the
           Loss He Incurs, Even When the Value of the Mortgaged
           Property Exceeds the Amount of the Debt, Including Its
           Principal and Interest? Or Is It the Custom for the Cred-
           itor to Sell the Mortgaged Property, Reimburse Himself
           Out of the Money Received from the Sale, and Return
           the Surplus to the Obligor?

GROUP I—ANSWERS

Tokyo.

Where a mortgage is security for a loan, the old practice was that
upon default of the obligor the obligee did not return the mortgaged
article to the obligor even when the value of the article exceeded
the debt, including its principal and interest. But, with the exception of some special cases of pawn, the usual practice today is that
upon default of the obligor, the obligee will sell the security and
apply the proceeds to the satisfaction of the debt. If there is any
surplus after payment of the principal and interest, he will turn it
over to the obligor. And if there is a deficit, he will demand its
payment.

Kyoto.

Observations have already been made, under the preceding topic,
on mortgages for commercial purposes. Mortgages of real property
in connection with lendings and borrowings of money between ordinary people have to pass through the office of the village or town
head, while personal property is handled by pawnbrokers, who
naturally have old customs of their own. A commercial secured loan
is an occasional transaction.[1] But the terms are specially agreed
upon each time such a loan is made, there being, we believe, no
fixed practice.

Each contract has its own provisions regarding the disposal of the
surplus that may result after payment of a debt from the proceeds

---

[1] *Hikiai (torihiki).*

of the sale of a security. Sometimes the contract may provide that when the debt is past due, the obligee is free to dispose of the security, and is under no obligation to turn over the surplus to the obligor, but also has no right to claim payment of any deficit that may occur after the sale of the security. Or it may sometimes provide that the obligor keep the amount advanced and the obligee keep the security, and before the debt is due, the obligee sell the security and settle the account with the obligor, turning over any surplus to, and claiming payment of any deficit from, the latter. We believe there is no fixed practice.

Osaka.

When the debt is due, the mortgagee never proceeds to appropriate the entire security when the value exceeds the debt, including principal and interest, unless there is a special provision to that effect. A commercial mortgage is transacted between parties who have hitherto had business dealings with each other. The parties deem mutual good faith so important that when the debt is due or past due, the obligee will give notice of it to the obligor, and upon receipt of reply, will sell the security, and apply the proceeds to the satisfaction of the debt, including principal and interest, turning over any surplus to the obligor or claiming payment of any deficit.

Though rare there are some mortgagors, who, when the debt is past due, will not reply to the mortgagee's note demanding payment of the debt. In such cases the value of the security is always below the amount of the debt, including its principal and interest, and is never enough to leave any deficit. For if the value of the security exceeded the principal and interest of the debt, the mortgagor would not wait for the demand of the mortgagee to pay his debt, but would consign the pledged goods to the mortgagee for sale, or ask for the postponement of the payment.

Yokohama.

The practice here with respect to the security for a loan, is that upon default of the obligor, the obligee will sell the security and apply the proceeds of the sale to the satisfaction of the debt, turning over any surplus to the debtor, or demanding payment of any deficit.

Hyôgo.

If a debt for which payment has been secured by a mortgage is not paid when due, the mortgagee, according to the local practice, does not proceed at once to appropriate the security, but will sell it and apply the proceeds to the satisfaction of the debt, including principal and interest, turning over any surplus to the obligor.

The following are the proceedings of the Investigation Committee here:

No. 27 [Arima]: It is the custom here that, upon default of the obligor, the obligee sells the security and applies the proceeds of the sale to the satisfaction of the debt, including principal and interest, turning over any surplus to the obligor.

No. 11 [Horiuchi]: Even if the debt is past due, there is no practice whereby the obligee will appropriate the security. After repeated notice to the obligor, he will proceed to sell it, according to the custom here.

Chairman [Kashima]: I will then submit a report to the effect that, according to local practice, upon default of the obligor, the obligee will not at once appropriate the security, but will sell it and apply the proceeds to the satisfaction of the debt, turning over any surplus to the obligor.

Ôtsu.

The local practice is that the obligee will apply the proceeds of the sale of the security to the satisfaction of the debt, including principal and interest, turning over any surplus to the debtor, and demanding payment of any deficit.

Kumamoto.

If in commercial transactions the obligor does not pay a debt secured by a mortgage when due, the obligee usually appropriates the security at once, even when its value exceeds the debt, including principal and interest. This is a commercial mortgage, generally called *buiri,* and is very different from a civil mortgage.

Okayama.

If the debt is not paid when due, the mortgagee sells the security for the loan and applies the proceeds to the satisfaction of the debt, including principal and interest, demanding payment of any deficit from the debtor, or turning over any surplus to him. However, formerly, the mortgagee used to appropriate the security at once.

Bakan.

Upon default of the mortgagor, the local practice is that the obligee will immediately appropriate the security if its value exceeds the debt, including principal and interest. If the value of the security falls short of the debt, the obligee will appropriate the security and demand payment of the deficit from the obligor.

Sakai.

The practice prevailing until recent times regarding security for a loan was that upon default of the obligor, the obligee would appropriate the security, and neither turn over any surplus to, or demand payment of any deficit from, the obligor, regardless of whether the value of the mortgaged article exceeded or fell short of the debt, including principal and interest. At present some merchants, such as pawnbrokers, still follow the old practice. But the general practice today is that, in other sorts of security for a loan, upon default of the obligor, the obligee will sell the security after conferring with the obligor, apply the proceeds to the satisfaction of the debt, including principal and interest, and either turn over any surplus to the debtor, or demand payment of any deficit from him. In the opinion of this association, the new practice is a more equitable proceeding than the old.

Iida.

Whether, upon the default of the obligor, the obligee shall appropriate the security or value it and turn over any surplus to the obligor depends upon the contract that is concluded either at the time the loan is made or later.

Takamatsu.

In the days when there was no civil court, upon default of the obligor, the obligee did not turn over any surplus to the obligee even if the value of the security exceeded the debt, including principal and interest. But nowadays, when it is not a chattel mortgage, the obligee is required to turn over any surplus to the obligor.

Fukui.

Upon default of the obligor, the obligee is at once entitled, according to the local custom, to appropriate the security. Therefore, when he sells it and finds a surplus after covering the debt, including principal and interest, the obligee does not turn it over to the obligor.

Tokushima.

If the obligor cannot pay a debt when due that is secured by a mortgage, the obligee will sell the security, and apply the proceeds to the satisfaction of the debt, turning over any deficit to the obligor.

Takefu.

When there is a surplus, it will of course be turned over to the obligor. Sometimes it may be provided that any deficit shall be paid by the obligor.

Miyagi.

Upon default of the obligor, the obligee, as a rule, sells the security, and after applying the proceeds to the satisfaction of the debt, turns over any surplus to the debtor, or demands payment of any deficit from him. However, according to an old provision, the obligee used to appropriate the security at once, regardless of whether the value of the security exceeded or fell short of the debt, including principal and interest.

Matsuyama.

Regarding the point in question, there are two kinds of mortgage. One is mortgage in the form of a pawn,[1] according to which neither the obligee nor the obligor generally gives or receives any surplus or deficit. However, in the case of mortgages[2] of [ordinary] chattels or immovables, which by regulation require attestation by the village or town head, the obligee sells the security and applies the proceeds to the satisfaction of the debt, turning over any debt to the obligor.

This rule, however, is not applicable to a mortgage which has different provisions from the above.

GROUP II—ANSWERS

TOKYO METROPOLIS

Pawnbrokers.

The security that we have to do with is not called *teitô*. At the expiration of six months' term, if the pledgor does not redeem the pledged article upon receipt of proper notice, the pledgee may foreclose the pledge and appropriate it. Whether the sale of the pledged article brings in more than enough or too little to cover the loan, the pledgee does not turn over the surplus to the pledgor [nor demand payment of the deficit].

Oil Wholesalers.

The bailment of goods as described in Topic 1 is nothing other than a mortgage. And if the mortgage is not paid when due, the

---

[1] *Shichi-ire-teitô.*

[2] *Kakiire-teitô.*

mortgagee may, according to the practice here, sell the security and apply the proceeds to the satisfaction of the debt, turning over any deficit to the mortgagor.

Dry Goods Wholesalers.

We have no practice of mortgage in our trade.

Timber Wholesalers.

The practice of mortgaging timber has already been described in Topic 1. There is also a practice of pledging. This consists in leaving some article in bailment with the pledgee and sometimes getting a receipt therefor. Upon default of the pledgor, the pledgee is entitled at once to appropriate the pledged article. But usually the pledgee, by way of compromise,[1] turns over the surplus to the pledgor.

Grain Wholesalers.

The obligor's inability to pay a debt which has been secured by a mortgage, as described in Topic 1, always arises from fluctuations of price in the market.[2] In such a case the obligor generally sells the pledged goods at reduced prices.[3] But when there is a heavy fall in the price, some obligors deliver the security to the obligee. Then when the obligee, who has the title to the goods, judges that the market situation justifies it, he will sell them. And even if the proceeds exceed the principal and interest of the debt, he will not turn over the surplus to the obligor.

Fish Wholesalers.

No.

Fuel Wholesalers.

Upon default of the obligor—if, for instance, the obligor has mortgaged his forest land to one merchant but ships the fuel produced from the forest to another merchant, which is tantamount to a failure in repayment—the first wholesaler will, according to the practice here, negotiate for a settlement with the person to whom the goods have been shipped. If the second wholesaler is found to be holding another mortgage, then the wholesalers will proceed to establish, by the priority of dates, who the first mortgagee is, when and if necessary, the goods will be re-shipped to the

---

[1] *Jidan.*

[2] *Sôba-no-hendô.*

[3] *Mikiri-baikyaku (mikiriuri).*

first mortgagee. Sometimes they resort to the practice[1] of dividing the pledged goods equitably among the mortgagees.

Saké Wholesalers.

No.

Dried Bonito Wholesalers.

Any surplus or any deficit after payment of the principal and interest of the loan will be accounted for to the obligor.

Salt Wholesalers.

The transaction of a mortgage is no different from an ordinary loan transaction. If the obligee takes possession of the security and sells it, he will turn over any surplus to the obligor after payment of the principal and interest of the loan.

Kôjimachi Ward.

If there is any surplus, the obligee, according to the custom here, will turn it over to the obligor.

Nihombashi Ward.

There is no fixed practice in the matter, but in the case of an ordinary mortgage the obligee turns over the surplus to the obligor. With respect to a pawn, it depends upon the contract, and is usually subject to the will of the obligee.

Kyôbashi Ward.

According to the custom here, the obligee sells the security, and after payment of the loan, turns over any surplus to the obligor.

Asakusa Ward.

With the exception of pawnbrokers, the second of the methods named in Topic 2 applies throughout this district.

Honjô Ward.

According to one practice, the obligee at once appropriates the security, as, for example, pawnbrokers, who do not turn over any surplus to the obligor.

There is also another practice, according to which the obligee usually sells the security, and after payment of the principal and interest of the loan, turns over any surplus to the obligor.

Ebara *kôri*.

It is not the practice here, on default of the obligor who has secured his debt with a mortgage, for the obligee to appropriate the security in satisfaction of the debt, even though the value of the

---

[1] *Tsuwake.*

security may exceed the principal and interest of the loan. Sometimes the obligee and the obligor may confer, and the obligee will sell the security in satisfaction of the loan including principal and interest, turning over any surplus to the obligor.

Higashi-tama *kôri* and Minami-toshima *kôri*.

It depends upon the contract whether, upon default of the obligor, the obligee may at once appropriate the security. When it is sold, the obligee is usually not obligated to turn over any surplus to the obligor, unless otherwise provided.

Kita-toshima *kôri*.

Even if the obligor fails to pay when due a debt whose payment ha has secured by a mortgage, the obligee has no right to appropriate the security without consent of the obligor, unless there is a provsion to that effect. In such a case usually the obligor and the obligee confer with each other, and, upon fixing the price of the security and calculating the interest on the loan, settle the accounts between them, the obligee turning over any surplus to the obligor and the obligor paying any deficit to the obligee.

Minami-adachi *kôri*.

With the exception of pawnbrokers, no pledgee may appropriate the security in satisfaction of the loan, unless there is a special agreement to that effect, something which is rather rare.

Shitaya Ward.

The usual practice hitherto has been that upon default of the obligor, with the exception of the pawned article, the obligee sells the security and pays the principal and interest of the loan, turning over any surplus to, or demanding payment of any deficit from, the obligor.

Kanda Ward.

Ordinarily there is no such practice, unless there is a special agreement about the matter.

Akasaka Ward.

The practice of appropriating the security in satisfaction of the loan as described in the Topic 2 prevailed until regulation in the 13th year of Meiji [1880]. However, if the value[1] of the security permitted it, some obligees would bestow some "consolation money"[2]

---

[1] *Shinagara;* quality.

[2] *Namida,* tears; *kin,* money.

on the obligor. The obligor, on the other hand, would never have to pay any deficiency[1] to the obligee.

Azabu Ward.

Formerly there prevailed the sort of practice described in Topic 2. However, there were some obligees who, according to the value of the security, would bestow some "consolation-money" on the obligor. The latter, however, never returned any deficiency to the obligee.

Hongô Ward.

When the value of the security exceeds the principal and interest of a debt, whether the obligee appropriates the difference himself or returns it to the obligor depends somewhat upon the moral sense of the obligee and the amount of the difference. In short, there is no fixed practice about the matter.

Chiba Prefecture

Awa *kôri*, Hei *kôri*, Asai *kôri* and Nagasa *kôri*.

Suppose some fishermen leave their fishing apparatus, such things as an eight-armed scoop-net and other fishing nets, sails and oars, in bailment, borrow money from the pledgee, and when their loan is due, fail to repay it even after repeated demands. The obligee, according to the local custom, may either sell the pledged articles or appropriate them. But this practice is resorted to only when the obligors are very untrustworthy and there is no other course of action. Usually the obligee makes a new contract with the obligors and gives them an extension of time for payment until their next large catch. But the obligee, if he does sell the security in satisfaction of the loan, seldom finds any surplus. For the obligors themselves would in such a case usually undertake the selling, without waiting for the obligee to do it.

Katori *kôri*.

There is no practice here whereby upon default of the obligor the obligee may at once appropriate his security. However, if the obligee sells the security after having conferred with the obligor, and there is any surplus, he is not deemed to be bound to turn it over to the obligor.

Yamabe *kôri* and Muza *kôri*.

Upon default of the obligor, the obligee, according to the custom

---

[1] *Sakin.*

here, appropriates the security, regardless of whether its value exceeds or falls short of the loan, unless otherwise provided in the contract.

Unakami *kôri* and Sôsa *kôri*.

According to the first sort of contract referred to in Topic 2, including pawns and other mortgages, the obligee at once appropriates the security regardless of whether its value exceeds or falls short of the loan, so that any gain or loss will be the obligee's. For the second sort of contract, the rule is the same as for a civil mortgage.

Higashi-katsushika *kôri*.

There is no fixed practice; it varies according to the contract. Sometimes the obligor may deliver the security to the obligee. Sometimes the obligee may sell it in satisfaction of the loan, and if there is any deficit, demand payment by the obligor.

IBARAGI PREFECTURE

Nishi-katsushika *kôri* and Sashima *kôri*.

The practice here is that the obligee sells the security and, after redeeming the loan, turns over any surplus to the obligor.

KANAGAWA PREFECTURE

Miura *kôri*.

The custom here is that the obligee sells the security, and after payment of the loan, turns over any surplus to the obligor.

Tachibana *kôri*.

There is no custom here of the obligee immediately appropriating the security, nor of the obligee turning over any surplus to the obligor after satisfaction of the loan.

Kita-tama *kôri*.

When a person borrows money upon a security and is unable to pay his debt when due, the mortgaged article will be put to public auction, the obligor being responsible for payment of any deficit and entitled to receive any surplus. Even the obligee has no right to sell the security, though he has a prior claim to it.

Prefectural Industrial Bureau.

Upon default of the obligor, the custom here is that the obligee sells the security, and after payment of the principal and interest on the loan, turns over any surplus to the debtor, or demands payment of any deficit from him.

TOCHIGI PREFECTURE

Shimo-tsuga *kôri* and Samukawa *kôri*.

If the obligor does not pay when due a debt secured by a mortgage, the obligee sells the security, and after satisfaction of the loan, including principal and interest, out of the proceeds, turns over any surplus to the obligor.

Ashikaga *kôri* and Yanada *kôri*.

It is only the banks here that, upon default of the obligor, sell his security and, after payment of the principal and interest of the loan, turn over any surplus to the obligor. All other obligees make demand of payment of the loan, and when it is not paid, appropriate the security. In actual practice, however, there are very few who do not pay their loan when they are pressed for payment.

Prefectural Office.

There is such a practice among fellow merchants of the same trade. However, the surplus is not turned over to the obligor. Between merchants of different trades the conditions of a loan are more elaborate, and the transaction is the same as others of the kind.

MIE PREFECTURE

Suzuka *kôri*.

Whether, upon default of the obligor, the obligee appropriates the security, even though its value exceeds the principal and interest of the loan, depends upon the contract. There is no fixed practice about this. However, even when it is explicitly provided that upon default of the obligor the obligee shall be free to dispose of the security at his pleasure, the obligee usually returns it, according to the custom here, to the obligor if the latter repays the principal and interest of his debt immediately after it is due. And even if the obligor fails to pay the whole debt but pays a portion of the principal and interest, the obligee customarily gives to the obligor an extension of time for payment. If the obligor fails to take one of these steps and the obligee has already sold the security, he will not return any surplus to the obligor.

Isshi *kôri*.

According to the custom here, the obligee at once proceeds to appropriate the security, and even if there is any deficit or surplus, he does not ask payment of the deficit nor turn over the surplus to the obligor.

Asake *kôri*.

Upon default of the obligor in payment of a debt secured by a mortgage, the obligee cannot at once appropriate the security. According to the custom here, he must notify the obligor of his intention to sell it. Then he applies the proceeds of the sale to the satisfaction of the loan, including principal and interest, and turns over any surplus to the obligor. On the other hand, if there is a gradual fall in the market price of the security, so much so that its value will not be enough to cover the principal and interest of the loan, and despite the obligee's demand, the obligor refuses to give additional security,[1] the obligee sometimes proceeds at once to sell the security.

Nabari *kôri* and Iga *kôri*.

The matter is determined by contract. But the general rule is that upon default of the obligor, the obligee may not immediately appropriate the security even though its value is less than the sum of the loan. Instead he sells the pledged goods, and after payment of the loan, settles accounts with the obligor.

However, a mortgage which has been made solely for a loan is not different at all from a civil mortgage.

AICHI PREFECTURE

Nakajima *kôri*.

Upon default of the obligor, the obligee, according to the usage here, sells the security, and applies the proceeds to the satisfaction of the principal and interest of the loan, turning over any surplus to the obligor.

Nagoya Ward.

We have no usage here corresponding to that described in the first half of Topic 2 or to that described in the second half. In such a case the obligee makes it a rule to dispose of the security only after securing the consent of the obligor. There are indeed some (though few) obligees who immediately appropriate the security, even though the loan, including principal and interest, is less than the value of the security. But generally they make it a rule to sell the security, and after payment of the principal and interest of the loan, to turn over any surplus to the obligor.

Chita *kôri*.

Whether the obligee may immediately appropriate the security

[1] *Mashi-teitô.*

upon default of the obligor depends upon the terms of the contract, there being no fixed practice about this. But the general custom is for the obligee to confer with the obligor and then to sell the security in satisfaction of the loan, turning over any surplus to the debtor or demanding payment of any deficit from him.

Minami-shidara *kôri*.

There is no fixed usage about the matter. It is generally decided according to circumstances.

Atsumi *kôri*.

It is dependent upon the terms of the contract. But generally it is the practice for the obligee to turn over any surplus to the debtor and to demand payment of any deficit from him.

Kaitô *kôri* and Kaisai *kôri*.

There is no such custom here that upon default of the obligor, the obligee at once appropriates the security even though its value exceeds the principal and interest of the loan. The obligee sells the security, and after paying the principal and interest of his loan, turns over any surplus to the obligor.

Aichi *kôri*.

Customarily the obligee neither appropriates the security at once, nor turns over any surplus to the obligor.

Niwa *kôri* and Haguri *kôri*.

Whether the obligee shall return any surplus to the obligor when the value of the security exceeds the principal and interest of the loan is dependent upon the terms of the contract as agreed upon when it was made or at the time of the sale of the security, there being no fixed practice about this.

SHIZUOKA PREFECTURE

Prefectural Office.

It depends upon the terms of the contract, there being no fixed practice.

Udo *kôri* and Abe *kôri*.

Since the sole aim of commerce is making a monetary profit, an obligor would never leave a security whose value exceeds the principal and interest of his loan in bailment with his obligee even after the mortgage is due. If by some chance such an obligor did exist, and the obligee sold the security, the later would not turn over any surplus to the obligor.

Inasa *kôri* and Aratama *kôri*.

When the obligor defaults in paying his debt, the obligee demands payment. If the obligor still fails to pay it, the terms of the contract [such as a provision that upon default of the obligor the obligee shall be free to appropriate the security] will take effect. The obligee may sometimes appropriate the security even though its value is greater than the principal and interest of the loan. But customarily the obligee does not appropriate it immediately after the loan becomes due. Nor is it customary for an obligee to turn over any surplus to the obligor after redeeming the principal and interest of the loan.

Saya *kôri* and Kitô *kôri*.

Whether a security is foreclosed or not depends upon the terms of the contract. But usually this does not take place unless there is no other course of action.

Kamo *kôri* and Naka *kôri*.

In the case described in Topic 2, the obligee seldom appropriates the security at once. In most cases the obligee sells the security, and applying the proceeds of the sale to the satisfaction of the loan, turns over any surplus to the obligor. Any deficit is the obligee's loss.

GIFU PREFECTURE

Mugi *kôri*.

It is the custom here that, when the debt is due, the obligee disposes of the security at the request of the obligor. No fixed practice exists.

Ampachi *kôri*.

The practice here is that, upon default of the obligor, the obligee does not appropriate the security at once. But, depending on the obligor's reply to his notice, he sells it or has it publicly valued. In case there is any surplus after paying the principal and interest of the loan, he generally turns it over to the obligor.

Fuwa *kôri*.

Upon default of the obligor, the custom here is that the obligee and the obligor sell the security in each other's presence. If there is any surplus after payment of the principal and interest of the loan, it is turned over to the obligor. However, it sometimes happens in particular circumstances that the obligee appropriates the security at once, and after redemption of the principal and interest of the loan, does not turn over any surplus to the obligor.

Atsumi *kôri*, Kagami *kôri* and Katagata *kôri*.

We have adhered to the practice described in the latter half of Topic 2. However sometimes, after consultation between the obligor and the obligee, the security is appropriated by the obligee.

Tagi *kôri* and Kami-ishizu *kôri*.

According to the custom here, upon default of the obligor, the obligee does not appropriate the security at once, and the sale or appropriation of the security is done only after conference with the obligor. However, if they agreed on some special provisions when their contract was made, the transaction will be completed according to said provisions.

Ôno *kôri* and Ikeda *kôri*.

Upon default of the obligor, the obligee may of course appropriate the security, even if its value is greater than the loan. However, in fact, this practice is very seldom resorted to. For when the security deposited by the obligor is greater in value than the loan, including principal and interest, it is more natural to sell it before the pledge period expires and to turn over the surplus to the obligor.

Haguri *kôri* and Nakajima *kôri*.

The practice as described in the first half of Topic 2 is rarely followed here. The practice described in the second half of Topic 2 is largely observed.

Ena *kôri*.

Sometimes the obligee may appropriate the security at once. In other cases he may return any surplus to the obligor.

Kamo *kôri*.

Upon default of the obligor, the obligee sells the security and applies the proceeds of the sale to the satisfaction of the loan, turning over any surplus to the obligor. If there is any deficit, he asks payment from the obligor; but usually he has to bear the loss.

Kani *kôri*.

The procedure as described in the first half of Topic 2 has hitherto been practiced here. But when the mortgage is due, the obligee makes it a rule to notify the obligor.

Atsumi *kôri*, Gifu Township.

Both practices as described in the first and the second half of Topic 2 have been followed here.

Ôgaki.

The practice prevailing here is that, upon default of the obligor, the obligee does not appropriate the security at once, but after proper notice to the obligor, sells it or has it publicly valued. If there is any surplus, he turns it over to the obligor.

Ena *kôri*, Nakatsugawa Village.

The security is sold in satisfaction of the loan. If there is any surplus, it is turned over to the obligor.

Shimo-ishizu *kôri*, Takasu Township.

If the obligor is unable to pay his debt when due, the obligee notifies the obligor and invites him to a conference to determine whether he consents to sale of the security in satisfaction of the loan, or, in case the obligee wishes to appropriate it, to decide upon the sales price. The obligee then proceeds to dispose of the security, and if there is any surplus after payment of the loan, turns it over to the obligor.

Haguri *kôri*, Takegahana Village.

There is no fixed practice in the matter. Hitherto, the obligee has sometimes appropriated the security. At other times he has sold the security, turning over any surplus to the obligor after payment of the debt.

Yamagata *kôri*, Takatomi Village.

Upon default of the obligor, the obligee sells the security and, after payment of the principal and interest of the loan, turns over the surplus to the obligor.

Mugi *kôri*, Kôzuchi Village.

When his debt becomes due, the obligor usually asks the obligee to grant him an extension of time. The commercial security, however, continues to be left in bailment with the obligee. Though its title belongs to the obligor, the security is disposed of by the obligee even when its value exceeds the principal and interest of the loan.

Haguri *kôri*, Kasamatsu Village.

The practice as described in the latter half of Topic 2 generally prevails here.

Fuwa *kôri*, Tarui Village.

Disposition of the security is usually made by the obligee after consultation with the obligor.

Ôno *kôri*, Miwa Village.

Both practices described in Topic 2 prevail here.

Ampachi *kôri*, Gôdo Village.

No.

Tagi *kôri*, Shimada Village.

No.

Ena *kôri*, Iwa Village.

Customarily the obligee appropriates the security at once.

Toki *kôri*, Tajimi Village.

Upon default of the obligor, the security is sometimes delivered to the obligee. At other times, if it is marketable, the obligee sells it and applies the proceeds to the satisfaction of the loan, turning over any surplus to the obligor.

Kamo *kôri*, Hosome Village.

When the loan becomes due, the obligee may ask the obligor to pay him the difference if he thinks the security is not worth enough to cover the loan. If the obligor leaves his debt unpaid without expressing his wishes about it, the obligee sometimes proceeds to sell the security. In such a case if there is any surplus after payment of the principal and interest of the loan, the obligee turns it over to the obligor, according to the custom prevailing here.

Toki *kôri*, Takayama Village.

As such matters are of course stipulated in each contract, we cannot say that there is any general rule. If, for instance, there is a provision such as the following, this provision will be observed.

"If I default in payment of my debt when it is due, I agree to the sale of my security for immediate payment of the principal and interest of the debt. If there is any deficit, I will pay it, and you are requested to return to me the surplus, if there is any." If, however, there are different provisions, the contract will be executed in accordance with these.

Kani *kôri*, Mitake Village.

The practice as described in the latter half of Topic 2 prevails here.

Ena *kôri*, Akechi Village.

According to the practice prevailing here, the security may be appropriated by the obligee, or it may be sold, and the surplus after payment of the debt be turned over to the obligor.

Mugi *kôri*, Seki Village.

Upon the failure of the obligor to pay, when due, a debt secured by a mortgage, the obligee may, according to the custom here, appropriate the security even if its value exceeds the debt, including principal and interest.

Ôno *kôri*, Takayama Township.

It depends upon the terms agreed upon at the time the mortgage was given. Upon default of the obligor, the security may sometimes be turned over to the obligee in keeping with the terms of the document. In other instances the obligee may, under the provisions of the contract, apply the proceeds of the sale of the security to the satisfaction of the debt, having the debtor pay any deficit, and turning over any surplus to him.

Motosu *kôri*, Kita-kata Village.

Upon the failure of the obligor to pay a debt secured by a mortgage, the obligee appropriates the security in satisfaction of the debt, even if the value of the security exceeds the principal and interest of the debt.

Kamo *kôri*, Ôta Village.

Upon the failure of the obligor to pay, when due, a debt secured by a mortgage, the obligee may sometimes ask the obligor to pay him the difference if he thinks the security not worth enough to cover the loan.

Kaisai *kôri* and Shimo-ishizu *kôri*.

If the obligor is unable to pay, when due, a debt secured by a mortgage, the obligee communicates with the obligor reminding him of the maturity of the debt, and the two confer to determine whether the obligor wishes to have his security sold and its proceeds applied to the payment of his debt, or, should the obligee desire to keep the mortgaged article as his own, whether the obligor agrees to part with it at an agreed price. If there is any surplus, it is the rule here for the obligee to turn it over to the obligor.

Gujô *kôri*.

Even when the obligor fails to pay, when due, a debt secured by a mortgage, the obligee never proceeds to appropriate the security without communicating with the obligor. When the obligee wishes to sell the security, he cannot do so without securing the consent of the obligor. Even if the contract provides explicitly for the obligee's right to dispose of the security at his will, he cannot do so without negotiating with the obligor. However, if the obligor delays, without any good reason [in taking proper steps], the obligee may sometimes bring the matter to the court and ask for a decision about it.

Topic 3:   When an Obligor Becomes Insolvent, Does any Obligee Besides the Holder of a Mortgage Take Priority[1] over Other (General) Creditors? (For Example, is There Any Custom According to Which a Land Rent,[2] a House Rent,[3] an Employee's Wage, or Money Due for Food Supplied to the Obligor, etc., Takes Priority over Other General Claims?)

GROUP I—ANSWERS

Tokyo.

This is a matter to be decided by law, and there is no fixed practice. Therefore, if such a case occurs, we have to follow what the law says with respect to priority.

Kyoto.

In a case like the present one, a loan made on either of the two kinds of securities described in the preceding topic, i.e. a loan made on the understanding that [upon default of the obligor] the obligee will be authorized to sell the security, is quite distinct from other [ordinary] kinds of loan. A loan of goods made on the security of immovables is regarded as of the same nature as an ordinary loan of money, and disputes regarding it are, in our opinion, to be brought to the court.

Osaka.

In a case, not of a bankruptcy declared by judgement of the office of the town magistrate, but of insolvency as agreed upon in private negotiations between obligor and obligee, no sort of priority is to be recognized. However, it often happens that the house rent, medical charges, wages of employees and bills for food and clothing are paid before other commercial claims are proportionately satisfied. But any priority in the satisfaction of those charges is in accord with the moral sense of the obligees.

Further, a rented house[4] has some appurtenances[5] that belong to

[1] *Sakidori-tokken.*
[2] *Jidai.*
[3] *Yachin.*
[4] *Yachin;* i.e., house rent.
[5] *Ietsukimono.*

the tenant.[1] These appurtenances are possessed of fair value as accessories to the house. But when they are removed from the house, they will lose nine-tenths or more of their value. Therefore, in order to maintain their value, it will be necessary for the outgoing tenant to sell the appurtenances to the party who will occupy the house after him. However, in an urgent occasion of insolvency, the outgoing tenant does not have time to wait for the new incoming tenant to sell the appurtenances to him and is therefore compelled to sell them to the owner of the house.[2] The landlord will then naturally subtract the house rent due to him from the purchase price of the appurtenances. Moreover, if the tenant wishes to remove to some other place after he has become insolvent, in the preparation of the removal notice[3] to be presented to the registry office,[4] he must obtain his landlord's attestation, which is effected by the latter affixing his seal to the paper. Thus the landlord is customarily in a position to require that his debt be paid by the obligor prior to other claimants. This does not constitute, however, what we should call a priority.

Yokohama.

Whether someone has a preferential right or not is decided by law. There are no fixed customary practices regarding this.

Hyôgo.

According to local practice, no one except the holder of a security has any priority claim over other creditors.

Below are the opinions of the members of the investigation committee on the subject.

No. 14 [Funai]: When goods are mortgaged, no one except the mortgagee has any priority claim.

No. 4 [Kishi]: Besides the obligee who is the holder of a security, there are some who have priority of claim. I once came across such a case. When an obligor became insolvent, his obligee made a priority claim on certain goods in mortgage which had been left with a certain wholesaler and demanded possession of them. But as the latter refused to deliver the goods to him, the obligee had to pay to the wholesaler the storage charges payable by the obligor in order to have the mortgaged goods delivered to him. From this, I conclude that, besides a mortgagee,

[1] *Shakuya-nin.*
[2] *Yanushi.*
[3] *Tenkyo-todoke.*
[4] *Koseki-yakuba.*

there are sometimes parties who have priority over other claimants.

No. 3 [Kondô]: When one takes goods stored in a warehouse as security, one must of course be aware that one has to pay the storage charges on the goods. Hence it was only natural that he paid them.

No. 11 [Horiuchi]: Regarding the storage charges, he paid them because he could not take possession of the goods in the warehouse otherwise.

No. 1 [Ikeda]: I also once took as security certain goods in storage with a wholesaler and paid storage charges for them, as No. 4 said. However, these things, like the house rent in the case of a house or the land rent in the case of land, do not, generally speaking, I believe, take priority over other claims.

No. 19 [Funai]: The question of priority cannot be decided once for all by a general rule. For whether the house rent, land rent, etc. take priority over other claims or not must depend upon the arrangement between obligee and obligor, and we cannot make any sweeping statement in the negative.

No. 4 [Kishi]: As I have already said, goods that are in storage with some wholesaler can never be taken out unless the storage charges are paid. Therefore the general practice is to recognize the priority of claims for storage charges.

No. 11 [Horiuchi]: As to the storage charges, I agree with No. 4. The land rent, house rent, wages of employees, etc., also, I am inclined to think, take priority over other claims. But I have not yet met with any actual cases. We cannot always make that inference from the example of the storage charges.

No. 19 [Funai]: Because a house is indispensable for sheltering ourselves from the rain, etc. and cannot be dispensed with even momentarily, the house rent takes priority over general claims.

No. 2 [Tamba]: There is no practice of house rent and other charges taking priority over other claims. When a tenant becomes insolvent, the landlord of the house will be treated on an equal basis with other claimants.

As the majority are of the opinion that, with the exception of a creditor holding some security, there are no creditors having priority over other claimants, it has been decided to submit a report to the effect that no such practices exist.

Ôtsu.

With the exception of public taxes[1] and special levies,[2] no claims

---

[1] *Kôso* (*sozei*).
[2] *Fueki.*

are entitled to priority among those in the position of creditors.

Kumamoto.

When an obligor becomes insolvent, no claimant, with the exception of the creditor holding some security, is entitled to priority.

Okayama.

With the exception of a creditor holding some security, whether a certain claim takes priority over others or not is decided by law, there being no customary practice regarding this.

Bakan.

With the exception of secured credits, no claims are entitled to priority.

Sakai.

There is just one sort of credit whose priority has been recognized since ancient times. When the vendee of goods has become insolvent after delivery of the goods to him but before his payment for the same, the obligee is entitled to a prior claim on the goods and may recover them even before a creditor holding a security.

Iida.

When an insolvent debtor wishes to make a composition[1] with his creditors, he has to put aside sums equivalent to the land rent, house rent, tuition fee,[2] medical charges, employees' wages and debts due to those who have supplied food, allotting what money he has left for distribution among the rest of his creditors.

Takamatsu.

Before the [present] law came into effect, land rent, house rent, employees' wages and debts due to those who supplied [food to the obligor], etc., used to take priority over other claims. But the practice has now undergone a slight change, for land rent no longer takes priority over debts due to secured creditors.

Fukui.

There are no preferential rights.

Tokushima.

According to the custom here, upon insolvency of an obligor, no one, with the exception of secured creditors, is entitled to any priority over other creditors.

Takefu.

---

[1] *Jidan.*

[2] *Kyôshi-no-sharei.*

With the exception of the land tax[1] and the land rent, no debt is entitled to any priority.

Miyagi.

According to the practice here, upon insolvency of an obligor, no one, with the exception of secured creditors, has been entitled to any priority claim. However, upon the consent of creditors, wages of the obligor's employees are sometimes paid before other debts. But this should not be called a preferential right, as it is entirely a benevolent act of the creditors.

Matsuyama.

Upon insolvency of an obligor, the priority the creditors are entitled to is limited to that which is provided in the law, and no other priority is recognized.

GROUP II—ANSWERS

Tokyo Metropolis

Tokyo Prefectural Office.

Pawnshops.

There is no practice of such a priority.

Oil Wholesalers.

None.

Dry Goods Wholesalers.

There obtains no such practice for mortgages in our trade.

Timber Wholesalers.

None. However, if a fellow trader becomes insolvent but wishes to carry on his trade, creditors engaged in the same trade will arrange, with a view to giving him moral support, for payment by yearly installments[2] on the basis of the pro rata distribution among the creditors of the trade, leaving him, on the other hand, enough property to pay all the debts due to his consignors. If he has no desire to continue in the same trade, then, according to the practice here, his property will be distributed among all the creditors proportionately to the amount of each debt due.

Rice Wholesalers.

According to the practice hitherto prevailing, upon insolvency

---

[1] *Chiso.*

[2] *Nenki;* nowadays the expression *nempu* is generally used.

of an obligor, all his creditors are paid proportionate dividends according to the amount of each debt due. There are no preferred claims recognized.

Fish Wholesalers.

None.

Fuel Wholesalers.

A composition upon insolvency between debtor and creditors consists merely in providing for proportionate payment of debts among the creditors, and never allows preference to any of the debts.

Saké Wholesalers.

None.

Dried Bonito Wholesalers.

None.

Salt Wholesalers.

None.

Kôjimachi Ward.

Land rent, house rent, etc., are customarily paid before other debts. During the Tokugawa period, rice bills used to be paid before other debts, and saké bills after the rest of the debts. But this practice does not obtain at present, those bills being classed together with other general debts.

Nihombashi Ward.

There is no practice of recognizing any preference in payment.

Kyôbashi Ward.

With the exception of creditors none is entitled to preferential payment.

Yotsuya Ward and Ushigome Ward.

Though it may not be called a fixed practice, land rent, house rent, employees' wages, etc., are, from the nature of the debt, distinguished from other debts, being paid apart from the other group.

Asakusa Ward.

Upon insolvency of an obligor, with the exception of secured creditors, none is entitled to preferential payment.

Honjo Ward.

Upon insolvency of an obligor, with the exception of secured creditors, none is entitled to preferential payment.

Ebara *kôri*.

Upon insolvency of an obligor, with the exception of secured creditors, none is entitled to preferential payment.

Higashi-tama *kôri* and Minami-toshima *kôri*.

Upon insolvency of an obligor, with the exception of secured creditors, none is entitled to preferential payment.

Kita-toshima *kôri*.

Upon insolvency of an obligor, with the exception of secured credit,[1] all claims, including even land rent, house rent and rent for tenanted rice field,[2] are accorded equal treatment.

Minami-adachi *kôri*.

Upon insolvency of an obligor, land rent and house rent are entitled to preferential payment, while other claims, with the exception of secured credits, do not take any priority over one another.

Shitaya Ward.

In a case of insolvency, settlement of which used to be made by a composition between debtor and creditors, land rent, house rent, etc., were formerly, we understand, entitled to preferential payment. But at present, when bankruptcy[3] is decreed by the court, those matters have to be decided by the law.

Kanda Ward.

In a case of insolvency, whose settlement by a composition between debtor and creditors consists in distributing [what property the debtor has left] among the creditors, there can be no claims of priority in payment. In a case of bankruptcy, however, only taxes in arrears[4] are entitled to prior payment.

Akasaka Ward and Azabu Ward.

No sort of debt has priority in payment. Land rent, house rent, etc., must be paid before what property the obligor has left is distributed among his creditors. This appears to be a customary practice, but in fact it is not.

Hongô Ward.

With the exception of taxes, etc., as provided by law, no kind of claim is entitled to payment prior to secured debts. Not even ar-

---

[1] *Teitô-fusai.*

[2] *Kosaku-mai-kin.* When it is paid in rice, this is called *kosaku-mai*, i.e., rent paid in rice.

[3] *Shindai-kagiri.*

[4] *Sozei-tainô-kin.*

rears[1] such as land rent, house rent, and board[2] are entitled to priority.

CHIBA PREFECTURE

Awa *kôri*, Hei *kôri*, Asai *kôri* and Nagasa *kôri*.

With the exception of secured creditors, nobody exercises a right to priority in payment. To give an instance, the employees of the insolvent will not have the heart to ask their employer to pay their wages due when they consider how heavily indebted he must be now that he has become insolvent. Also, it is not likely that the landlords of his land or house will be anxious to have their rents paid before other debts. On the other hand, it sometimes happens that the insolvent pays off these small debts first, and then asks that what property is left be distributed among those creditors to whom large debts of his are owing.

Katori *kôri*.

There is no practice whereby creditors apply to the authorities for preferential payment of land rent, house rent, etc., even if they are entitled to prior payment, when the obligor becomes insolvent.

Yamabe *kôri* and Muza *kôri*.

The wages of employees, charges for board, house rent, land rent, etc., used to be paid before other debts. But as the law has become more elaborate since the Meiji Restoration[3] [1868], this practice has gradually been discarded until at present there are no traces of it left.

Unakami *kôri* and Sôsa *kôri*.

Upon insolvency of an obligor, no debt is entitled to priority, with the exception of secured debts, land rent and house rent.

Higashi-katsushika *kôri*.

With the exception of secured creditors, no one is entitled to preferential payment.

IBARAGI PREFECTURE

Nishi-katsushika *kôri* and Sashima *kôri*.

With the exception of secured creditors, no one is entitled to preferential payment.

KANAGAWA PREFECTURE

Miura *kôri*.

[1] *Tainô-kin.*
[2] *Shokuryo (makanai-ryo).*
[3] *Go-isshin (Meiji-ishin).*

With the exception of secured creditors, no one is entitled to preferential payment.

Tachibana *kôri*.

There is a practice of priorities. For instance, farm rent paid in money or grain[1] is entitled to prior payment.

Kita-tama *kôri*.

Upon insolvency of an obligor, with the exception of secured creditors entitled to some special privilege, all creditors are of one general class [having no priorities].

Ashigara-shimo *kôri*.

Secured creditors apart, no one is entitled, according to the custom here, to preferred payment.

Prefectural Industrial Bureau.

Land rent, house rent, wages of employees and charges payable to those who have supplied food to the obligor are not entitled to preferential payment.

However, apart from the question of insolvency, silk commission agents of Yokohama[2] entrusted with the sale of goods to foreign merchants have the right to be paid, out of the proceeds of the sales, for their claims for various expenses incurred in connection with the goods, including commission, advances or other loans made to the consignor, the amount of the bill of exchange[3] paid and interest thereon, and the balance due[4] from any preceding account and interest thereon, provided they have received the goods on commission to sell and are free to dispose of them.

TOCHIGI PREFECTURE

Prefectural Office.

Secured debts (which include forwarding charges, packing charges,[5] land rent, house rent, etc.) are entitled to preferential payment.

Shimo-tsuga *kôri* and Samukawa *kôri*.

Upon insolvency of an obligor, with the exception of secured creditors, no one is entitled to prior payment.

Ashikaga *kôri* and Yanada *kôri*.

---

[1] *Kosaku-kinkoku; kosaku*, farm tenancy; *kin*, money; *koku*, grain.

[2] *Kito-urikomi-toiya*.

[3] *Nigawase*.

[4] *Kashikoshi-daka*.

[5] *Nizukuri-hi*.

Formerly there used to be some cases of insolvency in this district. But since the laws regarding bankruptcy, disposition of property by public sale,[1] etc., were put into effect, there has been no case of commercial insolvency.

MIE PREFECTURE

Suzuka *kôri*.

Upon insolvency of an obligor, with the exception of secured creditors, no one is entitled to preferential payment.

Isshi *kôri*.

If warehousing of goods, etc., has been done at the request of the obligor, then the storage charges are not entitled to preferential payment [when the obligor becomes insolvent]. But if it has been done at the request of his obligee, then the storage charges, forwarding charges, etc., are, by custom, entitled to preferential payment, as long as payment on delivery[2] has been expressly promised by the party directing the storage.

Asake *kôri*.

Upon insolvency of an obligor, apart from secured debts, those debts that have priority by natural usage[3] include land rent, house rent and the wages of employees. And if they are paid before other debts by the obligor, it is apparently connived at by the other creditors. However, the more important of his employees—such persons as the head clerk[4] and other clerks[5]—are under the necessity of sharing their fortunes with the insolvent, so they never make any claim to prior payment.

Nabari *kôri* and Iga *kôri*.

Upon insolvency of an obligor, no one is entitled to prior payment, there being no difference between a commercial and a civil case.

AICHI PREFECTURE

Nakajima *kôri*.

With the exception of secured creditors, no one is entitled to prior payment. However, fourteen or fifteen years ago, we under-

---

[1] *Kobai-shobun.*

[2] *Saki-barai.* The expression may mean payment on delivery or payment in advance, but the passage apparently implies "payment by the instructor" as well.

[3] *Shizen-no-kanrei.*

[4] *Bantô.*

[5] *Tedai.*

stand that land rent, the money due for food supplied and so on were entitled to priority.

Nagoya Ward.

In such cases, with the exception of secured creditors, no one is entitled to priority.

Chita *kôri*.

With the exception of secured creditors, no one is, by custom, entitled to priority.

Minami-shidara *kôri*.

From ancient times, debts due the public funds, such as the Shinto shrine funds,[1] or the town or village community funds,[2] were entitled to priority. After these debts were deducted, the rest of the insolvent's property was, by custom, distributed among his creditors. But at present nothing but the legally prescribed rules are in effect.

Atsumi *kôri*.

With the exception of those provided in the laws, no debts are entitled to priority.

Kaitô *kôri* and Kaisai *kôri*.

With the exception of secured creditors, no one is entitled to prior payment. Generally speaking, the creditors are, by custom, paid on the basis of a pro rata distribution.

Aichi *kôri*.

With the exception of secured creditors, no one is entitled to prior payment.

Niwa *kôri* and Haguri *kôri*.

With the exception of secured creditors, no one is entitled to prior payment. However, if the insolvent is a peasant, the land rent and the farm rent paid in rice[3] which are due are entitled to prior payment. In case of a merchant becoming insolvent, the house rent which is due has priority.

SHIZUOKA PREFECTURE

Prefectural Office.

Our answer for this topic is the same as that for the preceding topic.

Udo *kôri* and Abe *kôri*.

---

[1] *Shidô-kin.*

[2] *Kyôyû-kin.*

[3] *Kosaku-mai.*

We have never heard that there are any fixed practices about the matter. When some creditor or vendor of the insolvent is found to be in a distressing financial predicament, it sometimes happens that by conference among the creditors, the creditor who is in that condition is granted priority in payment.

Inasa *kôri* and Aratama *kôri*.

Upon insolvency of an obligor, none but [secured] creditors is entitled to priority. But it sometimes happens that by a sense of moral obligation the insolvent asks his creditors to allow him to pay the land rent, the house rent, the wages of his employees and the debts due to those who have supplied food to the obligor, etc., before other debts.

Kamo *kôri* and Naka *kôri*.

None but [secured] creditors is entitled to priority.

Saga *kôri* and Kitô *kôri*.

We have never heard that any but [secured] creditors is entitled to priority.

GIFU PREFECTURE

Mugi *kôri*.

It is the usual practice here that no one is entitled to priority. But there is also a custom, it is said, whereby the land rent, the house rent, etc., are paid before other debts.

Ampachi *kôri*.[1]

The usual practice prevailing here is that the obligee does not at once proceed to appropriate the security, but after receipt of the obligor's reply to his notice, sells it or gets it valued publicly, according to the reply, and after payment of the principal and interest, turns over any surplus to the obligor.

Fuwa *kôri*.

The land rent and the house rent are entitled to prior payment, according to the custom here. There are no other kinds of debts having priority.

Atsumi *kôri*, Kagami *kôri* and Katagata *kôri*.

No one is privileged to have his debt paid before others'.

Tagi *kôri* and Kami-ishizu *kôri*.

Upon insolvency of an obligor, none but secured creditors is

---

[1] It may be noted that this answer is the same as that for the preceding topic, and is here not applicable [*Translator*].

entitled to preferential payment.

Ôno *kôri* and Ikeda *kôri*.

Regarding the question of priority of creditors upon insolvency of an obligor, there is no fixed practice. But the land rent, the wages of employees, etc., are, by custom, usually paid before other debts.

Haguri *kôri* and Nakajima *kôri*.

With the exception of secured creditors, no one is entitled by custom to prior payment.

Ena *kôri*.

No debt is entitled to priority.

Kamo *kôri*.

Upon insolvency of an obligor, with the exception of secured debts and the land rent, including the rent paid in rice[1] for cultivated land[2] as well as residential land,[3] no kind of debt is entitled to prior payment, according to the custom here. However, regarding the wages of employees, the obligor often resorts, from sentimental considerations,[4] to the practice of paying those debts before he proceeds to distribute what property he has left among other creditors.

Kani *kôri*.

Before the Meiji Restoration, there prevailed here the practice described in the latter half of the present topic, i.e., land rent, house rent, wages of employees and debts due to those who had supplied food to the obligor were mostly entitled to preferential payment. At present these debts are usually accorded no better treatment than other debts in the distribution of the insolvent's property.

Atsumi *kôri*, Gifu Township.

No kind of debt is entitled to priority.

Ôgaki.

We have no custom of recognizing any priority.

Ena *kôri*, Nakatsugawa Village.

There is no distinction.

Shimo-ishizu *kôri*, Takasu Township.

---

[1] *Okite-mai.*
[2] *Kôchi.*
[3] *Taku-chi.*
[4] *Jôjitsu.*

Upon insolvency of an obligor, the secured creditors have their debts paid first. However, regarding land rent, house rent, etc. in arrears, the surety[1] of the obligor is made to pay those debts. If there is no surety, the claimants of those debts are classed together with other creditors, so that they may be entitled to distribution of the insolvent's property. There is no custom here whereby the land rent, the house rent, etc., are entitled to prior payment.

Haguri *kôri*, Takegahana Village.

With the exception of secured creditors, there is no one who is entitled to preferential payment.

Yamagata *kôri*, Takatomi Village.

Upon insolvency of an obligor, there are no debts having priority, with the exception of secured debts and the taxes levied by the office of the village head.

Mugi *kôri*, Kôzuchi Village.

Upon insolvency of an obligor, with the exception of secured debts, all other claims belong to a general class. But the land rent, house rent, wages of employees, etc., are given a special treatment apart from the general debts by the obligor.

Haguri *kôri*, Kasamatsu Village.

With the exception of secured creditors, there is no one entitled to priority.

Fuwa *kôri*, Tarui Village.

Land rent and house rent are entitled to prior payment, but there are no other debts having priority.

Ôno *kôri*, Miwa Village.

Upon insolvency of an obligor, besides the secured debts, the following are, generally speaking, entitled to priority. Land rent, house rent, etc., are by custom paid before other general debts, although the strictness of this usage is not euqal to the right of secured creditors, but is virtually recognized.[2]

Ampachi *kôri*, Gôdo Village.

None.

Tagi *kôri*, Shimada Village.

Upon insolvency of an obligor, the secured debts, land rent,

---

[1] *Mimoto-hikiukenin.*

[2] *Kamben-suru.*

house rent, wages of employees, etc., are, by custom, paid before other debts.

Ena *kôri*, Iwa Village.

There is no usage here whereby some creditor is entitled to prior payment.

Toki *kôri*, Tajimi Village.

Upon insolvency of an obligor, besides secured debts, the house rent alone is entitled to prior payment, according to the custom here.

Kamo *kôri*, Hosome Village.

They say there is a practice here whereby land rent, house rent, wages of employees, debts due to those who have supplied food to the obligor, etc., are entitled to preferential payment. But we have never observed an instance where such preferential payment was made, it being understood that the insolvent himself would exercise as much precaution as possible to satisfy their claims.

Toki *kôri*, Takayama Village.

Yes, there is.

Kani *kôri*, Mitake Village.

There is a custom here whereby once in a while some creditor is paid before secured creditors.

Ena *kôri*, Akechi Village.

No creditor is entitled to priority.

Mugi *kôri*, Seki Village.

Upon insolvency of an obligor, land rent, house rent, wages of employees, etc., are, by custom, paid before secured debts, and the debts for board are paid at the same time as the secured debts.

Ôno *kôri*, Takayama Township.

In case of mortgaged property which is found in the house of an obligor, no obligee other than the holder of the mortgage has a right to take it. On registering the mortgaged property, when there is a description of household properties but no statement of merchandise in detail, the obligor may pay land rent, house rent and wages of employees before such registration is made. But after the insolvency of the obligor is made public, the obligor is not entitled to the property in the list. But the property, with a special statement, may be delivered to the obligees designated in it.

Motosu *kôri*, Kita-kata Village.

Upon insolvency of an obligor, besides secured debts, the land rent and the house rent are, by custom, entitled to payment before other general debts. However, the wages of employees and other claims do not have any priority.

Kamo *kôri*, Ôta Village.

Upon insolvency of an obligor, with the exception of secured creditors, no one is entitled to priority in payment, according to the custom here.

Kaisai *kôri* and Shimo-ishizu *kôri*.

Upon insolvency of an obligor, secured debts are entitled to preferential payment. As to the land rent, the house rent, etc., in arrears, the surety of the obligor is made to pay them. In case no surety is available, the rents in arrears are classed together with other debts and are entitled to pro rata distribution of whatever property the obligor has left. There prevails no custom here that the rents in question are entitled to prior payment.

Gujô *kôri*.

Upon insolvency of an obligor, those claims, besides secured debts, that are entitled to priority, include money left in trust with the obligor merely for keeping, the land rent and the house rent. They are, by custom, paid before other general debts here.

Topic 4:   May a Merchant Who Is Holding a Mortgage Given
by Another Merchant Execute a Second Mortgage[1] on
the Security in Favor of a Third Merchant, Without Obtaining the Consent of the Second Merchant?

GROUP I—ANSWERS

Tokyo.

Formerly there generally prevailed a custom that a merchant who
was holding a mortgage given by another merchant might execute
a second mortgage on the security in favor of a third merchant,
without securing the consent of the second merchant. Even today
it often happens that a second mortgage is executed on such goods
as rice, oil, dried sardines and silk.

Kyoto.

In commerce, we believe they have no usage of the kind referred
to in the present topic, evidence of which may be found in cases
among those who are engaged in the pawnbroking business, a loan
society,[2] or a bank. We know by hearsay that there prevails a practice whereby a second mortgage[3] or transfer of mortgage[4] is executed
upon goods already mortgaged.

Osaka.

There is a custom here whereby a merchant who is holding as
security another's property in bailment may execute a second mortgage on the security in favor of a third merchant without securing
the consent of the second party.

Yokohama.

The practice generally prevails that a merchant who is holding
a mortgage given by another merchant executes a second mortgage
on the security in favor of a third merchant without securing the
consent of the second merchant. The majority of the commission
merchants of Yokohama entrusted by provincial merchants with
sale of their goods to foreign traders resort to this practice.

Hyôgo.

---

[1] *Fuku-teitô.*

[2] *Kashitsuke-kaisha.*

[3] *Fuku-jichi (shichi).*

[4] *Okuri-jichi;* literally, "sending a pledge."

The practice of mortgaging the same goods for the second time [as above described] is resorted to in some trades.

Following are the proceedings at the meeting of the investigation committee on the subject.

No. 3 [Kondô]: Such merchants as silk dealers never resort to the practice of executing a second mortgage on the security given by another merchant, without securing his consent.

No. 2 [Tamba]: Pawnbrokers sometimes practice mortgaging for the second time the mortgage given by another. No. 19, being a pawnbroker, is familiar with the circumstances. So I ask the Chairman to put questions to him about the matter.

No. 19 [Funai]: The pawnbrokers here have a practice called *uwa-jichi*,[1] whereby a pawnbroker pledges again with another pawnbroker an article pledged by an ordinary person. For that, the first pledgee does not always try to secure the consent of the first ordinary pledger.

No. 3 [Kondô]: There is a great difference between a pawn and a mortgage. A genuine merchant will never practice mortgaging for the second time the security given by another.

No. 9 [Takahama]: A pawn is naturally different from a mortgage, as No. 3 has stated. A mortgagee may sell his security when the mortgage is due, and after payment of the debt, turn over any surplus to, or ask payment of any deficit from, the mortgagor. But this is not so with a pawn, and the pledgee in this case is entitled to any surplus and suffers any deficit. Such is the difference between a mortgage and a pawn. There is a commercial custom whereby a merchant executes, for financial purposes, a second mortgage on the security given by another.

No. 2 [Tamba]: A second mortgage is sometimes executed on a security. When, for instance, a wholesaler is consigned successive lots of goods by his regular customers and wishes to remit money on them to the consignees but finds himself already short of funds, he often resorts to the method of raising the money temporarily by executing a second mortgage on the consigned goods. When the consignor brings with him money enough to cover the principal and interest, and wishes to redeem the goods in bailment, the merchant who is holding the second mortgage on the goods, not infrequently, immediately allows him to negotiate for his recovery of the goods.

Chairman [Kashima]: So let us submit a report to the effect that in some trades they have the practice of executing a second mortgage on a security.

---

[1] "On top of (second)—pledge?"

Ôtsu.

Such a practice prevails generally among merchants.

Kumamoto.

There are many instances in commerce of the practice of a merchant who is holding a mortgage given by another merchant executing a second mortgage in favor of a third merchant on the security without securing the consent of the second merchant.

Okayama.

In actual practice one sometimes meets with the practice of a merchant who is holding a mortgage given by another merchant executing a second mortgage on the security in favor of a third merchant without securing the consent of the second merchant.

Bakan.

A holder of a mortgage cannot execute a second mortgage on the security without obtaining the consent of the mortgagor.

Sakai.

Under the old [Tokugawa] regime it was prohibited for a mortgagee to execute a second mortgage on the security in the manner described in the present topic. But in actual practice this was sometimes resorted to. In such a case, however, the mortgagee tried not to enter into any agreement with the third merchant that might infringe upon the rights of the second merchant.

Iida.

The practice here is that even if the holder of a mortgage executes a second mortgage on the security without obtaining the consent of the mortgagor, the mortgagor cannot blame the mortgagee.

Takamatsu.

According to the custom here, a second mortgage may be executed on a security, as long as it concerns commercial goods.

Fukui.

A mortgagee cannot execute a second mortgage on the security without the consent of the mortgagor.

Tokushima.

A holder of a mortgage cannot execute a second mortgage on the security without the consent of the mortgagor.

Takefu.

A mortgagee cannot execute a second mortgage on the security without the consent of the mortgagor.

Miyagi.

The practice that a merchant who is holding a mortgage given by another merchant may execute a second mortgage on the security without obtaining the consent of the mortgagor is limited to cases where the given security consists of movable property.

Matsuyama.

Formerly there prevailed a custom that a merchant who was holding a mortgage given by another merchant might execute a second mortgage on the security in favor of a third merchant without securing the consent of the second merchant. But in recent years it has become the rule for the mortgagee to secure the consent of the mortgagor.

GROUP II—ANSWERS

Токуо Metropolis
    Prefectural Office.
    Pawnbrokers.

It sometimes happens, that for financial purposes, a pawnbroker may repledge a pawn given by his customer with a rich fellow pawnbroker. This is called a "transferred pledge"[1] and also a "sub-pledge"[2] in some quarters. When the pledgor comes back to redeem the pawn, the pledgee at once goes to the sub-pledgee, and redeeming the pawn, gives it back to the pledgor. As a sub-pledge is a credit transaction, each redemption is not always accompanied by payment. That may be made later, or the place of the redeemed article may be taken by another pledge later.

    Oil Wholesalers.[3]

No second mortgage on a security may be executed without the consent of the mortgagor.

    Dry Goods Wholesalers.

We have no such practice for mortgages.

    Timber Wholesalers.

No.

    Rice Wholesalers.

They sometimes execute a second mortgage on, for instance, the

---

[1] *Okuri-jichi.* See also page 273 above.

[2] *Shita-jichi.*

[3] The following traders deny the existence of the custom of second mortgage.

so-called mortgage of warehoused goods.[1] However, they are unable to transfer the actual goods, so the warehouse keeper[2] acts as witness.

Fish Wholesalers.

No.

Fuel Wholesalers.

No.

Saké Wholesalers.

No.

Dried Bonito Wholesalers.

No.

Salt Wholesalors.

No.

Kôjimachi Ward.

It is permissible to execute a second mortgage on a security, but there is no one here who does this.

Nihombashi Ward.

Pawnbrokers sometimes resort to a practice called subpledge; but we have never heard of a second mortgage.

Kyôbashi Ward.

A merchant may execute a second mortgage on B merchant's security in favor of C merchant without securing B's consent.

Yotsuya Ward and Ushigome Ward.

No one who is holding a security given by another may execute a second mortgage on it without securing the consent of the mortgagor.

Asakusa Ward.

No merchant who is holding a mortgage given by another merchant may execute a second mortgage on the security in favor of a third merchant without securing the consent of the second merchant.

Honjo Ward.

A merchant who is holding a mortgage given by another merchant may not execute a second mortgage on the security in favor of a third merchant without securing the consent of the second merchant.

---

[1] *Kura-jichi;* "warehouse-mortgage."

[2] *Kura-mori (kura-ban).*

Ebara *kôri.*

A merchant who is holding a mortgage given by another merchant sometimes executes a second mortgage on the security in favor of a third merchant without securing the consent of the second merchant.

Higashi-tama *kôri* and Minami-toshima *kôri.*

One who is holding a mortgage given by another may never execute a second mortgage on the security in favor of a third party without securing the consent of the second party. However, such a practice, known by the name of "sub-pledge," prevails among pawnbrokers.

Kita-toshima *kôri.*

It is a habitual practice with a merchant that, when he is holding a mortgage given by another merchant, he may execute a second mortgage on the security in favor of a third merchant without securing the consent of the second merchant. In such a case, the first mortgagee always holds himself responsible for the release of the second mortgage. For he is afraid that if the second mortgage inflicts any loss on his mortgagor, it will bring popular discredit upon himself and injury to the business of his firm. On the other hand, the first mortgagor himself has full confidence in his mortgagee, so he usually consents tacitly, even if he is aware that a second mortgage has been executed by his mortgagee on the security he gave.

Minami-adachi *kôri.*

With the exception of pawnbrokers, merchants have no practice whereby a mortgagee may execute a second mortgage on the security he is holding.

Shitaya Ward.

The practice of a merchant who is holding a mortgage given by another merchant executing a second mortgage on the security in favor of a third merchant without securing the consent of the second merchant used to be limited to pawnbrokers, with regard to the pledges they were holding, and to rice merchants holding a mortgage on warehoused grain, and could not be regarded as a general practice. But today there are, it is said, many instances of a second mortgage executed on gold, silver, public loan bonds,[1] silk, etc.

---

[1] *Kôsai-shôsho.*

Kanda Ward.

Sometimes merchants execute a second mortgage on some kinds of goods, such as rice and silk.

Akasaka Ward and Azabu Ward.

Formerly there existed such a practice in some trades. But it now apparently no longer remains, with the exception of the practice of "sub-pledging" which still prevails to this day.

Hongô Ward.

A mortgagee may not execute a second mortgage on the security without the consent of the mortgagor.

CHIBA PREFECTURE

Awa *kôri*, Hei *kôri*, Asai *kôri* and Nagasa *kôri*.

Sometimes a merchant who is holding a mortgage given by another merchant executes a second mortgage on the security in favor of a third merchant without securing the consent of the second merchant. To give an instance, a merchant who is holding an instrument of debt for ¥20 of a second merchant, accompanied by a security, may execute a second mortgage on the bond and give it, along with a written statement, to a third merchant, so that he may borrow ¥20 from the latter. This is of the same nature as the "sub-pledge" practiced by pawnbrokers.

Katori *kôri*.

According to the custom here, a merchant who is holding a mortgage given by another merchant may not execute a second mortgage on the security in favor of a third merchant.

Yamabe *kôri* and Muza *kôri*.

There is a practice here whereby a mortgagee may execute a second mortgage on the security in favor of a third party without the consent of the mortgagor.

Unakami *kôri* and Sôsa *kôri*.

We have never heard of the practice of a mortgagee executing a second mortgage on the security, once mortgaged, without the consent of the mortgagor.

Higashi-katsushika *kôri*.

No mortgagee may execute a second mortgage on the security without the consent of the mortgagor.

IBARAGI PREFECTURE

Nishi-katsushika *kôri* and Sashima *kôri*.

No mortgagee may execute a second mortgage on the security

in favor of a third merchant unless he secures the consent of the mortgagor.

KANAGAWA PREFECTURE

Miura *kôri.*

There has never been such a practice here.

Tachibana *kôri.*

There is such a usage here; for instance, in the case of a pledge of grain, the repledge by a pawnbroker with a richer pawnbroker,[1] etc.

Kita-tama *kôri.*

If a merchant who is holding a mortgage given by another merchant executes a second mortgage on the security in favor of a third merchant without securing the consent of the mortgagor, we deem it to be an improper act. But it is not criticized as long as the security is redeemed before the time for the payment of the first mortgage is due. Consequently, we do not know whether we ought to say we have such a practice or not.

Ashigara-shimo *kôri.*

We cannot make any general statement, for it happens sometimes that, due to some business circumstances, a merchant who is holding a mortgage given by another merchant may execute a second mortgage on the security in favor of a third merchant without securing the consent of the mortgagor, in order to obtain credit with the third merchant.

Prefectural Industrial Bureau.

According to the custom here, a merchant who is holding a mortgage given by another merchant may execute a second mortgage on the security in favor of a third merchant without securing the consent of the second merchant.

TOCHIGI PREFECTURE

Prefectural Office.

According to the practice here, a merchant who is holding a mortgage given by another merchant may execute a second mortgage on the security in favor of a third merchant without securing the consent of the second merchant.

Shimo-tsuga *kôri* and Samukawa *kôri.*

---

[1] *Oya-jichi;* "parent-pledge."

No merchant executes a second mortgage on the security given by another, with the exception of pawnbrokers, who have a practice of repledging a pawn, without securing the consent of the pledgor.

Ashikaga *kôri* and Yanada *kôri*.

Remortgaging is allowed here, as is repledging by a pawnbroker, the latter being a civil affair. The independent pawnbrokers here are divided into two classes, large and small pawnbrokers; there are eight or nine small pawnbrokers and only one or two large ones. When a small pawnbroker has exhausted his funds and is short of money to advance on pawns from his customers, he at once repledges them with a large pawnbroker; this is commonly called a "transferred pledge."[1] In the transaction of repledging, the second pledgee,[2] that is, the large pawnbroker, does not know to whom the pledged article belongs, but only the first pledgee,[3] that is, the small pawnbroker. The first pledgee does not let his pledgor know that his pawn is going to be made a repledge.[4] But even if the pledgor learned that his pawn had been repledged, he would not be surprised.

This civil practice having been brought over to the sphere of commercial matters, nobody is surprised now even if a mortgage is remortgaged without the consent of the mortgagor.

MIE PREFECTURE

Suzuka *kôri*.

No merchant who is holding a mortgage given by another merchant may execute a second mortgage on the security in favor of a third merchant without securing the consent of the second merchant.

Isshi *kôri*.

No merchant may do this.

Asake *kôri*.

No merchant who is holding a mortgage given by another merchant may execute a second mortgage on the security in favor of a

---

[1] *Okuri-jichi.*
[2] *Fuku-kashinushi;* "second-lender."
[3] *Saki-kashinushi;* "former-lender."
[4] *Fuku-tembutsu.*

third merchant unless the consent of the second merchant is secured.

Nabari *kôri* and Iga *kôri*.

It is a general rule that, unless the consent of the mortgagor is secured, or it is specially provided for in the agreement between mortgagor and mortgagee, the mortgagee may not execute a second mortgage on the security given by the mortgagor. But as long as no actual difficulty results therefrom, or arises when he proceeds to conclude some sales transaction on the spot and negotiates about price, the mortgagee may in fact execute a second mortgage.

AICHI PREFECTURE

Nakajima *kôri*.

It is possible that a merchant who is holding a mortgage given by another merchant may execute a second mortgage on the security without securing the consent of the second merchant.

Nagoya Ward.

No mortgagee may execute a second mortgage on the security without the consent of the mortgagor.

Chita *kôri*.

According to the local custom, no merchant who is holding a mortgage given by another merchant may execute a second mortgage in favor of a third merchant without securing the consent of the second merchant. However, circumstances may give rise to the possibility of a second mortgage being transacted by the mortgagor in favor of a third party.

Minami-shidara *kôri*.

No mortgagee transacts a second mortgage on the security without the consent of the mortgagor.

Atsumi *kôri*.

A practice exists whereby a mortgagee may execute a second mortgage on the security. But nobody may do this without the express consent of the mortgagor.

Kaitô *kôri* and Kaisai *kôri*.

No mortgagee may execute a second mortgage on the security, according to local practice.

Aichi *kôri*.

Unless the consent of the mortgagor is obtained, a mortgagee may not deal with the security to suit himself.

Niwa *kôri* and Haguri *kôri*.

No merchant who is holding a mortgage given by another merchant may execute a second mortgage on the security in favor of a third merchant unless the consent of the mortgagor is secured.

SHIZUOKA PREFECTURE

Prefectural Office.

A mortgagee may never do that.

Udo *kôri* and Abe *kôri*.

No.

Inasa *kôri* and Aratama *kôri*.

Some mortgagees execute a second mortgage on the security. It may be noted, however, that this can be done only as long as the first mortgage is in effect.

Kamo *kôri* and Naka *kôri*.

No merchant may execute a second mortgage on the security in favor of a third merchant unless the consent of the mortgagor is obtained.

Saya *kôri* and Kitô *kôri*.

Some mortgagees may possibly execute a second mortgage on the security in favor of a third party without securing the consent of the mortgagor. If this could not be done, commercial firms might be confronted with many difficulties. However, since this is not legally permissible, the second mortgage will be null if it turns out to be a breach of faith and results in litigation.

GIFU PREFECTURE

Mugi *kôri*.

There is no such practice here. The people of this place apparently have the idea that that kind of thing is not permissible.

Ampachi *kôri*.

It is sometimes practiced in commercial transactions, and we have never heard of any trouble resulting from it.

Fuwa *kôri*.

They have the practice here that a mortgagee may execute a second mortgage on the security without securing the consent of the mortgagor.

Atsumi *kôri*, Kagami *kôri* and Katagata *kôri*.

As this would give rise to great evils, it is not resorted to unless the consent of the mortgagor is secured.

Tagi *kôri* and Kami-ishizu *kôri*.

They never execute a second mortgage on a security. The mortgage discussed in the preceding four topics is a commercial transaction, but it is contracted according to general civil regulations.

Ôno *kôri* and Ikeda *kôri*.

No mortgagee-merchant may execute a second mortgage[1] on the security in favor of a third party without securing the consent of the mortgagor-merchant.

Haguri *kôri* and Nakajima *kôri*.

It may sometimes happen that a mortgagee executes a second mortgage on the security.

Ena *kôri*.

They sometimes transact a second mortgage.

Kamo *kôri*.

The practice prevails to a certain extent among silk, timber and other merchants that a merchant who is holding a mortgage given by another merchant executes a second mortgage on the security in favor of a third merchant without securing the consent of the mortgagor.

Kani *kôri*.

It is unusual that a person who is holding a mortgage given by another executes a second mortgage on the security in favor of a third party. If the mortgagee wishes to do this, needless to say, he always has to secure the consent of the mortgagor.

Atsumi *kôri*, Gifu Township.

There is no such practice as that of transacting a second mortgage on a security here.

Ôgaki.

Such a commercial practice is often found, and we have never heard of any trouble resulting from it.

Ena *kôri*, Nakatsugawa Village.

No mortgagee may transact a second mortgage on a security without securing the consent of the mortgagor.

Shimo-ishizu *kôri*, Takasu Township.

When a merchant who is holding a mortgage given by another merchant wishes to execute a second mortgage on the security in favor of a third merchant, it is the general rule for the mortgagee not to carry out the transaction without conferring with the mortgagor.

Haguri *kôri*, Takegahana Village.

[1] *Jû-teitô (fuku-teitô).*

Mortgagees who execute a second mortgage on a security are sometimes found.

Yamagata *kôri*, Takatomi Village.

Though the mortgage is given by another merchant, the mortgagee is free to deal with it as he likes, as long as the mortgage is in effect.

Mugi *kôri*, Kazuchi Village.

A merchant who is holding a mortgage given by another may execute a second mortgage on the security in favor of a third merchant.

Haguri *kôri*, Kasamatsu Village.

Sometimes a mortgagee may transact a second mortgage on the security.

Fuwa *kôri*, Tarui Village.

The custom prevails that a mortgagee may execute a second mortgage on the security.

Ôno *kôri*, Miwa Village.

No.

Ampachi *kôri*, Gôdo Village.

There is no such practice here.

Tagi *kôri*, Shimada Village.

No.

Ena *kôri*, Iwa Village.

Sometimes.

Toki *kôri*, Tajimi Village.

A merchant who is holding a mortgage given by another merchant sometimes transacts a second mortgage on the security in favor of a third merchant.

Kamo *kôri*, Hosome Village.

A merchant who is holding a mortgage given by another merchant sometimes makes use of it as a remortgage for raising funds.[1] But he may not transfer the mortgage to a third merchant unless the consent of the mortgagor is secured.

Toki *kôri*, Takayama Village.

This is not permissible.

Kani *kôri*, Mitake Village.

This is impossible unless the mortgagor's consent is secured.

---

[1] *Kinsaku.*

Ena *kôri*, Akechi Village.

A mortgagee sometimes transacts a second mortgage on the security.

Mugi *kôri*, Seki Village.

A mortgagee may not execute a second mortgage on the security in favor of a third merchant.

Ôno *kôri*, Takayama Village.

A second mortgage on a security may be executed by the mortgagee with the consent of the mortgagor. But a case may arise in which a third person promises orally to lend money or to execute a second mortgage on the security.

Motosu *kôri*, Kita-kata Village.

Unless the consent of the mortgagor-merchant is secured, the mortgagee-merchant may not transfer, with his endorsement[1] or explanatory statement,[2] the mortgage to a third merchant, subject to the time limit of the original mortgage.

Kamo *kôri*, Ôta Village.

The practice sometimes occurs, with some sorts of mortgaged goods, that a merchant who is holding a mortgage given by another merchant may execute a second mortgage on the security in favor of a third merchant without securing the consent of the mortgagor.

Kaisai *kôri*, Shimo-ishizu Village.

When a security which has been mortgaged by merchant A to merchant B will be mortgaged again to merchant C, the mortgage is executed to merchant A.

Gujô *kôri*.

The practice whereby a merchant holding a mortgage given by another merchant may execute a second mortgage on the security in favor of a third merchant without securing the consent of the mortgagor applies to personal property. But real property cannot be remortgaged.

---

[1] *Uragaki;* "back-writing."

[2] *Riyû-sho.*

CHAPTER III
AGENTS FOR SALE

Topic 1: What Marks the Difference between the Trade of a *Toiya* and That of a *Nakagai*?[1]

GROUP I—ANSWERS

Tokyo.

According to the traditional usage of the terms, *toiya*, or wholesaler, commonly includes, not only those who, carrying on business at their own risk, buy goods direct from producers and sell them, but also those who engage in the sale, for a commission, of goods entrusted to them by consignees. *Nakagai*, or broker, commonly signifies both those who, buying goods from wholesalers, sell them in turn to retail merchants, and those who, buying goods direct from producers, bring them to the market and sell them to wholesalers.

Herewith, we submit to you for your inspection a separate volume[2] that has been prepared by us after investigation into the matter. This contains the old regulations regarding the business and history of wholesalers and brokers in the rice, salt, oil, cotton and drapery trades. We hope that it may give you some idea about the difference in the nature of the trade.

Kyoto.

As to the distinction between a wholesaler and a broker, you are referred to Title I, Topic 1, where the description of the distinction between a merchant and a non-merchant contains also a brief statement on this point.

Osaka.

Before we proceed to answer the question of the present topic, let us describe how commercial conditions in Osaka characteristically differ from those in Tokyo and other cities.

Osaka is situated in the center of the country and is an important port of the Kansai district. Formerly the produce of all the provinces

---

[1] Literally, "middle-man."

[2] Printed in the Appendix to Book I herewith.

used to be assembled here and then distributed throughout the land. There was thus no district in the country which was not a market for Osaka merchants, who might, with some justice, be said to have dominated the market of the land. Although Osaka was not equal to Tokyo in the level of activity and prosperity, commerce in the latter was limited to satisfying local needs and sales in the neighboring provinces. Tokyo was the metropolis where the 300-odd feudal lords used to repair annually, and the local needs were vast. Leaving aside the question of the amount of business, and referring rather to its trade characteristics, it can be said that Osaka has thrived for the past 200 years on selling and distributing goods throughout the country, although its own local needs were small.

Thus, compared with Osaka, Tokyo might well be called a retail market,[1] as indeed it used to be commonly called.

In view of these facts, it may be stated that although there is not much difference in the characteristics of trade between Tokyo, Saikyo[2] and other flourishing commercial cities, including Nagoya, Niigata, Hyogo and Shimonoseki, Osaka alone is characterized by much that is distinct from Tokyo and other cities.

Regarding the distinction between a commission agent (*toiya*)[3] and a broker (*nakagai*), although each association had its own rules, neither side venturing to encroach upon the other's territory in the days when there were trade associations known by the name of *kabu-nakama*,[4] the distinction between the two sometimes varied with the particular trade. To cite an instance of the practices of some of the well-known organizations, it is the proper business of a *toiya* to sell to *nakagai* those goods with whose sale he is entrusted by their consignors, or to buy goods from consignors and sell them to *nakagai*. The proper business of a *nakagai* consists, on receipt of orders from merchants of other provinces and retailers, in buying goods from *toiya* and reselling them to customer-retailers, or in buying goods

---

[1] *Ko-uri-ba;* "small-sell-place."

[2] Old name for Kyoto.

[3] In this answer, the word *tonya* (not *toiya*) is used with a special meaning. The translation thus indicates a difference in usage here from that in other places.

[4] "Share-guilds"; an institution found at Yedo, Kyoto, Osaka and other large cities during the Tokugawa period. The associations were organized with government permission, and aimed at monopolizing business for the benefit of members. But sometimes they were organized at the government's suggestion for convenience of supervision. See Part I, Chap. 7.

on speculation[1] from *toiya* to resell to merchants of other provinces or retailers, sometimes making the goods more marketable. Some *nakagai* even buy goods direct from their producers and sell them direct to consumers.[2] A *toiya* cannot sell goods direct to consumers or to merchants of other provinces. On the other hand, a *nakagai* cannot buy goods direct from a consignor, according to the usage here.

The above rule mostly applies, with slight modifications according to the goods, to those goods that are transported here by sea, including rice and other cereals,[3] fuel, sugar, indigo,[4] fertilizer,[5] oil, raw fish,[6] dried fish,[7] salted fish,[8] dried bonito, timber, bamboo, iron, lacquer,[9] medicines[10] and rapeseed.[11]

Those persons are also called *toiya* (commission-agents), who employ craftsmen to manufacture certain goods, or contract with craftsmen to manufacture them, or buy them from the craftsmen who produce them, and then sell them to merchants of other provinces, retailers or consumers.

Again, some *toiya* (for instance, of dry goods and cotton goods) buy goods from merchants of other provinces, or direct from their producers, and sell them to merchants of other provinces, *nakagai* or retail merchants. On the other hand, *nakagai* buys goods direct from the producers and sells them to *toiya*, or buys them from *toiya* and sells them to merchants of other provinces, etc. A broker is one who cannot engage in the same kind of business as *toiya* because of lack of funds. The ordinary distinction between *nakagai* and *toiya* does not hold good in the present case.

Those who deal in paints,[12] books, soap,[13] etc. are called dealers-

[1] *Mikomi-gai.*
[2] *Juyônin (shôhisha)* (modern usage).
[3] *Zakkoku.*
[4] *Ai.*
[5] *Koyashi-mono.*
[6] *Nama-zakana.*
[7] *Hoshi-uwo.*
[8] *Shio-zakana.*
[9] *Urushi.*
[10] *Yakushu.*
[11] *Natane.*
[12] *Enogu.*
[13] *Sekkin* [?].

in-such-and-such-goods, and buy the goods direct from the producers or from the consignors, and sell them to general consumers, there being here no distinction between a *toiya* and a *nakagai* as far as these trades are concerned.

The distinction between a *toiya* and a *nakagai* as regards the usage of the two terms is occasionally reversed, for instance, in the case of dealers in sugar[1][?] and cotton. Those who are called *toiya* in these trades buy the goods from consignors or brokers of other provinces, and making them more marketable, sell them to merchants of other provinces or retailers, while a broker buys the goods from local producers or from producers of the neighboring provinces and sells them to *toiya*.

A glance at the above statements may, we are afraid, give an impression that the business of *nakagai* is in a subordinate position to that of a *toiya*. The *nakagai* of dry goods, sugar, etc., their capital not being equal to that of *toiya*, naturally appear to be in a position subordinate to *toiya*. But regarding rice dealers and other merchants engaged in ordinary trades, *nakagai* are by no means in a position subordinate to *toiya*. Not only does the former have business dealing with the latter on an equal footing, but it often happens that the former has more funds at his disposal than the latter, maintaining a position superior to the latter in the business world. Therefore, here in Osaka, there is no fundamental distinction, in the standing[2] and the amount of business, between a *toiya* and a broker.

The origin of the terms *toiya* and *nakagai* cannot be learned. But in view of the prevailing conditions of the rice traffic and other ordinary sorts of trade, it will be seen that both a *toiya* and a *nakagai* are resident merchants who act as agents for sale or purchase between producers and consumers of different provinces for the convenience of both parties; that although they belong to different organizations, the relations between a *toiya* and a broker are as close as if they were one; and that, to outsiders, including consignees and customers, they hold exactly the same status as merchants.

However, within this group of merchants themselves, that is,

---

[1] *Tô (Satô)* [?].
[2] *Kakushiki.*

among the local merchants of the Osaka Metropolis,[1] there are substantial distinctions between a *toiya*, a *nakagai* and a retailer. The *toiya* makes it his main business to sell, as agent of his consignee, the goods shipped by the latter; while the broker is an agent for his customers, who entrust him with the purchase of the goods they want. Looked at from the standpoint of the business they conduct, with their own funds, for the benefit of outsiders, a wholesaler makes it his main business to *buy* goods, while the main business of a broker consists in the *sale* of goods.

However, the business tax regulations[2] instituted in the 12th year of Meiji [1879] established the classification of merchants into companies,[3] *oroshi-uri*,[4] brokers and retailers, thus classifying the *toiya*, or commission agents, as *oroshi-uri*, and doing away with the old Osaka customs, to the considerable inconvenience of the merchants. What is called *oroshi-uri*, or wholesaler, in Osaka refers to sale in bulk[5] to "outsiders," in contrast to sale in small quantities, and forms the proper business of the [formerly termed] *nakagai*; so that we believe it would be more fitting to classify merchants into companies, *toiya* (or commission agents), *oroshi-uri* (or wholesalers) and retailers. Brokerage refers to the transaction in which a merchant, at the order of his customer, buys goods, in the capacity of agent, from a *toiya*, receiving a reasonable commission therefor. But when a merchant, taking advantage of an opportune moment, *buys* goods on his own responsibility from a *toiya* or the producers or his fellow merchants, with his eyes fixed upon future profits that may be derived from selling them or from working over the goods, and *sells* them to others, that is *oroshi-uri*.

However, if sale of goods in great quantity means the same thing as *oroshi-uri*, then it may be said that a *toiya* might justly be called *oroshi-uri*, since his sale to a *nakagai* is on a larger scale than that of a *nakagai* to his customer. However, a *toiya*'s sale to a *nakagai* is a dealing conducted *within* the trade, among merchants themselves, and is not of the sort that would be classified into big sale and small

---

[1] The text has *fu*, i.e., prefecture.

[2] *Eigyô-zei-soku.*

[3] *Kaisha.*

[4] This word is also usually translated as "wholesaler," but it is used here with some special connotation.

[5] *Ô-uri;* "great sale."

sale by *outsiders*. And when we consider that in actual practice the largest part of a *toiya*'s business consists in the sale to others of goods entrusted to him by the consignor, what he buys out of the consignment himself constituting only 20 or 30 percent, while a *nakagai*, taking an opportune moment of the market situation, buys goods and sells them to customers at large, only 10 or 20 percent of his business being to buy goods for his customers on receipt of their orders, it will be clear that, both in theory or practice, *oroshi-uri* should be another name for *nakagai*.

There are sometimes merchants who call themselves "wholesalers and retailers in such and such goods," or put up a sign[1] reading "wholesalers and retailers in such and such goods." They are, for the most part, engaged in some trade on the borderline between wholesale and retail. They sell manufactured goods of their own to general customers, or, on purchasing goods from the manufacturers, they sell them to customers at large. The term *oroshi-uri* is used in reference to customers, and it applies to a *nakagai* who makes it his main business to *sell* goods in the manner described above, and not to a *toiya* whose chief business consists in *buying* goods.

Yokohama.

According to the hitherto prevailing usage, the merchants commonly called wholesalers are those who buy goods from producers and sell them to merchants, or sell goods with the sale of which they are entrusted by consignors. Those are generally called brokers who buy goods from wholesalers and sell them to retailers, or buy goods direct from their producers and sell them to wholesalers in the market. However, the merchants whom we usually call *nakagai*, or brokers, in connection with the trade of this port are those who go between two parties and act as agents for sale or purchase of goods, receiving a commission for this. Although they are called *nakagai*, they are, in fact, of the same nature as those merchants who are called "margin-earners."[2]

Hyôgo.

A wholesaler is one who buys goods direct from producers and sells them to merchants, or sells goods on commission from con-

---

[1] *Shôhai* (*hamban*).

[2] *Sayachigai* (margin)-*tori* (taker).

signors. A broker is one who buys goods from wholesalers and sells them to retailers, or buys goods direct from their producers and sells them to wholesalers.

The following are the proceedings of the investigation committee on the subject.

No. 2 [Tamba]: As to the difference in the nature of their business, I believe a wholesaler is one who buys goods direct from producers and sells them to brokers, while a broker is one who buys goods from wholesalers and sells them to retailers.

No. 9 [Takahama]: A wholesaler is one who sells to brokers goods that are consigned to him by their producers, charging a commission for it or storage for the goods. Or a wholesaler may buy goods direct from their producers and sell them to brokers.

No. 14 [Funai]: It is very difficult to establish the distinction between a wholesaler and a broker. A *jōki-tonya*,[1] for instance, has the combined function of a wholesaler and a broker. Also [one who is called] a dry goods wholesaler is not, in reality, a wholesaler, but does the business of a broker.

No. 1 [Ikeda]: A merchant usually called *toiya* is one who buys goods from producers and sells them to brokers, but not to retailers. That is, it is another name for *oroshi-toiya*, or wholesaler. A *nakagai-nin* is one who buys goods direct from the producers and sells them to retailers, or, buying goods from their producers, sells them to wholesalers.

Chairman [Kashima]: Shall we submit a report to the effect that a wholesaler is one who buys goods direct from producers and sells them, or sells goods under commission of consignors; while a broker is one who buys goods from wholesalers and sells them to retailers, or buys goods direct from the producers and sells them to wholesalers?

The motion was unanimously adopted.

No. 2 [Tamba]: The nature of the business of a wholesaler has greatly changed today from former days. Thus most wholesalers today sell goods to retailers. I wish to make this statement for the sake of accuracy.

Ōtsu.

According to the usage that prevailed until the early modern period, a wholesaler, of rice, for instance, was allowed to purchase imported rice direct, but a broker was not. The practice is no longer in existence today. There is a slight difference between the two in their commercial preferences.

This is practically the same with other trades.

---

[1] *Jōki*, steamship. *Jōki-tonya* usually simply means a shipping agent; but the one referred to in this passage apparently was engaged in some other business as well.

Kumamoto.

As to the distinction in the nature of their business between a wholesaler and a broker, he is generally called a wholesaler who receives consignments of goods from the place of their production and sells them, or acts as agent for sale of goods at the request of others, receiving a commission therefor. A broker, meanwhile, is one who goes out to the place of production and buys goods there and sells them to wholesalers in the market, or, at the request of others, goes as intermediary between buyers and sellers. Such is the difference between a wholesaler and a broker.

Okayama.

He is called a wholesaler who buys goods at the place of their production, or from brokers, and exports them outside his district. One who goes out to the place of production, buys goods and sells them to wholesalers is called a broker.

Bakan.

A wholesaler is one who sells goods which come from consignors, or who buys goods for others at their request. A broker is one who buys goods from wholesalers and sells them to other merchants.

Sakai.

The merchants who have been called *toiya* since old times are those who, at their own risk, buy goods direct from the place of their production and sell them, or sell goods consigned to them, on commission from consignors, receiving some percentage therefor. A *nakagai* is one who buys goods from a *toiya* and sells them to retailers, or buying goods direct from the place of their production, sells them to *toiya* in the market.

Iida.

A *toiya* is one who buys goods at a price limit,[1] or at a price to be fixed by him according to the market price, from the producers of the goods or from merchants who bring them from other provinces, and resells them to others. A broker is one who goes between *toiya* and other merchants and acts as agent for sale or purchase of goods, receiving a percentage or commission therefor.

Takamatsu.

According to the usage here, the *toiya* in our locality, unlike those of other places, does not go out himself to the place of production

---

[1] *Sashi-ne.*

to buy goods at his own risk and sell them. He only engages in the sale of goods on commission from consignors, for which he receives a percentage. A *nakagai*, meanwhile, buys goods from *toiya* and sells them wholesale to retailers, or retails direct to consumers.

Fukui.

A *toiya* is one who receives goods consigned for sale by vendors, while a *nakagai* is one who is entrusted by vendees with the purchase of goods for them.

Tokushima.

A *toiya* is engaged in the sale of goods on commission, while it is the business of a *nakagai* to act as intermediary between buyers and sellers of goods.

Takefu.

A *toiya* is one who is consigned goods by a merchant and acts as intermediary for sale of the goods to another merchant, receiving therefor a commission or storage charges. A *nakagai* goes between a merchant and an ordinary consumer as intermediary for the purchase of goods, deriving some profit out of it. But it is not his business to receive a consignment of goods and to charge storage, etc., for it.

Miyagi.

It is the main business of a *toiya* to buy from middlemen[1] of various places and to keep a large quantity of goods in stock to sell wholesale. A *nakagai* buys various goods and sells them to a *toiya* as well as to retail merchants, or sometimes sells them retail himself.

Matsuyama.

The merchants who have been called *toiya* hitherto are those who make it their business to sell goods in the market on commission from consignors, or to buy goods imported or to be exported and sell them. A *nakagai* is a merchant who, with the exception of brokers in the rice exchange,[2] buys goods from the place of production, or from their manufacturers, and sells them to *toiya* or other firms.

---

[1] *Kaitsugi-shōnin.* See the following page.

[2] *Kome-shōkaisho (kome-kaisha);* a term that was in use before the 9th year of Meiji (1876).

GROUP II—ANSWERS

Tokyo Metropolis
Prefectural Office.
Oil Wholesalers.

A *toiya* is a merchant who, sending out orders for goods to places of production or receiving shipments of goods from consignors, sells them to *nakagai*, receiving a commission therefor. A *nakagai* buys goods from a *toiya* and sells them to retail merchants.

Dry Goods Wholesalers.

In the places where dry goods are produced there are middlemen called *kaitsugi-shônin*. A *toiya* sends his orders to these middlemen, or sometimes buys goods consigned to him direct from the producers, and is engaged in the sale of the goods with a view to profit. There is, in this trade, no merchant called *nakagai* acting as intermediary, and a *toiya* is engaged in retail business as well.

Timber Wholesalers.

A timber wholesaler is engaged in the sale of goods on commission from consignors, for which he receives a percentage. There is no special class of merchants called *nakagai* in this trade, as a timber wholesaler is at the same time a retailer of the goods.

Rice Wholesalers.

Formerly it was the custom for a rice wholesaler to order goods at the place of production, or to receive shipment of goods from consignors, which he then sold to brokers and retailers to make a profit, the brokers reselling to retailers. Nowadays, however, it is the rule for a wholesaler always to get the goods consigned, according to his financial status, direct from the place of production.

Fish Wholesalers.

A *toiya* is one who invests purchase money[1] in the fishing community[2] [to secure the goods], or accepts consignment of the goods shipped direct from the place of production, and *sells* them to *nakagai*. A *nakagai* is one who buys goods from a *toiya* and sells them to retailers, or sells them retail himself for profit. Some *toiya* are engaged in retail business as well. This is called "wholesale retail,"[3]

---

[1] *Shiire-kin-wo-dasu.*

[2] The text has *sanchi*, i.e., the place of production.

[3] *Te-uri*, "hand-sale."

and is resorted to by those *toiya* who are evading the sale of goods through *nakagai.*

Fuel Wholesalers.

The answer to the present topic is given under that on the wholesaler.

Saké Wholesalers.

A *toiya* is one who is engaged in the sale of goods shipped to him by consignors, for which he receives a percentage. A *nakagai* is one who buys goods from *toiya* and sells them to retailers to make a profit.

Dried Bonito Wholesalers.

A *toiya* is one who is engaged in the sale of goods shipped direct to him by consignors, for which he receives a percentage. A *nakagai* is one who buys goods from *toiya* and sells them to retailers for profit. However, dried bonito *toiya* are at the same time *nakagai,* and are engaged in retail as well as wholesale business.

Salt Wholesalers.

A wholesaler is one who, fixing the prices of the goods and securing the consent of the consignors therefor, concludes a sales contract with them. Then charging the consignors a 5 percent commission, he gives the consignors an invoice and sells the goods to *nakagai.* A *nakagai* is engaged in retail business, and in sales in bale[1] as well.

With respect to business methods, a *toiya* makes it a rule to immediately settle his account with his consignors; and he asks the *nakagai* to pay installments.[2]

Kôjimachi Ward.

It is the business of a *toiya* to get consignments of goods from producers[3] and sell them, and for a *nakagai* to buy goods from *toiya* and sell them to retailers.

Nihombashi Ward.

A *toiya* is a merchant who gets shipments of goods from consignors or from middlemen, or buys them direct from craftsmen.[4] He is influential in raising or lowering the prices of goods.

Kyôbashi Ward.

---

[1] *Tawara-uri.*

[2] *Waritsuke-sumashikata.*

[3] *Seizô-nin (seisansha).*

[4] *Kôsaku-nin.*

The distinction in the nature of their business between a *toiya* and a *nakagai* is as follows. A *toiya* makes it his business to buy goods at the place of production and to sell them to *nakagai*, while the business of a *nakagai* is to buy goods from *toiya* and to sell them to retailers, consumers, or to fellow traders.

Yotsuya Ward and Ushigome Ward.

A *toiya* is one whose business is to buy goods direct from the place of production or from producers,[1] and to sell them to merchants, or to sell goods on commission from consignors. A *nakagai* is one whose business is to buy goods from *toiya* or other merchants and to sell them to merchants.

Asakusa Ward.

Although there is a difference in name, there is no fixed distinction between a *toiya* and a *nakagai*.

Honjo Ward.

There is a distinction between a *toiya* and a *nakagai*. Those merchants who, for instance, buy goods direct from the mountainous districts[2] are called *toiya*, while those who buy goods from *toiya* and sell them to retailers are called *nakagai*.

Ebara *kôri*.

There is some distinction in the nature of business between a *toiya* and a *nakagai*.

Higashi-tama *kôri* and Minami-toshima *kôri*.

A *toiya* buys goods in advance from producers[3] and keeps them in stock to sell wholesale to *nakagai* or retail merchants at current prices.[4] A *nakagai* buys goods from *toiya* in advance and sells them to retailers.

Kita-toshima *kôri*.

A *toiya* makes a practice of selling to *nakagai* goods imported from various provinces, for which he openly receives a commission, the percentage being different with each trade. It is also his business to buy goods directly from the consignors in advance, and then sell them to *nakagai*. A *nakagai* is not allowed to openly receive a commission, but earns his profit in the form of what they call *kawa*,[5]

---

[1] *Seizô-mono (seizô-nin).*

[2] *Yamakata;* implies here the place of production.

[3] *Motokata.*

[4] *Sôba.*

[5] Literally, "skin" or "peel"; probably used here in the sense of "margin."

for instance, in so many *sho*[1] *kawa* or so many *go*[2] *kawa* in the case of rice and other cereals. If, for instance, one *yen* could buy for him one *to*[3] four *sho* of rice, a *nakagai* might sell the goods at the rate of one *to* three *sho* per yen, thus earning one *sho kawa*. Such is the distinction between a *toiya* and a *nakagai*.

Minami-adachi *kôri*.

The distinction in the nature of business between a *toiya* and a *nakagai* is as follows. A *toiya* is a merchant who is consigned goods for sale by farmers or manufacturers, and who sells them to *nakagai*, receiving some percentage. Sometimes he also resorts to a practice called *shikiri*, whereby he buys goods from farmers or manufacturers at the market price of the day and sells them to *nakagai*. A *toiya* also sometimes sells the goods direct to retail merchants, but this is a rather exceptional practice. A *nakagai* makes it his business to buy goods from *toiya* and to sell them to his customer-consumers or to retail merchants.

Shitaya Ward.

The term *toiya*, as hitherto used, is a general name for merchants who, on their own account, buy goods direct from the place of production or buy them through *nakagai* and sell them. It also refers to those who sell goods on commission from consignors, receiving a percentage therefor. *Nakagai* are merchants who on their own account buy and collect goods at the place of production or from craftsmen, or from *toiya*, and sell them; or go between merchants as intermediary for sale or purchase of goods; or sell goods to retailers on commission.

Kanda Ward.

A *toiya* is one who sells goods shipped to him by consignors, while a *nakagai* sells goods kept in stock by a *toiya*.

Akasaka Ward and Azabu Ward.

A *toiya* is one who receives shipments of goods direct from consignors, while a *nakagai* receives goods from a *toiya* and sells them to retailers. A retailer buys goods from the *nakagai* and sells them to ordinary customers.[4] Formerly there used to be a monopoly of

---

[1] A measure of capacity, i.e., 1.588 quart or 0.48 standard gallon.

[2] Also a measure of capacity: 1/10 of *sho*.

[3] 10 *sho*.

[4] The text has *jiyô-nin*, lit., "man who needs the goods for his personal use."

customer-retailers[1] for each *nakagai* in all lines of trade, and a *toiya* who was at the same time also a *nakagai* used to have his own customer-retailers. Of late, however, with the exception of some trades, the distinctions have become very much confused.

Hongô Ward.

A *toiya* is one who buys goods direct from the place of production or from craftsmen, while a *nakagai* buys goods from *toiya* and sells them to merchants.

CHIBA PREFECTURE

Awa *kôri*, Hei *kôri*, Asai *kôri* and Nagasa *kôri*.

A *toiya* is one who receives any shipment made to him by a consignor, and executes any order for goods received. He makes an invoice to the consignor on the basis of the appraisal of the goods by *nakagai*, and also sends an invoice to the orderer stating the sales price, receiving a percentage as his profit. If it happens, therefore, that the purchaser of the goods finds the prices too high and enters a protest with him, a *toiya* may show him the entries in the *shikiri-moto-chô* account book to clear up his doubts. Such occasions seldom arise among the merchants here, however.

A *nakagai* is one who goes between *toiya* and retailers, or between *toiya* and consumers, as intermediary for the sale or purchase of goods, and makes his profit by receiving a percentage or commission for it. The percentage system is known by the name of "*ryô-ichi*"[2] or "one *momme* for one *ryô*."[3] Thus a *nakagai* receives, for a transaction worth one *yen*, a reward the equivalent of one *momme* of silver, which is equivalent to 1.66 *sen* (0.0166 *yen*). Most of the business in fish and other marine products here is carried on through *nakagai*.

Katori *kôri*.

The business of a *toiya* is to receive consignments of goods from various places and buy them, in a lump, fixing their prices; while it is generally the business of a *nakagai* to sell goods. The latter buy goods from *toiya* or their producers and sell them to fellow traders or retail merchants.

Yamabe *kôri* and Muza *kôri*.

---

[1] *Kabumise;* "share-shop."

[2] One *ryô*.

[3] 1 *momme* = 1/60 *ryô*. *Momme* is the name of a silver coin and *ryô* that of a gold coin, used during the Tokugawa period; see Part I, Chap. 9.

Those who are called *toiya* in our *gun*[1] are, in other words, whole-salers, and they make it their business to buy goods from *nakagai* or producers and sell them wholesale to retail merchants. It is the business of a *nakagai* to buy goods from producers and sell them to *toiya*.

Unakami *kôri* and Sôsa *kôri*.

A *toiya* makes it his business to sell goods on commission from consignors. It is the business of a *nakagai* to go as intermediary be-tween buyers and sellers of goods or to buy and sell goods on his own account. Thus the distinction between *toiya* and *nakagai* is clear.

Higashi-katsushika *kôri*.

A *toiya* is one who buys goods from craftsmen or *nakagai*, etc. and sells them to merchants. A *nakagai* is one who acts as intermediary between merchants, receiving a commission therefor, or, buying goods with his own funds, sells them on his own account without putting them on show in his stock.

IBARAGI PREFECTURE

Nishi-katsushika *kôri* and Sashima *kôri*.

A *toiya* buys and collects goods in which he deals, at the current prices, distinguishing between finer and coarser goods, and sells them to others. A *nakagai* does not indiscriminately buy and sell goods in his line, but only those he selects among the goods in which he deals.

KANAGAWA PREFECTURE

Miura *kôri*.

A *toiya* is one who, receiving shipments of goods from consignors, fixes their prices and buys them. A *nakagai* is one who buys goods from a merchant and sells them to another. There are no merchants here who may be called *toiya*, their business being of the nature of a *nakagai*.

Tachibana *kôri*.

A *toiya*, for example in the vegetable market,[2] gets his commission without moving about, while a *nakagai* earns his profits by bustling about for his transactions.

Kita-tama *kôri*.

A *toiya* is one who, buying goods in advance, sells them to *nakagai*

---

[1] *Gun (kôri).*

[2] *Aomono-ichiba.*

and retailers; he is what is called a wholesale merchant.[1] A *nakagai* is one who goes between a *toiya* and a *nakagai* and acts as intermediary for the sale or purchase of goods. Sometimes the business of a *toiya* and a *nakagai* varies depending upon the trade. It is a matter of usage and it is impossible to make any generalized statement.

Ashigara-shimo *kôri*.

As far as Odawara and vicinity is concerned, with the exception of fish wholesalers, there is not much difference in the nature of the business of a *toiya* and that of a *nakagai*.

Prefectural Industrial Bureau.

The merchants who are publicly called *urikomi-toiya* or *hikitori-toiya* in the trade port [of Yokohama] are those who sell goods that are consigned to them by others or bought by them in advance, conducting the business in their own name or that of their company. A *nakagai* is just the same as the merchant called "percentage-earner."[2] He goes between other merchants as intermediary for the sale or purchase of goods, although he cannot conduct business in his own name.

TOCHIGI PREFECTURE

Prefectural Office.

Here it is generally the business of a *toiya* to receive goods in trust from *nakagai* or producers, sometimes allowing advances on them, or sometimes buying them. Then, putting them on the market in his own premises, he sell them to merchants, making a statement of account to the consignors and receiving a percentage for the sale. According to the usage here, it is generally the business of a *nakagai* to buy goods from producers and sell them to *toiya* or retailers for profit, or to act as intermediary between other merchants for the sale or purchase of goods, receiving a commission therefor.

Shimo-tsuga *kôri* and Samukawa *kôri*.

The distinction in the nature of business between a *toiya* and a *nakagai* consists in the fact that a *toiya* sells goods wholesale to retail merchants, while a *nakagai* buys goods from farmers or manufacturers and sells them to wholesalers. In practice, however, the distinction is hard to establish in most cases, for most *toiya* are, at the same time, engaged in the business of *nakagai*.

---

[1] *Oroshiuri-eigyonin.*

[2] *Saitori, sayatori.*

Ashikaga *kôri* and Yanada *kôri*.

Here anything and everything offered for sale by merchants is dealt with separately in each particular line of trade, and those merchants in each line who wish to buy come together and, fixing the price, take away the goods with them. But no merchant should be called *toiya* who receives percentages from both the seller and the buyer of the goods. Merchants who buy goods, such as textile fabrics, at the respective market,[1] do so with a view to reselling them to others or, at the order of their customers, delivering the goods immediately to their purchasers. Therefore, despite some modifications to be made (according to the trade), they must generally be called *nakagai*.

MIE PREFECTURE

Suzuka *kôri*.

Toiya are merchants who go between artisans and merchants and act as intermediaries for the sale and purchase of goods. The transaction ends with the delivery of the goods and payment, the *toiya* receiving a percentage, or sometimes, buying goods themselves and selling them to merchants. *Nakagai* are merchants who run about between artisans and merchants and act as intermediary for the sale or purchase of goods, receiving a percentage, or, sometimes, buying the goods themselves and selling them to merchants. Thus the business of a *toiya* and that of a *nakagai* appear to be the same, and they are hardly distinguishable from each other. The difference between them, however, consists, in short, in the fact that sellers and buyers of goods flock to the place of a *toiya* to transact their business, while the *nakagai* runs about between sellers and buyers to help them transact their business.

Isshi *kôri*.

A *toiya* maintains premises for his goods and makes it his business to receive goods from consignors, advancing money on them in part payment to the consignors, and after sale of the goods, takes a percentage out of the prices at which the goods have been sold. A *nakagai* does not keep a store of his own, but goes between merchants, acting as intermediary for the sale and purchase of goods, and receiving a percentage.

---

[1] *Ichi.*

Asake *kôri.*

The distinction between a *toiya* and a *nakagai* consists in the fact that a *toiya* sells goods consigned to him by others and buys goods for others at their request, receiving a commission, while a *nakagai* buys goods from *toiya* and sells them to consumers or fellow merchants.

Nabari *kôri* and Iga *kôri.*

Generally a *toiya* does not sell his own goods but sells those consigned to him by others. He receives and transmits payment of the prices, attends to the shipment and delivery of the goods, etc., receiving a percentage in proportion to the amount of the business done. *Toiya* also refers to those who buy and collect goods from non-merchants and *nakagai*, sometimes making them more saleable and bringing them to market in a lump to sell. *Nakagai* are merchants who buy goods from non-merchants and sell them to *toiya*, or, borrowing money from *toiya*, buy and collect goods on order[1] for which they earn thereby a middleman's profits.

AICHI PREFECTURE

Nakajima *kôri.*

A *toiya* is a firm where buyers and sellers of goods come together to transact business, paying the firm a commission. Such is the business of a *toiya*. A *nakagai-nin* makes purchases of goods,[2] sometimes direct from *toiya*, and sells them at a profit to consignees.[3] Such is the business of a *nakagai*.

Nagoya Ward.

A *toiya* is a firm that receives goods shipped from provincial consignors and serves as a place for selling the goods. A *nakagai* buys goods from *toiya* and sells them to retail merchants.

Chita *kôri.*

The distinction in the nature of their business between a *toiya* and a *nakagai* consists in the fact that a *toiya* acts, at the order of his customers, as intermediary between sellers and buyers of goods, paying temporarily on behalf of his customers and receiving a commission for his services, or sells in a large way in his own name the goods consigned to him by his customers, receiving therefor a com-

---

[1] *Ukemono-hin.*

[2] *Kaidashi.*

[3] *Buppin-itaku-nin;* literally, "one to whom goods are consigned."

mission, while *nakagai* goes between buyers and sellers of goods and acts as intermediary without making a temporary payment for them, and receives therefor a commission. *Nakagai* also usually refers to merchants who buy goods from producers with their own money and sell them to *toiya* or others.

Minami-shidara *kôri*.

In our region, the businesses of *toiya* and *nakagai* have been pursued as a combined business since old times, so it is impossible to assert a definite distinction between the two.

Atsumi *kôri*.

Though both names, *toiya* and *nakagai*, are in use here, in actual practice there is no difference between the two in their business.

Kaitô *kôri* and Kaisai *kôri*.

Toiya means merchants who buy goods from *nakagai* and producers and sell them to dealers in the goods; while *nakagai* are persons who act as intermediary between sellers and buyers of goods, receiving therefor a percentage.

Aichi *kôri*.

Toiya are those who receive goods from consignors and sell them to *nakagai*, making a profit in the form of a commission, commonly called *niwa-kôsen*,[1] in proportion to the amount of business done. *Nakagai* are those who buy goods from consignors or *toiya* and sell them to retail merchants, for a profit, as well as those who act as intermediary for the sale of goods between one merchant and another.

Niwa *kôri* and Haguri *kôri*.

Those who have heretofore been called *toiya* are merchants who act as intermediaries for the sale and purchase of goods between one merchant and another, receiving therefor *niwa-sen*,[2] commission, etc. *Nakagai* are persons who buy goods from a merchant and sell them to another at a profit.

SHIZUOKA PREFECTURE

Prefectural Office.

There is no term, "*toiya*," in use here at present. A *nakagai-nin* is one who acts as intermediary for the sale of goods. Those who used to engage in business under the name of *toiya* received pay for

---

[1] Lit., "space-charge."

[2] *Niwa-sen* (*niwa-kôsen*); see the preceding paragraph.

storage, commission, etc., like the present shipping agent or the ground transporter, but did not have anything to do with the sale of the goods themselves. There were some *toiya*, however, who employed a sort of *nakagai* to attend to certain business transactions, the latter, in turn, depending upon the *toiya* for patronage.

Udo *kôri* and Abe *kôri*.

Toiya are those who keep a store and act as intermediary for sales to *nakagai* and retail merchants of agricultural, manufactured and marine goods, lumbermen's products, etc., receiving therefor a commission in proportion to the amount of business done. *Nakagai* are those who go between farmers, manufacturers, and fishermen on the one hand and merchants on the other to help them transact their business, earning thereby a profit.

Inasa *kôri* and Aratama *kôri*.

The *toiya* buy goods from manufacturers, producers,[1] and *nakagai* and (sometimes making them more saleable) sell them to merchants. The *nakagai* buy goods from manufacturers or producers, with a commitment to sell them to certain buyers or act as intermediary for sale or purchase of goods between others, receiving therefor a commission.

Kamo *kôri* and Naka *kôri*.

The *toiya* sell goods shipped from consignors and receive a commission representing a certain percentage of the amount of the sale. *Nakagai* buy goods from *toiya* [and sell them to others], or at the request of their customers buy goods from producers for them, receiving a commission representing a certain percentage of the price. *Nakagai* who do business in a small way are also sometimes called *saitori*.

Saya *kôri* and Kito *kôri*.

There are two kinds of *toiya*. The first are those who act as intermediaries at the request of their customer-merchants for the sale and purchase of goods for which they merely receive a commission; they do not undertake to buy and sell goods on their own account. The second class of *toiya* are those who buy goods from *nakagai* and sell them wholesale to provincial merchants, and are also engaged in retail trade in their own shops.

---

[1] *Sôgyô-sha* (操業者).

There are also two kinds of *nakagai*. The first are those who merely act as intermediaries for the sale and purchase of goods between *toiya* and producers, or between *toiya* and consumers, receiving therefor a commission. The second class are those who buy goods from producers and sell them to *toiya* on their own account. In short, *toiya* obtain goods which are brought to them by various consignors, without bustling about for them, while the *nakagai* run about to get their customers.

GIFU PREFECTURE

Mugi *kôri*.

Toiya receive and hold on trust a consignment of goods with instructions about their price limits, and sell such goods to buyers as they present themselves. *Nakagai*, meanwhile, act as intermediaries for the sale or purchase of goods between one merchant and another, receiving therefor some commission.

Ampachi *kôri*.

Although the terms are subject to slight modifications according to particular cases, a *toiya*'s business is to act, while staying in his premises, as intermediary between buyers and sellers, receiving therefor a commission from the sellers. A *nakagai-nin*, meanwhile, upon receipt of an order from a buyer or a seller, runs about to effect a transaction between them, and upon its conclusion receives a commission from the orderer.

Fuwa *kôri*.

A *toiya* is one who sells goods sent to him by consignors, making an advance on them. Upon their sale, he receives a percentage out of the sales price, or, for allowing the use of his warehouse, a rental charge called *niwa-sen*. A *nakagai*, on the other hand, acts as intermediary for the sale of goods between one merchant and another, receiving therefor some commission.

Atsumi *kôri*, Kagami *kôri* and Katagata *kôri*.

A *toiya* keeps a shop and acts as intermediary for the sale and purchase of goods between merchants, while a *nakagai* runs about in all directions and acts as agent for others.

Tagi *kôri* and Kami-ishizu *kôri*.

Though it is hard to assert a clear distinction between a *toiya* and a *nakagai* in the nature of their business, generally speaking, a *toiya* makes it his special business to buy and collect goods direct from the manufacturers and other producers and to sell them to merchants and consumers; while it is the special business of a *nakagai* to sell goods direct to merchants which he has bought from manufacturers or other producers.

Ôno *kôri* and Ikeda *kôri*.

As there are no merchants here who correspond to the types described in Title III, Topics 1–6, we have nothing to report in answer to your questions as to their practices.

Haguri *kôri* and Nakajima *kôri*.

Toiya collect goods for others and receive a fixed sum of commission[1] therefor; while *nakagai* sell or buy goods to or from *toiya*.

Ena *kôri*.

There are two kinds of *toiya*. One buys goods at the place of their production or from the artisans and sells them wholesale to others. The other keeps a shop and acts as an intermediary for sale or purchase of goods between one merchant and another, receiving therefor a percentage or commission. *Nakagai*, on the other hand do not keep shops themselves and act as intermediaries for the sale or purchase of goods between others.

Kamo *kôri*.

The distinction in the nature of business between a *toiya* and a *nakagai* is that a *toiya* is a place of assemblage for prospective buyers and sellers of goods, who for sales or purchases are charged a "space-charge,"[2] storage, commission, and exchange fees.[3] A *nakagai*, meanwhile, buys and collects goods to resell immediately to others, for which he receives a small profit or commission.

Kani *kôri*.

A *toiya* acts as agent for the sale of goods consigned to him on commission from the consignors, receiving therefor a storage fee or commission. A *nakagai* sells the goods himself and earns the profit.

Atsumi *kôri*, Gifu Township.

The distinction in the nature of business consists in the fact that those referred to as *toiya* keep a shop and act as intermediaries for the sale and purchase of goods, while the *nakagai* run about in all directions, acting as intermediaries for the sale and purchase of goods.

Ôgaki.

[1] *Tei-kôsen.*

[2] *Niwa-chin (niwa-sen).*

[3] *Kawase-tesûryo.*

Although it is subject to slight modifications according to the case, a *toiya*'s business is, while staying in his house, to act as intermediary between buyers and sellers, receiving therefor a commission from the sellers. The *nakagai-nin*, on the other hand, upon receipt of an order from a buyer or seller, runs about to effect a transaction between them, and upon its conclusion receives a commission from the orderer.

Ena *kôri*, Nakatsugawa Village.

Both a *toiya* and a *nakagai* act as intermediary for business transactions between a merchant and non-merchant, or between one merchant and another. But a *toiya* has a fixed place of business, while a *nakagai* does not.

Shimo-ishizu *kôri*, Takasu Township.

Toiya, referred to in the present topic, are mostly provided with business funds, and are engaged in the sale of goods consigned to them by others, for which they receive a percentage or commission. *Nakagai* are little different from *toiya* in that they are also engaged in the sale of goods consigned to them by others, for which they receive a commission. However, *nakagai* do not need business funds, but have only to hustle around to carry on their business, for which they generally receive about one half as much in commission as a *toiya* gets for his services.

Haguri *kôri*, Takegahana Village.

A distinction in the nature of business between a *toiya* and a *nakagai* is found in the circles of merchants dealing in *Yûki* striped cloth[1] and *Santomé* striped (silk) cloth.[2] The party called *toiya* in this trade accomodates his customer-buyers from various provinces with free lodging and board in his house, and, inviting the manufacturers or *nakagai* of the goods to his place, acts as intermediary between the buyers and the manufacturers or *nakagai*, giving them an opportunity for direct negotiations. As to the commission to be paid to the *toiya* for his services, 2 percent of the sales price is [or used to be?] the regular rate paid by the party selling the goods. Those who are called *nakagai* buy goods from producers and sell them to *toiya*, receiving a middleman's profit.

[1] *Yûki-jima;* a name originally given to the cloth produced at the Yûki district, Shimotsuke Province.

[2] *Santomé-jima;* a name given to the silk cloth of a certain striped pattern. It was originally the name given to the silk fabric imported from Santomé, India.

Yamagata *kôri*, Takatomi Village.

Toiya stay at their places of business and wait for buyers and sellers to assemble, set the prices[1] of the goods in a public way, selling the goods to buyers at a small profit. *Nakagai*, meanwhile, go to the houses of buyer and seller, convey the opinion of the one to the other, and [thus acting as intermediaries between them] receive a commission for this.

Mugi *kôri*, Kôzuchi Village.

As to the distinction in the nature of business between a *toiya* and a *nakagai*, the former receives goods in consignment at his place of business and sells them, while the latter sells the goods of one merchant to another.

Haguri *kôri*, Kasamatsu Village.

The distinction is that *toiya* collect goods for others and get a fixed sum of commission for the service, while *nakagai* sell or buy goods to and from *toiya*.

Fuwa *kôri*, Tarui Village.

There are no merchants here called *toiya* or *nakagai*, so nothing is known about them.

Ôno *kôri*, Miwa Village.

There is no such business as *toiya* here.

Ampachi *kôri*, Gôdo Village.

There is no *toiya* here at present.

Ena *kôri*, Iwa Village.

There are two kinds of *toiya* here. The first are wholesalers; the second are persons who, offering the use of their places of business, act as intermediary for the sale and purchase of goods between one merchant and another. *Nakagai* are persons without shops who collect goods and sell them to *toiya*.

Kamo *kôri*, Hosome Village.

A *toiya* receives a consignment of goods and looks after their sale. He makes an advance[2] to the consignor in settlement of the sales account, receiving therefor a commission. A *nakagai* sometimes goes out to make a purchase of goods. *Nakagai* also engage in the transportation of the goods in which they deal.

Toki *kôri*, Takayama Village.

---

[1] *Sôba-o-tateru.*

[2] *Shikiri-tatekai-kin;* "settlement-advance-money."

A *nakagai-nin* buys goods directly from artisan-producers[1] and sells them to *toiya*, while a *toiya* engages in the sale of those goods to ordinary customers in general.

Kani *kôri*, Mitake Village.

There are no commercial *toiya*.

Ena *kôri*, Akechi Village.

There are two kinds of *toiya*. One group is usually called *oroshi-uri* or wholesaler. The other class includes those who, receiving goods in consignment from artisan-producers, sell them to merchants, receiving therefor a commission. *Nakagai* are those who, without keeping a shop, buy and collect goods and resell them [to merchants].

Mugi *kôri*, Seki Village.

A *toiya* is one who acts as intermediary between one merchant and another for the sale or purchase of the goods they deal in. According to the regulations of *toiya*, upon their reaching an agreement [and the conclusion of the transaction], the *toiya* charges both parties a commission ranging from 1/1000 to 5/1000 the value of the total sales price of the goods.

Ôno *kôri*, Takayama Village.

A *nakagai*, acting as intermediary between one merchant and another for the sale or purchase of goods, receives from the selling party a commission fixed according to the amount of the business done and the market price of the goods. The rate of the commission is variable.

Motosu *kôri*, Kita-kata Village.

A *toiya* is a firm which receives goods in custody or allows merchants to transact their business with one another on its premises, for which it receives a reasonable rate of commission. A *nakagai-nin* is one who acts as intermediary between merchants for sales or purchases, for which he receives a commission.

Kamo *kôri*, Ôta village.

The distinction in the nature of business between a *toiya* and a *nakagai* is that the *toiya* makes it his business [to receive goods in custody from consignors and] to make a "space-charge"[2] and take a commission. A *nakagai* merely buys goods and sells them at once,

---

[1] *Shokkô*. This may mean artisan or factory worker, the modern usage being almost exclusively the latter.

[2] *Niwa-chin*.

earning thereby a profit or commission.

Kaisai *kôri* and Shimo-ishizu *kôri*.

A *toiya* generally has business funds and is engaged in the sale of others' goods, receiving therefor a percentage, commission, or the like. A *nakagai* is also engaged in the sale of others' goods, receiving therefor a commission, but differs from a *toiya* in not having business funds, having to run about actively to get business. A *nakagai* usually gets half as much commission as a *toiya*.

Gujô *kôri*.

There are no merchants called *toiya* here, so there is no distinction to report in the nature of business between a *toiya* and a *nakagai*. A *nakagai* is one who, on receipt of orders, buys goods for others or acts as intermediary for the sale of goods, securing thereby a profit.

Topic 2: Is There Any Other Class of Persons Who, Acting as Agents for Sale between Two Parties, Receive a Commission, Other Than Those Who Are in General Usage Called *Toiya* and *Nakagai*? If There Are, What Are the Varieties?

GROUP I—ANSWERS

Tokyo.

Besides those persons who are in general usage called *toiya* and *nakagai*, there are many other agents for the sale of goods between two parties. The varieties include the rice exchange,[1] the stock exchange,[2] the fish and fowl companies,[3] the vegetables market,[4] the second-hand clothes market,[5] and the auction market,[6] and, as individual merchants, *saitori*.

Kyoto.

As has been stated in our answer to Title I, Topic 1, each commercial pursuit is given an appellation according to the nature of the business. It happens, however, that the same kind of business may sometimes be called by a different name in the three metropolises and other places. *Toiya* is a common comprehensive name, but it sometimes has different characteristics according to the case, as, for example, marine *toiya*,[7] loading *toiya*,[8] shipping *toiya*,[9] rice *toiya*,[10] timber *toiya*[11] and many others. There are also market *toiya*,[12] such, for example, as fish *toiya*, vegetable *toiya*, mulberry leaves

---

[1] *Kome-shôkai-sho (kome-kaisha)*, a term used until the 9th year of Meiji (1876), when a new rice exchange law was put into effect. See Part I, Chap. 10.

[2] *Kabushiki-torihiki-sho*. See Part I, Chap. 7.

[3] *Uo-kaisha* (fish company), an old time usage for *uo-ichiba* (fish-market); *uo-tori-kaisha* (fish and fowl company).

[4] *Aomono-ichiba; ichiba*, market.

[5] *Furugai-ichiba*.

[6] *Seriuri-sho; (seriuri-ichiba)*.

[7] *Kaisen-toiya*. See *kaisen-shonin* in Title I, Topic 1, page 4.

[8] *Tsumini-toiya*.

[9] *Unsô-toiya;* shipping agents.

[10] *Kome-toiya*.

[11] *Zaimoku-toiya*.

[12] *Ichiba-toiya;* a *toiya* who runs a market, or a *toiya* forming part of a general market.

toiya,[1] cocoon *toiya*[2] and probably many others. Each class of *naka-gai-nin* also has a name by which it is called, such as rice *nakagai*,[3] silk *nakagai*,[4] etc. To cite further examples, there are such and such *kaisha*,[5] such and such *kaisho*,[6] such and such *torihiki-sho*,[7] etc. These institutions or persons are called by different names, but in the end their businesses are no different from those of a *toiya* or a *nakagai*. They have different names according to the locality, and the institutions differ from one another in their importance.

Osaka.

There is such a class of intermediaries besides *toiya* and *nakagai* in almost every important trade here. They are called *suai*[8] or *tombi*, and are almost the same as those called *saitori*[9] in Tokyo, forming, apart from *toiya* and *nakagai*, a group of brokers licensed to charge a commission for their services in acting as intermediaries for sales or purchases within the same trade. To this class belong, for instance, the *ukemochi-nin* in the indigo trade and *toritsugi-nin*[10] in the sugar trade.

Yokohama.

Besides those who are generally called *toiya* and *nakagai*, there are some others who act as intermediaries for sale or purchase between two parties, receiving therefor some commission. They are called *sachigai-tori*,[11] or in the case of the tea trade, *nakatsugi*.[12] They are most numerous in the group of middlemen to whom is consigned

---

[1] *Kuwa-toiya*. Mulberry leaves are the food of cocoons.

[2] *Mayu-toiya*.

[3] *Kome-nakagai*.

[4] *Ito-nakagai*.

[5] *Kaisha*, in modern usage, means a company or share corporation; but formerly it used to mean simply an association or, in special usage, a market.

[6] *Kaisho:* 1. a place of assembly for some particular purpose; 2. an exchange or market.

[7] An exchange.

[8] *Su*, trading; *ai*, assembling of traders. *Suai* is a sort of commercial intermediary, and compared with *nakagai*, does his business in a smaller way; a pedlar-broker.

[9] A minor broker, a pedlar-broker. The word *saitori* is often said to be a shortened form of *suai-tori*, i.e., one who earns *suai* or brokerage.

[10] Intermediary.

[11] Literally, "margin-earner."

[12] Intermediary.

the sale of provincial products to foreign merchants in the port.
Hyôgo.

Besides those who are generally called *toiya* and *nakagai*, there are some others who go between two parties and act as intermediaries for the sale or purchase of goods between them. They are the rice exchange, the American dollar exchange,[1] the auction market, *saitori*, and those who are called *kudari-mono-ya* in the local dialect, etc.

The proceedings of the investigation committee on the subject follow:

No. 9 [Takahama]: There are others besides *toiya* and *nakagai* who act as intermediaries for sales or purchases between two parties, receiving therefor a commission. Examples are *saitori* and *tobi*. These persons do not make use of any business funds, even if they can afford to, but make it their chief occupation to act as intermediary for sale in business, for which they receive a commission.

No. 26 [Kuriyama]: In Hyôgo, there are, besides *toiya* and *nakagai*, some people called *kudari-mono-ya*, who, without the need of any business funds, make it their chief occupation to go between two parties and act as intermediary for sales or purchases between them, receiving therefor a commission. These people have business relations exclusively with the merchant ships from the north.[2] When the people of these ships, which enter this port every year, have disposed of their stock of goods and wish to set sail on their voyage home, they always make it a rule to buy goods by letting the *kudari-mono-ya* act as intermediary in their purchases from the vendees.

No. 11 [Horiuchi]: The American dollar exchange and the rice exchange also belong to the class of intermediaries, do they not?

No. 9 [Takahama]: So does the auction market, I believe.

After deliberations by the members present, it was agreed to submit a report to the effect that, as instances of the intermediary in question, there are, in our district, *saitori*, the rice exchange, the American dollar exchange, the auction market and *kudari-mono-ya*.

Ôtsu.

Those who are called *suai* and who act as intermediary for sale or purchase of rice and other cereals may be an instance of the intermediary in question. No other trade has any such intermediary.

Kumamoto.

---

[1] *Yogin-torihiki-sho; yogin*, American dollar.

[2] *Hokkoku-sen; hokkoku*, the north country.

Besides those who are publicly called *toiya* and *nakagai*, there are none here who act as intermediaries for sale or purchase between two parties. It may be added, however, that those people who may be called *saitori* and *tobi* merchants in Tokyo and Osaka, respectively, are all called, according to the local usage, *nakagai*.

Okayama.

Besides those who are generally called *toiya* and *nakagai*, there is not any definite class of persons here who go between two parties and act as intermediary for sales or purchases, receiving therefor a commission. However, we have hitherto met with some who are called *nibushi*, these persons corresponding to those who are called *saitori* in Tokyo and elsewhere.

Bakan.

Except for *toiya* and *nakagai-nin*, there are none here who act as intermediaries between two parties for sales or purchases.

Sakai.

Besides those people who are generally called *toiya* and *nakagai*, there are some in every trade here who go between two parties and act as intermediaries for their sales or purchases, receiving therefor some commission. They are called *tobi*, and in case of the saké trade alone, *nakatsugi*.

Iida.

Those who have no need of any business funds, and who go between parties and act as intermediaries for their sales or purchases, are called *saitori* in the local trade usage. These people, equipped with information about the goods to be sold by one party and their prices, make it their sole business to run about in all directions looking for buyers for the goods, and to bring about a transaction between the two parties, being paid some commission for their services.

Takamatsu.

Besides *toiya* and *nakagai*, who call themselves commercial intermediaries, there are some who act as intermediary for sales or purchases of goods. They are called *tobi* or *nibu* in the local usage, and form a special class of *nakagai* who make it their business to go between *toiya* and *nakagai*, or between consignors and consumers, and act as intermediaries between them for sales or purchases of goods.

Fukui.

There are none here who correspond to the intermediary as described in the present Topic.

Tokushima.

Other than *toiya* and *nakagai*, there are none here who act as intermediaries for sale or purchase between buyer and seller.

Takefu.

With the exception of the two classes of people mentioned in the preceding topic, there are no special people that correspond to those described in the present topic.

Miyagi.

Besides the generally known *toiya* and *nakagai*, there are some who act as intermediaries for sales or purchases. They are called *saitori*, although they are seldom met with here.

Matsuyama.

There are here, apart from *toiya* and *nakagai-nin*, agents who act as intermediaries for sales or purchases between two parties, receiving a commission for it, who are called swallow merchants[1] in the local usage. It is characteristic of these merchants that they regularly frequent commercial houses, furnishing them with daily reports of the market situation and quotations of goods, and act as sub-intermediaries[2] to *toiya* and *nakagai*, or introduce themselves to [new] commercial houses.

They resemble *nakagai*, but they belong to a slightly inferior class.

GROUP II—ANSWERS

TOKYO METROPOLIS
Prefectural Office.
Oil Wholesalers.
Those who are called *saitori* are such persons.
Dry Goods Wholesalers.

---

[1] *Tsubame-shonin*. The probable analogy is between the frequent visits of the intermediary to commercial houses and swallows' frequent flights into and out of a house. Swallows used to be, and sometimes still are, allowed to make their nests under the ceilings of houses in provincial districts.

[2] *Shita-shusen; shita*, under, *shusen*, mediation.

Those that are called *saitori* make it their occupation to run about between *toiya* and retail merchants, and to act as intermediaries for sales or purchases, receiving therefor a commission.

Timber Wholesalers.

Those who are called *saitori* run about in timber trades for example, between *toiya* and retail merchants.

They make it their occupation to act as intermediaries in the sale or purchase of goods, for which they receive a commission from the buyer.

Rice Wholesalers.

There are two classes of the so-called *saitori*.

To the first class belong those who, being men of some social standing, leave with consignors money equal to 5 or 10 percent of the price of the goods, thus temporarily assuming the position of the purchaser of the goods, and then, running about in all directions, act as intermediaries for their sale, from which they derive some profit. The second class consists of those who, being of the lowest social standing and living in humble quarters, make the rounds of consignors and *toiya* to learn about their stock[1] and to get quotations for the prices of their goods; they then act as agents for their sale. For example, when they find rice priced at one *to*, one *sho* for one *yen* they transact its sale either to obtain goods by way of a margin, which they will later resell, or to earn a commission. They are not always engaged in selling only rice and other cereals. They may undertake the sale of anything, depending on the market situation.

Fish Wholesalers.

None.

Fuel Wholesalers.

Those who are called *saitori* belong to this class.

Saké Wholesalers.

There are no agents who go between *toiya* and *nakagai*. But there are intermediaries, called *saitori*, who go between restaurant keepers and retail saké merchants of little means. These people, equipping themselves with information about the quality, quantity and prices of the goods for sale by *toiya* and *nakagai*, take some sample saké[2]

---

[1] *Arini.*

[2] *Kiki-zaké.*

with them, and going between restaurant keepers and retail saké merchants, transact a sale between them, receiving a commission for their services.

Dried Bonito Wholesalers.

There are such intermediaries, called *saitori* here. In most cases they do not transact business in their own name.

Salt Wholesalers.

None.

Kôjimachi Ward.

Other than *nakagai-nin*, agents who act as intermediaries for the sale of goods between two parties [transacting the sale or purchase without any business funds of their own], and receive therefor a commission, are called *saitori*, *karekore-ya*[1] or *sedori-ya*.[2]

Nihombashi Ward.

Apart from *toiya* and *nakagai*, agents who act as intermediaries for sale between two parties are called *saitori* or *hatashi*. However these people do not have the funds and influence possessed by *nakagai*.

Kyôbashi Ward.

There are some such intermediaries, commonly called *saitori*, and they form a class by themselves.

Yotsuya Ward and Ushigome Ward.

Apart from the *nakagai* mentioned in the first topic, there are agents called *saitori*. These, without assuming the position of a buyer or seller themselves, make it their business merely to act as intermediaries between two parties, for which they receive a commission. The varieties include those connected with the sale or purchase of real estate, the loan of money or grain, and those who arrange such transactions as a third party and receive therfor a commission.

Asakusa Ward.

Besides those who are called *toiya* and *nakagai*, there are some who act as intermediaries for sale or purchase of goods between two parties. In such trades as rice, timber, fuel, saké, oil, tea, paper

---

[1] "This-'n-that-er"; a kind of intermediary who has no settled line of business but takes on any lucrative-looking line as the occasion offers.

[2] Literally, "one who takes a commission."

and silk, they are called *saitori*,[1] and are restricted to wholesalers. In the second-hand furniture,[2] second-hand clothes and second-hand book trades, they are called *hatashi*. The latter are found among retailers as well as wholesalers.

Honjo Ward.

There are some, besides those who are publicly called *toiya* and *nakagai*, who act as intermediaries for sale or purchase between two parties. They are commonly called *saitori*, and are found in such trades as rice, cereals,[3] dried produce,[4] imported goods,[5] ironware,[6] silks, saké and soy sauce,[7] tobacco, paper and oil.

Ebara *kôri*.

There are many, besides those who are publicly called *toiya* and *nakagai-nin*, who act as intermediaries between two parties in the sale or purchase of goods. The varieties are almost innumerable.

Higashi-tama *kôri* and Minami-toshima *kôri*.

They are commonly called *saitori*. They are not called *toiya* or *nakagai*, and they act as intermediaries between two parties in sales or purchases, for which they receive a commission. They may be found in every trade, but here in this *gun* they are met with only in such trades as tea, silk, cereals, rice-bran[8] and dried sardines.

Kita-toshima *kôri*.

There are some intermediaries, besides *toiya* and *nakagai*, called *saitori* here. They do not keep a shop, but go out to the market every day to do business as an intermediary, receiving a trifling commission for their services.

Minami-adachi *kôri*.

Besides those that are publicly called *toiya* and *nakagai*, there are, in every trade, some who act as intermediaries for the sale or purchase of goods between two parties. These people are commonly called *saitori*, and are most numerous in the rice trade.

Shitaya Ward.

[1] Literally, "difference-earner."
[2] *Furu-dôgu-ya.*
[3] *Zakkoku.*
[4] *Kambutsu.*
[5] *Hakurai-mono.*
[6] *Tetsu-mono.*
[7] *Shoyu.*
[8] *Nuka.*

There are some, besides those that are called *toiya* and *nakagai*, who go between two parties and act as intermediaries for the sale or purchase of goods. They are called *saitori*, and make it their occupation to equip themselves with information about the stock of goods up for sale by a *toiya*. Going among other merchants, they act as intermediaries for sales, sometimes doing this at the request of their customers.

Kanda Ward.

Those who act as intermediaries for the sale or purchase of goods are commonly known as *saitori*. They are found, to cite some examples, in the trades of rice, dried produce, medicine,[1] saké, oil, money exchange,[2] leaf tea,[3] imported goods,[4] and others.

Akasaka Ward and Azabu Ward.

Those who act as intermediaries for sale or purchase of goods are commonly called *saitori*. *Saitori*[5] is, it is said, a corrupted form of 才取, and 才取 means *tobi* or 鳶.[6] Almost every trade has such intermediaries, and it is hardly possible to enumerate the varieties of these *saitori*, some of whom receive a percentage and others a service-fee.[7]

Hongô Ward.

Those people that are commonly called *saitori* here probably belong to this class. In the trades of rice, money exchange, art and curios[8] and others, there are a great many varieties of such agent.

CHIBA PREFECTURE

Awa *kôri*, Hei *kôri*, Asai *kôri* and Nagasa *kôri*.

Besides those who are generally called *nakagai-nin*, there are merchants who act as intermediaries for sale or purchase of goods be-

---

[1] *Yakushu.*

[2] *Ryôgaye.*

[3] *Ha-ja; ha,* leaf, *ja (cha)* tea. The word is used in distinction from powdered tea and stem tea.

[4] *Yôhin (hakurai-hin).*

[5] 才取.

[6] The reasoning is probably based on the fact that a kind of commercial intermediary is often called *tobi* as well as *saitori*, and *tobi* 鳶 means the bird "kite," when it is written in Chinese characters. As already stated elsewhere a great etymological authority believes that *saitori* is an abridged form of *sai-tori.*

[7] *Tesûryô.* This translation is purposely adopted here to distinguish it from *kôsen* (percentage), although it is rendered as "commission" elsewhere in the book.

[8] *Kottô-shô,* curio dealer.

tween two parties. They are called *saitori*. On receipt of information of the arrival of goods shipped by a merchant, the *saitori* goes to the merchant and learns their prices. Bringing the matter immediately to the consideration of another merchant, he effects a sales transaction between them, receiving from the seller some money as percentage or service fee. There are a great many *saitori* in this district.

Katori *kôri*.

There are few merchants here who, without being generally called *nakagai-nin*, act as intermediaries for sale or purchase of goods between two parties, receiving therefor a commission. In the rice trade, there are merchants who deposit funds with another and ask him to buy for them goods to be imported from the provinces.

Yamabe *kôri* and Muza *kôri*.

In our *gun*, there are no merchants other than *nakagai-nin* who act as intermediaries for sale or purchase of goods between two parties, for which they receive a commission.

Unakami *kôri* and Sôsa *kôri*.

Yes, there are. They are called *saitori* here. They may in fact, however, be regarded as *nakagai* of the lowest class.

Higashi-katsushika *kôri*.

Other than *toiya* and *nakagai*, there are no merchants who act as intermediaries for sale or purchase of goods between two parties.

IBARAGI PREFECTURE

Nishi-katsushika *kôri* and Sashima *kôri*.

Merchants who act as intermediaries for sale or purchase of goods between two parties, receiving therefor a commission are called *saitori*. They are found in this district among tea manufacturers, cocoon and silk merchants, etc.

KANAGAWA PREFECTURE

Miura *kôri*.

Those merchants who do not have their own goods to sell, but who act as intermediaries for sale or purchase between two parties are called *saitori* in the local usage. They are a minor kind of *nakagai*.

Tachibana *kôri*.

Intermediaries, who are commonly called *saitori*, and who are met with in connection with the sale or purchase of rice and cereals, fodder, etc., belong to the class.

Kita-tama *kôri*.

With the exception of *toiya* and *nakagai-nin*, there are no merchants in this *gun* who act as intermediaries for sale or purchase of goods and receive a commission for it. However, some such merchants may be found in Tokyo and vicinity. Those who are commonly called *shûsen-ya*[1] are an example. They make it their occupation to act, at the request of others, as intermediaries in the sale or purchase of goods, for which they receive a commission, the rate of the commission having no definite limit.

Ashigara-shimo *kôri*.

In Odawara and vicinity there are no others who may be regarded as intermediaries.

Prefectural Industrial Bureau.

Those who, in this trade port, are [commonly] called *saitori*, or *nakatsugi*, etc. have all been given their trade license[2] as *nakagai* and are engaging in their trade in such capacity. Therefore, with the exception of those who are generally called *toiya* and *nakagai*, there are no merchants who go between two parties and act as intermediaries for sale or purchase of goods between them, receiving therefor a commission.

TOCHIGI PREFECTURE

Prefectural Office.

With the exception of *toiya* and *nakagai*, there are no merchants here who act as intermediaries between two parties, publicly receiving a commission for this.

Shimo-tsuga *kôri* and Samukawa *kôri*.

With the exception of *nakagai-nin*, there are no merchants here who act as intermediaries for sale or purchase of goods between two parties and receive a commission for this.

Ashikaga *kôri* and Yanada *kôri*.

There are no such intermediaries. But in the textile market[3] here there are some merchants, called *seri*, who make it their object to get a profit in some other way than by earning a commission. When they learn the demands of one merchant and also learn that a second merchant has a desire to sell those goods that are in demand by the first merchant, these *seri* people buy the goods from the second merchant and sell them to the first, before the first mer-

---

[1] *Shûsen-ya;* intermediary.

[2] *Kansatsu.*

[3] Literally, "competition," "auction."

chant can buy the goods themselves and the second merchant learns about the demands of the first merchant. Thus these people try to compete with and out-buy and out-sell the first and the second merchants, thereby making some profit. Hence the name *seri*. These *seri* sometimes are an advantage to both buyer and seller. For when these find difficulty in disposing of or buying goods, they can, thanks to the *seri*, quickly effect the sale or purchase, without running about for it themselves. However, there are many *seri* who, taking advantage of new visitors' ignorance of the local circumstances, sell goods to them in tricky ways, thereby making excessive profits. So there is a common local saying that *seri* and *suri*[1] are the same thing. In short, these *seri* are very harmful and of little benefit. There are still some of them who are engaging in business under the name of second class *nakagai-nin*,[2] but their doings are not much different from what they used to be.

MIE PREFECTURE

Suzuka *kôri*.

Besides those who are publicly called *toiya* or *nakagai*, there are some merchants that go between two parties, and act as intermediaries for sale between them, receiving a commission for this. They are called *bakurô*,[3] and are engaged in the sale or purchase of horses and cattle [as agents for others].

Isshi *kôri*.

There are merchants called *saitori*, who, acting on orders from others, buy and collect goods from them, and receive a commission for this. However, they are not at all different from *nakagai*. They are called either *nakagai* or *saitori* simply on the basis of the scale of the business they customarily handle.

Asake *kôri*.

Apart from those who are generally called *toiya* or *nakagai*, merchants who act as intermediaries for sale and purchase of goods between two parties, and receive a commission for this, are called here *sashi*. These people do not keep a shop. Carrying just a memo-book[4] and a Japanese pen[5] with them, they run about between

---

[1] *Suri;* pickpocket.

[2] *Nitô-nakagai-nin.*

[3] Horse-dealer; cattle-dealer.

[4] *Tebikae-chô.*

[5] *Yatate.*

prospective buyers and sellers and receive a commission for their services. They belong to the same class of merchants elsewhere called *nakatsugi* or *saitori*.

Nabari *kôri* and Iga *kôri*.

There used to be merchants, besides those who are generally called *toiya* or *nakagai*, who acted as intermediaries for sale or purchase between two parties, receiving therefor a commission—in the rice trade, for instance, none are found in the trade now, however. Nowadays, there are just a few such merchants in the trades of tea, timber, beef[1] and others; but as they do not form a single class, no mention will here be made in detail of their different activities.

AICHI PREFECTURE

Nakajima *kôri*.

Besides those who are called *toiya* or *nakagai-nin*, there are merchants called *sashitori* who act as intermediaries for sale between two parties, and receive a commission for this in proportion to the amount of the business done.

Nagoya Ward.

There are some merchants here, called *saitori* in the local usage, who make it their occupation to act as intermediaries for sale and purchase of goods between two parties, and receive a small commission for this. Since a *saitori* proceeds to act in response to orders from customers, there is no restriction regarding the varieties of *saitori*.

Chita *kôri*.

We do not know of any such merchants who go between two parties and act as intermediary for sale and purchase of goods.

Minami-shidara *kôri*.

There are none here who correspond to the merchants mentioned in the present topic.

Atsumi *kôri*.

There are some merchants who act as middlemen between two parties, but none of them are professional brokers.

Kaitô *kôri* and Kaisai *kôri*.

Other than *toiya* and *nakagai*, there are none here who act as intermediaries for sale and purchase of goods between two parties.

---

[1] *Gyutai.*

Aichi *kôri*.

All merchants who act as intermediaries for sale and purchase of goods between two parties are called *nakagai-nin*. So, apart from the *nakagai-nin*, there are none here who act as intermediaries for sale or purchase of goods between two parties, and receive a commission for this.

Niwa *kôri* and Haguri *kôri*.

Besides those who are publicly called *toiya* or *nakagai-nin*, there are quite a few today who go between two parties and act as intermediaries for sale or purchase of goods between them, receiving a commission for this. Hence, there are no fixed varieties of these, nor any regular names by which they are called.

SHIZUOKA PREFECTURE

Prefectural Office.

None.

Udo *kôri* and Abe *kôri*.

All persons are known as *nakagai*, whether generally or locally, who go between two parties and act as intermediary for sale or purchase of goods between them.

Inasa *kôri* and Aratama *kôri*.

There are none here who make it their sole occupation to act as intermediaries for sale or purchase and to receive a commission for this.

Kamo *kôri* and Naka *kôri*.

Some keepers of inns[1] for sailors or ship passengers in a sea port town or village, at the request of the captain of a passenger boat or the owner of the cargo, sell the cargo or buy local products, as the representative of the captain or owner of the cargo, and receive a commission representing a certain percentage of the price.

Saya *kôri* and Kitô *kôri*.

There are no *nakagai-nin* of the A class,[2] except those who have been granted an official license in accordance with the regulations. There are, however, many *nakagai* of the B class.

GIFU PREFECTURE

Mugi *kôri*.

There are such merchants, called *saitori*; but they are, after all,

---

[1] *Funayado*. This may also mean a shipping agent.
[2] The meaning of the term "A class" here is unclear.

nothing but a low class of *nakagai*.

Ampachi *kôri*.

Their varieties are not fixed, but those merchants that are commonly called *saitori* belong to this class.

Fuwa *kôri*.

There are merchants who, besides being engaged in their main business, sometimes act as intermediaries for sale or purchase between two parties. They are called *saitori* or *batsukuri-nin*. Excepting these merchants, there are none of this kind.

Atsumi *kôri*, Kagami *kôri* and Katagata *kôri*.

There are merchants, called *kaitori-nin*, but they are scarcely distinguishable from *nakagai-nin*.

Tagi *kôri* and Kami-ishizu *kôri*.

Apart from *toiya* and *nakagai-nin*, there are none who act as intermediaries for sale or purchase of goods, and receive a commission for this.

Ôno *kôri* and Ikeda *kôri*.

The answer to the present topic has already been given under the first topic.[1]

Haguri *kôri* and Nakajima *kôri*.

Apart from *toiya* and *nakagai-nin*, those who act as intermediaries for sale or purchase of goods between two parties are called *saitori* in the local usage.

Ena *kôri*.

There are such merchants here, and they are called *saitori*.

Kamo *kôri*.

Besides those who are generally called *toiya* or *nakagai-nin*, there are merchants who go between two parties and act as intermediaries for sale or purchase of goods and receive a commission for this. They are called *saitori* or *tesaki*.[2]

Kani *kôri*.

There are merchants, besides *toiya* and *nakagai*, who go between two parties and act as intermediaries for sale or purchase. There are no fixed names by which their varieties are called, but those who have traditionally been called *saitori*, as well as those who are

---

[1] See page 308 above.

[2] A dialectical usage; the word ordinarily means "tool," "agent," "subordinate," etc.

now called *kaitsukai*,[1] belong to this class, and act as intermediaries, receiving some slight commission for this.

Atsumi *kôri*, Gifu Township.

There are none here who act as such intermediaries.

Ogaki.

Though their varieties are not fixed, those merchants that are commonly called *saitori* belong to this class.

Ena *kôri*, Nakatsugawa Village.

There is no such variety here.

Shimo-ishizu *kôri*, Takasu Township.

Besides those who are generally called *toiya* or *nakagai-nin*, as mentioned in the text, there are some merchants who go between two parties and act as intermediaries for sales between them, receiving some trifling commission for this. They are commonly called *saitori* in the rice trade.

Haguri *kôri*, Takegahana Village.

Besides *toiya* and *nakagai*, there are sometimes found, in the rice trade and among merchants dealing in the *yûki-jima*[2] and the *santomé-jima*[3] silk fabrics, persons who act as intermediaries for sale or purchase of goods between two parties, receiving a commission for this.

Yamagata *kôri*, Takatomi Village.

Apart from those who are generally called *toiya* or *nakagai*, there are none who go between two parties and act as intermediary for sale or purchase of goods. If there are, they are all called *nakagai-nin*.

Mugi *kôri*, Kôzuchi Village.

Apart from *toiya* and *nakagai*, those who act as intermediaries for sale or purchase of goods between two parties are a lower class of *nakagai*, but of the same profession.

Haguri *kôri*, Kasamatsu Village.

The kind of merchants mentioned in the present topic are called *saitori* here.

Fuwa *kôri*, Tarui Village.

There is no class of merchants who, working for a commission,

---

[1] *Kai*, "purchase," *tsukai*, "errand," "messenger."

[2] See page 309 above.

[3] See page 309 above.

are called by the general name of intermediary.[1] However, in sales transactions between merchants, there are found some people who occasionally act as such an intermediary.

Ôno *kôri*, Miwa Village.

None.

Ampachi *kôri*, Gôdo Village.

There are some people who act as such intermediaries and receive a commission for this, but they are restricted to the rice trade.

Ena *kôri*, Iwa Village.

Such people are called *saitori*.

Kamo *kôri*, Hosome Village.

Apart from *toiya* and *nakagai*, those who act as intermediaries for sale or purchase of goods between two parties are, in the local dialect, called *saitori* or *tesaki*. They are of the class of merchants who rely upon their activity in bustling about as their capital.

Toki *kôri*, Takayama Village.

None.

Kani *kôri*, Mitake Village.

With the exception of *nakagai-nin*, there are none.

Ena *kôri*, Akechi Village.

There is such a kind of merchants here, they are called *saitori*.

Mugi *kôri*, Seki Village.

Apart from *toiya* and *nakagai-nin*, those who act as intermediaries for sale or purchase between two parties, receiving a commission for this, have heretofore been commonly called *saitori* in local usage. Besides these people, there are no other kinds of intermediaries. *Saitori* would be a corrupted form of *suai-tori* (difference-earner).

Motosu *kôri*, Kita-kata Village.

There are merchants, besides those who are generally called *toiya* and *nakagai-nin*, who go between two parties and act as intermediaries for sale or purchase of goods, receiving a commission for this. They are called *shôgyô-sewanin*.[2]

Kamo *kôri*, Ôta Village.

Apart from *toiya* and *nakagai-nin*, those who go between two parties and act as intermediaries for sale or purchase of goods are, in the local usage, called *saitori* or *tesaki*. They are of the class of

---

[1] *Baikai-nin.*

[2] Literally, "commercial helpers."

merchants who rely upon their activity in bustling about as their "capital."

Kaisai *kôri* and Shimo-ishizu *kôri*.

There are merchants, besides those generally called *toiya* or *naka-gai-nin*, who go between two parties and act as intermediaries for sales, receiving a commission for this. They belong to the class of merchants commonly called *saitori-sashi* in the rice, second-hand clothes and second-hand furniture trades.

Gujô *kôri*.

There are merchants, besides *nakagai-nin*, who go between two parties and act as intermediaries for sales of goods receiving a commission (*kôsen*) for this. They are a kind of *nakadachi-nin*.[1]

---

[1] Literally, "stand-between."

Topic 3: Does the Agent Make Contracts with Other Parties in His Own Name, When Executing Any Sale or Purchase Transaction Committed to Him? Or Does He Act as Representative of His Principal, Concluding a Contract in the Name of His Principal?

GROUP I—ANSWERS

Tokyo.

Those who are called *toiya* or *nakagai* ordinarily conclude such contracts in their own name. However, such intermediaries as *saitori* conclude the contracts sometimes in their own name and sometimes in the name of their principal, there being no fixed practice about this.

Kyoto.

Business transactions, large or small, are, as mentioned above under the first and second titles, often carried out like a military campaign, tactically and confidentially, in bargaining[1] and in various ways. Therefore, the transactions are sometimes carried out in the name of the agents; or their execution may even sometimes be committed to the agents, either in the name of a party other than the principal, or in the name of the principal himself. Or again, the transactions are sometimes executed in the name of the representative of the principal. There is nothing illegal in these proceedings. And in view of the fact that any movement of goods may affect the market, it is natural that both buyers and sellers of goods should be careful in their negotiations, often assuming different names and resorting to different procedures. It is all a matter of custom, and there is no prescribed rule about it.

Osaka.

Toiya and *nakagai-nin* make contracts for sale or purchase in their own name, while *suai, tombi* and other intermediaries conclude contracts in the name of the principal. However, sometimes even the intermediaries of the latter group make contracts in their own name. This happens when they have gained enough credibility with the principal.

[1] *Kakehiki.*

Yokohama.

Such intermediaries as those called *saitori* never conclude sales contracts in their own name, according to the local usage, when they sell goods consigned to them for sale. They always make the contracts in the name of the consignor.

Hyôgo.

Toiya and *nakagai-nin* make contracts for sale or purchase in their own name, and other intermediaries, such as *saitori*, sometimes conclude it as representative of the principal.

The following are the proceedings of the investigation committee on the subject:

No. 4 [Kishi]: Intermediaries who act as agents for sale or purchase of goods conclude sales contracts in their own name. I do not know of any such agents making contracts in the name of the representative of the principal.

No. 10 [Ômori]: All steamship agents[1] act as representative of the owner of the ship,[2] according to the usage here. Reports to the custom-house[3] of the arrival and departure of the ships whose firm he is representing is, for instance, made by the agent on behalf of the owner of the ship.

No. 6 [Hamada]: The agents sometimes sell or buy goods in their own name. When, for instance, a *saitori*, taking with him some samples[4] of the goods of a *toiya*, succeeds in closing a deal with a customer, the latter usually makes the contract with the *saitori*. If the *saitori* has not sufficient credibility or is suspected of sharp dealing, the customer will conclude the contract directly with the principal, that is, the *toiya* in this case. Even in this case, however, the settlement of the sales price, etc. is made between the buyer and the *saitori*, and a reasonable commission is paid to the agent, according to the usage here.

No. 16 [Kimura]: Both *toiya* and *nakagai-nin* of course conclude such contracts in their own name. Others too, like *saitori*, if they are trusted, conclude sales contracts as representative of the principal.

No. 25 [Shinagawa]: The intermediary does not profess himself to be a representative and will not conclude a contract without obtaining the permission of the principal.

No. 27 [Arima]: It is rather difficult to say definitely if there are any agents acting as representative of the principal or not. When a deal is

[1] *Kisen-doiya.*
[2] *Senshu.* ⁒
[3] *Kaikan;* now called by a more general term, *zeikan.*
[4] *Mihon.*

closed, the papers exchanged between the buyer and the agent [of the seller] are never signed by the latter as the representative of the principal.

No. 25 [Shinagawa]: No sales contract is concluded by the agent of the selling party as the representative of the latter. When, for instance, a *saitori* takes some samples with him to his customer, he is regarded by the latter as the seller of the goods himself; so the contract is not concluded by him as representative of the principal.

No. 6 [Hamada]: Not all intermediaries like *saitori* can be regarded in the same light. Some of them handle just one kind of goods, while others handle several kinds of goods. Manufacturers of lacquered ware[1] in Kii Province, for instance, with a view to cutting down their expenses in selling their goods, form themselves into a trade organization and, bringing their products together, ask an intermediary to sell their goods to his customer *toiya* in other provinces, securing from him an advance in payment equivalent to 50 or 70 percent of what the goods are worth. The intermediary, after disposing of the goods, pays the balance of the prices to the producers and receives a reasonable commission from them. An intermediary like this concludes the sale contract as representative of the producers.

No. 3 [Kondô]: The importing and exporting merchants[2] here have no practice of trading in the name of their intermediaries.

No. 11 [Horiuchi]: Even *toiya* and *nakagai-nin* do not always trade in their own name. According to the nature of the goods they handle, they sometimes take their consignor to foreign firms and, as intermediary, help the foreign merchants and the consignor close a deal, the *toiya* and *nakagai-nin* merely receiving a commission. Therefore, we could not make a sweeping statement that *toiya* and *nakagai-nin* always trade in their own name.

Chairman [Kashima]: Then, shall we present a report to the effect that *toiya* and *nakagai-nin* conclude the sales contracts in their own name, while other intermediaries like *saitori* sometimes become the representative [of a party to a sales contract]?

No. 6 [Hamada]: I believe it is better to submit a report that such intermediaries as *saitori* sometimes become the representative of the principal at his instruction.

No. 33 [Kawanishi]: Here in Hyôgo, when the port is crowded with incoming ships, intermediaries like *toiya* and *nakagai-nin* conclude sales contracts as representatives of the principal, according to local practice.

---

[1] *Shikki.*

[2] *Boeki-shô.*

No. 10 [Ômori]: There are people called hotel touts,[1] who make it their business to solicit customers to the hotels for which they are working and to receive a commission for it. In acting as intermediary between the customers and the hotel, they are representative of the hotel.

No. 27 [Arima]: I believe that when an oral promise is made with an intermediary, the intermediary is regarded as representative of his consignor. Also, the intermediary himself is acting and making all contracts under the belief that he is the representative.

The opinions expressed in the discussion on the subject have been found so divergent from one another that they cannot be summarized in any accordant statement. Therefore, it has been decided to select those opinions which are considered appropriate, prepare a draft report based on them and bring it up for discussion at the meeting for decision.

Ôtsu.

Intermediaries conclude sales contracts mostly in their own name, but sometimes they make use of the name of the principal.

Kumamoto.

According to the requirements of the business, sales contracts are sometimes concluded in the name of the principal and sometimes in the name of the intermediary. Thus it may be said that there is no fixed practice about this.

Okayama.

According to the local practice, the intermediaries that conclude sales contracts in their own name are the *toiya* and *nakagai*, while other intermediaries like *nibushi* sometimes make contracts in their own name and sometimes in the name of the principal.

Bakan.

When a *toiya* executes a sales of purchase transaction committed to him, he always concludes the sales contract in his own name.

Sakai.

It is presumed that the intermediaries in question are not those who are in general usage called intermediaries, but others, such as *tobi* and *nakatsugi*, who have been described above in the preceding two topics.[2] If this is the case, the *tobi* concludes the sales contract in his name, while the *nakatsugi* makes it in the name of the principal, according to the usual practice here.

---

[1] *Kyakuhiki.*
[2] See pages 294 and 316.

Iida.

Those who are called *nakagai* conclude the sales contract in their own name, while those who are called *saitori* make it in the name of the principal.

Takamatsu.

Those who are generally called *toiya* always conclude the sales contract in their own name. Others like *nakagai, tobi* and *nibu* sometimes make it in their own name and at other times in the name of the principal, there being no fixed practice about this.

Fukui.

The sales contract is usually concluded in the name of the principal, but sometimes in the name of the representative of the principal as well, as convenience dictates.

Tokushima.

Intermediaries signify *nakagai*, who, at the instruction of the consignor, sometimes conclude the sales contract in their own name.

Takefu.

The sales contract may be concluded in two ways, either in the name of the agent or in that of the principal, but in practice it is most often concluded in the name of the agent.

Miyagi.

Both *toiya* and *nakagai-nin* always conclude the sales contract in their own name. However, others like *saitori* may do it in their own name or in that of the principal, according to the requirements of the occasion, there being no fixed practice about it.

Matsuyama.

The sales contract may sometimes be concluded in the name of the agent, and at other times in the name of the principal. There is no fixed practice about this.

GROUP II—ANSWERS

Tokyo Metropolis

Prefectural Office.

Oil Wholesalers.

The *saitori* sometimes concludes the sales contract in his own name, and at other times in that of his principal. There has been no fixed practice about this hitherto.

Dry Goods Wholesalers.

A *saitori* does not receive orders directly from a seller or buyer. He makes it his business merely to equip himself with information about the stock of goods for sale at a *toiya*'s and then to go from one merchant to another to act as intermediary for the sale of the *toiya*'s goods. When the sales contract is made or the deal is closed, however, it is sometimes done in the name of the intermediary, depending on the requirements of the consignor.

Timber Wholesalers.

When a *saitori* acts as intermediary for a sale and concludes a sale contract, he always does it in the name of the buyer or seller as his representative.

Rice Wholesalers.

When a *saitori*, taking with him some sample rice,[1] closes a deal with a buyer, he always concludes the sale contract in his own name. And when the time arrives for the delivery of goods, he issues, in the name of the consignor or sometimes in his own name, a kind of weight note[2] as follows:

Note

Name of Warehouse
100 bales Bushu rice   Bought by
   at _____ a *ryo*   So-and-so

   Please deliver the above to the
buyer on receipt of the payment.

   Date

                      [From] Salesroom agent
                             So-and-so

[Addressed to]
Warehouse-keeper
Mr. So-and-so

---

[1] *Sashimai.* More usually, however, this meant an amount of rice given, by a tenant to his landlord, in excess of the exact amount of rice to be given to the landlord in payment of the rent, for the purpose of making up for a deficit in the measurement of the rice due to drying, worm-eating, etc. See Part I, Chapter 5 (*kuchi-mai*).

[2] *Kuradashi-kitte.* A warrant instructing the warehouse-keeper to deliver certain goods to a certain buyer, on payment of so much money. See a fuller explanation in Part I, Chap. 10.

Fish Wholesalers.

There is no such practice.

Fuel Wholesalers.

Intermediaries like *saitori* sometimes conclude the sales contract in their own name. But when a bargain is closed, generally the buyer and the seller deal directly with each other, including the delivery of goods.

Saké Wholesalers.

All *saitori* conclude the sales contract in their own name.

Dried Bonito Wholesalers.

When they do a small amount of business, *saitori* sometimes conclude the sales contract in their own names.

Salt Wholesalers.

There is no such practice.

Kôjimachi Ward.

It depends upon the nature of the goods or upon the circumstances whether a *saitori* concludes the sale contract in his own name or the intermediary introduces the goods of one party to another, and the deal between them is made respectively in their own names, the intermediary sometimes acting as representative.[1]

Kyôbashi Ward.

The intermediaries make the contracts with others in their own names.

Yotsuya Ward and Ushigome Ward.

The *saitori*, or intermediaries, mentioned in the preceding topic, do not conclude the contract in their own name, but in that of their principal.

Asakusa Ward.

When the intermediaries transact business, both of the practices mentioned in the present topic are resorted to.

Honjo Ward.

When an intermediary conducts a sale or purchase on commission, he does not do it in his own name, but in that of his principal.

Ebara *kôri*.

When an intermediary conducts a sale or purchase on commis-

---

[1] The original text is ambiguous on this point.

sion, he seldom concludes the contract in his own name. Mostly, acting as representative, he makes the contract in the name of his principal.

Higashi-tama *kôri* and Minami-toshima *kôri*.

The intermediaries mentioned in the preceding topic may sometimes conclude the contract in their own name, but most often they do it in the name of their principal.

Kita-toshima *kôri*.

When a *saitori*, or intermediary, offering goods committed to him for sale, finds the quantity and the price of the goods offered for sale acceptable to the buyer, all he has to do is to meet the demand of the buying party. In such a case, the *saitori* makes the sales contract in the name of his principal. However, when a *saitori* buys goods from *toiya* or *nakagai-nin* and keeps them in stock, on his own account, with a view to waiting for others' orders to sell them, he concludes the contracts in his own name.

A *baikai-nin* or an intermediary is, as the name indicates, nothing more than one who mediates. However, though he is not a man of means, he is well versed in business. There is no kind of business which could not be transacted without his help, but he is a necessary character in business circles, as it is to the good of both for the principal to entrust his intermediary with the transaction of certain business.

Minami-adachi *kôri*.

In transacting a business entrusted to him, an intermediary makes the contract in his own name. However, intermediaries like those called *saitori*, mentioned in the preceding topic, mediate between two parties only in the initial stage of a transaction. When it comes to contract making, the two principals conclude it between themselves.

Shitaya Ward.

All *toiya* and *nakagai-nin* make the contract in their own name, while a *saitori* [usually] does it in the name of his principal, although there is no fixed practice about this. However, when it comes to the delivery of goods, it is mostly done in the name of the buyer and seller.

Kanda Ward.

The intermediaries sometimes conclude the contract and even make or receive the payment in their own name, but sometimes make the contract in the name of their principal on his behalf.

Akasaka Ward and Azabu Ward.

Both of the practices are prevalent.

Hongô Ward.

Suppose some one has brought some goods here for sale from a different locality, and having no regular *toiya* here with whom he has had dealings, has become for the time being short of funds. He then entrusts the sale of his goods to some company, *toiya* or *nakagai*. The intermediary, in such a case, sometimes advances money to him, and makes a contract with him, providing for his lien in recovering his loan out of the proceeds of the sales.

CHIBA PREFECTURE

Awa *kôri*, Hei *kôri*, Asai *kôri* and Nagasa *kôri*.

It is impossible to apply one and the same rule to answer the question. But in most cases the agent makes the contract with others in his own name in a case when the principal entrusts the sale or purchase to the intermediary because he is not acquainted with anybody here or because he puts special trust in the intermediary. Especially when goods are brought here from other localities, not only is the consignor put to inconvenience in disposing of the goods if he has no acquaintance here, but the buyer too generally feels hesitant about the transaction. For such reasons, the sales contract is mostly made in the name of the intermediary.

However, an intermediary like a *saitori-nin* merely mediates the sale or purchase between the two parties and seldom becomes a party to the sales contract.

Katori *kôri*.

The sales contract for some goods is made in the name of the intermediary. Rice and dried sardines, for instance, are a case in point.

Yamabe *kôri* and Muza *kôri*.

The answer for this topic is the same as that for the preceding topic.

Unakami *kôri* and Sôsa *kôri*.

Most intermediaries conclude the sales contract in their own name, but a *saitori-nin* sometimes does it in the name of his principal.

Higashi-katsushika *kôri*.

When the intermediaries transact a sale or purchase entrusted to them, they mostly conclude the sales contract in the name of their principal, acting as his representative.

IBARAGI PREFECTURE

Nishi-katsushika *kôri* and Eshima *kôri*.

The intermediary may sometimes conclude the sale contract in his own name, and sometimes in the name of his principal, depending on the agreement with his principal.

KANAGAWA PREFECTURE

Miura *kôri*.

An intermediary makes the sales contract in his own name, according to the local practice.

Tachibana *kôri*.

As to rice and other goods, the intermediary makes the sales contract in his own name, while in the sale of land and houses the contract is made in the name of his principal.

Kita-tama *kôri*.

When an intermediary is entrusted with the sale or purchase of goods, he makes the sales contract in his own name in eight or nine cases out of ten. He also sometimes brings the buyer and the seller to deal directly with each other, according to the occasion, but in such a case he does not like to act as their representative.

Ashigara-shimo *kôri*.

[Generally speaking] there is none here who makes it his proper occupation to act as intermediary for sale. But this rule cannot hold for all occasions, there being possible exceptions. As to whose name is to appear as a party to a sales contract, this would be decided each time according to the convenience of those concerned; there is no fixed practice about this.

Prefectural Industrial Bureau.

When he transacts a sale or purchase entrusted to him, a *nakagai-nin* never does it in his own name.

TOCHIGI PREFECTURE

Prefectural Office.

When they transact a sale or purchase entrusted to them, most of the intermediaries, including *toiya* and *nakagai*, conclude the sale contract in their own name. Also, depending on their agreement with the principal, they sometimes make the sale contract as representative of their principal. However, it is only, according to the local custom, on the occasions when they make part payment[1] to their principal that the intermediaries conclude the sales contract with the buying party in their own name.

Shimo-tsuga *kôri* and Samukawa *kôri*.

When they transact the sale or purchase on commission, the intermediaries sometimes make it in their own name, and sometimes in the name of their principal. There is no settled practice about this.

Ashikaga *kôri* and Yanada *kôri*.

All contracts are made in the name of the intermediaries, the names of their principals never coming to the surface.

MIE PREFECTURE

Suzuka *kôri*.

When they carry on a sale or purchase entrusted to them, the intermediaries sometimes make the sales contract with a third party in their own name, and sometimes in the name of their principal, acting as their representative.

Isshi *kôri*.

Some intermediaries conclude the sales contract in their own name, while others do it in the name of their principal. This point is decided each time the principal gives his commission to his intermediary. Consequently there cannot be said to be any fixed rule about this.

Asake *kôri*.

In carrying on a sale or purchase on commission, the *toiya* makes the sales contract in his own name. He is under the obligation of settling the account with the consignor for the goods entrusted to him for sale when the party that has bought the goods goes bankrupt.

However, intermediaries like the *sashi* mentioned in the preceding topic all make the contract in the name of the seller.

Nabari *kôri* and Iga *kôri*.

When they transact a sale or purchase on commission, some intermediaries act as representative of their principal and conclude the contract in the name of the same; while others, acting not as representative of their principal but merely as intermediary, may make the contract in their own name. These intermediaries are

---

[1] *Uchi-kin.*

under the obligation of acting as guarantors[1] when there is a breach of the agreement on the part of either one or the other party to the contract or some other trouble.

AICHI PREFECTURE

Nakajima *kôri*.

No intermediaries conclude the contract in their own name.

Nagoya Ward.

According to the circumstances or the nature of the goods handled, the intermediaries may sometimes conclude the contract in their own name and sometimes in the name of their principal.

Chita *kôri*.

The intermediaries, according to the local practice, transact business and conclude the contract in their own names. However, regarding the sale of ships, houses, lands, etc., the contract is made in the name of the selling party.

Minami-shidara *kôri*.

The intermediaries conclude the contract as representative of their principal.

Atsumi *kôri*.

The intermediaries sometimes make the contract in their own names, and sometimes in the name of their principal. There is no fixed practice about this.

Kaitô *kôri* and Kaisai *kôri*.

The intermediaries make the contract in their own name in nine cases out of ten.

Aichi *kôri*.

The intermediaries, that is, those who are called *nakagai-nin* here and who mediate in a sale or purchase between two parties, never make a contract in their name alone, but sometimes conclude it in the name of the intermediary of the buyer so-and-so.

Niwa *kôri* and Haguri *kôri*.

When they transact business on commission, selling or purchasing goods for another, some intermediaries make the contract in their own name, while others make it in the name of their principal, acting as his representative. There is no settled practice about this here.

---

[1] *Shô-nin.* This word sometimes means only "witness," sometimes "guarantor."

SHIZUOKA PREFECTURE

Prefectural Office.

As stated in the preceding topic, the intermediaries make the contract in their own name.

Udo *kôri* and Abe *kôri*.

Most intermediaries make the contract in their own name.

Inasa *kôri* and Aratama *kôri*.

We have nothing to report on this question, as it will be seen in our answer to the second topic.[1]

Kamo *kôri* and Naka *kôri*.

Those intermediaries who receive a percentage or commission out of the proceeds of sale, make the contract in their own name, and never in that of their principal.

Saya *kôri* and Kitô *kôri*.

Nakagai-nin, certainly those of the B class, and even those of the A class, make it a rule to conclude the contract in their own name.

GIFU PREFECTURE

Mugi *kôri*.

Either one of the practices is resorted to according to the circumstances.

Ampachi *kôri*.

There is no fixed practice about this; the matter is decided according to the circumstances of the occasion and place. For instance, the name of the person who enjoys the greater trust with the other party will be made use of in making the contract.

Fuwa *kôri*.

The intermediaries may sometimes make the contract in their own name, and sometimes in the name of their principal. Both practices are in use here.

Atsumi *kôri*, Kagami *kôri* and Katagata *kôri*.

Some intermediaries make the contract in their own name, and others in the name of their principal.

Tagi *kôri* and Kami-ishizu *kôri*.

Except for *toiya* and *nakagai-nin*, there are no professional intermediaries here, as has been observed in the second topic.[2] But when someone acts as intermediary for sale at the request of an-

---

[1] See page 326 above.

[2] See page 327 above.

other or of his own will, he always concludes the contract in the name of his principal.

Ôno *kôri* and Ikeda *kôri*.

The answer to the present topic has already been given in the answer to the first topic.[1]

Haguri *kôri* and Nakajima *kôri*.

In making a contract, either one of the practices is resorted to, depending on the circumstances of the occasion.

Ena *kôri*.

The intermediaries make the contract in their own name.

Kamo *kôri*.

When an intermediary transacts a business committed to him by another, he makes it a rule to act as representative of his principal and make the contract in the name of the principal.

Kani *kôri*.

The intermediaries mostly conclude the contract in their own name.

Atsumi *kôri*, Gifu Township.

Both practices are in use here.

Ôgaki Township.

There is no fixed practice about this, but the matter is decided according to the circumstances of the occasion and place. For instance, the name of the person who enjoys the greater trust of the other party will be made use of in making the contract.

Ena *kôri*, Nakatsugawa Village.

Both practices are in use here.

Shimo-ishizu *kôri*, Takasu Township.

Those kinds of intermediaries called *toiya* or *nakagai* in these answers mostly conclude the contract in their own name, although there are occasionally found some who make the contract in the name of their principal. [Strictly speaking], there is no fixed practice about this.

Haguri *kôri*, Takegahana Village.

The matter in point, whether the contract is to be made in the name of the intermediary or in that of his principal, is decided according to the circumstances. Consequently, there is no fixed practice about this.

---

[1] See page 308 above.

Yamagata *kôri*, Takatomi Village.

When an intermediary transacts a business entrusted to him by another, he concludes the contract in the name of his principal, acting as the representative of the same.

Mugi *kôri*, Kôzu Village.

When an intermediary transacts business committed to him by another, he does not make the contract in his own name, but does it in the name of his principal, acting as the representative of the same.

Haguri *kôri*, Kasamatsu Village.

The contract here in question may be made in the name of the intermediary, or in that of his principal, according to the circumstances.

Fuwa *kôri*, Tarui Village.

The contract may be made in the name of the intermediary or in that of his principal, according to the circumstances under which he has come to act as intermediary, as has been observed in the preceding topic.[1]

Ôno *kôri*, Miwa Village.

Both practices are in use here.

Ampachi *kôri*, Gôdo Village.

When an intermediary transacts business on commission, he makes the contract in his own name, and not in that of his principal.

Ena *kôri*, Iwa Village.

Some intermediaries conclude the contract in their own name, while others do it in the name of their principal, acting as his representative.

Kamo *kôri*, Hosome Village.

It occasionally happens in the timber trade here that the intermediaries make the contract in their own name when they transact business committed to them. In the other trades, however, most intermediaries conclude the contract in the name of their principal, acting as representative of the same.

Kami *kôri*, Mitake Village.

In such a case, the intermediaries mostly conclude the contract

---

[1] See pages 328 and 329 above.

in the name of their principal, although once in a while they do it in their own names.

Ena *kôri*, Akechi Village.

The contract may be made in the name of the principal, or in that of the intermediary.

Mugi *kôri*, Seki Village.

When an intermediary transacts business committed to him, he may conclude the sales contract in his own name or in that of his principal, according to the occasion. Both practices are prevalent here.

Motosu *kôri*, Kita-kata Village.

When *toiya* and *nakagai-nin* transact business entrusted to them, they sometimes conclude the contract in their own name, but intermediaries like *shôgyô-sewa-nin* make the contract in the name of their principal, acting as the representative of the same.

Kamo *kôri*, Ôta Village.

When an intermediary transacts business entrusted to him, he makes it a rule to conclude the contract in the name of his principal.

Kaisei *kôri* and Shimo-ishizu *kôri*.

Those sorts of intermediaries that are called *toiya* or *nakagai* mostly mediate [and conclude the contract] in their own name, although there are occasionally found some who make the contract in the name of their principal. [Strictly speaking,] there is no fixed practice about this.

Gujô *kôri*.

Either one of the practices described in the present topic has heretofore been resorted to, depending on the circumstances.

Topic 4: If the Agent Advances Money to His Principal on the Goods with Whose Sale He Is Entrusted, Does He Have Any Prior Claim on the Proceeds to Reimburse Himself for the Money He Has Advanced?

GROUP I—ANSWERS

Tokyo.

If the agent advances money to his principal on the goods with whose sale he is entrusted, it has hitherto been the general practice here that the agent has a prior claim on the proceeds to recover the money he has advanced.

Kyoto.

It is a matter of course that the agent has a prior claim on the proceeds to recover the money he has advanced to his principal in the way described in the present topic. However, the matter may be variously modified according to the contract concluded between the agent and the principal.

Osaka.

If the agent advances money to his principal on the goods with whose sale he is entrusted, he has, according to the general usage here, a prior claim on the proceeds to recover the money he has advanced, with interest. Then he returns any surplus to the consignor and demands payment of any deficit.

Yokohama.

There is no practice here by which the agent advances money to his principal on the goods with whose sale he is entrusted. Consequently there is no general usage here on the point of priority.

Hyôgo.

The agent has a prior claim on the proceeds, according to the practice here.

The proceedings of the investigation committee on the subject are as follows.

No. 25 [Shinagawa]: The agent has a prior claim on the proceeds.

This view was agreed to by all present without dissent.

Ôtsu.

It has hitherto been the general practice here that in such a case the agent has a prior claim on the proceeds.

Kumamoto.

According to the local practice, the agent has a prior claim on the proceeds of sale to reimburse the money he has advanced to his principal.

Okayama.

If the agent advances some money to his principal on the goods with whose sale he is entrusted, he has a prior claim on the proceeds to recover the money he has advanced.

Bakan.

If the agent advances money to his principal on goods with whose sale he is entrusted, he has a prior claim on the proceeds to recover the money he has advanced.

According to the circumstances of their shipment, the goods are sometimes unloaded from a ship and left in trust with the agent, who puts them in a warehouse and advances money on them to his principal. If, in such a case, the goods are disposed of according to the directions of the consignor, the agent has, of course, a prior claim on the proceeds of sale to recover the money he has advanced, interest, warehouse charges, etc. If the consignor wishes to transport the goods to some other place, the agent allows him to take the goods out of the warehouse after payment of his debt, including principal and interest, warehouse charges, etc.

Sometimes the consignor, who has already shipped goods to his agent by a chartered vessel, may later ask to borrow some money on the goods. In such a case the agent sends him the money by a bill of exchange and dispenses with the formalities of requiring an I.O.U. of the consignor. For all this, when the goods are disposed of by the agent, he has, as observed above, a prior claim on the proceeds of the sale to recover the loan, including principal and interest, storage charges, etc.

Sakai.

If the agent advances money to his principal on goods with whose sale he is entrusted, then, according to the general practice here, he at once reimburses himself for the whole sum of the loan out of the proceeds of the sale and returns any surplus to his principal.

Iida.

The agent sometimes advances money to his principal on goods with whose sale he is entrusted. According to the practice here, he has a prior claim on the proceeds to recover money he advanced.

Takamatsu.

When the agent advances money to his principal on goods with whose sale he is entrusted, it has hitherto been the general practice here that the agent has a prior claim on the proceeds to recover the loan. However, if the case is brought to the court, the agent is not entitled to a prior claim on the proceeds unless he has an I.O.U. signed by his principal.

Fukui.

The agent has no prior claim on the proceeds.

Tokushima.

When the agent advances money to his principal on goods with whose sale he is entrusted, he has a prior claim on the proceeds to recover the money he has advanced.

Takefu.

The agent sometimes advances to his principal money, known as *tetsuké*,[1] equivalent to 10 to 20 percent of the price of the goods with whose sale he is entrusted. The agent has a prior claim on the proceeds, which is a natural consequence of the advance he has made.

Miyagi.

It is a matter of course that when the agent advances some money to his principal on goods with whose sale he is entrusted, he is entitled to a prior claim on the proceeds of sale. Also, if there is any deficit, it is apparently the general practice for the agent to demand its payment from his principal, but in actual practice, this sometimes varies with the agreement.

Matsuyama.

When the agent advances money to his principal on goods with whose sale he is entrusted, he is entitled to a prior claim on the proceeds.

GROUP II—ANSWERS

Tokyo Metropolis
Prefectural Office.
Oil Wholesalers.

---

[1] Advance money, earnest-money.

None.

Dry Goods Wholesalers.

If the buyer promises the sale to the agent (*saitori*), the buyer often advances money and the balance is paid at the time of the settlement of accounts.

Timber Wholesalers.

None.

Rice Wholesalers.

None.

Fish Wholesalers.

None.

Fuel Wholesalers.

None.

Saké Wholesalers.

None.

Dried Bonito Wholesalers.

There is no such practice that the agent advances money to the consignor. All payment is made on the delivery of merchandise.

Salt Wholesalers.

None.

Kôjimachi Ward.

In case the dealer is an agent, the agent does not have a prior claim on the proceeds to reimburse himself for the money he has advanced.

Nihombashi Ward.

Average agents cannot advance money to the consignor. Those who advance money to their consignors on the goods with whose sale they are entrusted are mostly *toiya*. They have a prior claim.

Kyôbashi Ward.

If the agent advances money for the sale of the goods, he has a prior claim.

Yotsuya Ward and Ushigome Ward.

There are cases that even an agent mortgages the goods and advances money to the consignor and reimburses himself the money on the proceeds.

Asakusa Ward.

The agent has a prior claim on the proceeds.

Honjo Ward.

If the agent advances money to his consignor on the goods with whose sale he is entrusted, he has a prior claim on the proceeds.

Ebara *kôri*.

The agent can advance money to his consignor on goods with whose sale he is entrusted and has a prior claim on the proceeds.

Higashi-tama *kôri* and Minami-toshima *kôri*.

The agent has no prior claim.

Kita-toshima *kôri*.

The answer is stated in Topic 3.

Minami-adachi *kôri*.

When the agent advances money, he has a prior claim on the proceeds.

Shitaya Ward.

The *saitori* has no such prior claim. But when the *toiya* advances money to his consignor on the goods with whose sale he is entrusted, and then the latter does not pay the debt by selling the goods to another person, it has been the general practice here that the *toiya* has a prior claim to the goods or the proceeds from the buyer.

Kanda Ward.

In this case the agent has the right to indemnification.

Akasaka Ward and Azabu Ward.

An advanced payment to the consignor does not constitute a prior claim of the agent. When the agent delivers the proceeds, he subtracts the money advanced, and pays the balance to the consignor.

CHIBA PREFECTURE

Awa *kôri*, Hei *kôri*, Asai *kôri* and Nagasa *kôri*.

In some cases, the agent advances money to the consignor on goods with whose sale he is entrusted. After the sale of the goods, he subtracts the money advanced and pays the balance to the consignor.

Katori *kôri*.

Even when the agent is entrusted with the sale and advances money to the consignor, there is no practice here that the agent has a prior claim on the proceeds and gets indemnified.

Yanabe *kôri* and Muza *kôri*.

The same as is stated in Topic 3.

Unakami *kôri* and Sôsa *kôri*.

Usually the agent entrusted with the sale of the goods advances money to the consignor, and therefore has a prior claim on the proceeds and demands the payment of any deficit.

Higashi-katsushika *kôri*.

The agent has a prior claim and demands the payment of any deficit.

IBARAGI PREFECTURE

Nishi-katsushika *kôri* and Sashima *kôri*.

The agent has no prior claim and no right to indemnity.

KANAGAWA PREFECTURE

Miura *kôri*.

There are cases where the agent has a prior claim and the deficit can be paid.

Tachibana *kôri*.

Customarily the agent has a prior claim.

Kita-tama *kôri*.

It is the custom that the agent, entrusted with the sale of goods, advances money to the consignor at the latter's request (no matter whether the request is just or not), and puts the goods under his custody. Therefore, the agent naturally has a prior claim.

Ashigara-shimo *kôri*.

Even if the agent receives the money on behalf of the consignor, he has no prior claim for the advanced money paid to the consignor. However, this sometimes varies depending on the contract.

Prefectural Industrial Bureau.

There is no practice that the agent advances money to the consignor on goods with whose sale he is entrusted.

TOCHIGI PREFECTURE

Prefectural Office.

It is the custom that the agent has a prior claim, and the money is indemnified when the agent advances money to the consignor on goods with whose sale he is entrusted.

Shimo-tsuga *kôri* and Samukawa *kôri*.

The agent has a prior claim for the proceeds when he advances money to the consignor on goods with whose sale he is entrusted.

Ashikaga *kôri* and Yanada *kôri*.

The agent naturally has a prior claim for the proceeds here.

MIE PREFECTURE

Suzuka *kôri*.

The agent occasionally advances money to the consignor on goods with whose sale he is entrusted. He also has a prior claim on the proceeds to reimburse himself for the money he has advanced.

Isshi *kôri.*

The agent has a prior claim to the advanced money and is surely reimbursed.

Asake *kôri.*

The agent advances money to the consignor on goods with whose sale he is entrusted. He has a prior claim on the proceeds to be reimbursed.

Nabari *kôri* and Iga *kôri.*

If money is advanced on the goods, the agent has a prior claim on the proceeds to be reimbursed.

AICHI PREFECTURE

Nakajima *kôri.*

When the agent advances money to the consignor on goods with whose sale he is entrusted, the advanced money is balanced or sometimes is not balanced by the proceeds.

Nagoya Ward.

The agent in some cases has a prior claim on the basis of the contract made between the agent and the consignor, in which the latter entrusted the former with the sale of goods or the former advanced money on the goods.

Chita *kôri.*

The fact that the agent advances money to the consignor on goods with whose sale he is entrusted and has a prior claim on the proceeds means that the advanced money is regarded as prepayment of the proceeds and therefore the goods are mortgaged. The agent customarily has a prior claim. If, therefore, the proceeds fall short of the advanced money, the agent is able to claim for the balance.

Minami-shidara *kôri.*

If the agent advances money to the consignor, he customarily balances the amount of the money when the goods with whose sale he is entrusted are sold, irrespective of the presence of a contract thereof. There has been no case so far when the consignor caused trouble about the matter.

Atsumi *kôri.*

Yes he has.

Kaitô *kôri* and Kaisai *kôri.*

It is the custom that the advanced money is to be balanced

within the limit of the proceeds.

Aichi *kôri*.

Money being advanced to the consignor on goods with whose sale the agent is entrusted, the latter has a prior claim on the proceeds to reimburse himself for the advanced money.

Niwa *kôri* and Haguri *kôri*.

If the agent advances money to the consignor on goods with whose sale he is entrusted, he has prior claim on the proceeds to reimburse himself for the money he has advanced. If the proceeds fall short of the advanced money, the consignor naturally balances the shortage. However, that depends on the contract concluded when the money is advanced.

SHIZUOKA PREFECTURE

Prefectural Office.

The agent has a prior claim; however, only a few agents do advance money because most of them are not very wealthy.

Udo *kôri* and Abe *kôri*.

The agent has a prior claim.

Inasa *kôri* and Aratama *kôri*.

Nothing to be added to the answer to Topic 2.

Kamo *kôri* and Naka *kôri*.

The agent has a prior claim and is indemnified.

Saya *kôri* and Kitô *kôri*.

The *toiya* of the A class advance money on the goods and have a prior claim on the proceeds. It is rare that wholesalers request indemnification, because they would not advance so extravagant an amount of money on the goods. If there is any such case, the damage would be borne by *toiya*.

GIFU PREFECTURE

Mugi *kôri*.

The agent has a prior claim.

Ampachi *kôri*.

Customarily the agent has a prior claim.

Fuwa *kôri*.

Advancing money on goods, the agent has a prior claim on proceeds and is able to be indemnified. There is also a custom that the indemnification is shared jointly by the agent and the consignor through negotiation between them.

Atsumi *kôri*, Kagami *kôri* and Katagata *kôri*.

The agent has a prior claim.

Tagi *kôri* and Kami-ishizu *kôri*.

Those who, upon request, mediate the purchase and sale of goods act only for the conclusion of a contract and not for the monetary dealings.

Ôno *kôri* and Ikeda *kôri*.

Stated in Topic 1.

Haguri *kôri* and Nakajima *kôri*.

Cannot follow what the question is.

Ena *kôri*.

The agent has a prior claim.

Kamo *kôri*.

The agent occasionally advances money to the consignor on goods with whose sale he is entrusted. Then he customarily has a prior claim on the proceeds for the security of the advanced money.

Kani *kôri*.

The agent has a prior claim.

Atsumi *kôri*, Gifu Township.

The agent has a prior claim and the advanced money is to be reimbursed.

Ôgaki.

Customarily the agent naturally has a prior claim.

Ena *kôri*, Nakatsukawa Village.

The agent is to be reimbursed.

Shimo-ishizu *kôri*, Takasu Township.

If the agent advances money to the consignor on goods with whose sale he is entrusted, the agent naturally has a prior claim on proceeds. When the proceeds fall short of the advanced money, the agent is naturally to be indemnified. As a matter of fact, however, indemnification in that way is not put into practice.

Haguri *kôri*, Takegahana Village.

The agent might have a prior claim when he has at hand the goods with whose sale he is entrusted. He is not sure to have the prior claim if the goods are in the hands of the consignor.

Yamagata *kôri*, Takatomi Village.

Whether the indemnification is made or not depends upon the agreement. Usually the agent is indemnified.

Mugi *kôri*, Kôzuchi Village.

The agent advances money to the consignor on goods with whose sale he is entrusted and gets indemnified at the time of the sale of the goods.

Haguri *kôri*, Kasamatsu Village.

No answer.

Fuwa *kôri*, Tarui Village.

Any person who advances money as an agent has a prior claim on the proceeds. In case of deficit, both the agent and the consignor share it together through negotiation.

Ôno *kôri*, Miwa Village.

The agent has a prior claim and occasionally gets indemnified.

Ampachi *kôri*, Gôdo Village.

The agent has a prior claim and gets indemnified.

Ena *kôri*, Iwa Village.

The agent gets indemnified.

Kamo *kôri*, Hosome Village.

When advancing money on goods in the way described in Topic 4, the agent naturally has a prior claim on the proceeds.

Kani *kôri*, Mitake Village.

The advanced money enables the agent to have a prior claim on the proceeds.

Ena *kôri*, Akechi Village.

The agent has a prior claim.

Mugi *kôri*, Seki Village.

When the agent (B) advances money to the consignor (A) on goods with whose sale he (B) is entrusted and sells the goods to a merchant (C), the prior claim is held by the agent (B) and the indemnification is to be always made by the consignor (A).

Motosu *kôri*, Kita-kata Village.

If the agent advances money to the consignor on goods with whose sale he is entrusted, he has a prior claim on the proceeds to reimburse himself for the money he has advanced.

Kamo *kôri*, Ôta Village.

If the agent advances money to the consignor on goods with whose sale he is entrusted, he customarily has a prior claim on the proceeds to reimbursed himself for the money he has advanced.

Kaisai *kôri* and Shimo-ishizu *kôri*.

If the agent advances money to the consignor on goods with whose sale he is entrusted, he naturally has a prior claim and balance is to be settled. However, such settlements are rarely made.

Gujô *kôri.*

If the agent advances money to the consignor on goods with whose sale he is entrusted, and so long as he reaches an agreement on the sales price of the goods, he has a prior claim on the proceeds to reimburse himself the money he has advanced.

Topic 5:   Is There Any Sort of Business Transaction That Cannot
Be Done Except through the Agency of an Intermediary?

GROUP I—ANSWERS

Tokyo.

There is no kind of business transaction that cannot be done
except through the agency of an intermediary. Only there is some
difference in the expediency of transacting business, depending on
whether recourse is had to the agency of an intermediary or not.

Kyoto.

As has been observed in Topic 3 above, recourse may be had,
in the transaction of business, to the agency of an intermediary,
according to the convenience of the principal. There is no sort of
business transaction that cannot be done except through the agency
of an intermediary.

Osaka.

Here in Osaka, there are many kinds of business whose transaction
cannot be effected in direct dealings between the consignor and
the customer, but must depend, for realization, upon intermediaries,
including *toiya* and *nakagai*. The transaction of business between
merchants in Osaka can be effected without the agency (*suai* and
tombi) of an intermediary, but they sometimes resort to it because
it is convenient. It is impossible to transact business in the rice
trade and at the vegetable market here without the agency of some
intermediary.

Yokohama.

There is no kind of business here which cannot be transacted
without the agency of an intermediary.

Hyôgo.

There is no kind of business here which cannot be transacted
without the agency of an intermediary. However, if any rice merchant here transacts his business without the agency of an intermediary, his fellow traders resort to the practice called "shutting
out a deaf man,"[1] i.e., refusing thereafter to have any dealings with
him.

---

[1] *Tsunbo-fûji.*

The transactions of the investigation committee on the subject are as follows:

No. 25 [Shinagawa]: There are some kinds of business that cannot be transacted without the agency of an intermediary. The transaction of business with foreign merchants, for instance, cannot be done except through the agency of a trading merchant.[1]

No. 27 [Arima]: There is no kind of business that cannot be transacted without the agency of an intermediary; but it is necessary for merchants to depend upon the agency of an intermediary if they wish to enjoy advantages in the transaction of their business.

No. 6 [Hamada]: There is no sort of business that cannot be carried out without the agency of an intermediary. Lately there are some foreign merchants who go direct to the place of production to buy goods. In such a case the trading merchants get only a trifling commission.

No. 3 [Kondô]: The trading merchants are not always to be regarded as intermediaries. They may act as such only occasionally.

No. 18 [Tamba]: In transacting business, is it always necessary for a merchant to depend upon the agency of an intermediary? I say, it is not.

No. 33 [Kawanishi]: There are some kinds of business which cannot be transacted without the agency of an intermediary. If any rice merchant of Hyôgo, for instance, transacts his business without the agency of an intermediary, his fellow traders resort to the practice called "shutting out a deaf man," i.e., refusing thereafter to have any dealings with him. It is entirely a matter of usage.

Chairman [Kashima]: Then we will submit our report to the effect that there is no kind of business here which cannot be transacted without the agency of an intermediary, except only for the rice trade, where it is impossible for merchants to transact their business without the agency of an intermediary.

Ôtsu.

Hitherto there has been no kind of business that could not be transacted except through the agency of an intermediary.

Kumamoto.

There is no sort of business that cannot be transacted without the agency of an intermediary. There is merely some difference of expediency in transacting business, according to whether resort is had to the agency of an intermediary or not.

Okayama.

---

[1] *Bôeki-shô.*

There is no sort of business that cannot be transacted without the agency of an intermediary.

Bakan.

As there are no intermediaries other than *toiya* and *nakagai-nin* here, it naturally follows that there is no kind of business that cannot be transacted except through the agency of any intermediaries other than *toiya* and *nakagai-nin*.

Sakai.

Hitherto, it has been impossible, according to the general practice here, for saké manufacturers to distribute their goods in the provinces except through the agency of the intermediary called *nakatsugi-nin*; but no such practice prevails in any other trade.

Iida.

The fish and fowl *toiya* are the only merchants here who find it impossible to carry on their business without the agency of some intermediary.

Takamatsu.

There has never been any kind of business that cannot be transacted without the agency of some intermediary. However, there is much difference in the point of expediency, according to circumstances, in the transaction of some affairs, depending on whether recourse is had to the agency of an intermediary or not.

Fukui.

Yes, the silk auction market[1] is an example.

Tokushima.

There is no kind of business that cannot be transacted without the agency of an intermediary, that is, a *nakagai*.

Takeo.

Yes, but the varieties are too numerous to describe here.

Miyagi.

There is no kind of business that cannot be transacted without the agency of some intermediary, but dealers in seaweeds, fish, etc. derive great convenience from the agency of an intermediary.

Matsuyama.

With the exception of a market adopting rules to that effect, there is no kind of business that cannot be transacted without the agency of some intermediary.

---

[1] *Seriuri-ba.*

GROUP II—ANSWERS

TOKYO METROPOLIS
Prefectural Office.
Oil Wholesalers.
None.
Dry Goods Wholesalers.
None.
Timber Wholesalers.
None.
Rice Wholesalers.
None.
Fish Wholesalers.
None.
Fuel Wholesalers.
None.
Saké Wholesalers.
None.
Dried Bonito Wholesalers.
None.
Salt Wholesalers.
None.
Kôjimachi Ward.
Formerly retail merchants could not transact their business directly with *toiya*, but always had to depend upon a *nakagai*, according to the local practice. However, as far as the business within Kôjimachi Ward is concerned at present, there is no kind of business which cannot be transacted except through the agency of a *nakagai-nin*.
Nihombashi Ward.
At the rice exchange, the stock exchange,[1] etc., no dealings can be had except through the agency of some intermediary.
Kyôbashi Ward.
There is no kind of business which cannot be transacted except through the agency of an intermediary.
Yotsuya Ward and Ushigome Ward.

[1] *Kabushiki-torihikisho.*

There is no kind of business that cannot be transacted except through the agency of an intermediary.

Honjo Ward.

There is no kind of business which cannot be transacted except through the agency of an intermediary.

Ebara *kôri*.

There is no kind of business that cannot be transacted except through the agency of an intermediary.

Higashi-tama *kôri* and Minami-toshima *kôri*.

In selling to foreign merchants such goods as tea, silk, etc., traders always have to depend upon the agency of some intermediary; otherwise they cannot transact any business with foreign merchants. [In Yokohama, such intermediaries are called, for instance, *urikomi-toiya*, or *toiya* entrusted with sale of goods to foreign merchants, and are different from *saitori* as described in the first topic.[1] These *toiya* employ the service of *saitori*, but the consignors do not have any direct resort to the *saitori*.] However, as for business between the domestic merchants, there is no kind of business that cannot be transacted except through the agency.

Kita-toshima *kôri*.

The answer to the present topic has already been given in the answer to the third topic.[2]

Minami-adachi *kôri*.

No dealings in timber or building stone[3] can be had except through the agency of some intermediary. In some cases, however, buyer and seller have direct dealings with each other.

Shitaya Ward.

Formerly it was the local practice that no consignor could dispose of his goods unless he depended on the agency of some *toiya*, but today there is no such practice in effect. There is merely some difference in expediency for a consignor in disposing of his goods according to whether he resorts to the agency of an intermediary or not.

Kanda Ward.

At the rice exchange, the stock exchange, etc., no dealings can

---

[1] Should be the second topic instead of the first. See page 320 above.

[2] See page 338 above.

[3] *Sekizai*.

be had except through the agency of some intermediary.

Akasaka Ward and Azabu Ward.

None.

Hongô Ward.

Generally speaking, there is none.

CHIBA PREFECTURE

Awa *kôri*, Hei *kôri*, Asai *kôri* and Nagasa *kôri*.

There is no kind of business that cannot be transacted except through the agency of an intermediary. However, [the people of] the merchant ships from other places,[1] who are not familiar with the places they visit, find it convenient to have resort to the agency of intermediaries. Therefore, when ships of this kind enter port, they depend upon some inn for the sailors and passengers, or some reliable *nakagai* or other, and entrust them with the sale of their goods.

Katori *kôri*.

In this locality business in fish, silk, cotton, cocoons, hemp,[2] round stones,[3] etc. cannot be transacted without resorting to the agency of an intermediary.

Yamabe *kôri* and Muza *kôri*.

None.

Unakami *kôri* and Sôsa *kôri*.

There is no sort of business that cannot be transacted without falling back upon the agency of an intermediary.

Higashi-katsushika *kôri*.

None.

IBARAGI PREFECTURE

Nishi-katsushika *kôri* and Sashima *kôri*.

There are none in this locality.

KANAGAWA PREFECTURE

Miura *kôri*.

None.

Tachibana *kôri*.

There is no such business transaction here.

Kita-tama *kôri*.

---

[1] *Ryosen;* lit., "travelling ship."

[2] *Asa.*

[3] *Tama-ishi* may mean larger round stones that may be used in building walls, or it may refer to pebbles. In the latter case it is also called *kuri-ishi*, i.e., "chestnut stone."

Formerly, it was the practice here that, depending on the nature of the goods, no dealings in goods could be had except through the agency of some intermediary. Since the Meiji Restoration [in 1868], however, the practice has become obsolete.

Ashigara-shimo *kôri.*

In this prefecture, there are many such businesses at Yokohama, etc., but there are none here that always require, for transaction, some intermediaries.

Prefectural Industrial Bureau.

There is no sort of business that cannot be transacted except through the agency of some intermediary.

TOCHIGI PREFECTURE

Prefectural Office.

The noted products of this prefecture [such as the cereals, hemp, tobacco, silk, timber, textile fabrics, and cocoons] are not easy to dispose of unless resort is had to the *toiya, nakagai* and others; so it is necessary to use those intermediaries here.

Shimo-tsuga *kôri* and Samukawa *kôri.*

There is no kind of business that cannot be transacted without having recourse to the agency of some intermediary.

Ashikaga *kôri* and Yanada *kôri.*

In Ashikaga, of late years, they have laid down rules for the supervision of the market of textile fabrics, so that no goods which do not come up to the standard[1] may be marketed. Consequently, it is naturally necessary for merchants wishing to buy the goods to depend upon the agency of some intermediary. When business is done without the agency of an intermediary, the practice is called "street buying"[2] and is generally despised by other merchants.

MIE PREFECTURE

Suzuka *kôri.*

Those businesses which it is impossible to transact here without the agency of some intermediary are as follows:

1.   Dealings in futures,[3] as well as spot purchases,[4] at the rice exchange;

2.   Sale and purchase of cattle and horses;

---

[1] *Fusei-hin;* lit., "fraudulent goods."

[2] *Tsuji-gai.*

[3] *Teiki-baibai.*

[4] *Gemba-baibai.*

3. Sale of tea by the manufacturers.

It may be added that these transactions are not absolutely impossible without having resort to the agency of some intermediary, but it is, in most cases, the usual practice here for merchants to depend upon some intermediary.

Isshi *kôri*.

There is no business of that kind in this locality.

Asake *kôri*.

Those businesses which it is impossible to transact without having recourse to the agency of some intermediary include:

1. Sale in Tokyo of the rice produced here;
2. Sale in Yokohama of the silk and tea produced here;
3. Purchase of fertilizer in the Kyoto-Osaka district, Hakodate, Odaru and other places;
4. Purchase in Yokohama of reeled thread,[1] sugar, petroleum, etc.

For the transaction of such business, it is of course necessary to depend upon the agency of some intermediary. On the other hand, in the transaction of some local business it is apparently not necessary to depend upon the agency of any intermediary. But when merchants sell or purchase goods in large quantities, it is found convenient to have resort to the agency of some intermediary, supplying him beforehand with samples of the goods and entrusting him with their sale, or asking him beforehand to buy goods for them.

Nabari *kôri* and Iga *kôri*.

Hitherto it has been impossible for rice and other cereals *toiya* to transact their business without the agency of some *toiya*. The transaction of the sale of horses and cattle used to require the agency of some intermediary, but this undesirable practice is now no longer in effect.

AICHI PREFECTURE

Nakajima *kôri*.

It is not necessary to depend upon the agency of any intermediary.

Nagoya Ward.

---

[1] *Kase-ito*.

Here *isaba*,[1] spot rice,[2] and bean paste,[3] are among the goods, the sales transaction of which cannot be done except through the agency of an intermediary.

Chita *kôri*.

There is no kind of business which cannot be transacted except through the agency of an intermediary.

Minami-shidara *kôri*.

Generally speaking, there is none. However, in transacting the sale of timber, a bamboo grove, cattle and the like, merchants all have resort to the agency of some intermediary, as they find it more convenient to do so.

Atsumi *kôri*.

None.

Kaitô *kôri* and Kaisai *kôri*.

There is no kind of business transaction here which cannot be done except through the agency of an intermediary, but usually merchants find it more convenient to depend upon such agency.

Aichi *kôri*.

There is no kind of sales transaction which cannot be undertaken except through the agency of an intermediary.

Niwa *kôri* and Haguri *kôri*.

There is no kind of business transaction which cannot be done except through the agency of an intermediary.

SHIZUOKA PREFECTURE

Prefectural Office.

In the villages in Kamo *kôri* and Naka *kôri*, Izu Province in the prefecture, they make it a practice never to enter into any sales transaction of cattle between the buyer and the seller except through the agency of an intermediary.

Udo *kôri* and Abe *kôri*.

Yes, the sale of cattle is an example.

Inasa *kôri* and Aratama *kôri*.

For the reason stated in the second topic, we have nothing to report on this subject.

Kamo *kôri* and Naka *kôri*.

Any kind of sales transaction may be undertaken between the

---

[1] A local slang word meaning "salted fish."

[2] *Shomai.*

[3] *Miso.*

buyer and the seller without an intermediary. But merchants usually depend upon such agents, as they are well versed in the judgement of the quality of the goods and are familiar with the market prices of the goods.

Saya *kôri* and Kitô *kôri*.

When traders want to sell tea to foreign merchants, they always have recourse to the service of some intermediary. It is the same with silk. Excepting these, there are no other goods here, the sales transaction of which cannot be undertaken except through the agency of an intermediary.

GIFU PREFECTURE

Mugi *kôri*.

There is no kind of business, the transaction of which requires an intermediary.

Ampachi *kôri*.

It may be impossible to say that there is absolutely none; for there are some kinds of business which merchants will find it inconvenient in practice to transact unless they have recourse to the agency of an intermediary.

Fuwa *kôri*.

There is no such usage as is described in the present topic.

Atsumi *kôri*, Kagami *kôri* and Katagata *kôri*.

The transaction of a large trade in saké, cereals, bean paste, etc. requires the agency of some intermediary, although it is not impossible for the parties concerned to reach some agreement between them for dispensing with the services of the intermediary. They have resort to the agency of the intermediary, because they will find it difficult to transact their business unless they depend upon his services.

Tagi *kôri* and Kami-ishizu *kôri*.

There is no kind of business transaction which cannot be carried out unless resort is had to the agency of an intermediary.

Ôno *kôri* and Ikeda *kôri*.

The answer to the present topic has already been given in the first topic.[1]

Haguri *kôri* and Nakajima *kôri*.

There is no kind of business as is described in the present topic.

---

[1] See page 308.

Ena *kôri*.

There is some such business as is suggested in the present topic, for instance, export of goods abroad.

Kamo *kôri*.

There is no kind of business which cannot be transacted except through the agency of some intermediary. However, merchants apparently find it practically impossible to carry out the sale of horses and cattle without the agency of a cattle broker.[1]

Kani *kôri*.

Except the trade at the rice exchange, etc. which has some special provisions to that effect, there is no kind of business that cannot be transacted without the agency of an intermediary.

Atsumi *kôri*, Gifu Township.

Those goods, whose sales transaction cannot be carried out except through the agency of some intermediary, include, chiefly, cereals, saké, soy, bean paste, rapeseed oil, etc.

Ôgaki Township.

It may be impossible to say that there is no such business, for there are some sorts of business which merchants will find it practically difficult to transact without having recourse to the agency of an intermediary.

Ena *kôri*, Nakatsugawa Village.

There is no kind of business which it is impossible to transact without the agency of an intermediary.

Shimo-ishizu *kôri*, Takasu Township.

There is no kind of business, such as suggested in the present topic, which it is impossible to transact without the agency of an intermediary; but merchants resort to his services because they can derive some convenience from them.

Haguri *kôri*, Takegahama Village.

There is no kind of business which cannot be transacted except through the agency of an intermediary.

Yamagata *kôri*, Takatomi Village.

According to the nature of the trade, some kinds of business cannot be transacted except through the agency of an intermediary.

Mugi *kôri*, Kôzuchi Village.

---

[1] *Bakurô.* This may also mean exclusively a horse broker or horse dealer.

Sometimes merchants find it impossible to transact business unless they have recourse to the agency of an intermediary.

Haguri *kôri*, Kasamatsu Village.

There is no such business as is described in the present topic.

Fuwa *kôri*, Tarui Village.

There is no such practice as is described in the present topic.

Ôno *kôri*, Miwa Village.

There is no kind of business that cannot be transacted except through the agency of an intermediary.

Ampachi *kôri*, Gôdo Village.

Some people carry on their sales transactions without depending on the agency of an intermediary.

Ena *kôri*, Iwa Village.

The export of goods abroad cannot be carried on without the agency of an intermediary.

Kamo *kôri*, Hosome Village.

Those goods whose prices are liable to fluctuation are difficult to obtain on short notice, so merchants always make it a rule to rely upon the agency of an intermediary for an urgent transaction. Also they find it impossible to transact the sale of horses and cattle unless they have recourse to the agency of such a person.

Toki *kôri*, Takayama Village.

As there are no intermediaries here, there is no report on the present topic from us.

Kani *kôri*, Mitake Village.

None.

Ena *kôri*, Akechi Village.

Yes, the export of goods abroad for instance, cannot be carried on without the agency of an intermediary.

Mugi *kôri*, Seki Village.

There is no sort of business which cannot be transacted without the agency of an intermediary. But, according to the circumstances, when it is impossible to transact the sale of certain goods due to the fluctuation of their market prices, merchants always make it a practice to depend upon the agency of an intermediary.

Motosu *kôri*, Kita-kata Village.

We do not know of any sort of business which cannot be transacted without the agency of an intermediary.

Kamo *kôri*, Ôta Village.

There is no sort of business which cannot be transacted without the agency of an intermediary. As to the sale of horses and cattle, etc., however, merchants find it impossible to carry it on except through the agency of an intermediary.

Kaisai *kôri* and Shimo-ishizu *kôri*.

There is no sort of sales transaction which cannot be carried on without the agency of an intermediary. Merchants rely upon his agency because they find it more convenient for transacting their business. The sale of horses and cattle is the only sort of business which they cannot transact without depending upon the agency of an intermediary.

Gujô *kôri*.

A business which cannot be transacted without the agency of some intermediary is that of horses and cattles.

Topic 6:   Are There Any Intermediaries Who Act as Agents for
a Consignor in Connection with Transportation of Goods,
such as Those Who Make a Contract, on Behalf of a
Consignor, with a Shipowner or a Wagon-owner?

GROUP I—ANSWERS

Tokyo.

For marine transportation there are people called *shûsenya*[1] who
act as intermediary [for a consignor] in connection with shipment.
Also, apart from them, there are people called *kaisen-toiya*, or shipping agents who, acting as agents for some shipowner, take an
order for the carriage of goods by sea. There are again some people
called loading agents[2] and cargo-boat agents[3] who, acting as agents
for a consignor, conclude a contract in connection with the carriage
of his goods. However, there are no such intermediaries for transport by land.

Kyoto.

The shipping agents[4] in each port town make it their special
business to take care of goods to be transported by sea, acting as
agents for the consignor of the goods. For transportation by land,
there are nowadays some kinds of transport companies,[5] which,
acting on commission from the consignor, undertake the transport
of his goods, having secured his assent to their rate of charges. [In
the pre-Restoration[6] days there were, besides the post-horse agents[7]
at each stage,[8] baggage agents[9] at towns along a lake or a river,
who made it their specialty to handle only merchants' baggage.]

For overland transport of goods, there is a practice called "carriage with escort,"[10] according to which the consignor, or some agent

[1] *Shûsenya;* lit., "intermediary."
[2] *Tsumi-toiya.*
[3] *Hashike-yado.*
[4] *Kaisô-toiya;* same as *kaisen-toiya.*
[5] *Tsû-un-kaisha.*
[6] The Meiji Restoration in 1868.
[7] *Temma-toiya; temma* may also mean a sampan or a lighter.
[8] *Shukueki.*
[9] *Nimotsu-toiya.*
[10] *Sairyô-tsuki; sairyô* may also mean a superintendent or to supervise.

of his, accompanies his goods to their destination by way of protecting them. According to another practice known as "relay transport,"[1] the names of the forwarding agents at various places, one after another, are written together on the tag of the goods. And the goods, along with the money to be paid for carriage, are transported from one forwarding agent to another until the goods reach their destination. Although these practices have different names at different places, they were generally in effect hitherto throughout the country.

He who acts as agent for the consignor, in accompanying his goods in what is called the "transport with escort," is called *hikyaku*[2] or *nimawashi*.[3] He is a man of small means, but he makes it his business to undertake the overland transport of goods which may be worth several thousand pieces of gold. [The occupation was prohibited by Government Decree No. 230 in the 6th year of Meiji (1873). This was followed by its entire abolition by Government Decree No. 16 in the 12th year of Meiji (1879)].

Osaka.

There are some intermediaries here who act as agents for a consignor in connection with transportation of goods. Shipping agents and forwarding agents,[4] for instance, are such intermediaries.

Yokohama.

For marine transportation there are shipping agents, who, acting on behalf of the consignor, conclude a contract with the shipowner.

Hyôgo.

There are some persons who act as intermediaries in connection with transportation of goods.

The proceedings of the investigation committee on the subject are as follows:

No. 10 [Ômori]: There are some persons who act as intermediaries in connection with the transport of goods. They are called *shûsenya* in Kobe and *nakatsugi-nin* in Osaka. In case any damage or loss occurs to the goods whose transport they have undertaken, the intermediaries are

---

[1] *Furihanashi-nimotsu.* Literally, *furihanashi* means "shaking off," presumably with allusion to the manner of a carrier unburdening himself of his load before he gives it to the next man.

[2] Literally, "flying feet"; also an express messenger.

[3] *Kaisen-toiya.*

[4] *Unsô-toiya.*

held responsible. But for damage or loss that occurs after the goods are loaded aboard a ship, the shipowner is held responsible, according to the usage here.

No. 4 [Kishi]: The consignor makes it a practice to take from an intermediary a receipt for the goods whose transport has been entrusted to him. Then the intermediary takes a receipt for the goods from the shipping agents, who in turn take one from the shipowner. If some damage, etc. occurs to the goods, then the consignor holds the intermediary and the other parties who have issued the receipt for the goods, in the above order, responsible for the damage.

Chairman [Kashima]: Shall we present a report to the effect that for marine transportation there are intermediaries called *shûsen-toiya* and *nizumi-toiya*?[1]

No. 11 [Horiuchi]: There are intermediaries not only for marine transportation[2] but also for overland carriage.[3] Here in this port town, Kitamura-gumi & Co., for example, is such an agent for overland transport. They have an arrangement with the Railway Bureau whereby they undertake the transport of goods by rail. These people assume all the responsibilities relating to the transport of goods.

No. 14 [Funai]: Regarding goods with the transport of which they have been entrusted, the forwarding agents[4] are, according to the local practice, held responsible for all damage to the goods, even if it has been caused by some fault on the part of the shipowner.

No. 1 [Ikeda]: Once we had some goods shipped to our firm from Yokohama. On receipt of three boxes of the goods, it was plain that the contents of one box must have been damaged. Consequently we notified the shipowner that we could not accept the box of the goods, and we unpacked it in his presence, to find that its contents had been damaged as was feared. So we wrote to the consignor at Yokohama to that effect. There arose a controversy between the consignor and the shipowner as to which party was responsible. And finally, in accordance with the decision of the court, the consignor had to pay for the damage.

No. 6 [Hamada]: In Osaka there is such an agent called *hikyaku-ya*,[5] who makes it his business to undertake the delivery there of goods brought over to Osaka from Kaga and neighboring provinces, and, taking orders for the carriage of goods from Osaka to Kaga, to have the carriers who fetched a load with him to Osaka from Kaga transport

---

[1] Literally, "loading agents."

[2] *Kai-un.*

[3] *Riku-un.*

[4] *Nimotsu-atsukai-sho.*

[5] Couriers' agency.

the goods to Kaga. I mention this for your information.

No. 5 [Inoue]: There are light barges called *choki-bune* which ply between Osaka and Kobe, carrying coal, petroleum, etc. If the barge meets with a mishap and some damage is done to its cargo, the buyer and the seller of the goods share the loss thus incurred, according to the practice here.

Chairman [Kashima]: Let us submit a report to the effect that there are such intermediaries as *shûsen-toiya* and *nizumi-toiya*.

Ôtsu.

There are no intermediaries of the kind.

Kumamoto.

Excepting shipping agents,[1] there are no people who act as intermediaries for marine transport of goods. For overland transport of goods to a distant place or over a precipitous road, there are people called *ninushi-nakatsugi-nin*,[2] who act as agents of the consignor in connection with the transport of goods.

Okayama.

There are intermediaries for the transport of goods known by the name of forwarding agent,[3] who may conclude a contract with the consignor on behalf of the shipowner and undertake the carriage of goods. However, there are no intermediaries for the overland transport of goods.

Bakan.

The loading of goods aboard a steamship is undertaken by the steamship agents,[4] regardless of whether the owner of the goods is a passenger of the steamship or a resident of this port town. On the other hand, the loading of goods aboard a ship of old Japanese type[5] is undertaken by the ship agents when the goods are owned by a resident of this port town, who makes it a rule to conclude a contract with the shipowner for the carriage of the goods.

Sakai.

Those who act as intermediaries in various ways in connection with marine transport are *shûsen-ya*, shipping agents, loading agents, *uke-yado*,[6] etc. The *shûsen-ya* acts as intermediary in connection with

---

[1] *Funa-doiya.*

[2] Consignor's agent.

[3] *Unsô-doiya.*

[4] *Kisen-doiya.*

[5] *Wasen;* wooden sailing or other boats of old Japanese type.

[6] This word usually means a servants' agency, employment agency, etc.

the transport of goods; the shipping agents take orders for transport of goods on behalf of the shipowner; and the loading agents and *uke-yado* conclude a contract for transport of goods on behalf of the consignor. For overland transport, however, there are no intermediaries.

Iida.

There are intermediaries in connection with transport of goods, such as the general utility agency.[1]

Takamatsu.

The intermediaries indicated in the present topic are found more especially in connection with marine transport. Among the steamship agents, the shipping agents, ordinary *toiya*,[2] the keepers of inns for sailors or ship passengers, etc., there are some who, besides being engaged in their main occupation, work as such intermediaries to earn a brokerage. They are sometimes, though rather rarely, met with in connection with overland transport.

Fukui.

There are forwarding agents[3] and others[4] who make it their occupation to transport goods.

Tokushima.

The transport of goods is an enterprise always associated with, and undertaken by, a *toiya*. Hence there is no special intermediary here. There is no practice that the consignor transacts directly with the shipowner or the overland transporter for the carriage of the goods.

Takefu.

The forwarding agents and *nigawase-toiya*[5] are examples of such an intermediary, but apart from them there are none.

Miyagi.

There are some intermediaries connected with the transport of goods, such as the shipping agents and the goods agency.[6]

Matsuyama.

---

[1] *Naigai-yôtashi-kaisha; naigai*, within and without; *yôtashi*, executing a commission, running errands; *kaisha*, firm, company.

[2] *Tsûjô-toiya.*

[3] *Tsûun-kaisha.*

[4] *Nimawashi.*

[5] Wholesalers who draw a documentary draft or a letter of credit.

[6] *Unsoniyado;* lit., "hotel for goods to be transported."

There are some such intermediaries, called shipping agents and steamship agents, who, acting as intermediaries associated with marine transportation, conclude a contract with the shipowner on behalf of the consignor. There are no such intermediaries in connection with overland transport.

GROUP II—ANSWERS

Tokyo Metropolis
    Prefectural Office.
    Oil Wholesalers.
    The shipping agent is an example. However, he does not conclude any contract on behalf of the consignor with the shipowner.
    Dry Goods Wholesalers.
    There are marine shipping agents,[1] who make a contract with the shipowner on behalf of the consignor.
    Timber Wholesalers.
    None.
    Grain Wholesalers.
    None.
    Fish Wholesalers.
    None.
    Fuel Wholesalers.
    None.
    Saké Wholesalers.
    None.
    Dried Bonito Wholesalers.
    For the transport of goods between the metropolitan area and the outlying districts there are sea boat loading agents[2] and river boat loading agents,[3] who act as intermediary with regard to the carriage of the goods.
    Salt Wholesalers.
    Salt is bought from the consignors at the seaside and carried by boatmen[4] to sell.
    Kôjimachi Ward.

---

[1] *Kaisen-toiya; kaisen,* "sea boat."
[2] *Umibune-tsumi-toiya.*
[3] *Kawabune-tsumi-toiya.*
[4] *Sendô;* one who manages a small boat; one of the crew.

Besides forwarding agents,[1] there are none in this ward who are engaged in the transport of goods.

Nihombashi Ward.

There are no special people who are called intermediaries in the carrying trade. However, there are forwarding agents[2] for trains, steamships, horse carts and ox carts.[3] And those who are called *tsumi-doiya*, or loading agents, all correspond to the intermediaries mentioned in the present topic.

Kyôbashi Ward.

There are intermediaries in the carrying trade.

Yotsuya Ward and Ushigome Ward.

For convenience in forwarding, goods are sometimes committed to an intermediary.

Asakusa Ward.

There are no such intermediaries.

Honjo Ward.

There are intermediaries in connection with the transport of goods—the marine loading agents.[4]

Ebara Ward.

There are intermediaries in connection with the carriage of goods.

Higashi-tama *kôri* and Minami-toshima *kôri*.

There are some people who make it their occupation to act as intermediaries in connection with the transport of goods, of whatever sort they are. They are called *unsô-yado*[5] or *ni-yado*,[6] and act as agents of the consignor in handling the transport of his goods and advance the carriage charges for the consignor.

Kita-toshima *kôri*.

There are loading agents[7] for river transportation. They undertake the carriage of goods in their own boats. And when they have no boats of their own left, they engage boats of others and load them

---

[1] *Tsûun-kaisha.*

[2] *Unsôtsumini-toriatsukai-shô;* lit., "office handling goods to be loaded for transportation."

[3] *Basha,* horse cart; *gyusha,* oxcart.

[4] *Funazumi-doiya.*

[5] Forwarding house.

[6] Freight agency.

[7] *Tsumi-doiya.*

with the goods to transport. They take as a commission a part of the money which they have been given by the consignor in payment for the carriage rates for the goods.

For land transportation, with the exception of the forwarding company,[1] consignors make a contract directly with the wagon owner each time according to the circumstances.

Minami-adachi *kôri.*

The people who act as intermediaries in connection with the transport of goods are those whose business is called "ship-loading agency."

Shitaya Ward.

There are intermediaries in the carrying trade. In marine transportation they are called "loading agents" and act as intermediaries in the transport of goods. There are also people called "shipping agents," who undertake the carriage of goods, acting as agents for the consignor. If any damage is done to the goods by accident during the carriage by sea, they make the boatmen pay for it. In land transportation, too, the forwarding company, for instance, holds the carriers[2] responsible for damage that may be done to the goods during transport.

Kanda Ward.

It is the business of a loading agent to act as intermediary and conclude a contract with the shipowner or the wagon owner [for the consignor].

Akasaka Ward and Azabu Ward.

For marine transportation there were *shûsen-ya*; for river boat transportation, barge agencies[3] and loading agents; and for overland transport, freight forwarding agents,[4] etc. Generally speaking, they are called by different names at present, but they are engaged in the same sort of business.

Hongô Ward.

None.

CHIBA PREFECTURE

Awa *kôri*, Hei *kôri*, Asai *kôri* and Nagasa *kôri.*

There are no intermediaries in connection with the transport of

---

[1] *Tsûun-kaisha.*

[2] *Unsô-nin.*

[3] *Hashike-yado.*

[4] *Nimotsu-unsô-doiya.*

goods. However, there are some people who may entrust the sale of their goods with the shipowner to whom they entrust the transport of the goods. It digresses somewhat from the point of inquiry of the present topic, but an instance may be given as follows. Suppose a consignor makes a shipment of dried sardines and oil-cakes to some place where, however, there is no *toiya* with whom he has had any regular dealings. So he invests the ship captain with authority to sell the goods, which are now called "disposable goods."[1] Upon his entry into port, the captain makes inquiries among *toiya* and *nakagai-shô* of the place and sells the goods to the highest bidder.

Katori *kôri*.

There are intermediaries in connection with the transport of goods, mostly goods to be carried by sea. They make a contract with the shipowner on behalf of the consignor.

Yamabe *kôri* and Muza *kôri*.

In our *gun*, such goods as dried sardines are bought by *nakagai-nin* and forwarded to the places where they are in demand, through a series of forwarding agents[2] at various places, who are charged by the *nakagai-nin* to relay the goods[3] from one place to another. The forwarding agents are paid for the services of labor and relay horses they have supplied, and also charge storage for the goods in case they are stored in a warehouse.

Unakami *kôri* and Sôsa *kôri*.

Intermediaries are sometimes needed in the transport of goods. Also merchants may sometimes conclude a contract, on behalf of the consignor, with the shipowner or the wagon owner. The practice is restricted, however, to a very limited number of kinds of goods.

Higashi-katsushika *kôri*.

None.

IBARAGI PREFECTURE

Nishi-katsushika *kôri* and Sashima *kôri*.

There are none in these districts.

KANAGAWA PREFECTURE

Miura *kôri*.

---

[1] *Shihai*, "control"-*nimotsu*, "freight-goods."

[2] *Riku-un-ten;* used in contrast to *kai-un-ten* (shipping agents).

[3] *Tsugitate;* a word originally used in the sense of "to relay horses at the relay station."

None.

Tachibana *kôri*.

An example of this practice is when the producer consigns goods to the shipowner or the wagon owner in forwarding vegetables for the market.

Kita-tama *kôri*.

A company which acts as intermediary for the transport of goods is represented in this *gun* only by the branch office of Chuma Company. There are no other people here who make it their occupation to act as intermediaries in the carrying trade.

Ashigara-shimo *kôri*.

No intermediaries are required for the transport of goods. The consignor makes a contract directly with the shipowner or the wagon owner, according to the practice here.

Prefectural Industrial Bureau.

In marine transportation there are shipping agents,[1] who conclude a contract with the shipowner on behalf of the consignor.

TOCHIGI PREFECTURE

Prefectural Office.

The intermediaries in the carrying trade are the shipping agents and the forwarding agents, who at the request of the consignor, undertake the carriage of his goods, making a contract with the shipowner or wagon owner.

Shimo-tsuga *kôri* and Samukawa *kôri*.

Those who act as intermediaries in the carrying trade in Tochigi Town are represented by the forwarding agents[2] and shipping agents.

Ashikaga *kôri* and Yanada *kôri*.

There are no such intermediaries here.

MIE PREFECTURE

Suzuka *kôri*.

There are no intermediaries for the transport of goods here.

Isshi *kôri*.

The shipping agents and the forwarding agents[3] and the like are here engaged in the trade in question.

---

[1] *Kaisô-doiya.*

[2] *Tsûun-kaisha.*

[3] *Riku-unten.*

Asake *kôri*.

When merchants wish to send goods from this Yokkaichi Port to Tokyo, Yokohama or Osaka, they entrust the goods directly to Mitsubishi & Co., from whom they get a consignment-receipt[1] for the goods and send it by mail to the consignee. Then the consignee will get delivery of the goods in exchange for the receipt. Such is the procedure to be followed in the shipment of goods. However, it is very troublesome for them to follow this procedure themselves; hence they entrust the matter to freight agents,[2] that is, intermediaries. The freight agents are found both at this port and at the destinations of the goods, and in accordance with the above procedure, they deliver and receive the goods to and from Mitsubishi & Co., finally delivering the same to the consignee.

As to the freight charges, the consignor pays them to the freight agents, the rates being fixed in the deliberation between the consignor and the freight agents.

The practice of consigning the transport of goods to the freight agents is limited to goods that are billed for Tokyo, Yokohama or Osaka. Shipments to other places have hitherto all been handled directly by the consignor and the shipowner.

Nabari *kôri* and Iga *kôri*.

None.

AICHI PREFECTURE

Nakajima *kôri*.

Regarding the transport of goods, the loading agents act as intermediaries and conclude the contract.

Nagoya Ward.

There are no such intermediaries here.

Chita *kôri*.

The intermediaries for the transport of goods include the shipping agents and the forwarding agents,[3] etc.

Minami-shidara *kôri*.

In this district there are none, except the consignor, who may make a contract [about the transport of goods].

Atsumi *kôri*.

Yes. They sometimes entrust the matter to the inland forwarding

---

[1] *Azukari-shô.*

[2] *Nimotsu-atsukai-sho.*

[3] *Tsûun-ten.*

company[1] and other shipping agents.

Kaitô *kôri* and Kaisai *kôri*.

None.

Aichi *kôri*.

There are some agents, such as forwarding agents[2] and shipping agents,[3] that on behalf of the consignor undertake the responsibility for the transport of goods. But apart from them, there are none who act as intermediaries in the transport of goods.

Niwa *kôri* and Haguri *kôri*.

No special intermediaries are necessary in the transport of goods.

SHIZUOKA PREFECTURE

Prefectural Office.

For the transport of goods, forwarding agents[4] and shipping agents, etc. sometimes conclude a contract with the shipowner or the wagon owner on behalf of the consignor.

Abe *kôri* and Udo *kôri*.

There are no intermediaries for the transport of goods.

Inasa *kôri* and Aratama *kôri*.

There are none for the carriage of goods.

Kamo *kôri* and Naka *kôri*.

Those who are called ship agents[5] or shipping agents all act as intermediaries for the carriage of exported and imported goods; that is, they conclude a contract, on behalf of the consignor, with the shipowner or the wagon owner.

Saya *kôri* and Kitô *kôri*.

The transport of goods is handled by shipping agents, forwarding agents,[6] etc., who are usually left to deal with the matter in accordance with the rules of each of the firms. Excepting these people, there are no special intermediaries.

GIFU PREFECTURE

Mugi *kôri*.

For the transport of goods no intermediaries are necessary, according to the practice here.

---

[1] *Naikoku-tsûun-kaisha.*

[2] *Riku-un-ten.*

[3] *Kai-un-ten.*

[4] *Riku-un-ten.*

[5] *Funa-yado.*

[6] *Tsûun-kaisha.*

Ampachi *kôri*.

Those who are commonly called *ni-mawashi*[1] belong to this class.

Fuwa *kôri*.

There are some intermediaries for the transport of goods. They are, for instance, the marine and overland transport company[2] and shipping agents.

Atsumi *kôri*, Kagami *kôri* and Katagata *kôri*.

The firms engaged in the transport of goods are the intermediaries in point.

Tagi *kôri* and Ishizu *kôri*.

There are no intermediaries at all for the transport of goods.

Ôno *kôri* and Ikeda *kôri*.

The answer to the present topic has already been given in the first topic.

Haguri *kôri* and Nakajima *kôri*.

There are no commercial transactions as stated in the present topic.

Ena *kôri*.

There are.

Kamo *kôri*.

There are no intermediaries for the transport of goods.

Kani *kôri*.

The forwarding agents traditionally perform this kind of business, but it is rare that they proceed to conclude any special contract.

Atsumi *kôri*, Gifu Township.

Those firms that are engaged in the transport of goods are the intermediaries in point.

Ogaki.

Those who are commonly called *ni-mawashi* belong to this class.

Ena *kôri*, Nakatsugawa Village.

Those who are called freight agents[3] belong to this class.

Shimo-ishizu *kôri*, Takasu Township.

There are no persons here who make a contract with the shipowner or the wagon owner on behalf of the consignor for the trans-

---

[1] "Freight move-around."

[2] *Suiriku-unsô-kaisha.*

[3] *Ni-doiya.*

port of his goods. However, if it is especially undertaken at the request of the consignor, it is permissible.

Haguri *kôri*, Takegahana Village.

Excepting the freight forwarding agents[1] and the shipping agents, there are no other merchants of the kind.

Yamagata *kôri*, Takatomi Village.

Even for the transport of goods, there are such intermediaries.

Mugi *kôri*, Kôzuchi Village.

There are such intermediaries for the transport of goods. They make contracts with the shipowner or the wagon owner on behalf of the consignor.

Haguri *kôri*, Kasamatsu Village.

There are no such intermediaries as described in the present topic.

Fuwa *kôri*, Tarui Village.

There is no such practice here as is referred to in the present topic.

Ôno *kôri*, Miwa Village.

There are intermediaries for the transport of goods.

Ampachi *kôri*, Gôdo Village.

There are no persons who act as intermediaries for the transport of goods.

Kano *kôri*, Hosome Village.

It happens sometimes that the shipowners, the wagon owners, etc. who engage in the carriage of goods are entrusted with the sale of the goods. In this village, however, such a consignment is made only occasionally as the circumstances may demand; so such transport agents are not of a status entitling them to be called sales agents.

Toki *kôri*, Takayama Village.

There are.

Kani *kôri*, Mitake Village.

The forwarding agents[2] may be an example in question, but besides them there are none others here.

Ena *kôri*, Akechi Village.

There are.

---

[1] *Nimotsu-unsô-doiya.*

[2] *Riku-un-kaisha.*

Mugi *kôri*, Seki Village.

In transporting tea from this provincial district, they always make it a rule to depend upon the services of some intermediary. He concludes a contract with the shipowner; then in the capacity of supercargo,[1] [accompanies the goods aboard the ship, and] on his arrival at some port, draws a draft on some *toiya* or firm [to whom he has sold the goods]. Besides this kind of intermediary, there are none others who conclude such a contract.

Motosu *kôri*, Kita-kata Village.

In connection with the transport of goods by sea or land, there are persons called *nakagai-nin*, who, on behalf of the consignor, conclude a contract with the forwarding agents, and assume responsibilities relating thereto.

Kamo *kôri*, Ôta Village.

There are no intermediaries engaged in the transport of goods. However, it happens sometimes that the shipowner, the wagon owner, etc. are entrusted with the sale of some goods according to the nature of the goods.

Kaisai *kôri* and Shimo-ishizu *kôri*.

There are no shipowners, wagon owners, etc. who may make a contract, on behalf of the consignor, regarding the sale of his goods. However, if they are persistently asked to do so due to circumstances, they may sometimes act as intermediary for the consignor.

Gujô *kôri*.

There are no intermediaries engaged in the transport of goods, which is entrusted to forwarding agents.

---

[1] *Uwanori.*